BLACK FRANCE, WHITE EUROPE

BLACK FRANCE, WHITE EUROPE

YOUTH, RACE, AND BELONGING IN THE POSTWAR ERA

EMILY MARKER

CORNELL UNIVERSITY PRESS

Ithaca and London

Every effort has been made to trace the copyright holder(s) and to obtain permission for the use of figures 4.2 and 4.3, which were first published in Albert Tévoedjrè, *L'Afrique révoltée* (Paris: Présence Africaine, 1958) and are the presumed personal photographs of the author.

First published 2022 by Cornell University Press

Library of Congress Cataloging-in-Publication Data

Names: Marker, Emily, 1982– author.
Title: Black France, white Europe : youth, race, and belonging in the postwar era / Emily Marker.
Description: Ithaca, New York : Cornell University Press, 2022. | Includes bibliographical references and index.
Identifiers: LCCN 2022006075 (print) | LCCN 2022006076 (ebook) | ISBN 9781501765605 (hardcover) | ISBN 9781501765612 (epub) | ISBN 9781501765629 (pdf)
Subjects: LCSH: Youth—France. | Youth—Africa, French-speaking. | Decolonization. | Europeans—Ethnic identity. | France—Race relations—Political aspects. | France—Colonies—Africa—Race relations.
Classification: LCC DC34 .M275 2022 (print) | LCC DC34 (ebook) | DDC 305.800944—dc23 /eng/20220317
LC record available at https://lccn.loc.gov/2022006075
LC ebook record available at https://lccn.loc.gov /2022006076

For my family

Contents

Acknowledgments   ix

List of Abbreviations   xi

Introduction   1

1. Envisioning France in a Postwar World   25

2. Recalibrating *Laïcité* from Brazzaville
   to Bruges   66

3. Reconstructing Race in French Africa
   and Liberated Europe   101

4. Encountering Diversity in France
   and "Eurafrica"   139

5. Forging Global Connections   181

   Epilogue   216

Bibliography   229

Index   257

Acknowledgments

The research for and writing of this book would not have been possible without generous support from the Rutgers University Research Council; the Center for the Study of Race, Politics, and Culture at the University of Chicago; the Georges Lurcy Charitable and Educational Trust; and the Social Science Research Council/Mellon International Dissertation Research Fellowship.

Chapters of this book have benefited from the collective wisdom of participants at the Modern Europe Workshop at Indiana University Bloomington, the Beyond France Seminar at Columbia University, the Lees Seminar at Rutgers University–Camden, and the Philadelphia-area French History Group. Special thanks to Kelly Duke Bryant, Gregory Mann, and Judith Surkis for their thoughtful comments and detailed feedback on early chapter drafts.

I am deeply indebted to Emily Andrew, Durba Ghosh, Bethany Wasik, and the anonymous reviewers for Cornell University Press for their incisive critiques and perceptive suggestions. Richard Ivan Jobs, Semyon Khokhlov, and Sam Lebovic gave me generous, detailed feedback on the entire manuscript. This is a better book thanks to them.

The core idea for this book emerged from conversations with Leora Auslander more than a decade ago. From that initial spark to the finished product, Leora has helped me make sense of the chaos. Her unwavering belief in me and this project empowered me to think big and take risks. I am in awe of her intellect, generosity, and commitment to both her scholarly work and making the profession a more humane and equitable place than when she entered it. I am forever grateful to have her as a mentor and friend.

The conceptual repertoire and key arguments of this book developed dialogically with a wide circle of interlocutors at conferences, archives, and elsewhere. Thanks to Jennifer Boittin, Neilesh Bose, Sung Choi, Andrew M. Daily, Naomi Davidson, Muriam Haleh Davis, Jennifer Dixon, Flavio Eichmann, Charlotte Faucher, Darcie Fontaine, Elizabeth Foster, Elise Franklin, Harry Gamble, Adom Getachew, Burleigh Hendrickson, Rachel Kantrowitz, Suzanne Kaufman, Kathleen Keller, Emma Kuby, Daniel Lee, Etay Lotem, Stephanie

Maher, Elizabeth Marcus, Larry McGrath, Eric O'Connor, Roxanne Panchasi, Terrence Peterson, Erin Pettigrew, Christy Pichichero, Keith Rathbone, Louisa Rice, Julia Roos, Sandrine Sanos, and Emmanuelle Sibeud. Conversations with Laura Lee Downs, Carole Reynaud Paligot, and Michelle Zancarini-Fournel helped me refine earlier formulations of this project.

I have had the good fortune to work with inspirational mentors, scholars, and peers. Special thanks to Mark Bradley, Alice Conklin, Michael Geyer, Jan Goldstein, and Emily Lynn Osborn. I am particularly grateful for the intellectual fellowship and camaraderie of Emily Lord Fransee, Michael Kozakowski, Celeste Day Moore, Eleanor Rivera, and Jake P. Smith, as well as Jacob Betz, Brett Brehm, Christopher Dingwall, Madeleine Elfenbein, Susannah Engstrom, Dara Epison, Darryl Heller, Ke-chin Hsia, Amanda Michelle Jones, Elisa Jones, Ari Joskowicz, Ainsley LeSure, Cam McDonald, Sarah Miller-Davenport, Katya Motyl, Tessa Murphy, Becca Schlossberg, Diana Lynn Schwartz, Guo-Quan Seng, Caroline Séquin, Peter Simons, Lauren Stokes, Gwynneth Troyer, Erika Vauss, and Fei-hsien Wang. I am deeply indebted to Sébastien Greppo, director of the University of Chicago Center in Paris, for his unwavering support while I was in the field.

I am so fortunate to have been a part of the intellectual communities at Rutgers-Camden, Rutgers' Center for African Studies, and Rutgers' Center for European Studies. Thanks to all my Rutgers colleagues, and also to Sharon Smith for her administrative support and to Anaïs Faurt and Ariel Mond, two outstanding PhD students at Rutgers-New Brunswick, for their invaluable research assistance in the final stages of preparing the manuscript.

Thanks to my friends in Paris—Emily Bosch, Baptiste Fabre, Cormac Flynn, Sunayana Ganguly, Pascaline Lefebvre, David Lewis, Adam McBride-Smith, Meghna Prakash, Samantha Rajasingham, and Corentin Seznec—for hosting me, keeping me company, listening to me talk about this project, and making me want to come back to France, year after year.

Thanks, too, to friends in Philly and New York who saw me through the last leg of writing this book: Caren Beilin, Rachel Bobrick, Megan Brown, Jake Collins, Jean-Paul Cauvin, Katherine Clark, Mikkel Dach, Cassandra Fiore, Evan Few, Isabel Gabel, Michael Garber, Colin Hartz, Ruth Judge, Nabil Kashyap, Kinohi Nishikawa, Eileen Ryan, Victoria Sacks, David Suisman, Naomi Taback, and B. Trent Williams. I am also infinitely grateful to Relebohile Letsie, whose support was invaluable as I revised the manuscript.

Finally, thanks to my family, for their boundless love, patience, and compassion. To Jim and Marjorie Marker, Kate Walsh, Semyon Khokhlov and Cecilia Semyonovna Khokhlova Marker—this book is for you.

Abbreviations

AAPSO	Afro-Asian Peoples' Solidarity Organization
AEF	Afrique équatoriale française
AGED	Association générale des étudiants de Dakar
AGEFAN	Association générale des étudiants français en Afrique Noire
AHC	Archives de l'Histoire Contemporaine, Sciences Po, Paris
AHUE	Archives Historiques de l'Union Européenne, Florence
AMAE	Archives Diplomatiques, La Courneuve
AMEAN	Association musulmane des étudiants d'Afrique noire
AN	Archives Nationales, Paris
ANOM	Archives Nationales d'Outre-Mer, Aix-en-Provence
ANS	Archives Nationales du Sénégal, Dakar
AOF	Afrique occidentale française
CAC	Centre des Archives Contemporaines, Fontainebleau
CAME	Conference of Allied Ministers of Education
CFLN	Comité français de libération nationale
CNR	Conseil national de la Résistance
EAMA	États Africains et Malgache Associés
ECHR	European Court of Human Rights
ECSC	European Coal and Steel Community
EDC	European Defense Community
EEC	European Economic Community
EPC	European Political Community
EU	European Union
EUI	European University Institute
EYC	European Youth Campaign
FEANF	Fédération des étudiants d'Afrique noire en France
FIDES	Fonds d'Investissement pour le Développement Économique et Social
FLN	Algerian National Liberation Front
FOM	France d'outre-mer
GDR	German Democratic Republic

IHED	Institut des Hautes Études de Dakar
IIIC	International Institute for Intellectual Cooperation
IUS	International Union of Students
MEN	Ministère de l'Éducation Nationale
MFOM	Ministère de la France d'Outre-Mer
MRP	Mouvement Républicain Populaire
MSEUE	Mouvement Socialist pour les États-Unis d'Europe
RJDA	Rassemblement de Jeunesse Démocratique Africaine
TOM	Territoires d'outre-mer
UEF	Union of European Federalists
UGEAO	Union générale des étudiants d'Afrique occidentale
UNEF	Union nationale des étudiants français
UNESCO	United Nations Educational, Scientific, and Cultural Organization
WAY	World Association of Youth
WFDY	World Federation of Democratic Youth

BLACK FRANCE, WHITE EUROPE

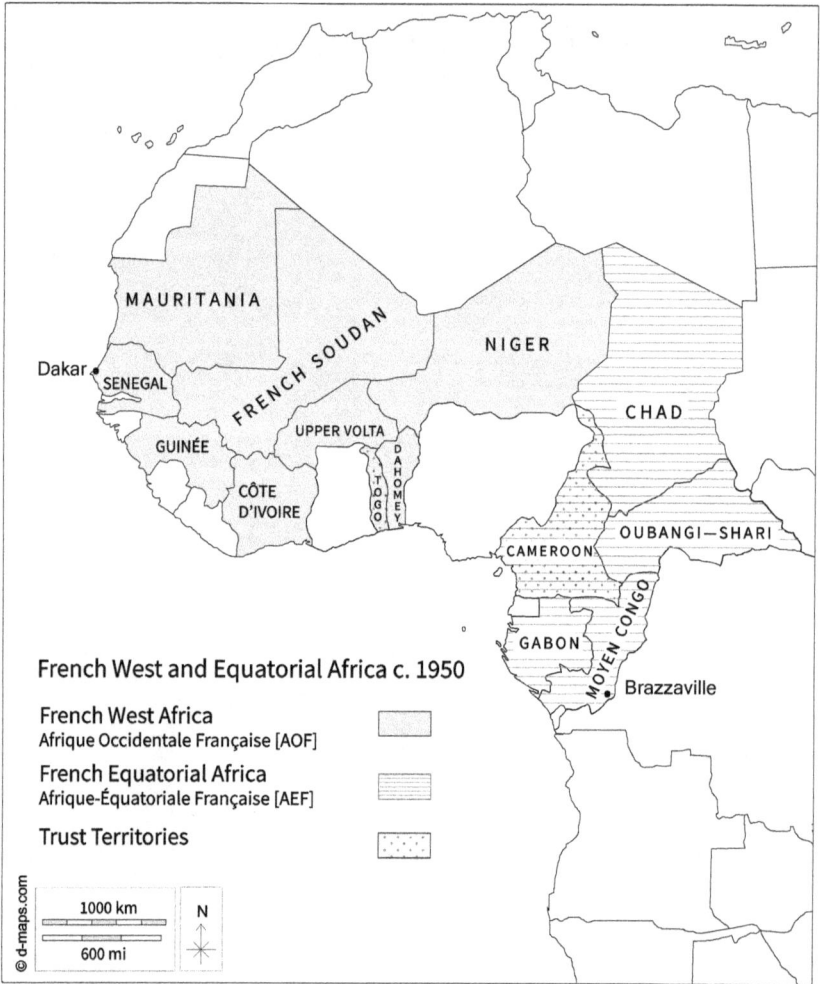

French West and Equatorial Africa c. 1950

French West Africa
Afrique Occidentale Française [AOF]

French Equatorial Africa
Afrique-Équatoriale Française [AEF]

Trust Territories

MAURITANIA

FRENCH SOUDAN

NIGER

Dakar

SENEGAL

GUINÉE

UPPER VOLTA

CÔTE
D'IVOIRE

TOGO

DAHOMEY

CHAD

CAMEROON

OUBANGI—SHARI

GABON

MOYEN CONGO

Brazzaville

1000 km

600 mi

N

© d-maps.com

French West and Equatorial Africa c. 1950. Created by Anaïs Faurt (adapted from dmaps.com), 2021.

Introduction

In late March 1953, one hundred and thirty high schoolers from across Western Europe arrived in Paris for a ten-day "gathering of European youth." After a couple of days of sightseeing in the City of Light, the group headed west to Brest, where they spent the remainder of their trip with local students attending lectures and roundtable discussions about the future of Europe during the day and going to dinners, concerts, and dances at night. The program was sponsored by the European Movement, the largest of the postwar activist networks for European unity, whose decade-long European Youth Campaign organized hundreds of similar events of various scale and scope in the 1950s. A few months later, some five thousand youth and student leaders attended the campaign's European Youth Congress in The Hague.

Although the gathering in Brest was comparatively small, important pro-Europe statesmen from opposite ends of the political spectrum still took the time to participate. French Socialist André Philip and Belgian Christian Democrat Étienne Vallée-Poussin came to publicize the new European Coal and Steel Community established the year before and to promote the proposed European Defense Community—which would have created an integrated European army and a supranational political authority—that was then awaiting final ratification by the national parliaments of potential members. With the prospect of more robust European union on the horizon, the students were shown a series of documentaries to learn about different parts of Europe and get to know their fellow Europeans better. On Easter Sunday, the students sat for a screening of short films on the fishing industry in the North Sea, sculpture in the Netherlands, the history of Luxembourg, and everyday life in Cameroon.[1]

When we think about the opening chapters of European integration, Cameroon does not usually come to mind. But in 1953, Cameroon, like the rest of France's African colonies, was part of the French Union (the postwar incarnation of France's overseas empire), and the 1946 constitution decreed that the Fourth Republic and French Union formed an indissoluble whole.[2] French leaders responded to the growing global movement for decolonization in the postwar conjuncture with more integration between metropole and colony, not less. A small but significant cohort of Africans entered French government at the end of the war, and their critical interventions helped turn African colonial subjects into French citizens. These auspicious French reforms drew Africa and Africans into the European project. By including the film on Cameroon in the program in Brest, its French organizers were inviting a rising generation of Europeans to envision French Africa not only as an integral part of France but also as part of Europe.

At least one adult in the room that day declined the invitation. In an angry letter to the chairmen of the European Youth Campaign, a local volunteer protested what he derisively referred to as "the supposedly European films" the students were shown. He proudly recounted how he had seized the floor between the films on Luxembourg and Cameroon to emphasize the immense gulf separating Europe and Africa. He congratulated himself for having impressed upon the students that travel to other continents, *especially* Africa, was the surest way for them to appreciate their own distinctive Europeanness. After hearing such a speech, we can easily imagine that at least some of his impressionable young audience came away with a sense that French Africa and French Africans were not and probably never could be "European."[3]

The controversy over the proceedings in Brest reflects a broader political debate about the horizons of belonging in postwar France. The incredulous volunteer in Brest was certainly not alone in believing that French Africa did

---

1. Rassemblement européen de jeunes lycéens à Brest à Pâques, undated, Archives Historiques de l'Union Européenne (AHUE): ME-218. Participants included groups of ten to twenty high school students from the Netherlands, Italy, Britain, West Germany, Belgium, Austria, Norway, Sweden, Denmark, and Finland.

2. As a United Nations "trust territory," Cameroon was not supposed to be integrated into the French Union, but the architects of the Fourth Republic ignored the formal terms of international trusteeship and included Cameroon (and Togo) anyway.

3. Rapport sur la rencontre internationale des lycéens Brest 2–10 avril 1953, à l'attention de MM. Moreau et Deshormes, April 9, 1953. AHUE, ME-218.

not quite fit in the new Europe-in-the-making. Gaullist senator and future prime minister Michel Debré vehemently argued that French participation in supranational European institutions would erode the foundations of the French Union. Indeed, while the European Movement was trying to mobilize young Europeans in support of the European Defense Community (EDC) at events like the one in Brest, Debré frequently invoked youth in his (ultimately successful) parliamentary campaign to defeat it. In a screed against the prospect of European sovereignty in the run-up to the French vote on the EDC, he warned, "European citizenship might have meaning for French youth who live in Europe, [but] it strongly risks having none for French youth who live outside of Europe, especially those of other religions and other races."[4]

These remarks are worth parsing carefully. In his reference to "other religions" and "other races," Debré coded Europe as white and Christian, even as he strongly affirmed that young people in overseas France, who were not necessarily white or Christian, were in fact French. In other words, for Debré "French" was racially neutral and religiously open, whereas "European" was an exclusive racial-religious category. There is certainly a long history of conceptualizing Europeanness in this way, but Debré was responding more immediately to the Europeanist rhetoric of Christian Democrats, the dominant political force everywhere in postwar Western Europe, who explicitly fused political and civilizational identity in their rationale for European unity. A few months after the gathering in Brest, Pierre-Henri Teitgen, then president of the French Christian Democratic party, vigorously championed the EDC at the founding congress of the International Union of Young Christian Democrats in Tours in civilizational terms. He modeled European self-understanding to the hundreds of young people assembled there: "Let us make Europe," Teitgen declared. "We shall be defending a civilization, a soul, a spirit, and—in my eyes, as in yours—lands, fields, towns, mountains, rivers, men and women, children, wealth, enjoyment of justice, coal and steel, the civilization, the Christian humanism, that means everything to us."[5] With this brand of Europeanism ascendant throughout Western Europe, it is little wonder that Debré

4. Michel Debré, "Proposition invitant le gouvernement à constituer une commission chargée d'étudier les rapports entre l'Union française et une organisation politique de l'Europe," undated, Archives de l'Histoire Contemporaine (AHC): Fonds Debré, 1/DE/513. Although we typically associate this kind of antisupranationalism with Gaullism, French Socialists also opposed the EDC on colonial grounds. See Brian Shaev, "The Algerian War, European Integration, and the Decolonization of French Socialism," *French Historical Studies* 41, no. 1 (February 2018): 63–94, https://doi.org/10.1215/00161071-4254619.

5. Cited in Paolo Acanfora, "Christian Democratic Internationalism: NEI and the Geneva Circles between European Unification and Religious Identity, 1947–1954," *Contemporary European History* 24, no. 3 (2015): 387n62, https://doi.org/10.1017/S0960777315000211.

worried about young metropolitan French considering themselves *too* European. "Europe for the Europeans," Debré insisted, was no different from and no less dangerous than the Pan-Africanist rallying cry, "Africa for the Africans."[6] Both threatened to reinforce racial and religious boundaries between French youth in the metropole and their new co-citizens overseas.

Debré's focus on youth was neither incidental nor symbolic. It reflected a decade's worth of public pronouncements by French and African leaders that framed the social promotion of African youth and the development of genuine bonds of solidarity between French and African young people as critical to the French Union's long-term success. But bringing young Africans into the social and cultural life of the French Union in a meaningful way would be no small feat. The infrastructure of colonial domination in France's African empire was solidly built; social and cultural institutions in French Africa were designed to maintain structural inequality and ensure racial reproduction across generations. At the French Union's founding, Africans in proximity to French colonial society typically resided in racially segregated urban centers and attended separate schools, if they attended school at all. For all the grand rhetoric about France's "civilizing mission," on the eve of the war barely 1 percent of the total population across the French African Federations had had any kind of schooling whatsoever.[7] Secondary education for Africans in the territories was almost nonexistent, and only a privileged few were able to pursue further study in France.

World War II was a turning point for education in French Africa and for the colonial administration's stance toward African youth. As the end of the war drew near, the dismal state of education in France's African colonies became a point of international embarrassment and anxiety for French leaders. Determined to restore France's global image and stave off international oversight in the education space, French colonial officials committed themselves to the expansion of African education at Charles de Gaulle's landmark Brazzaville Conference on colonial reform in early 1944. But what had begun as a defensive maneuver directed primarily toward international opinion became infused with more radical and emancipatory potential after the Liberation, as newly elected and enfranchised Africans seized on issues of educational access and youth empowerment as benchmarks of democratization in postwar French Africa more broadly. "It is well and good to tell us all men are equal,"

---

6. Michel Debré, "Sur le transfert de souveraineté," *Bulletin du Comité National de défense de la France et l'Union Française*, no. 4, September 1, 1953, Archives Nationales de la France (AN): C//15913, dossier 2.

7. "Éléments de rapport sur le développement de l'Enseignement dans les TOM," April 7, 1950, Archives Nationales de la France d'Outre-Mer (ANOM): 1AFFPOL/1015.

Guinean deputy Mamba Sano reproached colleagues in the French National Assembly in 1950. "It is well and good to tell us we now have rights and freedoms according to the constitution. Well, all those rights and freedoms are still only on paper." For his constituents in the rural villages and forest communities of Guinée to be truly free and equal, Sano insisted, they needed *schools*.[8]

French African leaders Léopold Sédar Senghor and Félix Houphouët-Boigny fought ceaselessly alongside lesser-known figures like Sano and many others to close the gap between French political rhetoric about improved education and social opportunities for African youth and realities on the ground. Those efforts bore some fruit. By the late 1950s, the construction of hundreds of new schools in the territories had raised the rate of primary school attendance in French Africa to 15 percent. Colonial authorities provided more scholarships for promising students to continue their studies in new or desegregated secondary schools in regional hubs in the territories or to complete their educations in the metropole. On the eve of African independence, there were some eight thousand African students enrolled in metropolitan middle schools, high schools, and universities (about half of whom received state aid), and a bevy of new youth exchanges and training programs—a signature policy of Houphouët-Boigny's—brought hundreds more young Africans to European France each year during school breaks and summer holidays.

Contrary to what we might expect from the reconstituted republic, whose constitution reaffirmed France's commitment to *laïcité*, the postwar expansion of colonial education and state-sponsored youth programs was not limited to secular public schooling. Beginning in 1946, billions of francs were allocated for social and economic development in France's overseas territories, and a significant portion of those funds supported mission schools and Catholic youth organizations. African Muslims leveraged state funding for Christian education to advance long-standing demands for subsidizing Qur'anic schools and adding Arabic to the public-school curriculum in Muslim-majority areas. This effort also yielded some results. By the early 1950s, territorial governments were experimenting with new kinds of "Franco-Muslim" and "Franco-Arabic" schools in Mauritania, French Soudan (contemporary Mali), and Chad, as well as incorporating Arabic language instruction in public school programs in other territories with large Muslim populations.

This openness to reform and apparent embrace of racial and religious pluralism seems to support a growing body of literature that considers the postwar conjuncture an unprecedented, if ultimately fleeting, moment of radical

---

8. *Procès-Verbal de la Commission d'Outre-Mer, séance du 6 décembre 1950.* AN C / / 15408.

FIGURE I.1.   A Franco-African exchange program in the French Alps in 1960. Courtesy of the Archives Nationales de France, CAC: 19770181/7.

possibility to remake the French colonial world.[9] Certainly, colonial youth and education initiatives in the 1940s and 1950s projected a powerful vision of what a multiracial and religiously inclusive France could look like (figure I.1), a vision that stands in stark contrast to the exclusivist conception of Europe and Europeanness that rose to the fore at the gathering in Brest. And yet, even before African independence in 1960, it once again seemed like common sense that France belonged in Europe and French Africans did not quite belong in European France. A decade of scholarship has insisted that this outcome was not inevitable. So how and why did it happen?

For all its emphasis on the "imagined possibilities" of the era, the literature on postwar empire has yet to give us a clear picture of what was actually possible for France and Africa, and Africa and Europe, in the ostensible world-historical opening of the postwar conjuncture. The onset of the Cold War and the Algerian Revolution certainly foreclosed many radical visions in both

---

9. Frederick Cooper, *Citizenship between Empire and Nation: Remaking France and French Africa, 1945–1960* (Princeton, NJ: Princeton University Press, 2014); Gary Wilder, *Freedom Time: Negritude, Decolonization and the Future of the World* (Durham, NC: Duke University Press, 2015); Andrew Smith and Chris Jeppesen, eds., *Britain, France and the Decolonization of Africa: Future Imperfect?* (London: University College London Press, 2017); Todd Shepard, *The Invention of Decolonization: The Algerian War and the Remaking of France* (Ithaca, NY: Cornell University Press, 2006); Kristen Stromberg Childers, *Seeking Imperialism's Embrace: National Identity, Decolonization, and Assimilation in the French Caribbean* (New York: Oxford University Press, 2016).

the colonial and European arenas, but not all. This book looks to youth at the crossroads of integration and decolonization as a fruitful, unexplored terrain for more answers. The book explores how colonial education reforms and public and private programs to promote solidarity between French and African youth collided with transnational efforts to make young people in Western Europe feel more European after World War II. If we approach Franco-African and European integration as overlapping and competing *generational projects*— that is, as concerted efforts to build new kinds of composite polities by targeting young people's sense of self, affective ties, and institutional pathways for solidarity—the contingent and structural limits of the early postwar years come into focus more clearly. Colonial reformers and European unity activists alike hailed the slogan "Unity in Diversity" as the ethos of their respective generational projects, but consideration of those projects side by side reveals that pluralism and diversity, as ideals and in practice, assumed radically different forms within Europe and between Europe and the wider world.

This book identifies new patterns of racial and religious exclusion nested in that divergence. It connects the vision of Europe that coalesced in postwar campaigns for European unity—a vision that defined Europe as both white *and* raceless, Christian *and* secular—to crucial decisions about how much France should invest in the promotion of African youth and what African education should entail. That vision of Europe also informed French responses to African demands for more robust racial and religious equality, responses that ultimately turned many young francophone Africans away from France irrevocably. In these and other ways, *Black France, White Europe* shows that the interconnected history of colonial and European youth initiatives is key to explaining why, despite France's efforts to strengthen ties with its African colonies in the 1940s and 1950s, France became more European during precisely those years.

Postwar Empire and United Europe: An Entangled History

The overarching historiographical intervention of this book is simple: that histories of African decolonization and European integration cannot be isolated from one another. The intensity, breadth, and long-term consequences of France's efforts to reconcile its commitments to its old African empire and the new Europe are obscured in conventional accounts of twentieth-century European history, which present World War II as a watershed when European powers, with the ambiguous exception of Britain, renounced their claims to world domination and abandoned their colonial vocations.[10] In these narratives, the brutality and devastation of the war shattered Europe's "civilizational confidence" such that continental leaders turned inward to focus on securing peace and prosperity within Europe.[11] Though many European powers continued to control vast territories overseas after the war, it was clear to all—so this line of thinking goes—that the age of empire was over in 1945; the only remaining question was how Europe could extract itself from its colonial entanglements as quickly, cheaply, and peaceably as possible. In this telling, then, European leaders felt they had to pursue European union *over* empire. The only relation posited between the two is sequential: first there was empire, then there was Europe. This narrative effectively detaches the history of colonialism from the history of European integration. The result, as Peo Hansen and Stefan Jonsson cheekily observe, is a whiggish history of the European Union (EU) in which the European project is spared the taint of associations with colonialism in the past that could add weight to accusations of European neo-colonialism in the present.[12]

Contrary to this general European narrative, the French case underscores that postwar leaders were trying to remake the European and colonial worlds simultaneously. It throws into relief the ways in which united Europe and postwar empire were not merely contemporaneous, parallel projects but fundamentally interconnected historical processes, whose points of intersection profoundly shaped the contours of decolonization and the longer trajectory of European integration. More instructive than exceptional, the particularities of France's wartime experience and postwar reconstruction across Europe and Africa help illuminate this "entangled history."[13]

---

10. Tony Judt, *Postwar: A History of Europe since 1945* (New York: Penguin, 2004); Mark Mazower, *Dark Continent: Europe's Twentieth Century* (New York: Vintage, 1997). Mazower has since complicated this line of thinking, without dispensing with it entirely. See his "End of Eurocentrism," in "Around 1948: Interdisciplinary Approaches to Global Transformation," ed. Leela Gandhi and Debbie Nelson, special issue, *Critical Inquiry* 40, no. 4 (Summer 2014): 298–213, https://doi.org/10.1086/676409. Konrad Jarausch's *Out of Ashes: A New History of Europe in the Twentieth Century* (Princeton, NJ: Princeton University Press, 2015) takes a more nuanced approach that considers how decolonization "crisscrossed" with other postwar developments, but the overarching tale of a Europe ridding itself of its "imperial baggage" remains the same (15).

11. Judt, *Postwar*, 5. Martin Conway makes a similar claim in his *Western Europe's Democratic Age, 1945–1968* (Princeton, NJ: Princeton University Press, 2020): 143–145.

12. Peo Hansen and Stefan Jonsson, *Eurafrica: the Untold Story of European Integration and Colonialism* (London: Bloomsbury, 2014).

13. Colonial and transnational entanglements are increasingly acknowledged in the subfield of European integration history. Far from considering these entanglements as unique to France, Kiran Klaus Patel characterizes the whole integration project as a "late colonial" undertaking in his *Project Europe: A History* (Cambridge: Cambridge University Press, 2020), 244. On the methodology of entangled history, see Michael Werner and Bénédicte Zimmerman, "Beyond Comparison: *Histoire Croisée* and the Chal-

After the humiliation of military defeat and the indignity of the collaborationist Vichy regime (1940–1944), France emerged from the war more attached to its empire, not less, in Africa especially. As Eric Jennings has shown, with the metropole under German occupation in the north and the racist Vichy government in the south, for four long years "Free France"—the good, republican France—*was* French Africa.[14] French African labor sustained the Free French war effort, and French African troops played a vital role in the liberation of European France. Consequently, when African colonial subjects started making demands for more political rights and social equality in the increasingly anticolonial international climate of the postwar conjuncture, French leaders listened. They responded with a massive overhaul of colonial governance in a bid to keep French Africa French, and African political participation became one of the basic premises of France's postwar democracy.

The contours of that participation were both groundbreaking and severely limited. A small group of French Africans took part in the constituent assemblies (1945–1946) that wrote the postwar republic's constitution and built the political architecture of the French Union. Many more then served at every level of representative government in African and European France for the duration of the Fourth Republic (1946–1958), from new local assemblies in their home territories and federal councils in Brazzaville and Dakar to the national parliament in Paris. Some even served on French delegations to international organizations, including the earliest European institutions. Léopold Senghor and his Senegalese counterpart in the French Senate, Ousmane Socé Diop, for instance, represented France for more than a decade in the Council of Europe's Parliamentary Assembly in Strasbourg, where they fought for the equitable inclusion of French Africa in the new Europe.[15] In all of these local, national, and international bodies, French Africans contested colonial relations of power and confronted their metropolitan and European colleagues on issues of racism and structural inequality—face-to-face, as ostensible equals—for the first time.[16]

Such extensive African representation within and beyond the empire was unprecedented in modern colonial history, but it was also discriminatory by

---

lenges of Reflexivity," *History and Theory* 45, no. 1 (February 2006): 30–50, https://doi.org/10.1111/j .1468-2303.2006.00347.x.

14. Eric Jennings, *Free French Africa in World War II: The African Resistance* (Cambridge: Cambridge University Press, 2015).

15. Yves Montarsolo, *L'Eurafrique: Contrepoint de l'idée de l'Europe. Le cas français de la deuxième guerre mondiale aux négociations des Traités de Rome* (Aix-en-Provence: Presses Universitaires de Provence, 2010), 73–79.

16. Emily Marker, "Obscuring Race: Franco-African Conversations about Colonial Reform and Racism After World War II and the Making of 'Colorblind France,'" *French Politics, Culture & Society* 33, no. 3 (Fall 2015): 1–23, https://doi.org/10.3167/fpcs.2015.330301.

design.[17] Separate electoral colleges were established in France's African territo-ries, one for whites and the few Africans with French civil status and another for everyone else. The *collège européen,* as it was commonly known, often com-prised fewer than two thousand individuals in territories with African popula-tions in the hundreds of thousands. The dual electorate ensured that at least half of the parliamentary delegations from French Africa were made up of white Frenchmen, typically Christian Democrats, who acted on behalf of mi-nuscule settler populations, colonial business interests, and the Christian mis-sions. This foundational inequity was compounded by the disproportionate total number of deputies allocated to the African territories in the National Assembly, the lone chamber of the French parliament with legislative power. The territories had a greater (though still not proportional) stake in the As-sembly of the French Union (AUF), a novel third parliamentary chamber that dealt with issues concerning overseas France. But the AUF was an exclusively consultative body whose recommendations were seldom heeded. By the early 1950s, the physical distance between the Versailles-based AUF and the real cor-ridors of power in Paris seemed to symbolize the AUF's marginal status, and its own members publicly questioned the significance of their work.[18] With these institutions, the relationship between France and French Africa under the Fourth Republic became less colonial but not truly democratic.

Sui generis French maneuvers like the dual electorate, whose express pur-pose was to reconstitute white supremacy in the renovated imperial republic, should not obscure how closely the shallow democratization of postwar France-Africa relations tracks with wider European trends. As Martin Conway has shown, the kind of democracy that took hold in postwar Western Europe was formal and indirect, not participatory. Popular democracy and a real plu-ralist democratic culture, Conway argues, were out of step with the conform-ist and conservative temper of postwar European societies. The dominant mentality of the era was "restoration, rather than revolution."[19] Europeans, he writes, "wanted to enter a new world, but without destroying the old," which lent "an air of revolution without revolution to the political rhetoric of liberation." Indeed, Conway emphasizes that a return to normalcy was already a top priority in 1945–1946, well before the Cold War partition of the conti-

---

17. Frederick Cooper, *Colonialism in Question: Theory, Knowledge, History* (Berkeley: University of California Press, 2005).

18. Even the AUF's president, Albert Sarraut, expressed his frustration at the apparent futility of the AUF's work in a pair of speeches before the chamber as early as 1951: Allocution prononcée le 9 janvier 1951 par M. Albert Sarraut; Allocution prononcée le 12 juillet 1951. AN C//16135.

19. Conway, *Western Europe's Democratic Age,* 8, 26, 50.

nent shrunk democratic Europe down to size and cemented its defensive stance in both its internal and external affairs.[20]

Franco-African negotiations over the configuration of the French Union fit squarely in this pattern of a pronounced West European pivot away from liberation politics toward formal democracy and structural continuity in the postwar conjuncture. The first proposal for France's postwar constitution, which French Africans fought hard for, would have established a more egalitarian democracy with a unicameral legislature elected through direct universal suffrage. That proposal was voted down in a national referendum in May 1946. When new elections were called, a wave of Christian Democrats was swept into office in a major rout of the parties of the Left. The Fourth Republic and French Union were creatures of that second, more conservative constituent assembly. The constitution that was ultimately adopted in October 1946 reined in popular democracy, narrowed the scope of colonial reform, and strengthened the Christian Right in a single stroke. Subsequent measures like the dual electorate reinforced those crosscutting currents; by institutionalizing white minority rule in the territories, the dual electorate further augmented Christian Democratic power across Europe and Africa. For all the give and take between French and African political actors over the next decade and a half, some potentialities were hamstrung, if not completely foreclosed, by this conservative *Euro-colonial* institutional framework from the start.

Still, it would be a mistake to characterize the political constellation that bound European and African France together in the early postwar era as a "restoration." Postwar colonial reform may not have produced a robust multiracial democracy, but it did open up new forms of scrutiny, critique, and accountability that had tangible effects on policy and the tenor of Franco-African encounters from the parliament floor to the lecture hall. Throughout the period, French politicians, officials, and youth and education workers continuously found themselves on the back foot precisely because some things had changed and others had not. Most no longer wanted to be associated with racism, religious persecution, or other forms of colonial domination, but they struggled to disrupt those relations of power in practice. That disjuncture was the real nub of Franco-African conflict after 1945. Bringing transnational and colonial perspectives into the same frame helps foreground the complexity of the postwar conjuncture as a moment of both rupture and continuity, and the subsequent decade as a period of both structural impasse and contingent politicking.

---

20. Conway, *Western Europe's Democratic Age*, 35, 49.

The tension between historical contingency and impersonal structural forces is a central interpretative and methodological point of contention in the literature on France's postwar empire.[21] This is exemplified in influential works by Frederick Cooper and Gary Wilder, who take contrasting approaches to French, African, and Antillean aspirations for new forms of postnational sovereignty and citizenship after the war. In his *Citizenship between Empire and Nation,* Cooper offers a narrative political history of French and African efforts from 1945 to 1960 to chart a path out of empire that did not end in national independence.[22] Wilder's *Freedom Time* is a conceptual and intellectual history of the political thought of Léopold Senghor and Aimé Césaire on related themes during the same period.[23] The advantages of the two approaches are almost perfectly inverse. Cooper's meticulously researched empirical account of the tit for tat of Franco-African political negotiations discounts any sort of structural explanation for why French and African leaders could not find a way to make decolonization without independence work, while Wilder's rich theoretical consideration of Senghor's and Césaire's ideas about global decolonization and political temporality is disconnected from everyday politics and social experience.

Building on these important works, my analysis draws on both explanatory strategies to tell a different kind of story, one that shifts the focus away from the formal politics and political forms of postwar empire to the social and cultural policies that accompanied them. I rely heavily on archival material that captures the pragmatic and contested aspects of real-world policymaking, but I read the archival record from the perspective of currents of thought that see certain configurations of power as irreducible to individual policy choices. The postwar play of contingent and structural forces, of ideas and institutions, is especially pronounced with regard to youth and education. In moments of great upheaval, the education sector is caught between the pull of social reproduction and the drive for societal transformation. Moreover, its central preoccupation, "youth," is never just a neutral demographic slice of the population based on chronological age but is instead a historically gendered, raced, and classed conceptual category (and thus a reflection of the existing power structure) that is itself an object of political contestation.[24] In this light, the social world of students, youth leaders, educators, bureaucrats, and academics consti-

---

21. Gary Wilder, "From Optic to Topic: The Foreclosure Effect of Historiographic Turns," *American Historical Review* 117, no. 3 (June 2012): 723–745, https://doi.org/10.1086/ahr.117.3.723.

22. Cooper, *Citizenship between Empire and Nation.*

23. Wilder, *Freedom Time.*

24. David M. Pomfret, *Youth and Empire: Trans-Colonial Childhoods in British and French Asia* (Stanford, CA: Stanford University Press, 2016).

tutes a vital part of the political archive of postwar reconstruction and "world-making."[25] This book is not a history *of* young people and adjacent social groups; rather, it explores the shifting coordinates of postwar belonging *through* them.[26] The educational infrastructure that was put in place after the war offered French, African, and West European young people "multiple and unequal paths to citizenship."[27] Those unequal paths, I argue, reflect a new constellation of exclusionary logics and practices—some that predated the war and others that were unleashed by it—that came together at the interstices of Franco-African and European integration.

Both Wilder and Cooper have considered elements of those intersecting integration stories in their attention to Senghor's support for a "Eurafrican" federation in the 1940s and 1950s.[28] For Senghor, postwar integration would proceed simultaneously on multiple scales in concentric circles, like Russian nesting dolls. French Africa would be more thoroughly integrated into France, but on an equal footing; that new Franco-African polity would be integrated into a larger

25. "Worldmaking" has become an important way of thinking about various levels of historical agency and global transformation in this era. See Wilder, *Freedom Time*; Adom Getachew, *Worldmaking After Empire: The Rise and Fall of Self-Determination* (Princeton, NJ: Princeton University Press, 2018); and Christopher Lee, ed., *Making a World After Empire: The Bandung Moment and Its Afterlives* (Athens, OH: Ohio University Press, 2010).

26. Sarah Maza makes this distinction with regard to histories of childhood in "'The Kids Aren't Alright: Historians and the Problem of Childhood," *American Historical Review* 125, no. 4 (October 2020): 1261–1285, https://doi.org/10.1093/ahr/rhaa380. There are excellent social histories of these groups and their role in wider processes of integration and decolonization throughout the period. On African teachers and students, see Boubacar Ly, *Les instituteurs au Sénégal, 1903–1945*, 6 vols. (Paris: L'Harmattan, 2009); Pascale Barthélémy, *Africaines et diplômées à l'époque coloniale (1918–1957)* (Rennes: Presses Universitaires de Rennes, 2010). On youth and student movements and decolonization, see Hélène d'Almeida-Topor and Odile Georg, eds., *Le Mouvement associatif des jeunes en Afrique noire francophone au XXe siècle* (Paris: L'Harmattan, 1989); Nicolas Bancel, Daniel Denis, and Youssef Fates, *De l'Indochine à l'Algérie. La jeunesse en mouvements des deux côtés du miroir colonial* (Paris: La Découverte, 2003); Amady Aly Dieng, *Les grands combats de la Fédération des étudiants de l'Afrique Noire: de Bandung aux indépendances, 1955–1960* (Paris: L'Harmattan, 2009); Burleigh Hendrickson, *Decolonizing 1968: Transnational Student Activism in Tunis, Paris, and Dakar* (Ithaca, NY: Cornell University Press, 2022). On youth and European integration, see Richard Ivan Jobs, *Backpack Ambassadors: How Youth Travel Integrated Western Europe* (Chicago: University of Chicago Press, 2017).

27. Clif Stratton, *Education for Empire: American Schools, Race, and the Paths of Good Citizenship* (Berkeley: University of California Press, 2016), 1.

28. Cooper, *Citizenship between Empire and Nation*, chap. 4, and Gary Wilder, "*Eurafrique* as the Future Past of 'Black France': Sarkozy's Temporal Confusion and Senghor's Postwar Vision," in *Black France/France Noire: The History and Politics of Blackness*, ed. Trica Danielle Keaton, T. Denean Sharpley-Whiting, and Tyler Stovall (Durham, NC: Duke University Press, 2012), 57–87. For earlier French-language scholarship on Eurafrica, see Montarsolo, *L'Eurafrique*; Guia Migani, *La France et l'Afrique sub-saharienne, 1957–1963: Histoire d'une décolonisation entre idéaux eurafricains et politique de puissance* (Bern: Peter Lang, 2008); Marie-Thérèse Bitsch and Gérard Bossuat, eds., *L'Europe Unie et l'Afrique: De l'idée d'Eurafrique à la convention de Lomé I* (Brussels: Bruylant, 2005); René Girault, "La France entre l'Europe et l'Afrique," in *The Relaunching of Europe and the Treaties of Rome: Actes du Colloque de Rome 25–28 Mars 1987*, ed. Enrico Serra (Brussels: Bruylant, 1989).

European agglomeration, securing for French Africa more equitable relationships with France's European partners; and that entity—Eurafrica—would itself be integrated into an increasingly interconnected and interdependent global order. Senghor's Eurafrica bore little resemblance to its original formulation in the early 1920s as an unabashedly colonial, extractive, and instrumental relationship between Europe and Africa, in which coordinated European development schemes in Africa would be a means to achieve political union and economic recovery in post–World War I Europe.[29] Variations on that theme were embraced by startlingly diverse constituencies in the years between the wars, from industrialists in German-speaking Central Europe and colonial officials and politicians with links to the Colonial Lobby in France, to Labour Party leaders in Britain and liberal internationalists in League of Nations circles.[30] As this varied following suggests, Eurafrica in the 1920s and 1930s was "more a vague space of dreams and projections than a clear political concept of any meaningful relevance."[31] The one through line of the interwar conceptual repertoire of Eurafrica was an underlying belief in Europeans' superior ability to maximize African resources, which justified European control of Africa's natural wealth and the privileging of European over African interests.

Senghor's redeployment of Eurafrica after the war as a genuinely global and democratic project was idiosyncratic, but his scalar vision was not. To many postwar observers, bigger seemed better, or rather bigger seemed necessary for survival in the new superpower age. With Europe and Africa emerging as key battlegrounds in the global Cold War, Africans and Europeans alike sought novel institutional arrangements that would ensure them the maximum amount of political, economic, and cultural autonomy in a bipolar decolonizing world.[32] As Todd Shepard, Michael Collins, and others have shown, the postwar era saw many experiments with supranational, federal, or other types of composite polities and extraterritorial economic zones, within and across Europe and Africa both.[33]

29. Antoine Fleury, "Paneurope et l'Afrique," in *L'Europe Unie et l'Afrique*, ed. Bitsch and Bossuat.

30. Charles-Robert Ageron, "L'idée d'eurafrique et le débat colonial franco-allemand de l'entre-deux-guerres," *Revue d'Histoire Moderne et contemporaine* 22 (1975): 446–475, https://doi.org/10.3406/rhmc.1975.2329; Chantal Metzger, "L'Allemagne et l'Eurafrique," Yves Montarsolo, "Albert Sarraut et l'idée d'Eurafrique," and Anne Deighton, "Ernest Bevin and the Idea of Euro-Africa from the Interwar to the Postwar Period," in *L'Europe Unie et l'Afrique.*, ed. Bitsch and Bossuat.

31. Patel, *Project Europe*, 246.

32. Odd Arne Westad, *The Global Cold War: Third World Interventions and the Making of Our Times* (Cambridge: Cambridge University Press, 2006).

33. Todd Shepard, "À l'heure des 'grands ensembles' et de la guerre d'Algérie. L'État-nation' en question," *Monde(s)* 1, no. 1 (2012): 113–134; Michael Collins, "Decolonization and the 'Federal Moment,'" *Diplomacy & Statecraft* 24, no. 1 (2013): 21–40, https://doi.org/10.1080/09592296.2013.762881;

The reemergence of Eurafrica in the 1940s as a salient geopolitical concept is a particularly evocative instance of this broader postwar trend. Many Eurafrica boosters from the interwar period, like veteran French colonial administrators Robert Delavignette and Albert Sarraut, continued to occupy prominent positions in the new postwar regime; they helped rebrand Eurafrica for the changed times as a more mutually beneficial relationship for Europe and Africa.[34] For many Europeans, though, Eurafrica largely remained an African solution to European problems. It regained its earlier transnational appeal as a way to strengthen Europe's internal unity, institutional integration, and economic independence and assumed newfound resonance as a counterweight to Europe's declining power base in Asia and waning global influence more broadly. For these reasons, although most closely associated with France in this period, Eurafrica found supporters even in generally hostile Germany and the Netherlands, including Dutch prime minister Willem Drees (1948–1958).[35] No longer the stuff of fantasy, Eurafrica became real in the 1950s as European colonies in Africa were included in institutional Europe, most notably in the decade's major institutional breakthroughs: the 1957 establishment of the European Economic Community (EEC) and European Atomic Energy Community (EURATOM). Just as postwar colonial reform brought French Africa into the European project, resurgent transnational interest in Eurafrica brought Europe into France's postwar empire.

In recent years Eurafrica has enjoyed a groundswell of scholarly attention that has begun to shine a much-needed spotlight on the interconnected history of the end of empire and the construction of Europe. Work on Eurafrica, much like the literatures on European integration and late colonialism that it brings together, centers on juridical and economic institutional arrangements and related questions of sovereignty, markets, geostrategy, and diplomacy. Its focal point has been the formal association between colonial African territories and the European Communities, the renegotiation of those terms after independence, and subsequent trade policy and development aid.[36] By using

---

Matthew Connelly, *A Diplomatic Revolution: Algeria's Fight for Independence and the Origins of the Post-Cold War Era* (Oxford: Oxford University Press, 2002).

34. Sarraut, for instance, served as the president of the Assembly of the French Union for the entirety of its existence (1947–1958); Delavignette served as a top official in the central colonial authority in Paris from 1947 to 1951 and as a professor at the École Nationale de la France d'Outre-Mer, the elite training ground for colonial personnel for the next decade.

35. Patel, *Project Europe*, 246, 249.

36. Hansen and Jonsson, *Eurafrica*; Martin Rempe, "Decolonization by Europeanization? The Early EEC and the Transformation of French-African Relations," *KFG Working Paper Series* 27 (May 2011): 1–21, http://dx.doi.org/10.17169/refubium-22834; Giuliano Garavini, *After Empires: European Integration, Decolonization, and the Challenge from the Global South, 1957–1986* (Oxford: Oxford University Press, 2012); Muriam Haleh Davis, "North Africa and the Common Agricultural Policy: From Colonial Pact to

youth as its primary lens, this book not only adds a social and cultural dimension to the history of Eurafrica; it also offers a fuller picture of postwar integration more broadly as a set of coordinated attempts to engineer new kinds of pluralist communities made up of socially rooted and enculturated human beings as opposed to abstract political and economic actors.

The literature on European integration, in particular, has struggled to link up the political project of European unity and the history of early European institutions with broader social and cultural processes of Europeanization in the mid-twentieth century.[37] "Europeanization" here refers both to large-scale patterns of social change and transnational cultural diffusion in which the lifeworlds of populations in different European contexts became more alike and also more closely identified with "Europe."[38] The world of youth is a natural place to explore such processes. In a recent study of independent youth travel, Richard Ivan Jobs compellingly argues that new forms of youth mobility "helped constitute the social space of Western Europe" from the immediate postwar years through the end of the Cold War. His examination of Europe's "backpack ambassadors" gives us a less EU-centric and top-down history of European integration, one that emphasizes "horizontal dimensions of integration emerging from social activity, rather than just the vertical dimensions descending from the political activity of diplomats negotiating international treaties."[39]

Scholars working on this kind of social and cultural integration are seldom concerned with the actual denouement of Europe's imperial extensions overseas, but they intuitively recognize that Europeanization encompassed "processes of delimitation and othering" both within Europe and between Europe and the wider world.[40] Sociologists, for instance, have suggested that the convergence of postwar demographic and sociological trends like rising incomes and aging populations made the distance between Europe and Africa more pronounced.[41] Cultural historians have made similar suggestions. Victoria de

European Integration," in *North Africa and the Making of Europe*, ed. Davis and Thomas Serres (London: Bloomsbury, 2018); Megan Brown, *The Seventh Member State: Algeria, France, and the European Community* (Cambridge, MA: Harvard University Press, 2022). See also notes 28 and 30.

37. Histories of the EU ignore the cultural dynamics and politics of European integration before the late 1960s. See Cris Shore, *Building Europe: The Cultural Politics of European Integration* (London: Routledge, 2000).

38. This is what political scientist Kevin Featherstone defines as the "maximalist" conception of Europeanization, as opposed to the "minimalist" understanding that refers to national adaptations to EU policy. See Kevin Featherstone and C. M. Radaelli, eds., *The Politics of Europeanization* (Oxford: Oxford University Press, 2003), 3–7.

39. Jobs, *Backpack Ambassadors*, 57, 3–4.

40. Jobs, *Backpack Ambassadors*, 6.

41. Göran Therborn, *European Modernity and Beyond: The Trajectory of European Societies, 1945–2000* (London: Sage, 1995).

Grazia argues that the relentless spread of US consumer culture across twentieth-century Europe helped forge a new transatlantic civilization—which she provocatively calls the "White Atlantic"—that detached Western Europe from the Third World and fostered a new "way of life racism."[42] Conway makes a parallel point about the democratic political culture of the "smaller Europe" that emerged from the war and the Cold War division of the continent, which, he argues, reinforced Western Europe's image as "a homogenously European and white society."[43]

Such broad societal trends were constantly shifting the racialized boundaries between a European "us" and a non-European "them," precisely as institutional Europe—and with it, Eurafrica—was taking shape. Though difficult to see in technical negotiations over customs unions or free trade zones, as the Brest proceedings show, confusion and contestation over those boundaries and their underlying racial logics bubbled to the surface in postwar campaigns for European unity that targeted youth. Those logics contributed to the consolidation of a new racial formation that I call "postwar racial common sense."[44] Without having to use the word "race," the outraged volunteer in Brest enacted "racial Europeanization" with his outburst on the immutable social and cultural difference between Africans and Europeans. As we shall see, that process of self-definition through the Other went hand in hand with a concerted effort to excise the language of race from discussions of *intra*-European diversity in post-Holocaust Europe. After more than a century and a half of racial discourse on European national, regional, linguistic, and religious difference, postwar Europe was consciously refigured as both white and *raceless*.[45] The transnational construction of European racelessness, I argue, dovetailed with specifically French maneuvers to avoid racial language and the appearance of racism in postwar colonial governance in the face of more robust public scrutiny and African critique. Those conceptual and rhetorical shifts strengthened political claims that racism was not (or no longer) a native European problem—that Africans and their demands for racial justice made it one. Transnational European forums, as well as Franco-African ones, were crucial venues where that kind of racial-cultural work took place.

---

42. Victoria De Grazia, *Irresistible Empire: America's Advance through Twentieth-Century Europe* (Cambridge, MA: Belknap Press of Harvard University Press, 2005), 11–13, 351.

43. Conway, *Western Europe's Democratic Age*, 86–87.

44. Michael Omi and Howard Winant, *Racial Formation in the United States from the 1960s to the 1980s* (New York: Routledge, 1994).

45. David Theo Goldberg, *The Threat of Race: Reflections on Racial Neoliberalism* (Oxford: Blackwell Publishing, 2009), chap. 5, "Precipitating Evaporation (On Racial Europeanization)," 151–198. On the racial categorization of Europeans in prewar France, see Elisa Camiscioli, *Reproducing the French Race: Immigration, Intimacy, and Embodiment in the Early Twentieth Century* (Durham, NC: Duke University Press, 2009).

Focusing too narrowly on the technical and bureaucratic aspects of European integration also obscures the importance of religion in European unity and the decisive role Christian Democracy played in setting institutional Europe on its course.[46] Many of the most ardent early European unity activists were motivated by their Christian faith, seeing supranational European federalism as a way to revive European Christendom and re-center Christianity in European life. It follows that the political and legal idea of Europe at the heart of Christian Democratic Europeanism was unabashedly Christian.[47] With the onset of the Cold War, the Christian Democrat pro-Europe movements overtook their Socialist counterparts, and significant US aid—both vocal and covert—ensured the predominance of a Christian vision of Europe in federalist circles and early transnational institutions, including the European Youth Campaign.[48]

The ascendancy of Christian Democratic Europe was not due to Cold War geostrategy alone; combining transnational and colonial perspectives offers a more complex portrait of the changing relationship between religion, politics, and European identity in the middle third of the twentieth century. European Christianity underwent epochal transformations midcentury, most significantly the rapprochement between Catholics and Protestants and political Catholicism's coming to terms with the modern secular state. A growing body of literature has shown that the roots of both of these historic shifts lay in older visions of European unity (including fascist ones) and deep-seated anxieties about Christianity's fate in the postcolonial world (especially in Africa).[49] Protestants and Catholics found common cause in making the secular

---

46. Wolfram Kaiser, *Christian Democracy and the Origins of the European Union* (Cambridge: Cambridge University Press, 2007).

47. Acanfora, "Christian Democratic Internationalism"; Rosario Forlenza, "The Politics of *Abendland*: Christian Democracy and the Idea of Europe after the Second World War," *Contemporary European History* 26, no. 2 (2017): 375–391, https://doi.org/10.1017/S0960777317000091. On Christianity and the establishment of a European human rights regime in this period, see Marco Duranti, *The Conservative Human Rights Revolution: European Identity, Transnational Politics and the Origins of the European Convention* (Oxford: Oxford University Press, 2017); Samuel Moyn, *Christian Human Rights* (Philadelphia: University of Pennsylvania Press, 2015).

48. Richard J. Aldrich, "OSS, CIA, and European Unity: the American Committee on United Europe, 1948–1960," *Diplomacy and Statecraft* 8, no. 1 (March 1997): 184–227, https://doi.org/10.1080/09592299708406035; Brian McKenzie, "The European Youth Campaign in Ireland: Neutrality, Americanization and the Cold War, 1950–1959," *Diplomatic History* 40, no. 3 (2016), 421–444, https://doi.org/10.1093/dh/dhv010.

49. Udi Greenberg, "Catholics, Protestants, and the Violent Birth of European Religious Pluralism," *American Historical Review* 124, no. 2 (2019): 511–538, https://doi.org/10.1093/ahr/rhz252, and "Protestants, Decolonization, and European Integration, 1885–1961," *Journal of Modern History* 89, no. 2 (2017): 314–354, https://doi.org/10.1086/691531; Elizabeth Foster, *African Catholic: Decolonization and the Transformation of the Church* (Cambridge, MA: Harvard University Press, 2019); James Chappel, *Catholic Modern: The Challenge of Totalitarianism and the Remaking of the Church* (Cambridge, MA: Harvard

order more hospitable to Christianity in postwar Europe and in dissociating Christianity from the late colonial state to preserve the Christian presence after the end of empire. Those motivations worked in tandem with presenting a united front against godless Communists in the global Cold War. The political discourse of "religious pluralism" and "religious liberty" served all of these purposes. That rhetoric also bolstered Western Europe's self-image as tolerant and democratic, even though, much like postwar European democracy itself, it was in fact quite narrowly conceived by and for European Christians.[50] Religious pluralism was embraced in the postwar European mainstream, not only as a core European value but also as a distinctly Christian legacy on Europe's democratic political culture. Indeed, as Christian ecumenism and Catholic modernism made Christian faith less politically and communally divisive in postwar Europe, Christianity itself became more available as a moral and historical resource to left-leaning and secular European integrationists, who emphasized Christianity's imprint on "European civilization" beyond theology and religious practice.

Anthropologists Talal Asad and Mayanthi Fernando argue that the contours of European secularism have always cast Christian modes of religiosity within the bounds of secular normativity while excluding all others.[51] This book approaches the postwar conjuncture as a particularly important chapter in that longer story, a time when a transnational European secular order was actively constituted in ways that simultaneously cast itself as an exemplar of religious pluralism *and* reprivileged Christianity over other faiths. I refer to this as the "culturalization of Christianity" in postwar Europe. Europe was becoming more internally united in a way that set itself against the anti-Christian Soviet Union and the doubly un-Christian, because also "nonsecular," Islamic world.[52]

University Press, 2018); Darcie Fontaine, *Decolonizing Christianity: Religion and the End of Empire in France and Algeria* (Cambridge: Cambridge University Press, 2016).

50. While some postwar Christians across Europe and Africa advocated for a more robust pluralism that would include Jews and Muslims, Christian ecumenism was the form that ultimately triumphed in the postwar European mainstream. Darcie Fontaine's analysis of European Christians' failed efforts to dissociate Christianity from colonial rule in Algeria mirrors James Chappel's discussion of the failure of the postwar Catholic European Left to push the Church to come to terms with its complicity in the development of modern anti-Semitism. Fontaine, *Decolonizing Christianity*; Chappel, *Catholic Modern*. The dogged silence on anti-Semitism and Jews in general in all of the sources on religious and racial pluralism in this period is truly stunning. I address this silence at discrete points in this book, but the topic deserves and requires further research in its own right.

51. Mayanthi Fernando, *The Republic Unsettled: Muslim French and the Contradictions of Secularism* (Durham, NC: Duke University Press, 2014); Talal Asad, *Formations of the Secular: Christianity, Islam and Modernity* (Stanford, CA: Stanford University Press, 2003).

52. Joan Scott, *Sex and Secularism* (Princeton, NJ: Princeton University Press, 2017); Samuel Moyn, "From Communist to Muslim: European Human Rights, the Cold War, and Religious Liberty," *South Atlantic Quarterly* 113, no. 1 (Winter 2014): 63–86, https://doi.org/10.1215/00382876-2390428. Moyn

Matthew Connelly, in his work on the Algerian Revolution (1954–1962), notes that it was precisely this perception of multiaxial civilizational conflict—not only East-West but also North-South—that made the idea of Eurafrica so appealing in the 1950s, not only to Europeans but also to the US foreign policy establishment.[53] Connelly focuses on the remaking of the postwar international order, but the same forces also contributed to the remaking of postwar Western Europe as both secular *and* Christian. That transnational European realignment of religion, (geo)politics, and identity, I suggest, is an often overlooked but crucial counterpart to what some scholars have called the "racialization of Islam" in France.[54]

Racial and religious exclusion in contemporary France is typically considered through a national lens that emphasizes the legacy of revolutionary universalism on France's distinct secular and color blind republican culture.[55] Even colonial approaches that locate the production of racial and religious difference in the historical experience of colonialism and decolonization generally stay within the bounds of the French "imperial nation-state."[56] Such national-colonial frameworks make it difficult to see how transnational processes like the culturalization of Christianity and racial Europeanization narrowed the horizons of belonging in postwar France and fundamentally recontextualized republican principles of *laïcité* and colorblindness that continue to frame debates about racial and religious pluralism in France today.

Bringing these sprawling and complex political and geopolitical, sociocultural and institutional, racial and religious dynamics together into a single frame may seem like a hopelessly gargantuan undertaking, but postwar French, African, and European integrationists' shared preoccupation with youth created a well-defined policy area where all of these concerns collided and con-

---

argues that the Cold War discourse of religious freedom and the equation of democracy and Christianity sought to marginalize secularism, whereas Scott, who I think makes the more persuasive case, argues that Christianity, democracy, *and* secularism became synonymous in Cold War rhetoric in opposition to Soviet *atheism*.

53. Connelly, *A Diplomatic Revolution*.

54. Naomi Davidson, *Only Muslim: Embodying Islam in Twentieth-Century France* (Ithaca, NY: Cornell University Press, 2012); Fernando, *The Republic Unsettled*. For a provocative new interpretation of the racialization of Muslims and Islam in France and its empire in this period through the lens of racial capitalism, see Muriam Haleh Davis, *Markets of Civilization: Islam and Racial Capitalism in Algeria* (Durham, NC: Duke University Press, 2022).

55. Alyssa Goldstein Sepinwall, *The Abbé Grégoire and the Making of Modern Universalism* (Berkeley: University of California Press, 2005).

56. Gary Wilder, *The French Imperial Nation-State: Negritude and Colonial Humanism between the World Wars* (Chicago: University of Chicago Press, 2004); Emmanuelle Saada, *Les enfants de la colonie: les métis de l'empire français entre sujétion et citoyenneté* (Paris: Découverte, 2007); Shepard, *The Invention of Decolonization*.

verged.[57] In a rare study of the European Movement's early interest in youth, Christina Norwig suggests that from the beginning, European unity activists approached European integration as a "generational project," adapting nationalist discourses about the "young generation" and political rejuvenation to forge Europe's postnational future.[58] I argue that the renovation of France's African empire was also pursued as a generational project, whose success hinged on decolonizing belonging throughout European and African France. French-educated Africans, who were themselves set apart from their societies because of their schooling and the special colonial status it conferred on them, were especially attuned to the way generations are actively *made* through historical processes, institutions, and social practice. The first African woman to serve in France's postwar parliament, Jeanne Vialle (who represented Oubangui-Chari in the French Senate from 1947 to 1952), dedicated her political career to making French education widely available to African girls because it was African women, she argued, who would ultimately "knead the dough from which tomorrow's men would be made."[59] (See figure I.2.) For Vialle, decolonization meant the obsolescence of the *évolué*, the elite French-educated African, through mass education and the uplift of the entire population. As Annette Joseph-Gabriel has argued, Vialle's political vision was not about "inclusion, moving a token few marginalized people from the periphery to the core of the imperial nation-state," but rather redefining the very terms on which "collective identities and belonging can be imagined."[60]

Conceived in this way, the confluence of the generational projects of Franco-African and European integration posed a vital, existential dilemma for France and the rest of Europe: Would future generations of Black Africans, particularly

57. A growing literature foregrounds the centrality of education in postwar global politics. See Charles Dorn and Kristen Ghodsee, "The Cold War Politicization of Literacy: Communism, UNESCO, and the World Bank," *Diplomatic History* 36, no. 2 (2012): 373–398, https://doi.org/10.1111/j.1467-7709.2011.01026.x; Damiano Matasci, "'Une 'UNESCO africaine'? Le ministère de la France d'Outre-Mer, la coopération éducative intercoloniale et la défense de l'empire," *Mondes* no. 13 (2018): 195–214, https://doi.org/10.3917/mond1.181.0195.

58. Christina Norwig, "A First European Generation? The Myth of Youth and European Integration in the 1950s," *Diplomatic History* 38, no. 2 (2014): 256, https://doi.org/10.1093/dh/dhu006. Generational thinking remained a powerful mode of envisioning national reconstruction in postwar Europe as well. See Richard Ivan Jobs, *Riding the New Wave: Youth and the Rejuvenation of France after the Second World War* (Stanford, CA: Stanford University Press, 2007); Tara Zahra, *The Lost Children: Reconstructing Europe's Families After World War II* (Cambridge, MA: Harvard University Press, 2011). On generations as both actor and analytical categories, see Emily Marker with Abosede George et al., "AHR Conversation: Each Generation Writes Its Own History of Generations," *American Historical Review* 123, no. 5 (December 2018): 1505–1546, https://doi.org/10.1093/ahr/rhy389.

59. Cited in Annette Joseph-Gabriel, *Reimaging Liberation: How Black Women Transformed Citizenship in the French Empire* (Champaign: University of Illinois Press, 2020), 107.

60. Joseph-Gabriel, *Reimaging Liberation*, 108, 12.

FIGURE I.2.   African young women and girls were a special target of Franco-African youth initiatives. A Franco-African exchange program on the Brittany coast in 1960. Courtesy of the Archives Nationales de France, CAC: 19770181/7.

Black African Muslims, be French? Would they then also be European? Could they be Black, African, Muslim, French, and European all at once? Which of those identifications might be mutually exclusive, and why? These were the fundamental questions youth and education initiatives in France, French Africa, and Western Europe in the 1940s and 1950s sought to address and ultimately failed to resolve. Three-quarters of a century later, Black and Muslim youth in France and across Europe, born in Africa or with African roots, still wrestle with these questions, and they are still demanding answers.[61] The unfinished business of decolonizing belonging remains as urgent today as ever.

Rethinking the Postwar

The temporal focus of this book spans the late war years to the end of the 1950s. A lot happened and a lot changed politically in European and African France in that mind-bogglingly eventful decade and half, but decolonizing be-

---

61. Gurminder Bhambra, Dalia Gebrial, and Kerem Nişancıolu, eds., *Decolonising the University* (London: Pluto Press, 2018); Fatima El-Tayeb, *European Others: Queering Ethnicity in Postnational Europe* (Minneapolis: University of Minnesota Press, 2011); Trica Danielle Keaton, *Muslim Girls and the Other France. Race, Identity Politics, and Social Exclusion* (Bloomington: Indiana University Press, 2006).

longing remained a serious and steady proposition despite the tumult and turmoil of two colonial wars, domestic regime change, Cold War escalation, and transnational institution building. That belonging was not in fact decolonized during those years cannot be fully explained by a series of notable events. I approach the era as an extended "postwar moment," a distinct period in which older modes of distinction in France and its empire were recalibrated and rearranged in response to a new, evolving set of historical conditions engendered by France's wartime experience and postwar reconstruction, the global movement for decolonization, and European integration.[62] The major political turning points of those intersecting historical arcs punctuate my analysis but do not drive the narrative. The competing generational projects of Franco-African and European integration followed their own rhythms.

The chapters in this book all move forward in time, but they are organized thematically with considerable chronological overlap among them. Chapter 1 sets up the war years (c. 1940–1944) as a transitional phase in the longer histories of French republican, colonial African, and transnational European education and approaches to youth, as France's European and African futures were reimagined and increasingly considered in explicit relation to one another. The second and third chapters take different thematic lenses—religion and race, respectively—to youth and education policies in the immediate postwar years (c. 1944–1950) that sought to promote pluralism and integration across European and African France. Chapter 2 focuses on policies and institution building that enacted the culturalization of Christianity; chapter 3 focuses on those that helped consolidate postwar racial common sense. The next two chapters pivot from policy to practice, exploring the experience of students, youth leaders, and educators as they navigated the institutional pathways that had been established for them after the war as political winds and global conditions changed over the course of the following decade. Chapter 4 centers on African students in European France in the 1950s; chapter 5 broadens the field of vision to youth exchanges and international mobilizations in the global arena from the late 1940s to the early 1960s. I then take a longer view of Franco-African and

---

62. Isser Woloch specifies a shorter "postwar moment" in France (1944–1947) that he equates with the rise and fall of liberation politics, whereas in Britain and the United States this "moment" lasted until 1951. Isser Woloch, *The Postwar Moment: Progressive Forces in Britain, France, and the United States After World War II* (New Haven, CT: Yale University Press, 2019). Global and entangled histories often rely on "moments" as an analytic to capture the crystallization of a new set of relations and emphasize the intersections or interconnections of diverse historical phenomena that often have their own logics and trajectories. The concept resonates strongly among historians of anticolonialism and decolonization. See Lee, ed., *Making a World after Empire: The Bandung Moment and Its Afterlives*; Collins, "Decolonization and the 'Federal Moment'"; Erez Manela, *The Wilsonian Moment: Self-Determination and the International Origins of Anticolonialism* (Oxford: Oxford University Press, 2007).

European integration as generational projects. The epilogue considers the consequences of the disjuncture between what had seemed possible and desirable to colonial reformers and European unity activists in the mid-to-late 1940s and what actually came to pass in 1950s, and concludes with some reflections on the afterlives of that entangled history up through the present day.

CHAPTER 1

Envisioning France in a Postwar World

Plans for postwar educational reconstruction in metropolitan France, colonial Africa, and transnational Europe converged on the desk of a single Free French official during the war. René Cassin served as national commissioner of justice and public instruction in Charles de Gaulle's shadow government in London from December 1941 to June 1943. One of Cassin's primary tasks in that capacity was to reconstitute French education along new lines in the wake of the national traumas of defeat, occupation, and collaboration. That entailed wading into entrenched ideological conflicts over schooling that had bitterly divided French leaders, educators, and the public for decades. More immediately, though, Cassin had to deal with the sudden influx of school-age French children to Britain. The logistical challenge of placing émigré children in British schools put Cassin in regular contact with his counterparts in the other European governments-in-exile in London, and ultimately involved him in initiatives for greater European educational cooperation once the war was won. At the same time, Cassin was also the titular head of public instruction in the vast lands of French Equatorial Africa (AEF), the only actual territory under Free French control during Cassin's tenure as Free France's top education official. On a monthslong tour of AEF in early 1942, Cassin visited schools in Chad, Congo, and Gabon and opened discussions about enhancing educational opportunities for French Africans with AEF's governor general, Félix Éboué.

This expansive constellation of national, colonial, and transnational concerns extended Cassin's responsibilities well beyond the normal purview of French ministers of education past. Before the war, international education was Foreign Affairs' bailiwick, and the Colonial Ministry and local administrations exercised complete autonomy over education in the overseas territories. The peculiar situation of Free France—with headquarters in London, Brazzaville, and ultimately Algiers—turned conventional distinctions between metropolitan French, colonial African, and transnational European space upside down, upending the traditional administrative and political geography of French youth and education policy. The wartime interregnum set an important precedent: national figures like Cassin were brought into the colonial policymaking process, and education policy in French Africa was considered alongside national and transnational agendas for education reform. The extraordinary circumstances of the war also inflated the stakes of debates about the spirit and the structure of education across all these contexts. Even the most wonkish policy discussions about curricula and pedagogy became lively outlets for envisioning French national renewal and France's European and African futures.

Cassin's unusual wartime portfolio is a useful lens onto how educational reconstruction in the postwar republic, French Africa, and Western Europe became entangled during the war in new and enduring ways. This chapter locates the origins of two postwar conceptual shifts in what it meant to be French, African, and European in that wartime entanglement. One such shift concerns attitudes about the place of religion in French society and culture. The complex political geography of wartime education planning contributed to the emergence of new rationales for embracing Christianity as an integral part of France's cultural heritage and tamping down the anticlerical edge of French *laïcité* as the overarching framework for school policy in both metropole and colony. The other shift pertains to the coordinates of racial distinction. Education reformers' wartime visions about the role of education in what would become the French Union and united Europe reified ideas about French, African, and European youth, reconstituting a stark Europe-Africa binary in racialized terms. These two shifts shaped subsequent colonial and transnational youth and education policy and the broader generational projects of Franco-African and European integration of which those policies were a part. In this sense, the war years were a moment of transition that opened a new, distinct period of contestation over the horizons of belonging in European and African France.

Education, Republicanism, and the War

As national commissioner for justice and public instruction, Cassin was responsible for preparing for both legal and educational reconstruction in post-Liberation France. This administrative pairing reflected a long French tradition going back to the Enlightenment and the French Revolution of linking the general political order and the structure of education. That tradition inspired wartime planners like Cassin and gave meaning and purpose to their work. Cassin is best known today as the driving force behind the 1948 United Nations Declaration of Human Rights. In the shadow of that historic achievement, Cassin's biographers have characterized his appointment as head of de Gaulle's Justice and Education Department as a "second-rate position" and a "painful political setback."[1] However, we should not discount Cassin's own reflections, many years later, on the capital importance of his work as Free France's top education official, which, in keeping with French tradition, he linked to the question of human rights: "My department, more than any other, worked simultaneously to restore France's moral and intellectual influence in the world and also human rights, so cruelly scorned by Hitlerism. . . . The honor fell to me to represent my country in the spiritual revolution that would accompany the war's victorious end."[2]

In the French revolutionary-republican tradition, education is regarded as the foundation of personal emancipation, societal transformation, and democratic consolidation. A dyed-in-the-wool republican, Cassin identified deeply with that legacy. On the lecture circuit in wartime Britain, he framed the conflict between totalitarianism and democracy as one of warring educational philosophies. In a talk at the Franco-Scottish Society in Edinburg in October 1942, Cassin declared, "Before he dreamed of forming enslaved races abroad, Hitler devised a totalitarian education for the young people of his own country." Cassin decried the extension of that assault on young hearts and minds to France, not only at the hands of the Germans but also in Vichy education reforms that abandoned "the French tradition" rooted in the "critical spirit" and "sought to turn French children into little Nazis."[3] For Cassin, educational reconstruction was vital for the restoration of both France's democracy and its national identity.

---

1. Jay Winter and Antoine Prost, *René Cassin and Human Rights: From the Great War to the Universal Declaration* (Cambridge: Cambridge University Press, 2013), 135, 150.

2. René Cassin, *Les hommes, partis de rien: Le réveil de la France abattue* (Paris: Plon, 1974), 408.

3. René Cassin, "L'éducation et l'avenir," Conférence donnée à la Franco-Scottish Society, le 5 octobre 1942. AN: 382AP/55.

The politicization of education in France from the revolutionary era onward made it a central issue for all subsequent regimes, Left and Right. In the 1790s, successive waves of revolutionaries saw the revolution itself as a pedagogical project to mold an active citizenry that would no longer be controlled by the aristocracy, the Catholic Church, and other corporate entities.[4] Napoleon's reorganization of French education into a national, centralized system in 1806–1808—known as "the University"—was a cornerstone of his efforts to unify the country and one of his most enduring legacies.[5] That centralized education system served as a bulwark of the liberal regime of the July Monarchy (1830–1848), which sought to re-found a stable society in the post-corporate world of nineteenth-century France by erecting a new hierarchy based on individual "capacity" and education.[6] Though primary schooling expanded under that regime, access to secondary education remained limited to a small bourgeois elite, which aligned with the constitutional monarchy's political culture of limited suffrage and elite politics.[7]

The architects of the Second Republic (1848–1852), the short-lived "republican experiment" between the July Monarchy and the Bonapartist Second Empire (1852–1870), envisioned a dramatic expansion of secular primary education to support a democratic republic based on universal male suffrage. But the idealistic "48ers" quickly lost control of the fledgling republic to the conservative bourgeoisie and Napoleon III. The legislature reinstituted Catholic education with the 1850 Falloux Laws, shortly before rallying behind Louis Napoleon's coup d'état that dissolved the republic altogether. Maurice Agulhon has argued that the great political lesson of the Second Republic was the necessity of universal public education to sustain a socially inclusive and democratic polity.[8]

That lesson was not lost on the next generation of French republicans. As soon as they consolidated their grip on France's Third Republic (1871–1940) in the early 1880s, republican leaders elevated the school as the bedrock of the new

---

4. R. R. Palmer, *The Improvement of Humanity: Education and the French Revolution* (Princeton, NJ: Princeton University Press, 1985); Mona Ozouf, *L'école de la France: Essai sur la Révolution, l'utopie de l'enseignement* (Paris: Gallimard, 1984); Isser Woloch, *The New Regime: Transformations in the Civic Order in France, 1789-1820s* (New York: Norton, 1994).

5. Christine Musselin, *The Long March of French Universities* (New York: Routledge Falmer, 2001).

6. Jan Goldstein, *The Post-Revolutionary Self: Politics and Psyche in France, 1750–1850* (Cambridge, MA: Harvard University Press, 2008); Alan Kahan, *Liberalism in Nineteenth-Century Europe: The Political Culture of Limited Suffrage* (New York: Palgrave, 2003); Jennifer Pitts, *A Turn to Empire: The Rise of Imperial Liberalism in Britain and France* (Princeton, NJ: Princeton University Press, 2005).

7. André Jardin and A.-J. Tudesq, *La France des notables*, 2 vols. (Paris: Editions du Seuil, 1973). The Guizot Law of 1833 mandated the creation of primary schools in every commune that reached a certain population threshold, which doubled the total number of primary schools under the July Monarchy.

8. Maurice Agulhon, *The Republican Experiment, 1848-1852*, trans. Janet Lloyd (Cambridge: Cambridge University Press, 1983). See also Sudir Hazareesingh, *From Subject to Citizen: The Second Empire and the Emergence of French Democracy* (Princeton, NJ: Princeton University Press, 1998).

regime. The Ferry Laws (1881–1886) secularized primary education; abolished fees and tuition in public elementary schools; made primary school attendance compulsory for boys and girls up to age thirteen; mandated the creation of public schools in communes with as few as twenty school-age children; and standardized teacher training programs, school inspections, and other bureaucratic controls. The extension of primary schooling into the French countryside was intended to "civilize" its supposedly backward inhabitants. In his classic study of the modernization of rural France, Eugen Weber highlighted the civilizational discourses associated with these education reforms, in which schools "were credited with the ultimate acculturation process that made the French people French" and "finally civilized them." Likewise, schoolteachers were cast as "the militia of the new age, harbingers of enlightenment and of the republican message that reconciled the benighted masses with a new world, superior in wellbeing and democracy."[9] For republicans of the era, that message was a militantly secular one, duly rejected by the Catholic hierarchy, Catholic educators, and Catholic parents. Thus began France's decades-long *querelle scolaire*, which epitomized the ferocious conflict between traditional Catholics and the anticlerical republic that rent France apart from the Dreyfus affair to Vichy.[10]

This 150-year political struggle over the structure and spirit of French education shaped how contemporaries interpreted France's shocking and humiliating defeat in June 1940. Critics on both the Left and Right attributed "the debacle" to the abject failure of the republican school to produce competent leaders and a united citizenry.[11] For *Vichystes*, the defeat directly resulted from school policies that had abandoned religion and traditional values. Pétain himself was heard to have said to the US ambassador that France lost the war because its teachers were not patriotic enough.[12] The Vichy regime set about dismantling the republican school accordingly. By November 1940, the regime had fired all Jewish teachers, abolished the national network of teacher training institutes (*écoles normales*), and added "duties to God" in the ethics syllabus. In the months that followed, religious instruction was reintroduced in the state curriculum and priests were welcomed back into public classrooms. However, the place of Catholicism in French public education was such a polarizing issue that even Vichy officials were wary of overreach. Worried about worsening

---

9. Eugen Weber, *Peasants into Frenchmen: The Modernization of Rural France* (Stanford, CA: Stanford University Press, 1974), 3–5, 303, 308–309.

10. The literal translation is "school quarrel," but it is often glossed as "battle over schools."

11. Jean-François Muracciole, *Les enfants de la défaite: La Résistance, l'éducation et la culture* (Paris: Presses de Sciences Po, 1998); Jean-Michel Barreau, *Vichy contre l'école de la République: Théoriciens et théories scolaires de la "Révolution nationale"* (Paris: Flammarion 2000).

12. Nicholas Atkin, "Church and Teachers in Vichy France, 1941–1944," *French History* 4, no. 1 (1990): 1, https://doi.org/10.1093/fh/4.1.1.

public morale, Vichy rescinded some of these measures a few months after implementing them. Catholic officials and educators committed to the principle of "neutrality" were sent in to replace the intransigents, and, in a move that presaged broader patterns in both the reconstituted republic and elsewhere in Western Europe after the war, the study of "Christian values and civilization" was substituted for the study of God in the public-school curriculum.[13]

The anticlerical stance of the Third Republic's school policies was equally divisive for the ideologically heterodox men and women who took a stand against Vichy, whether in the internal Resistance or Free French circles. To protect their fragile coalitions of Socialists, Communists, republicans, Catholics, and Gaullists, some anti-Vichy education reformers tried to sidestep the thorny issue of laïcité, focusing instead on the rigidity and classism of France's education system as the root problem.[14] The Third Republic had universalized primary schooling, but like its predecessors, it left secondary education to the preserve of the bourgeois elite. The classist structure of the higher orders of French education was not seriously challenged until the Popular Front came to power in 1936. The Popular Front made democratizing education a key plank of its radical political agenda, and thirty-two-year-old Jean Zay pursued that objective with gusto at the helm of the Ministry of National Education (MEN) until the onset of the war. In his three years as France's youngest minister, Zay raised the school-leaving age to fourteen; made the curriculum less narrow and elitist by introducing more active pedagogy, practical subjects, and physical education; and began to restructure the ministry itself.

A through line of Zay's democratic reforms was a more capacious view of young people's social, cultural, and moral formation beyond formal schooling. Since the late nineteenth century, not just in France but across Europe, the increasing salience of "youth" as a key social category in advanced capitalist societies raised the question of the modern state's role in organizing activities and programs for young people outside of the classroom.[15] During the early Third Republic, youth movements and cultural associations flourished, but they did so without national support. Beginning in the 1880s, municipal governments helped develop a vast network of colonies de vacances for working-class children.

---

13. The ultra-collaborationist circle around Marcel Déat and the German occupation authorities were also hostile to the complete abrogation of the secular school. Atkin, "Church and Teachers," 11–13.

14. Muracciole, Les enfants de la défaite.

15. Jobs, Riding the New Wave; Richard Ivan Jobs and David Pomfret, eds., Transnational Histories of Youth in the Twentieth Century (London: Palgrave, 2015). Scholars have linked the growing body of public policy and concerted state action directed at youth to processes of national consolidation and the development of the nascent welfare state. Patricia Loncle, L'action publique malgré les jeunes: Les politiques de jeunesse en France de 1870 à 2000 (Paris: L'Harmattan, 2003); Benedict Anderson, Imagined Communities (New York: Verso, 1983).

Zay wanted to scale up those kinds of programs to the national level. He established an "Undersecretariat for Youth and Sport" within the MEN in a bid to institutionalize a more expansive role for the national state in youth affairs, but most funding and logistical support for scout troops, youth clubs, and other forms of popular education and organized leisure for young people before the war continued to come from private groups and religious charities.[16]

Zay's overhaul of French youth and education infrastructure was just getting started when the war broke out, and it would ultimately fall to others to pick up where he left off. A Freemason, a Jew, and the face of the reviled republican school, Zay was a particular target of Vichy propagandists. He was captured trying to join the external Resistance in the summer of 1940 and spent the next four years outlining further youth and education reforms from a prison cell in Riom, until his abduction and brutal murder by the *milice* in June 1944.[17] That Zay was the only government minister of the late Third Republic to lose his life at the hands of Vichy or its agents underscores the extraordinary politicization of education policy in the wartime conjuncture.

The complexity of the politics of youth and education policy during the war years was no less extraordinary, for it was Vichy that ultimately realized Zay's vision of a more activist national state in the youth sector. As soon as it came to power, the Vichy regime brought the leadership of private youth organizations, including confessional ones, into the national bureaucracy. This proved to be the key institutional breakthrough; neither the post-Liberation provisional government nor the young Fourth Republic reversed course.[18] Clearly, then, key aspects of postwar youth and education policy had deep roots in both the late Third Republic and Vichy. This aligns with Philip Nord's contention that the mix of state-building, cultural and economic reconstruction, and social democracy that he calls "France's New Deal" was a "transwar" constellation. He stresses that however much the men and women of the Liberation moment thought they were starting anew, they found themselves in a context inherited from the Third Republic and Vichy.[19] Nord's account is compelling if we consider the metropolitan context in isolation. The real novelty of the postwar conjuncture—at least

16. Laura Lee Downs, *Childhood in the Promised Land: Working-Class Movements and the Colonies de Vacances in France, 1880–1960* (Durham, NC: Duke University Press, 2002); Arnaud Baubérot and Nathalie Duval, *Le scoutisme entre guerre et paix au XXe siècle* (Paris: L'Harmattan, 2006).

17. Antoine Prost and Pascal Ory, *Jean Zay, le ministre assassiné* (Paris: Taillandier / Canopé, 2015). Pierre Mendès-France, who was captured with Zay but managed to escape, gives a heartbreaking account of Zay's fate in Marcel Ophüls's *The Sorrow and the Pity* (1971).

18. Pierre Giolitto, *Histoire de la jeunesse sous Vichy* (Paris: Perrin, 1991); Loncle, *L'action publique malgré les jeunes.*

19. Philip Nord, *France's New Deal: From the Thirties to the Postwar Era* (Princeton, NJ: Princeton University Press, 2010), 11–15.

with regard to youth and education—lies beyond the national-metropolitan story, in the entanglement of education reform agendas across republican France, colonial Africa, and transnational Europe.

The politics of education in the metropole had always reverberated in the empire to varying degrees, but the development of colonial education prior to World War II largely followed its own contingent logics. For Louis Faidherbe, chief architect of French military expansion in West Africa in the mid-nineteenth century, the school was a crucial tool for legitimizing French rule. To that end, Faidherbe and his successors promoted the French school in direct opposition to Qur'anic schooling long before republican secularism took root in France.[20] Republican ideology began to shape education policy in sub-Saharan Africa in earnest in the 1880s, when the consolidation of the Third Republic and the colonization of the African interior converged. As Alice Conklin has shown, education was an integral part of the Third Republic's "civilizing mission" in French Africa, much as education played a key role in "civilizing" the countryside in the metropole.[21] To be sure, the purpose of colonial education differed from mass schooling in France: colonial education sought to create obedient and useful colonial subjects to sustain French colonial rule, not patriotic citizens of a republican nation-state.[22] However, as Harry Gamble has recently observed, the colonial administration had a model of "educational segregation" along *class* lines back in the metropole. Transplanted to the colonies, the metropolitan precedent for "parallel and unequal educational regimes" merely shifted the organizing principle from class to legal status and race.[23]

The contrast in the application of the republican principle of *laïcité* between metropole and colony was starker. Given the colonial state's limited financial and human resources, republicans and Catholics forged what J. P. Daughton has called an "informal, if rocky entente" throughout the empire. The early Third Republic did not outlaw mission schools in colonial Africa, and the missions channeled their project of evangelization into the republican civilizing mission.[24] The repression of the thousand-year tradition of Qur'an schools in

20. Rudolph T. Ware III, *The Walking Qur'an: Islamic Education, Embodied Knowledge and History in West Africa* (Chapel Hill: University of North Carolina Press, 2014), 191–192.

21. Alice Conklin, *A Mission to Civilize: The Republican Idea of Empire in France and West Africa* (Stanford, CA: Stanford University Press, 1997), 75–106.

22. Kelly Duke Bryant, *Education as Politics: Colonial Schooling and Political Debate in Senegal, 1850–1914* (Madison: University of Wisconsin Press, 2015), 9.

23. Harry Gamble, *Contesting French West Africa: Battles over Schools and the Colonial Order, 1900–1950* (Lincoln: University of Nebraska Press, 2017), 7.

24. J. P. Daughton, *An Empire Divided: Religion, Republicanism and the Making of French Colonialism, 1880–1914* (Oxford: Oxford University Press, 2006), 6; Elizabeth Foster, *Faith in Empire: Religion, Politics, and Colonial Rule in Senegal, 1880–1940* (Stanford, CA: Stanford University Press, 2013).

the region, which was official French policy until the early 1900s, suited the objectives of both parties just fine.[25]

French colonialism shared its civilizing project with other colonial powers, but the Third Republic's approach to colonial schooling, which prized French as the language of instruction, differed significantly from that in neighboring British Africa.[26] The emphasis on French-language instruction initially reflected an "assimilationist" orientation in French colonial policy, in which school programs were based on the metropolitan curriculum. However, the increasing salience of scientific theories of race, the imperatives of economic development, and the emergence of a vocal politicized francophone African elite turned French colonial officials away from assimilation around the turn of the twentieth century, even more so after World War I. Colonial administrators pivoted to more "adapted" forms of education that would mold Africans into productive workers in the colonial economy while keeping them fixed in their place at the bottom of the social order. By the 1920s, the colonial bureaucracy prioritized the creation of rural village schools that would concentrate on agriculture, manual trades, hygiene, and basic writing and arithmetic to avoid "alienating" African youth from their traditional milieus, and the administration softened its hostile stance on Qur'an schools for similar reasons.[27]

In the mid-1930s, Léopold Sédar Senghor and other African educators and activists tried to channel this new policy orientation in directions that would advance African empowerment instead of subordination. They briefly found high-ranking allies during the "Colonial Popular Front," but that opening proved fleeting as colonial education reformers were quickly chased from their posts.[28] Thus, the dominant conceptions of colonial education between the wars narrowed the "civilizing mission" considerably and proved to be very much in line with Vichy's openly racist policies in French West Africa (AOF) during its brief rule there (1940–1942). As Ruth Ginio has argued, most colonial officials in AOF experienced the fall of the Third Republic as a "great relief" insofar as they found Vichy's racial paternalism more in line with their actual practices than the egalitarian logic of republican universalism.[29] But the

---

25. Ware, *The Walking Qur'an*.

26. Bryant, *Education as Politics*, 17n30.

27. Wilder, *The French Imperial Nation-State*. On rural schools, see Gamble, *Contesting French West Africa*, chap. 2. On Qur'anic schools, see Ware, *The Walking Qur'an*, chap. 4.

28. James Genova, "The Empire Within: The Colonial Popular Front, 1934–1938," *Alternatives* 26, no. 2 (2001): 175–209, https://www.jstor.org/stable/40645015. On Senghor's educational activism in this period, see Gamble, *Contesting French West Africa*, chap. 5.

29. Ruth Ginio, *French Colonialism Unmasked: The Vichy Years in French West Africa* (Lincoln: University of Nebraska Press, 2006), chap. 4.

parallels and continuities of colonial education in AOF under the Third Republic and Vichy became embarrassing for French leaders during the war. Facing mounting pressure to dissociate postwar French rule from Vichy's vision
of empire, de Gaulle and his allies pushed the colonial administration to finally commit to meaningful reform at the Brazzaville Conference (1944), which
inaugurated a new era of national oversight and incessant conflict between
the national government and the colonial bureaucracy over the content, quality, and scope of education in French Africa.

Restoring French international prestige after Vichy also motivated wartime
planners to try to reclaim French leadership in European educational cooperation before the war. Much of that work had been conducted through organizations sponsored or supported by the League of Nations (1919–1939). Two
of the League's most significant initiatives to promote European intellectual
and cultural exchange were based in Paris: the Cité internationale universitaire, a housing complex for international students that sought to foster a transnational university environment, and the International Institute for Intellectual
Cooperation (IIIC), which anchored a steady stream of international education programs and scientific and cultural conferences in Europe between the
wars.[30] The spectacular failure of those initiatives to unify the continent and
prevent another internecine European war did not discredit the underlying
principle that cultural and educational cooperation was essential for European
postwar recovery. On the contrary, as the collective experience of occupation,
resistance, and exile invigorated calls for a "United States of Europe," wartime
planning bodies like the Conference of Allied Ministers of Education (CAME,
1942–1945) encouraged officials in the European governments-in-exile in London to think about cultural and educational reconstruction in a transnational
framework. The CAME launched a series of initiatives to "Europeanize" textbooks, curricula, and intellectual exchange that were picked up and expanded
on by the postwar pro-European movements. French figures like René Cassin
were determined to secure a leading role for France in those efforts.

Cassin was the senior French delegate to the CAME for the duration of the
war. He continued on in that role even after he had stepped down as Free
France's top education official in June 1943, when the bulk of the Free French
operations in London relocated to Algiers. At the war's end, Cassin helped

---

30. Though interwar institutions of international intellectual cooperation nurtured global ambitions, in practice their scope was European. See Akira Iriye, *Cultural Internationalism and World Order*
(Baltimore, MD: John Hopkins University Press, 1997), and Frank Séréni, "La Cité internationale universitaire de Paris, 1925–1950: De la Société des Nations à la construction de l'Europe," *Relations internationales* 72 (Winter 1992): 399–407, https://www.jstor.org/stable/45344479.

oversee the CAME's conversion to the United Nations Educational, Scientific, and Cultural Organization (UNESCO), and he was instrumental in winning Allied support for UNESCO's headquarters to be built in Paris. Cassin was well suited to that work. He had served as the representative of French veterans at the League of Nations for almost fifteen years (1924–1938), and his first assignment in Geneva had been to promote the IIIC.[31] Cassin was therefore especially plugged into inter-Allied networks and international milieus in wartime London, which regrouped many of his former colleagues from the League. Most of the people he recruited to his Education Department shared those connections and sympathies; others developed them through the experience of exile. When Cassin convened a special commission to prepare comprehensive education reform in post-Liberation France, its members were primed to reconsider many of the points of contention in France's historic *querelle scolaire* from more comparative and transnational perspectives.

Both the CAME and the Brazzaville Conference involved education officials and planners in the Free French orbit who were grappling with what post-Vichy France and the postwar international order would like, but place mattered in shaping their fields of vision. Though London and Brazzaville shared a national aura as headquarters of Free France, as the seat of most of the continental governments-in-exile, wartime London was a transnational European city, while Brazzaville was a long-neglected African colonial outpost. Education planners' postwar visions looked different depending on where the planners stood, but as they moved among these locales, they brought their perspectives and priorities with them. Cassin and others like him were connective tissue in an ongoing conversation about education, democracy, and postwar reconstruction that crisscrossed French "national," transnational European, and colonial African space. By mapping the contours of education planning from London to Brazzaville, another conversation also comes into view, about belonging, community, and what it might mean to be French, African, and European in an unsettled and unsettling postwar world.

The View from London—Transnational Capital of Occupied Europe

Cassin was one of twelve thousand French people who made their way to London after the defeat, only a minority of whom joined the Free French

---

31. Winter and Prost, *René Cassin*, 51–66.

movement.[32] The new arrivals and the French on the spot were a heterogeneous and ideologically diverse group; the political calculus of whether to support de Gaulle was idiosyncratic. Socialist Henry Hauck was a labor attaché in the French Embassy in London when Pétain signed the armistice. Hauck immediately pledged his allegiance to de Gaulle and became his top labor adviser. A committed leftist who had run a chapter of the secular-republican Ligue de l'Enseignement before the war, Hauck put his political differences with de Gaulle aside and served on the major committees on education reform in London and Algiers. De Gaulle's ambivalence about democracy, however, alienated other left-leaning potential allies. Denis Saurat, director of the French Cultural Institute in Kensington, offered his support the day after de Gaulle's famous radio appeal. Another contender to lead the Free French Education Department, Saurat coordinated "intellectual resistance" at the Institute, and de Gaulle sent him on an educational mission to Brazzaville in early 1941. But after losing the top education post to Cassin later that year, Saurat grew disillusioned with de Gaulle's undemocratic tendencies and became an outspoken *anti*-Gaullist among the French in London.[33]

Cassin and Hauck represented republican continuity in London, but their republicanism left them isolated in Free French circles. Cassin's Jewishness was an added political liability.[34] Anti-Semitism was pervasive among the French in London, Gaullist and anti-Gaullist alike. Saurat, for instance, derisively characterized de Gaulle's entourage as "mayhem, havoc, factions, parties, Jews."[35] In personal engagements and broadcasts on the BBC, Cassin occasionally spoke out about the plight of French Jews in Occupied and Vichy France, but his was a lonely voice, and he did not force the issue with regard to education policy.[36] Education planning during Cassin's tenure did not take French Jews—their con-

---

32. Charlotte Faucher and Laure Humbert, "Introduction," in "Beyond de Gaulle and Beyond London: The French External Resistance and Its International Networks," special issue, *European Review of History* 25, no. 2 (2018), 201.

33. Charlotte Faucher, "From Gaullism to Anti-Gaullism: Denis Saurat and the French Cultural Institute in Wartime London," *Journal of Contemporary History* 54, no. 1 (2019): 60–81, https://doi.org/10.1177/0022009417699866.

34. A Jewish professor in the Paris Law Faculty, Cassin was himself one of the first victims of Vichy's two-pronged attack on democracy and education. His colleague Georges Ripert, who served as Vichy's first secretary for youth and education and helped draft the first round of anti-Jewish statutes that removed Jews from all teaching positions, personally revoked Cassin's Paris appointment in absentia in fall 1940. Pierre Allorant, "Lettre de Jean Cassou à Jean Zay," *Parlement(s): Revue d'histoire politique* 11, no. 3 (2016): n11; see also Winter and Prost, *René Cassin*, 103.

35. Cited in Faucher, "From Gaullism to Anti-Gaullism," 74.

36. Transcripts of Cassin's radio addresses are reprinted in the appendix of his memoir, *Les hommes, partis de rien*. On French Jews, see "Israélites de France" from April 1941, 480–481.

cerns, preferences, or sheer existence—into consideration. Indeed, Jews were not mentioned at all.[37]

Cassin and Hauck may have been odd men out among the Free French, but they were warmly welcomed in international milieus. Many of Cassin's friends and former colleagues from Geneva became important players in inter-Allied politics, like Czechoslovak President Edvard Beneš and Belgian Prime Minister Paul-Henri Spaak, leaders of their respective governments-in-exile.[38] As the epicenter of interwar internationalism, the League had served as an incubator of what French scholars refer to as *la conscience européenne,* the conviction that Europe could secure its future peace and prosperity only through coordination and institutional organization.[39] For many continental exiles, the League's failure to check fascist aggression in the 1930s only deepened their European commitments and resolve. The association of former participants in the League-sponsored Czechoslovak "summer schools" in 1937–1938 is a case in point. Once in London, this association reorganized itself as the "New Europe Circle," broadening its original mandate from the study of central European problems to promoting European federalism. Its manifesto pointedly considered the League's shortcomings and emphasized how its approach to European integration would be different. Notably, that included radically expanding on the League's work in educational cooperation. The New Europe Circle proposed a vast system of student exchanges and subsidized youth travel to anchor their bolder vision of a federal Europe in social reality. Beneš had ties to this group, and Henry Hauck was the guest of honor at its third luncheon (December 1940). In his keynote address, Hauck focused on building a more just social system after the war not just in France but across Europe, an important signal that Socialists as well as Christian Democrats would embrace

---

37. Cassin would subsequently become involved with matters of Jewish education in a very different context. Though de Gaulle and Free France generally were deafeningly silent on Vichy anti-Jewish policy in the early war years, de Gaulle took up the issue instrumentally as part of his power struggle with Giraud in the run-up to the creation of the CFLN. In April 1943, de Gaulle appointed Cassin president of the Alliance Israélite Universelle (AIU), a French-Jewish organization with deep roots in North Africa. Giraud had upheld Vichy's abrogation of the Crémieux Decree (which had made Algerian Jews full French citizens). De Gaulle pledged to reinstate it. The AIU operated a network of French-language schools in the region; by installing a loyal supporter at its helm, de Gaulle sought to present himself as the true incarnation of France in North Africa. Cassin, who had no prior ties to Jewish organizations, would serve as the AIU's president for the next thirty years. Winter and Prost, *René Cassin,* 310–315.

38. Winter and Prost, *René Cassin,* 52.

39. French-language scholarship on European integration draws a sharp distinction between this and the ostensibly related idea of "European identity." The latter connotes "feeling European," whereas *la conscience européenne* reflects a commitment to Europe as a political project. See René Girault, ed., *Identités et consciences européennes au XXe siècle* (Paris: Hachette, 1994); Jean-Michel Guieu et al., *Penser et construire Europe au XXe siècle: Historiographie, bibliographie, enjeux* (Paris: Belin, 2006).

European unity after the war. "We are determined," Hauck concluded, "to make the united slaves of Europe rise into the United States of Europe."[40] Hauck was one of several French in London who got involved with the New Europe Circle. In early 1943, Cassin was named an honorary vice president.[41]

The League of Nations' "internationalism" had centered on Europe, and its residual organizations and networks in wartime London also had a decidedly Europeanist bent.[42] Many Free French who had no prior ties to the League latched on to this ambient Europeanism, especially as they came to feel France's diminished stature among the Allies. Michel Berveiller, for instance, a Borges scholar who spent the early war years in Mexico, did not have a history of promoting European unity before he joined the Free French in London in 1942.[43] But there, under a pseudonym, he penned an impassioned plea for the governments-in-exile to lay the groundwork for united Europe. Washington's steadfast refusal to break diplomatic relations with Vichy and the deepening Anglo-American alliance convinced Berveiller that France and the rest of continental Europe needed to chart their own path, quite literally. He called for a "European Charter" to complement its Atlantic counterpart, so that a "United States of Europe" could secure a place for itself in the postwar world of "giants"—Russia, China, and the Anglo-American bloc—forming before his eyes. Naturally, he concluded that it should fall to the Free French to take the lead in these conversations, for France was still "the most considerable among the continental allied nations."[44] Though born of the wartime conjuncture, Berveiller's Europeanism endured. He publicly promoted European federalism under his own name after the war.[45]

Berveiller's dream of a "European Charter" did not come to pass, but the Free French in London took solace in their ever-closer collaboration with the other governments-in-exile. Cassin later recalled that while the "Anglo-Saxons" had deliberately kept Free France down and out, "there was no such exclusion on the European level."[46] French ties with Paul-Henri Spaak's Belgian operations were particularly strong. Cassin and Spaak had met in Geneva in

40. New Europe Circle brochure, "Statement of Aims," undated, AN: 382AP/66.

41. Letter from Alexander Kunosi and Robert Auty to René Cassin, February 3, 1943, AN: 382AP/66.

42. On the League's Eurocentrism, see Iriye, *Cultural Internationalism*.

43. Jacques Michon, "Les éditeurs de littérature française aux États-Unis et en Amérique latine durant la Deuxième Guerre mondiale," *Papers of the Bibliographical Society of Canada* 33, no. 2 (1995): 165–88, https://doi.org/10.33137/pbsc.v33i2.17964.

44. Gilbert Vélaire, "Les gouvernements en exil doivent jeter les bases de l'Europe-Unie," manuscript, undated, AN: 382AP/66.

45. Michel Berveiller, "Fédéralisme interne et fédéralisme international," *Fédération*, August–September 1949; see also his "Letter to the Editors of *Le Monde*," in response to an article, "Fédéralisme et neutralité," by Georges Scelle, August 2, 1950.

46. Cassin, *Les hommes, partis de rien*, 278.

1935 and reconnected at the inaugural inter-Allied meeting at St. James in June 1941, where Winston Churchill first elaborated his own vision for the reorganization of Europe after the war.[47] Spaak, later known as "Monsieur Europe" for his leading role in postwar integration, explored different configurations of political and economic federation between France and the Benelux countries in his conversations with the Free French. He suggested that past attempts at such cooperation had failed because they had been too modest, "limited to metropolitan territories" even though France, Belgium, and Holland were all "great colonial empires." If they extended collaboration to their empires, Spaak urged, they could achieve more robust and lasting unity after the war.[48]

Colonialism had been an important part of Europeanism at the League, which had been as concerned with the management of European empires as it was with the preservation of peace and democracy in Europe.[49] Africa occupied pride of place in that realm of the interwar imagination. Richard Coudenhove-Kalergi's campaign in the 1920s for a "Pan-European Union" was predicated on coordinated development schemes in Africa. His *Paneuropa* necessarily entailed "Eurafrica."[50] The war gave Coudenhove an opportunity to extend his pan-European advocacy farther afield.[51] In exile in New York, he won new converts among the city's cosmopolitan elite and frequently traveled to Washington, where he lobbied top government officials, including Harry Truman. These efforts were effective. Coudenhove influenced US ideas about European unity and Eurafrica in ways that significantly affected US involvement in both European reconstruction and French colonial affairs after the war.[52]

Wartime meditations linking European unity and imperial renewal were not limited to longtime pro-Europe elites like Coudenhove and Spaak. Berveiller proposed joint sovereignty over Europe's colonies with an "equitable compensation" to colonial powers proportionate to their "civilizing" efforts.

---

47. Winter and Prost, *René Cassin*, 144.

48. Interview between M. Spaak and M. Dejean, March 6, 1942, Archives Diplomatiques—La Courneuve, France (AMAE): Guerre, 1939–1945 / Londres-CNF, 172.

49. Susan Pedersen, *Guardians: The League of Nations and the Crisis of Empire* (Cambridge: Cambridge University Press, 2015).

50. Antoine Fleury, "Paneurope et l'Afrique," in *L'Europe Unie et l'Afrique*, ed. Bitsch and Bossuat (Brussels: Bruylant, 2005).

51. Ageron, "L'idée d'eurafrique"; and Metzger, "L'Allemagne et l'Eurafrique," Montarsolo, "Albert Sarraut et l'idée d'Eurafrique," and Anne Deighton, "Ernest Bevin and the Idea of Euro-Africa from the Interwar to the Postwar Period," in *L'Europe unie et l'Afrique*, ed. Bitsch and Bossuat.

52. On Coudenhove-Kalergi's political impact in the United States, see Gérard Bossuat, *Faire l'Europe sans défaire la France: 60 ans de politique d'unité européenne des gouvernements et des présidents de la République française (1943–2003)* (Brussels: Peter Lang, 2005), chap. 1; on his impact on US ideas about "Eurafrica," see Connelly, *A Diplomatic Revolution*, chap. 2.

In fact, he thought France should take the lead in the European project precisely because France possessed "an empire superior to all the others."[53] Berveiller was not alone. In April 1942, Cassin received a letter from a lieutenant in Brazzaville who, having recently read one of Cassin's articles on European federalism in a Free French publication, enclosed his own detailed plan for a federal Europe that would perforce also be a "Europe-Africa Federation."[54] A common theme in the Eurafrica plans was that possessing an empire was itself a defining European trait. As a transnational European capital, wartime London was necessarily a transimperial one as well.

Postwar Education Planning: National Reforms and European Horizons

De Gaulle established Free France's first planning operation in late 1941. The creation of the Commission for the Study of Postwar Problems was announced to leaders in the empire to solicit their participation and publicize the commission's work.[55] Their responses stressed that the commission should pay special attention to the reorganization of the empire. French officials on the ground were already keenly aware that the war was disrupting the old colonial order.[56] That message registered rhetorically. Planners often spoke of national, colonial, and European reconstruction as intimately linked. In practice, though, colonial concerns were often tabled in the commission, and the subcommittee on colonial matters never got off the ground.[57]

By contrast, French planners closely monitored conversations in the postwar planning bodies of both the British and the other governments-in-exile. Summaries of those activities were published in a bimonthly journal and circulated among the Free French in London. The French followed British moves to democratize education with particular interest.[58] They compiled extensive reports on the landmark Beveridge Plan (1942), the blueprint for Britain's postwar social

---

53. Vélaire, "Les gouvernements en exil," 7, AN: 382AP/66.

54. Letter from Lt. Paul Petit to Cassin, April 4, 1942; Petit, "Étude sur possibilités pratiques d'organisation d'une fédération européenne après la victoire," Brazzaville, April 1942; AN: 382AP/66.

55. Décret no. 53, December 2, 1941; Télégram à MM. Haussaires Noumea, Brazzaville; DEL-FRANCE Caire; FRANCOM Beyrouth, January 14, 1942, AMAE: Guerre, 1939–1945/Londres-CNF, 172.

56. Télégram de FRANCOM Beyrouth à CNF-Londres, March 27, 1942, AMAE: Guerre, 1939–1945/Londres-CNF, 172.

57. Dossier Groupe Colonial—Secrétariat des Commissions d'après-guerre, 1943, AMAE: Guerre, 1939–1945/Londres-CNF, 180.

58. *Revue bi-mensuelle des questions d'après-guerre: Les Faits, Les Opinions*, Bulletin no. 30, December 1942, 13–27, AMAE: Guerre, 1939–1945/Londres-CNF, 172.

democracy that named education as one of the "five giants on the road to recon-struction," and the debates that led to the Butler Act (1944), which made public secondary education in Britain completely free.[59] Cassin felt it was imperative that Free France prepare similar measures. In June 1942, he formed a subcom-mittee to draft a comprehensive education plan. The Cathala Commission, as it was known, was the first of a "reforming chain" of education committees set up during the war in London, Algiers, and liberated Paris.[60] Although few of their recommendations were implemented by the Fourth Republic, their proceedings track the evolution of competing views about the role of education in national reconstruction and France's place in the postwar order.

With its eclectic mix of academics, professionals, teachers, military, and syn-dicalists, the Cathala Commission offers a rare snapshot of a cross section of general opinion on the ins and outs of education policy. Its members' views spanned the political spectrum. Some, like Hauck, were committed republi-cans and leftists; others were staunch conservatives, like Maurice Schumann, cofounder and future leader of France's Christian Democratic Party, the Mou-vement Républicain Populaire (MRP).[61] The commission's deliberations were often heated and divisive. However, even its diverse members agreed that their proposed reforms were suitable for the metropole only. For this group, it was so obvious that colonial and metropolitan education should not be based on the same principles that the underlying rationale was left unsaid.[62]

The first major issue the commission confronted was the most intractable: the decades-old conflict over schooling between the anticlerical republic and the Catholic Church. For many Free French, deep-seated contempt for the re-publican school and the Third Republic's militant anticlericalism fueled in-tense distrust of republicanism altogether. The very mention of "the French republic" in an early draft of the commission's mission statement caused an uproar. Some members insisted they should not presume the kind of political system France would have after the war; others felt it was inconceivable *not*

---

59. "Social Insurance and Allied Services," Report by William Beveridge, presented to Parliament by command of His Majesty, November 25, 1942. On French reporting on the Butler Act, see André D. Rob-ert, "La commission Cathala et le modèle anglais, Londres, 1942–1943," *Carrefours de l'Education* 41, no. 41 (May 2016): 71–76, https://doi.org/10.3917/cdle.041.0065. Vichy officials also followed Beveridge's work and felt pressure to make similar overtures toward social inclusion. Philippe Jean-Hesse and Jean-Pierre Le Crom, *La protection sociale sous le régime de Vichy* (Rennes: Presses Universitaires de Rennes, 2015), 343.

60. Robert refers to this as a "chaine réformatrice," 67. The Algiers and Paris commissions are discussed in chapter 2.

61. A convert to Catholicism (his father was Jewish), Schumann served as the MRP's first presi-dent from 1944 to 1949.

62. Compte-rendu de la Section intellectuelle et de l'enseignement de la session du 27 novembre 1942, AMAE: Guerre, 1939–1945/Londres-CNF, 186.

to invoke the republic.[63] Unable to come to an agreement on even this most basic issue, the commission set the whole task of writing up its first principles to the side.[64]

At an impasse from the outset, the commission would have to come to some kind of common understanding about the *querelle scolaire* if it was to proceed. The commission's president formed a task force of two Catholics (including Schumann), one Protestant, and two republican secularists (including Hauck) to work out a compromise. The task force's proposal called for an autonomous education system that would exercise a monopoly over all French schooling, public and private, effectively creating the single school system (*l'école unique*) long desired by republicans. But in a significant concession to opponents of the Third Republican model of *laïcité*, the task force also recommended the inclusion of more moral and civic education in the standard curriculum and the provision of religious instruction at parents' request in public school buildings after school hours.[65] These conciliatory proposals won the qualified support of most commission members. With the groundwork laid to imagine a different kind of postwar republic, references to "the republic" became more palatable. When the commission revoted on the mission statement, it passed overwhelmingly (16–2).[66]

The task force's proposals on moral, civic, and religious instruction were linked to broader concerns about the narrowness of the classic French curriculum and youth development beyond the classroom. In these concerns, the commission was following Cassin's lead. In a talk earlier that fall, Cassin worried that young people spent too much time in school and, more generally, that prewar education had been too intellectual. "Modern life," he argued, seemed to require other kinds of learning that would build character as well as intellect. In the past, this had been the preserve of the family, but now "society" needed to play a part as well.[67] Cassin's and the commission's interest in a more progressive approach to schooling and youth development was shaped by wartime conditions. Cassin and commission members closely followed the "ruralization" of education during the London Blitz, when more than two million

---

63. Compte-rendu de la Section intellectuelle et de l'enseignement de la session du 16 octobre 1942, AMAE: Guerre, 1939–1945/Londres-CNF, 186.

64. Procès-verbal de la réunion de la Section intellectuelle et de l'enseignement qui a eu lieu le vendredi 30 octobre 1942, AMAE: Guerre, 1939–1945/Londres-CNF, 172.

65. Texte proposé par M. Maisonneuve avec l'approbation de MM. Beuhror et Schaeffer, désignés avec lui pour étudier une modification à l'art, 3 de la note sur les principes fondamentaux, undated, AMAE: Guerre, 1939–1945/Londres-CNF, 186.

66. Procès-verbal de la Section intellectuelle et de l'enseignement de la séance du 13 novembre 1942, AMAE: Guerre, 1939–1945/Londres-CNF, 172.

67. Cassin, "L'éducation et l'avenir."

children (including those at the Lycée français) were evacuated to the English countryside. Evacuees' schooling followed different rhythms and emphasized physical education, cooking, gardening, and outdoor activities like scouting. The commission expressed enthusiastic support for incorporating more active pedagogy and *éducation nouvelle* methods in the French curriculum, although members felt it was not their place to make formal prescriptions at the level of pedagogy.[68] They did, however, include the need to complement formal schooling with youth programs and cultural activities beyond the classroom as a core principle of their postwar reform program.[69]

The commission also entertained the idea of creating a new "Ministry of Cultural Life" to organize youth and continuing education initiatives.[70] This proposal revived the polarizing issues of autonomy, monopoly, and *laïcité*. In a heated exchange, a lycée teacher on the commission announced his firm opposition to any kind of state centralization with regard to youth activities. He also questioned how confessional youth movements could be integrated into a state-run youth department without completely abandoning the principle of *laïcité*. Some commission members agreed they should not produce a "single youth" but rather a "united youth." Others pointed out the blatant contradiction between that position and the rationale of the *école unique*.[71] Raphael Vangrévelinghe, another lycée teacher on the commission, saw this debate as a fresh opportunity to renew his earlier objections to the proposals on expanding the moral and civic curriculum and religious instruction in public schools. Vangrévelinghe predicted that any attempt to reintroduce religious instruction would provoke such intense teacher protest that the whole education system would collapse. He also felt that commission members were wading into dangerous territory with their call for positive moral education. "To inculcate moral and civic duties in the spirit of a child as though with a waffle iron," he declared, "is a danger both to the intellectual development of the child and in the uses certain authorities or teachers would make of it." He concluded, "If the Fourth Republic wants to renovate democracy, it will have to clear away the morass in which the clerical and anticlerical bourgeoisie has mired the school."[72]

---

68. Robert, "La commission Cathala et le modèle anglais," 74, 71.

69. Projet de Réforme de l'Enseignement dans la France Métropolitaine, January 21, 1943, AMAE: Guerre, 1939–1945/Londres-CNF, 186.

70. Note sur le rapport intitulé "Les Bases d'un Ministère de la Vie Culturelle," undated, AMAE: Guerre, 1939–1945/Londres-CNF, 186.

71. Lt. Voisine, Note sur les questions de jeunesse, April 6, 1943, AMAE: Guerre, 1939–1945/Londres-CNF, 172; Procès-verbal de la Section intellectuelle et de l'enseignement de la séance du 28 mai 1943, AMAE: Guerre, 1939–1945/Londres-CNF, 186.

72. Note de M. Vangrévelinghe, November 1942; Note de M. Vangrévelinghe sur l'enseignement, December 7, 1942, AMAE: Guerre, 1939–1945/Londres-CNF, 186.

This stirring oratory did not convince his colleagues. The commission's final recommendations included religious or philosophical instruction in school for children whose families requested it as well as more moral and civic education in the regular curriculum. Vangrévelinghe's was the only vote against these recommendations.

The overwhelming support for these measures reflects the commission's determination to put an end to the *querelle scolaire*. Indeed, the way the commission framed the issue of moral and civic education underscores the commission's paramount concern to reconcile republicans and Catholics: "The common general education will include positive civic and moral instruction founded on the respect of the great traditions that form the spiritual patrimony of France: the Christian tradition of the dignity of the human person and the revolutionary tradition of the Rights of Man and Citizen—a tradition of human fraternity that is both Christian and revolutionary."[73] The use of "Christian" rather than "Catholic" is noteworthy, signaling a more ecumenical approach and a desire to downplay the historic conflict between the anticlerical republic and the Church. There is also a germ here of a larger process that will continue into the postwar years: the cleaving of *laïcité* from anticlericalism. By removing the anticlerical tenor of the revolutionary tradition, it becomes possible to define the "spiritual patrimony of France"—the essence of what it means to be French—as republican *and* Christian.

The expanded moral and civic curriculum was intended to solve this specifically French political-historical problem, but the commission also insisted that moral and civic education should mold French youth to be good citizens of both the "national and international community."[74] Commission members were quick to relate the need to "internationalize" their outlook to their situation in London. As one member put it, it was their special responsibility, "we, who live in contact with the Allies," to ensure that France "does not close itself off after the war in intellectual isolation, in a petty nationalism," for "most of the problems of education are common to all peoples who share the same civilization." He added they should take concrete action by setting up international accords to standardize curricula in civic education and history, guarantee the equivalence of diplomas, and facilitate faculty and student exchanges across national borders.[75]

---

73. Procès-verbal de la Section intellectuelle et de l'enseignement de la séance du 11 décembre 1942, AMAE: Guerre, 1939–1945 / Londres-CNF, 186.

74. Procès-verbal de la Section intellectuelle et de l'enseignement de la séance du 11 décembre 1942, AMAE: Guerre, 1939–1945 / Londres-CNF, 186.

75. Georges Ungar, Remarques sur le Rapport intitulé "Les Bases d'un Ministère de la Vie Culturelle," April 5, 1943, AMAE: Guerre, 1939–1945 / Londres-CNF, 172.

These ideas were couched in the universal language of internationalism, but in these discussions "international" often really meant "European." The equation of the two is especially pronounced in the wartime rhetoric of Julian Huxley, British biologist, educationalist, and antifascist, whose articles and speeches were translated and circulated widely in Free French circles.[76] In a January 1943 article that was distributed to the Cathala Commission, Huxley anticipated the commission's proposals. He hoped to see a transnational group of European experts prepare new textbooks with a "European outlook" so that young Europeans would no longer receive "mutually contradictory" history instruction. He also called for a "truly European system of Universities" in which students and teachers would be free to move among universities in different European countries. More broadly, he proposed an "International Education Office" as a necessary complement to "whatever supranational political organization is set up for Europe." Such an undertaking, he insisted, "could make a solid and substantial contribution towards the development of a European system of education, and so towards that of a culturally and politically more unified Europe." Huxley concluded by energetically affirming the underlying unity of European societies and culture upon which his proposals sought to build: "There *is* a reality behind the phrase, 'European Civilization'; there *are* definite and inescapable trends that are now molding the development of the nations which are the inheritors of that civilization."[77]

Thus, as the Cathala Commission was struggling to redefine the fundamental principles of French education and overcome France's historic conflict between secular republicanism and "Christianity," the London environment kept its members keenly attuned to France's place within a broader "European civilization." A widening cohort of European federalists, both individuals like Berveiller and transnational organizations like the New Europe Circle, were elaborating competing views of what exactly that meant. For Denis Saurat, continental Western Europe formed a single spiritual community rooted in democracy and Christianity. In weekly public lectures at the French Institute, Saurat advocated for a *cultural* Western European Union in addition to postwar European political integration. That entity would be anchored in a network of "Western European Institutes" in the "civilizational triangle Amsterdam-Lisbon-Naples,"

---

76. Huxley had been a central figure in pro-Europe circles in interwar Britain. See Luisa Passerini, *Europe in Love, Love in Europe. Imagination and Politics in Britain between the Wars* (London: I.B. Tauris, 1999). Although he was a lifelong eugenicist, Huxley coauthored a scientific refutation of Nazi race theory, dismissing racial divisions among Europeans. *We Europeans: A Survey of "Racial" Problems* (New York: Harper & Brothers, 1936). His racial ideas about non-Europeans, however, were deeply ambivalent and anticipated wider postwar shifts in racial conception explored in chapter 3.

77. Julian Huxley, "German Education and Re-education," reprinted from the *New Statesman and Nation*, February 13, 1943 (emphasis in the original), AMAE: Guerre, 1939–1945/Londres-CNF, 186.

whose core, naturally, was Paris. The institutes would have two courses of study to highlight Europe's "diversity in its unity." The first would have regional specialists familiarize European publics with local cultures; the second would "distill and explain democratic and Christian principles common to all the regions in the cultural triangle." In this way, Europeans would come to appreciate Europe's cultural diversity and develop a meaningful sense of solidarity.

Saurat's conception of the Christian basis of Western Europe had nothing to do with "religious orthodoxy" or "any particular political form." Rather, for him, Europe was *culturally* Christian, in values like respect for the human person and social practices like the family.[78] Saurat's vision of a postwar European union rooted in Christian and democratic traditions, brought to life by transnational European education, mirrors the twinning of Christianity and the revolutionary-republican legacy in the Cathala Commission's proposals for national education reform in a renovated postwar republic. This synergy between French national and transnational European registers would intensify after the war as pro-Europe activist networks expanded and new European institutions were created.[79]

A forerunner of those institutions was then taking shape across town from Saurat's Institute. A month after Cassin convened the Cathala Commission, British education minister Richard Butler announced the formation of the Conference of Allied Ministers of Education. Cassin represented the French National Committee at the CAME's inaugural session at the British Board of Education, where he joined top education officials from the governments-in-exile of Belgium, the Netherlands, Czechoslovakia, Greece, Norway, Poland, and Yugoslavia. Everyone there had worked with the British Council to place their nationals in British schools. British Council president Malcolm Robertson opened the proceedings by declaring that this was their chance to go beyond that initial collaboration and build a lasting "educational fellowship," which he hoped "would be the solution to many of the problems of the future." Together, they would develop the tools to dismantle the Nazis' warped education in occupied Europe and replace it with "the Allied outlook on life."[80]

---

78. Denis Saurat, Projet de formation d'une Union Culturelle des Pays de l'Europe Occidentale, undated; for reports on Saurat's lectures, see Note par Steigerhof à M. Gros, October 19, 1942, AN: 382AP/66.

79. Joan Scott argues that the conjoining of democracy and Christianity was always part of discourses of secularism in Protestant countries and was then embraced by Catholic Europe in the context of the Cold War. *Sex and Secularism.* My analysis here and in subsequent chapters suggests a wider set of factors specific to the French wartime experience and the conjunction of French colonial and European imperatives.

80. Draft Report of a Conference held at the Board of Education on Monday, November 16, 1942, in *CAME, London 1942–1945 vol 1: Records of Plenary Meetings,* 2–4, UNESCO Archives.

One of the CAME's areas of interest concerned the teaching of European history. Its first proposal was to commission a brief history of the war that would "give some conception of the European civilization for which the Allies are fighting" to European schoolchildren.[81] The CAME also wanted to design a manual for history teachers on how to teach contentious episodes in European history and break out of the "diseased national megalomania" that had distorted the way European history had been taught before the war.[82] The CAME hoped to develop a new European history textbook that would be translated into the major European languages and used across the continent after its liberation.[83] One of René Cassin's handpicked associates, Paul Vaucher, took the lead on this last project. Vaucher was one of three coauthors of the resultant multivolume work, *The European Inheritance*, whose treatment of race will be discussed in chapter 3.

By the end of 1943, the CAME had expanded from its initial group of continental exiles to include representatives from the United States, the Soviet Union, China, and the British Empire.[84] The organization continued to pursue its various efforts to "Europeanize" history instruction and prepare for the denazification of education in liberated Europe, but its European focus started to shift. French participants and observers were wary of the predominant roles played by the British—with their expanded delegation of representatives from their empire—and the United States, which provided the lion's share of the CAME's funding. In April 1944, a US delegation led by J. William Fulbright proposed reorienting the CAME's operations. He outlined its conversion into an international organization affiliated with the United Nations.[85]

This US-led initiative was particularly worrisome to Cassin and Vaucher, who did not want to see French predominance in interwar international education superseded by France's Anglo-American allies. More precisely, the initiative jeopardized the position of the International Institute for Intellectual Cooperation in Paris, which Cassin was particularly keen to revive.[86] Free French officials in the Foreign Affairs Department were also distrustful of the CAME, which "grew up

81. Draft Report of the Second Meeting of the Conference of Ministers of Education of the Allied Governments and the French National Committee, January 19, 1943, *CAME, London 1942–1945, vol. 1: Records of Plenary Meetings*, UNESCO Archives.

82. Olgierd Gorka, "Spirit of History in the Handbook of Suggestions for Teachers of History," *CAME, London 1942–1945, vol. III: Books and Periodicals Commission: History Committees and Subcommittees*, UNESCO Archives.

83. Draft Report of the Fifth Meeting of the Conference of Ministers of Education of the Allied Governments and the French National Committee, July 27, 1943, *CAME, London 1942–1945, vol. 1: Records of Plenary Meetings*, UNESCO Archives.

84. Canada, Australia, New Zealand, South Africa, and India began sending delegates in July 1943.

85. Introduction, *CAME, London 1942–1945, vol. 1: Records of plenary meetings*, UNESCO Archives.

86. Winter and Prost, *René Cassin*, 231–232.

in London during a period marked by the eclipse of France and continental Europe." Cassin and others were encouraged to try to prevent the transformation of the CAME into a permanent international organization from within.[87] When those attempts failed, they changed course and successfully lobbied for the new organization to be based in Paris. In 1946, the CAME was reborn as UNESCO, whose headquarters remain in Paris today.[88]

French unease with the changing composition of the CAME in mid-1943 reflected broader anxieties and resentment over the persistent exclusion of Free French leaders from top-level planning among the Allies. With the liberation of French North Africa and the creation of the French Committee of National Liberation (CFLN) in June 1943, de Gaulle expected to be recognized as the head of the legitimate government of France. He was cruelly disappointed when the United States continued its diplomatic relations with Vichy. Worse, that fall, Britain, the United States, and the Union of Soviet Socialist Republics (USSR) formed a "European Advisory Committee" on the postwar occupation of Germany and Austria. The CFLN was once again excluded. A year of angry protests from Free French officials in London and Algiers made little headway. The French would eventually be invited to serve on the committee, but only after the liberation of metropolitan France.[89]

The marginalization of CFLN within the Allied camp in 1943–1944 inspired further interest in united Europe and Eurafrica, including from within the internal Resistance. Jean Cassou, a founding member of the Musée de l'Homme Resistance network who had served in Jean Zay's Education Ministry, proposed a French-led "Mediterranean Pact" or "Latin Union" as an alternative to Atlantic partnership. Relations between the CFLN and its "Anglo-Saxon allies" made it clear to him that France had to look elsewhere to secure its future. France must "recover its metropolitan and imperial sovereignty," Cassou insisted, but France could not achieve this on its own. Rather, France should form a political and economic union with Italy, Spain, and Portugal—each with its own African colonies—to prevent France's subordination in a Europe "dominated by Anglo-Saxon capital." Significantly, Cassou's proposal was not just a defensive maneuver; he also saw it as an instrument of national reconciliation.

---

87. Communication du Ministre de l'Education Nationale a/s d'un projet de création d'une organisation internationale de l'Education et de la Culture, élaborée par la CMAE à Londres, undated, AN: F60/427.

88. Denis Mylonas, *La genèse de l'Unesco: La Conférence des Ministres Alliés de l'Education (1942–1945)* (Brussels: Bruylant, 1976). Cassin tried and failed, however, to secure the first presidency of the new organization for a Frenchman. That post went to Julian Huxley.

89. Telegram Vienot (London) to CFLN-Algiers, October 26, 1943, AMAE: Guerre, 1939–1945/ Alger, CFLN-GPRF, 657; Letter from D. Cooper to Georges Bidault, November 11, 1944, AMAE: Y-Internationale, 1944–1949, 133.

By uniting itself with "the other great Catholic nations of the Occident, Republican France would integrate the most vibrant elements of Catholicism among the popular masses . . . into the fight against Nazism, the defense of French freedoms and the project of national reconstruction." Such a union would thereby ensure the "political equilibrium of the country and the construction of a Republic that is social, human, comprehensive and audacious."[90]

There are interesting parallels and contrasts among this proposal, the Cathala Commission's national reform project, and Saurat's Western European Union. They each conjoin the republic / democracy with Catholicism / Christianity and elide the historical tension there. Both Cassou and the Cathala Commission tried to reposition the republic in a way that would embrace France's Catholic identity and preserve the alliance between republicans and Catholics forged in resistance. Cassou and Saurat both grounded their respective transnational projects in religion, but Cassou's emphasis on Catholicism, rather than Christianity, sets his thinking apart from the Cathala Commission's proposals and the "triangular" geography of Saurat's vision of Europe. Cassou's "Latin" Union drew on a particular vision of European civilization anchored around the Mediterranean that was long a hallmark of French colonial discourse.[91] Indeed, the central place of empire and Africa in particular in Cassou's proposal distinguishes it from the others. There are also interesting contrasts of a more personal nature, in terms of politics and temperament. While Saurat often made casual anti-Semitic remarks, Cassou would tolerate none (his wife and many of his inner circle came from Jewish families). Politically, Cassou's prewar stance on education policy was close to Raphael Vangrévelinghe's, and yet Cassou's proposal for a Latin Union was motivated by the same logic that had been put forth in support of the reform program that Vangrévelinghe voted against. What is more, Cassou's Eurafrican vision was most popular among colonial officials whose policies and practices Cassou, a lifelong leftist, would probably have found quite troubling.

In the inside-out world of the wartime conjuncture, old patterns of political commitment were often as muddled as the conventional distinctions between national, colonial, and European space. War, occupation, and exile make strange bedfellows. On the ground in Free French Africa, resisters of all political stripes newly arrived from the metropole encountered deeply conservative colonial

---

90. Jean Cassou, *Pour une Union Latine*, undated, AMAE: Z-Europe, Generalités 1944–1949, 40. The treatise was circulated among the CFLN in Algiers and the London Commission for the Study of Postwar Problems.

91. Camiscioli, *Reproducing the French Race*; Patricia Lorcin, "Rome and France in Africa: Recovering Colonial Algeria's Latin Past," *French Historical Studies* 25:2 (Spring 2002): 295–329, muse.jhu.edu /article/11923.

officials, an openly antirepublican professional military, wizened missionaries, and idealistic teachers. Bitter rivals René Cassin and Denis Saurat discovered this reality on their respective missions to Free French Africa in the early war years. If we follow them there, we can see what the view from London looked like *in Africa.*

Saurat and Cassin in Free French Africa

Before their relationship soured, Charles de Gaulle sent Denis Saurat on an educational mission to AEF for several months in 1941. From February to May, Saurat toured schools and talked with teachers, missionaries, and local officials across the vast territories of Free French Africa.[92] Like the overwhelming majority of French who found themselves in sub-Saharan Africa during the war, Saurat had no prior African experience or known interest in the place or the people. But he seems to have been genuinely fascinated by his travels there, which he described in lively prose in a slim volume, *Watch over Africa,* published (in English) the following year.

Cassin left a much thinner record of his time in Free French Africa, which was one leg of a longer tour across Africa and the Middle East. For most of his journey, Cassin traveled more as an ambassador of Free France than as head of public instruction. He left London for Cairo in December 1941, making stops in Damascus, Jerusalem, and Tel Aviv before arriving in Fort Lamy (Chad) in early February 1942. For the next two months, Cassin traveled widely in the region. Besides touring AEF, where he visited several schools and discussed education policy with AEF governor general Éboué, Cassin made official visits to Léopoldville in the Belgian Congo and Lagos and Bangui in British West Africa.[93] Perhaps Cassin did not wish to reflect long on his African travels because he, unlike Saurat, had less pleasant memories of his time there. Eric Jennings has noted that as a standard-bearer of republican continuity, Cassin was "persona non grata" in Free French African military circles. High-ranking officers protested his visit and refused to participate in official ceremonies to greet him.[94] In London, Cassin may have felt himself and Free France slighted by the British, but after receiving such humiliating treatment by his countrymen on "French" soil, his trips to Lagos and Bangui, where he was greeted with the respect typically accorded a foreign dignitary, must have come as a welcome relief.

---

92. Chad, Congo, Gabon, Cameroon, and Oubangui-Chari (present-day Central African Republic).
93. Winter and Prost, *René Cassin,* 151–157.
94. Jennings, *Free French Africa,* 93–94.

For all their personal animosities—and there were several[95]—Saurat and Cassin both came away from their travels in Africa convinced of the importance of maintaining close relations with Britain, and they were not alone.[96] While in Brazzaville, Saurat heard Edgard de Larminat, a general and high-ranking military leader in Free French Africa, deliver a speech in ardent support of British plans to reorganize Europe after the war. In *Watch over Africa*, Saurat reprinted the full text of this address, whose concluding thoughts on the "Europe of tomorrow" linked Franco-British rapprochement and a path forward for France:

> Anglo-Saxon civilization is exactly the same as our Christianized Greco-Latin civilization, polished and refined through time and struggle. This civilization must stabilize and save the world. . . . It is alongside Great Britain that we will remake a Europe that stands against totalitarian barbarisms. [It is in that Europe that] France will reclaim its historic role.[97]

We have seen that Saurat construed European civilization rather differently, but this speech must have impressed him deeply, for it was one of only three documents he appended at the end of his little book and the only one that he translated into English in the middle of a chapter for the benefit of his British audience. Indeed, Saurat seemed to find Larminat generally impressive, noting after dining with him one evening in Brazzaville that he was young and good-looking, athletic, bronzed, very tall. Saurat then mused, "So many of de Gaulle's men are tall. Has some ancient race waked up in France in answer to France's need?"[98] This droll quip was in keeping with the ethnographic and ethnoracial tenor of the book. Saurat constantly commented on African physiques and skin tones and meditated on the ancient origins of "the Bantu races."

Race was the primary lens through which Saurat narrated his journey. As his ship approached Port Gentil (Gabon) and he caught first sight of the African coast, Saurat thought to himself: "France used to begin at Calais, one hour's sailing from England. Now negroes—and France—begin here, forty-one days

---

95. For the first two years of the war, Cassin and his wife were given lodgings at the French Institute, but Saurat, who resented Free French demands on Institute space, evicted them while Cassin was on his *tournée* of the empire. Winter and Prost, *René Cassin*, 151.

96. This position alienated them both from de Gaulle, though perhaps more intensely for Saurat. Indeed, Saurat delivered a very pro-British address on Radio-Brazzaville during his mission. This was very poorly received by the Free French in London, who hindered his media appearances and blocked a series on postwar order he had proposed to the BBC. Faucher, "From Gaullism to Anti-Gaullism," 74.

97. Denis Saurat, *Watch over Africa* (London: J.M. Dent & Sons, 1941), 164. Cited from the original French, reprinted as appendix II: Larminat, "Position des Français libres vis-à-vis des problèmes nationaux," February 18, 1941, Brazzaville. The speech appears in translation in English in chapter 4.

98. Saurat, *Watch over Africa*, 46.

from Liverpool."[99] The existential situation of France was now racially marked. His inquiries into African education also passed through this racial filter. Saurat recounted a long conversation he had with an education official who had taught in remote villages in AOF for decades before he rallied to de Gaulle and joined the education service in Brazzaville. Saurat wrote that this old *broussard* "was the first white man to startle me with the theory that the blacks are potentially wiser and cleverer than the whites. I met several experienced administrators later who held the same view." Saurat initially qualified this theory, noting that most of his informants seemed to think of "fully developed intelligent negroes as exceptions in a mass of rather inferior people," but he quickly added, "but then is not this also the situation among the whites?" Whatever their own equivocations, Saurat's interlocutors left him with the firm impression that "a true system of education could produce results that would astonish Europeans, and that since in this climate black bodies were in every way better than any white physique, the future of equatorial countries went with the future of the black races." Even more remarkably, he concluded France should educate Africans so that *they* "could utilize the amazing wealth of the land."[100] In this stunning collection of ideas, which mixes climatological racial theory with a vision of education for African empowerment, Saurat suggested relations between elites and masses in Europe and Africa were essentially the same, and he envisioned a future in which African resources would be developed by and for Africans.

Saurat's reflections on religion and education in France and Africa turned on a similarly productive tension between inherited racist mental categories and more supple and idiosyncratic turns of thought. Saurat detailed a long exchange he had with a local bishop who urged Saurat to convince the colonial administration to work more closely with the missions. Secular education was totally unsuitable for Africans, the bishop argued, because Africans needed religion. If state schooling succeeded in turning them away from their "witch doctors" and "witchcraft," he argued, something else would have to take its place. "Do you know what would happen if you really did teach them that there is no religion, that there is nothing?" the bishop asked. "They would die. Just die." He continued, "And do you know besides why France is dying? Because you have taught France that there is nothing to believe in. No one to believe in. No Christ. No Resurrection. No Virgin Birth. So France has decided, deep within her soul, that life is not worth living." After telling the bishop he more or less

---

99. Saurat, *Watch over Africa*, 37. Saurat always referred to Africans as "negroes" or "blacks"; he used Bantu only in certain circumstance (typically, in the formula "Bantu races") and "Africans" not at all. I use "Africans" in my discussion of Saurat's thoughts and impressions except when citing him directly.

100. Saurat, *Watch over Africa*, 59–61.

agreed, Saurat then marveled to himself: "Curious that the same problems should exist in France and the Congo." He came away from the exchange with a new conviction: "In short, our whole system of education must be reformed: both in the Church schools and in the State schools, both for the whites and the blacks."[101] Saurat then attempted to put this conviction into practice. He initiated talks between the regime and a group of missionaries who he hoped could take control of village schools whose white teachers had been mobilized, but Saurat returned to London before an agreement was reached.[102]

That Saurat waded into these issues at all is a testament to the depth of his newfound personal interest in African education, for de Gaulle had sent Saurat to AEF for another purpose entirely. His official mandate was to organize secondary schooling for French children who could no longer be sent back to France. Like Cassin and many others, Saurat was a fierce critic of prewar French education, which he felt had been too intellectual and too specialized for children aged nine to fifteen. He opined, "It is obvious that our educational system is fundamentally wrong. It is obvious also that this system is one of the main factors in the diseases of our civilization." He imagined a new kind of "natural education" in its place, in which young children would be taught by teachers without any specialist training so that they could "grow naturally, under the direction of a real human being, into human beings." The wartime situation made Africa an ideal testing ground for this new pedagogy and the children who had been too young to send to France in 1939 ideal test subjects. "Their elder brothers and sisters were lost, under who knows what Vichy system," Saurat reflected wistfully, but the eleven- and twelve-year-olds in the territories could be educated "in a new way for a new world, since the old one has perished partly because its training had been evil."[103] On these grounds, he forcefully opposed a proposal to build a new boarding school along metropolitan lines in Brazzaville. Instead, he suggested a decentralized system of "centers" where students would learn closer to nature and their families. This alternative schooling structure never came to pass; if it had, French and African schooling in the territories would have become much more similar. As we shall see, the colonial administration took the opposite tack: three years after Saurat had insisted *in Brazzaville* that formal schooling was harmful to French children, colonial educators at the Brazzaville Conference would insist that "Europeans" were uniquely suited for such schooling to justify Africans' exclusion from metropolitan-style secondary schools.

---

101. Saurat, *Watch over Africa*, 65.

102. Saurat, *Watch over Africa*, 95–96. As we shall see, soon after Saurat's departure, Governor-General Éboué would make encouraging this kind of collaboration official policy for all of AEF.

103. Saurat, *Watch over Africa*, 102.

Cassin leaned more in that latter direction. When Cassin arrived in AEF the following year, there were only two postprimary schools for Africans in the entire federation. Both were technical schools, the *écoles professionelles* in Brazzaville and Libreville (Gabon). Cassin found this situation woefully insufficient and urged Éboué to develop new secondary programs in all major urban centers.[104] But Cassin was more interested in developing new village schools, open-air *"écoles de brousse."* Unlike Saurat, he does not seem to have made a connection between these and the English rural schools that he and the Cathala Commission had so admired. Perhaps the reason is that Cassin saw African children and "European French" children as intrinsically different. In a handwritten aside that he eventually cut from a lecture he gave on African education back in London, Cassin reflected: "In truth, there is an immense difference between French citizens of Europe and black French subjects."[105] For Cassin, that difference warranted a simpler kind of schooling for Africans. Cassin found rural African schools "remarkable" for teaching young Africans basic reading, writing, and arithmetic, while prioritizing handicrafts and farming to prepare them for a "better" rural life. He hoped that "within a few years AEF will be covered in these kinds of schools."[106]

More of *those* schools was probably not what Gabonese notable Félix Adandé Rapontchombo had in mind when he asked for more institutional support to help Africans attain "a superior evolutionary stage" in a written appeal to Cassin when he passed through Libreville. Rapontchombo relayed his ardent hope that France would invest more in the development of higher-quality education in Gabon and AEF more broadly. "Generous France," he added, would surely not regret it, and signed off: "Vive la France! Vive de Gaulle! Vive Gabon!"[107] Descended from a royal lineage among the Mpongwe clans, Rapontchombo was part of the tiny francophone elite in the region and was most likely one of the few Africans with whom Cassin had an actual exchange.[108] Rapontchombo's polite, patriotic, and personal request marks the closing of an era. After the war, officials in French Africa and France would be confronted with widening African networks collectively demanding equal access to equal education.

---

104. Bilan de l'activité du Service de l'Instruction Publique, Note Préliminaire, undated, AN: 382AP/55.

105. Cassin, "La France en Proche-orient et en Afrique," Conférence de M. le Prof. René Cassin, Faite au Hyde Park Hotel, May 5, 1942, 17, AN: 382/AP/59.

106. Cassin, "La France en Proche-orient et en Afrique," 22.

107. Letter from Prince Félix Rapontchombo to René Cassin, Libreville, March 4, 1942, AN: 382AP/59.

108. Cassin lamented his limited contact with Africans during his trip. "La France en Proche-orient et en Afrique," 21.

The peculiar wartime situation brought men like Cassin and Saurat to central Africa, a place where neither had been and where both probably never thought they would go. For that very reason, their thinking was not limited by a strict colonial formation. They brought different perspectives to bear on colonial problems, even if neither man could break completely free of inherited racist ideas. Cassin's view of African education was shortsighted, but he did contest colonial policies that he considered discriminatory. He was appalled by a plan by Governor-General Éboué to codify a hierarchy of local statuses that would consign some social strata of Africans to forced labor, a practice Cassin wished to see abolished entirely.[109] Saurat, on the other hand, was perfectly at ease with explicit racial categories, but, to his great amazement, found colonial problems bore a striking resemblance to metropolitan ones. The relationship between public and Christian schools and the postwar parameters of *laïcité* was a shared concern linking the Cathala Commission in London and missionaries in AEF, even if Saurat was one of the few to recognize it. From Brazzaville to European milieus in London and even underground networks in occupied France, the question of Christianity's place in French national culture intersected with debates about how France would fit into a future united Europe or "Europe-Africa Federation." Other concerns were also shared across this complex and multilayered geography. What kind of schooling would help build more socially inclusive, democratic societies? What activities beyond the classroom would prepare young people for modern life and teach them to be good citizens? Cassin and Saurat, the Cathala Commission, the other European governments-in-exile, and the British were all asking these questions as they debated the kind of postwar world they wanted. Colonial officials and educators were doing likewise in wartime French Africa.

The View from Free French Africa: Reimagining "Black France"

While Cassin represented republican rectitude in Free French London, Félix Éboué and Henri Laurentie were the "standard-bearers of republican continuity" in Free French Africa.[110] In just a few crucial years, these career colonial civil servants reoriented French colonial policy in the region. Together they pursued a moderate reformist agenda that put greater emphasis on African well-being and elite Africans' participation in local affairs, which culminated

109. Jennings, *Free French Africa*, 224–228.
110. Jennings, *Free French Africa*, 93–94.

in the Brazzaville Conference in January 1944. Most important, they orchestrated a lasting rapprochement between the administration and the missions, reversing a long-standing policy that construed mission interests and the interests of the colonial state as distinct and, at times, fundamentally opposed. Although neither man held important positions in the postwar republic—Éboué died of a stroke shortly after the Brazzaville Conference, and Laurentie, too reformist for the conservative colonial bureaucracy in liberated Paris, was pushed out in early 1947—their wartime leadership shaped postwar debates about colonial reform and the contours of youth and education policy across French Africa for years to come.

Éboué and Laurentie initially appear an unlikely pair. The descendant of enslaved people in his native Guyane, Éboué was the first (and only) Black colonial governor in France's empire, while Laurentie, son of a civil servant, came from an established bourgeois family in the Loire. Éboué was a Socialist and a Freemason, Laurentie a devout Catholic with no partisan ties. But they shared a rare independence of mind with regard to colonial policy (neither had attended the École nationale de la France d'Outre-Mer, where most mid-century colonial bureaucrats developed their acute *esprit de corps*), and both happened to be in the same remote place at an unusual time. They met in Chad on the eve of the war, where Éboué was serving as governor and Laurentie as a district officer. Éboué was impressed by Laurentie and brought him to Chad's capital, Fort Lamy, to serve as his chief of staff. From there, they rallied to de Gaulle in August 1940 and helped bring the rest of AEF and Cameroon into the Free French fold. When de Gaulle named Éboué governor-general of AEF, Éboué retained Laurentie as his second-in-command, and the two relocated to Brazzaville that fall. They worked together there for the next three years, until Laurentie was appointed director of political affairs in the CFLN's Commissariat for Colonies in Algiers. In that post, Laurentie oversaw preparations for the Brazzaville Conference, whose proceedings Éboué helped preside over despite his failing health.[111]

When Éboué and Laurentie arrived, Brazzaville was little more than a large town, with fewer than fifty thousand residents. Like many colonial African cities, it was racially segregated, with an administrative district situated on the best land reserved for a tiny white population of less than fifteen hundred. A rigid racial hierarchy governed every aspect of daily life; the use of forced labor

111. Philippe Oulmont, "Félix Éboué: Un jaurasien inattendu," *Cahiers Jaurès* 200, no. 2 (2011): 147–161, https://doi.org/10.3917/cj.200.0147; Martin Shipway, "Thinking Like an Empire: Governor Henri Laurentie and Postwar Plans for the Late Colonial Empire-State," in *The French Colonial Mind*, vol. 1, *Mental Maps of Empire and Colonial Encounters*, ed. Martin Thomas (Lincoln: University of Nebraska Press, 2011), 219–250.

in the city's environs was widespread, as it was throughout the region, and even Éboué and Laurentie felt they could not suppress the practice in wartime.[112] Neither Éboué nor Laurentie had very radical visions of colonial reform, but they both bucked racist norms and everyday practice in Brazzaville as the only Frenchmen in the administration who did not *tutoyer* African notables and civil servants, according them the respect and dignity expected by all white French adults.[113]

Their brief tenure at the helm of the civilian administration of Free French Africa did little to uproot the deeply entrenched racial order in AEF, but Éboué and Laurentie had a lasting impact on the government's relationship with the missions. As Elizabeth Foster has shown, they both personally reached out to local Catholic leaders who had supported Vichy in 1940 and invited those willing to embrace Free France to help shape policy, particularly in the domain of education. In a momentous November 1941 circular on "indigenous policy," which was signed by Éboué but which Foster suggests was likely written by Laurentie, they declared the goals of public schools and mission schools to be identical and therefore equally deserving of government support. What is more, the circular explicitly characterized "Christianity" as a vital force for advancing French civilization in Africa more broadly. This was a departure from the dominant interwar administrative stance that was wary of missionary activity, especially schooling. Before the war, occasional subsidies had been granted to mission schools, but only in exceptional cases and on a temporary basis. With the November 1941 circular, mission schools throughout AEF effectively became "subcontractors" of the colonial state, an arrangement that was later extended to AOF and that continued after the war.[114]

This public-private collaboration in education is exactly what Saurat had hoped for and tried himself to arrange during his *tournée* of AEF in spring 1941. His position on the matter did not stem from personal piety. "I am not known, even to myself, as a particularly devout Christian," Saurat mused during his African travels.[115] Rather, like so many others, he blamed the French defeat on the Third Republic's anticlerical approach to youth and education policy.

---

112. Éboué's stance on forced labor caused a major row with Cassin and Henry Hauck back in London, both of whom found Éboué's proposal to codify a new "evolved native status" to exempt African elites ridiculous. However, as Eric Jennings has noted, Éboué saw that status as a way to "avoid infantilizing a tiny slice of African society" and elaborated the rationale for it in the language of rights. Jennings, *Free French Africa*, 50–55, 95, 224–228.

113. Oulmont and Shipway both highlight this practice, citing Brian Weinstein's *Éboué* (Oxford: Oxford University Press, 1972).

114. Foster, *African Catholic*, 34–41. The full text of the circular was republished after the war: Félix Éboué, *La nouvelle politique indigène pour l'AEF* (Paris: Office Français d'Edition, 1945).

115. Saurat, *Watch over Africa*, 69.

Months before the November circular, Saurat already felt he had found a kindred spirit in Éboué in this regard. On April 4, Saurat praised Éboué's moral leadership on Radio-Brazzaville in effusive terms. He cited an earlier Éboué circular that identified "unity" and "freedom" as twin pillars of France's "spiritual renovation," which Saurat insisted needed to begin with the school:

> Our task must be to make all children realize from an early age those common principles of action to which Governor-General Éboué refers. For instance, during those hours in which the *aumônier* or the *pasteur* come to teach the children the religion chosen by their parents, let the children whose parents prefer it listen to the headmaster or headmistress on morality or behavior. . . . Let all children, whether Catholic, Protestant, or anything else, learn in a real way those common principles of practical morality, of true patriotism, of just collaboration between men and nations.[116]

Saurat's ecumenism and retreat from anticlericalism were widely shared among French educators and policymakers during the war—in the Cathala Commission; in the internal Resistance; and, of course, within the Vichy regime itself. Éboué and Laurentie had personal, pragmatic, and local reasons for initiating a lasting rapprochement between the colonial administration and the missions, but their November 1941 circular and all the related policies and material investments that followed should be considered within a broader geography of wartime reappraisals of *laïcité* and the place of Christianity in French society and culture that outlasted the war.

Éboué and Laurentie also helped initiate a new approach to colonial youth and education policy more generally. After the Allied landing in Morocco and Algeria in late 1942, their moderate reformism was extended to the rest of French sub-Saharan Africa as AOF left the Vichy fold. From then on, Éboué and Laurentie's emphasis on increasing African well-being and participation in local affairs took on added international significance. The year before, the Atlantic Charter (1941) had stoked French anxieties about US views on French colonialism. The predominant role played by the United States in the "liberation" of so much of France's African empire further heightened those fears. As a result, local education reforms started to be elaborated with a more global audience in mind. Shortly after the African federations were reunited under de Gaulle's leadership in August 1943, the director of public education in AOF

---

116. Saurat, appendix I, "A Broadcast Given from Brazzaville on April 4, 1941, at 9:45 p.m.," *Watch over Africa*, 143–149.

called for massive investment in "indigenous" primary education, emphasizing that such a move would command the respect of foreign observers. The expansion of African education, he argued, "could present itself, externally, as one of the solid elements, as one of the successes of our colonization of these territories."[117] Educating Africans was becoming a crucial part of a nascent international public relations campaign to justify continued French rule on African soil.

Six months later, the official program of the Brazzaville Conference further drove the point home. The preamble to the proceedings affirmed: "The world is watching us. We must respond to these enquiring looks not only with a presentation of our past successes, but also with a program . . . that will show that France is an active and methodical nation, a worthy steward of the Empire which it has under its care."[118] By highlighting France's "past successes" alongside calls for reform, the conference organizers blunted critical evaluation of prewar French colonial policy from the outset. Indeed, they avowed that the "indigènes" had always been the raison d'être of the French presence in Africa and insisted that if this was not always evident in practice, it was because colonial administrators had misunderstood the "real interests" of Africans. "Without waiting for the Atlantic Charter," the organizers proudly declared, "France had already enshrined, if not in words, but more importantly, in deeds and in intentions, the principle 'Africa for the Africans.'"[119]

Laurentie began preparations for the Brazzaville Conference in late 1943, while he was still overseeing the reorganization of the administrative apparatus in AOF following the Vichy interlude there.[120] He sent directives to AOF's new governor-general, Pierre Cournarie, to promote and subsidize youth programs for both metropolitan French and Africans.[121] Laurentie took pains to underscore that the youth and education services were there to serve "the entirety of AOF youth, European and indigenous, 'evolved' and 'non-evolved,' male and female, school-educated and not, and especially those categories enumerated above that are the most backward." It was the administration's responsibility, Laurentie continued, to promote young people's "moral, spiritual, physical and

117. Rapport au sujet des activités du Service de l'Enseignement AOF, préparé par M. Mus, Direction-Générale de l'Instruction Publique en AOF, August 9, 1943, Archives Nationales du Sénégal—Dakar, Senegal (ANS): O/1 (31).

118. Programme général, Conférence de Brazzaville (January 1944), 2, ANOM: 1AFFPOL/2201, dossier 5.

119. Programme général, Conférence de Brazzaville, 3, ANOM: 1AFFPOL/2201, dossier 5.

120. Ginio, *French Colonialism Unmasked.*

121. Letter from the Commissariat aux Colonies (signed Laurentie) to the Gouverneur-Général Pierre Cournarie, December 16, 1943, ANOM: 1AFFPOL/872.

intellectual development" and prepare young Africans for the ever-greater role they would surely be called on to play in *both* "imperial and French life."[122]

Laurentie's approach to colonial youth policy combined colonial paternalism with a vision, however limited, of African empowerment. That volatile combination was a recurrent theme of the Brazzaville Conference. In late 1943, Laurentie compiled extensive reports from officials in AOF and AEF on the state of colonial education and youth programming to present at the conference. A profound tension emerges in this material between two key objectives: (1) the expansion of primary education, basic training, and youth activities to reach "the masses"; and (2) the cultivation of a new generation of francophone elites who would be loyal to France. This tension can be seen in Laurentie's own report on African youth programs in the run-up to the conference. He praised scout movements and sporting clubs for their "beneficial effect, not only to fortify the body of the *indigènes,* but also to develop a sense of responsibility, loyalty, and team spirit." At the same time, he called for more local educational circles, which, he argued, promoted the "cultural evolution of the race" and enabled "the *évolué* elite to develop its intelligence and especially its character and capacity for critical thinking." Laurentie concluded, "This *éducation* of the *évolués* constitutes the lynchpin of our colonial policy."[123]

Laurentie's vision for formal schooling hinged on the same tension. He proposed a system of public schools at the primary, secondary, and higher levels, but though he used the terminology of the metropolitan educational system, each order of African education meant something radically different. His "secondary schools" would prepare Africans for low-level administrative positions or to become primary school teachers for other Africans and so would be closer to upper primary schools (*écoles primaires supérieures*) than to metropolitan middle schools (*collèges*), let alone lycées. Laurentie was unequivocal that African and metropolitan higher education should have "nothing in common." Colonial "tertiary education" would comprise a few specialized technical institutions in medicine, agriculture, and pedagogy. This three-tiered system would be supplemented by other kinds of state-supported institutions that responded to local conditions: rural schools to give a practical education to the peasantry; "*médersas*" to provide education to the sons of Islamic chiefs and other Muslim notables in the "Arab" regions of Chad and Mauritania; and now also mission schools, with which Laurentie envisioned "the most fertile collaboration." Thus although "one of the objects of the Brazzaville Confer-

---

122. Note pour la Direction-Générale—Instruction Publique-AOF, January 9, 1944, ANS: O/87 (31).
123. Note sur l'enseignement des Indigènes et les oeuvres de jeunesse indigène dans les colonies françaises préparée par Henri Laurentie, December 12, 1943, ANOM: 1AFFPOL/874, dossier 3.

ence [would] be to organize mass schooling," under Laurentie's plan only the tiniest fraction of the population would have had access to anything beyond the most basic education.[124]

Nevertheless, even Laurentie's modest proposal was too radical for top education officials in AOF. Edmond Cabrière, headmaster of the lone lycée in Dakar and director of secondary education for the federation, felt the conference should focus on adapting formal education to the needs and capabilities of the local population, which, in his view, absolutely precluded secondary schooling in the metropolitan sense of the term. He strongly opposed admitting any Africans to lycées. His vision of African education was much more limited: "Before we *instruct* them, [our project] hopes to *educate* them: it hopes for the progressive elevation of the whole population, not the artificial culture of a few uprooted plants." Secondary education in French Africa, Cabrière continued, should offer the same education to "European" youth in the territories as they would receive in the metropole, but precisely for this reason the administration should not recruit African students at the secondary level. For him, the "nature of this schooling" and the "character of the exams which it entails both forbid it."[125]

Cabrière did not justify the exclusion of Africans from secondary education with rehearsals of racist stereotypes of African intelligence, aptitudes and discipline; he offered a reified portrait of *Europeans*. Cabrière maintained that secondary education was about "classical culture," and so he asked, "Who could doubt that young Europeans, conscious or unconscious inheritors of Mediterranean civilization, are more apt than the local population to receive this culture?" He insisted that secondary education could not be "adapted" to local conditions without perverting its very essence; everything about it was "conceived for Europeans."[126] For Cabrière, then, young "Europeans" belonged to a common culture and civilization and were inheritors of qualities that made them uniquely fit for a specific kind of education. Contrary to the tenets of republican universalism, Cabrière construed French education as profoundly particular. Its particularity, however, was rooted, not in a narrowly conceived French nation, but rather in a broader "classical culture" and "Mediterranean civilization"—that is, in a certain vision of Europe.

Cabrière's deployment of the category "European" in this way was part of a long tradition of coded language in French colonial discourse, but it also

---

124. Note sur l'enseignement des Indigènes et les oeuvres de jeunesse indigène dans les colonies françaises préparée par Henri Laurentie, ANOM: 1AFFPOL/874, dossier 3.

125. Edmond Cabrière, Rapport à M. le Directeur-Général de l'Instruction Publique sur l'Enseignement secondaire et la question indigène, undated [1943], ANS: O/171 (31).

126. Cabrière, Rapport, ANS: O/171 (31). Harry Gamble discusses this document in his *Contesting French West Africa*, 204–205.

points to a historically specific crisis of political vocabulary. In the postwar conjuncture, "European" emerged as *the* racial code word for both "French" and
"white," terms that became politically untenable as Africans attained French
citizenship and explicit racial language was tabooed.[127] Efforts to define what
being "European" actually meant—indeed, to imagine what "Europe" would
actually be—in discussions about postwar European integration brought educators in French Africa like Cabrière into dialogue with transnational European federalists in wartime London and clandestine pamphleteers like Jean
Cassou in Occupied France.

Not all French colonial officials who invoked Europe did so to justify excluding Africans from advanced levels of education. Local administrators in French
Soudan (contemporary Mali) suggested in a report for the conference that
their task was to find a way to reconcile the two "educative forces" operating
on African society, "tradition" and "European civilization." Ideally, colonial education should strike a balance between cultural preservation and transformation. But colonial educators must acknowledge that education had an inherent
emancipatory quality and that their African students "have learned from us that
schooling is the key that opens all doors." The report concluded that the administration should not fear the emancipatory power of the school. Schooling
was perfectly suited to AOF, the report's authors argued; the administration
just had to expand its reach.[128]

Yves Aubineau, the top federal education official in AOF, had a more cautious
view. In his preparatory report, he summed up his philosophy of African education in two words: "happiness" and "progress." African education, Aubineau argued, "is essentially about penetrating the masses, teaching them how to live
better, to give them a life that is more productive, healthy and comfortable—in a
word, a better life." He cautioned, however, that colonial officials needed to be
aware of the specificity of their own conceptions of "happiness." "Without a
doubt," he wrote, "our European ideas, as seductive, honest and generous as
they may be, have a totally different nature in the eyes of the Blacks." Education
may be a "work of social promotion," but it is also "a lever that can upset, and if
we are not careful, totally destroy, the entire edifice of indigenous social and fa-
milial organization." Aubineau then exclaimed, "And so it must be undertaken
with infinite precaution! It is the herald of emancipation, a potential disaster."[129]

Like the Cathala Commission before him, Aubineau thought it impossible
to reorganize colonial education on the same basis as metropolitan education

---

127. On race and the crisis of political terminology in the late 1940s, see Marker, "Obscuring Race."
128. Rapport sur l'Education pour la Conférence de Brazzaville (Soudan), undated, ANS: O/171 (31).
129. Rapport a/s de la Conférence de Brazzaville, signed Yves Aubineau, Directeur-Général de
l'Instruction Publique (AOF), January 10, 1944, ANS: O/171 (31).

reform. Unlike his London predecessors, though, he was bracingly candid about his rationale: if the colonial administration applied metropolitan principles in the territories, it would have to admit "the equality of all children to the right to schooling." In theory, he conceded, it would not only be just but also in France's interest to provide all African children with equal access to education. But given the paucity of schools, teachers, and resources, getting all school-age African children into classrooms would be a pipe dream, especially at the secondary level. Aubineau then quickly layered onto this stark material reality a moral justification for not educating more Africans at a higher level, citing at length the passages discussed earlier from Cabrière's report on secondary education as the unique preserve of Europeans. Aubineau therefore proposed the conference set a modest target: two hundred thousand children enrolled in *primary* schools in AOF over the next ten years.[130]

Raising the rate of primary school attendance became the central focus of conversations about education during the Brazzaville proceedings. The conference's resolution on education called on colonial governors to submit fifteen-year plans for the rapid construction of new teacher training institutes, primary schools, and upper primary schools by August 1944.[131] But educational philosophy and school curricula were also discussed, and it was widely accepted that the purpose of colonial education was to reproduce African racial difference, not overcome it. The AOF delegation, which was led by Aubineau, was particularly insistent that their objective should be "the making of the Black," by which they meant "protecting the race, assuring its harmonious development, in short, making the *indigène* an *indigène* of quality."[132] And yet, conference participants also rejected schooling in African languages. French-language instruction was deemed essential not only for the formation of a loyal African elite but also for strengthening ties between metropole and colony.[133] The Brazzaville resolutions mandated French-language instruction in *all* African schools.[134] Arabic instruction would no longer be permitted in Muslim-majority regions, a policy that had significant repercussions after the war.[135]

---

130. Rapport a/s de la Conférence de Brazzaville, signed Yves Aubineau, ANS: O/171 (31).

131. Exécution des Recommandations: Enseignement, Brazzaville Conference, January 1944, ANOM: 1AFFPOL/2201, dossier 5. The plans would be reviewed by a special education committee within the Commissariat of Colonies in Algiers, which would also study the creation of new professional and secondary schools in the territories.

132. Rapport no. 1 sur la politique indigène en AOF, Brazzaville, undated, ANOM: 1AFFPOL/2201, dossier 5.

133. Rapport relations metropole-colonies, January 1944, ANOM: 1AFFPOL/2201, dossier 5.

134. Exécution des Recommandations, enseignement, 1944, ANOM: 1AFFPOL/2201, dossier 5.

135. I return to this issue in chapter 5.

It remained unclear exactly what kind of African elite conference-goers had in mind. The AOF delegation conceded, "An autochthonous elite, very small at least at the outset, could integrate itself, in the fullest sense of the term, in the universal French community where they will join our Frenchmen of color from our oldest colonies." However, this integration would be possible only for those who acquired a level of culture and "moral standing" comparable to those of "the most distinguished Frenchmen." What is more, the AOF delegation hoped that this "incorporation" would occur elsewhere in the empire, not in their home territories.[136] Colonial officials' inability to imagine African elites' integration into local French milieus construes the territories as exceptional spaces unfit to foster a genuine Franco-African community.

The official Brazzaville education plan did not resolve these tensions. Primary education would last for six years, and those who completed the cycle would receive a *Certificat d'études*, a diploma with no equivalent in metropolitan France. Primary schooling would be modeled on the metropolitan system *and* "adapted" to local life, with parts of the curriculum devoted to manual work, agriculture, household training, and physical education. Instruction would be in French, but the curriculum would be "the least literary possible." In this way, colonial education would instill "love and respect for France" without disrupting traditional African milieus. This aligned with the "new" colonial doctrine outlined at Brazzaville more broadly: "It is essential that peoples develop according to their own spirit and that Black France, firmly rooted in African soil, be an original, vibrant and fertile creation."[137]

For all its limitations, the Brazzaville education plan required significant financial investment. After the conference, the CFLN's Commissariat of Colonies in Algiers requested an additional 675,000 francs for its 1944 budget to create its own education department to carry out the Brazzaville resolutions on expanding African primary education.[138] Any sum may seem substantial given the penury of wartime conditions, but it is worth comparing it to other funding requests for colonial projects at the time. Consider, for instance, a concurrent request for 800,000 francs to help complete the construction of a Catholic cathedral in Brazzaville, and another for 500,000 francs to renovate a Protestant church in Douala (Cameroon). The completion of the Brazzaville cathedral was characterized as directly in line with French interests, since the curacy in Brazzaville had "fostered national sentiment which contributed profoundly to achieving a climate of

---

136. Rapport no. 1 sur la politique indigène en AOF, 51–52, ANOM: 1AFFPOL/2201, dossier 5.

137. Plan d'Enseignement-Conférence Africaine Française de Brazzaville, undated, ANS: O/171 (31).

138. CFLN: Budget 1944, AN C//15268, dossier 2.

national unity in AEF."[139] As for the Protestant church, officials noted that the French Protestant mission in Douala represented the beginning of "Christian civilization in Cameroon" and had achieved great works "as much from the point of view of evangelization as the penetration of French influence among indigenous milieus."[140] Clearly the central colonial authority in Algiers considered Christianity—in its Catholic *and* Protestant forms—a crucial vector for the spread of French influence and French interests in sub-Saharan Africa. As the central authority requested almost twice as many funds for these projects as it did to create and operate its entire Education Department, we may well wonder whether colonial officials in Algiers considered schooling or churchgoing more effective in nurturing the authority's vision of "Black France."

Educational reconstruction in the postwar republic, French Africa, and Western Europe became entangled during the war in new and enduring ways. As Free French planners from London to Brazzaville elaborated new agendas for national, colonial, and transnational education reform, they also mapped new, often overlapping coordinates of belonging—based on religion, race, and "civilization"—that crisscrossed French, African, and European space. The Brazzaville Conference and the Conference of Allied Ministers of Education encapsulate the wartime evolution of ideas and expectations about France's European and African futures. This chapter has considered these events in their wartime context, but they also serve as points of departure for thinking about ongoing conversations about the role of education and the horizons of belonging in the French Union and united Europe in the early postwar years. The next chapter will revisit the Brazzaville Conference proceedings in relation to postwar ideas about belonging and religion, and chapter 3 will return to both the Brazzaville Conference and the CAME from the perspective of shifting postwar conceptions of race.

---

139. Observations sur la subvention pour l'achèvement de la cathédrale de Brazzaville, undated, AN: C//15268, dossier 2.
140. Observations sur l'église protestante du centenaire à Douala, undated, AN: C//15268, dossier 2.

CHAPTER 2

Recalibrating *Laïcité* from Brazzaville to Bruges

Postwar efforts to devise new approaches to national, colonial, and transnational youth and education policy engendered extensive reflection on the role of the Christian tradition in French society, the French colonial project in Africa, and "European civilization" more broadly. The quest for national unity after Vichy and Catholic participation in the Resistance created an opening to reconcile Catholicism and republicanism in metropolitan France and francophone Africa, and one of the key strategies education officials adopted in trying to reach out to Catholic educators was to characterize French culture, even *laïcité* itself, as culturally Christian. At the same time, French participation in European youth and education forums offered new venues and an additional impetus for acknowledging the centrality of Christianity in French culture and social life. Indeed, affirming the relationship between Christianity and transnational Europeanness rendered such recognition more acceptable and commonsensical in postwar French political discourse.

This chapter follows the political, social, and geopolitical developments that drove the postwar culturalization of Christianity through time and across space. During the war, French education officials from London and Free French Africa to Vichy saw a robust organized youth sector, made up of secular and confessional groups, as an antidote to everything that seemed wrong with education under the Third Republic—its rigidity, its intellectualism, and its militant anticlericalism. The first two critiques had long traversed the political spectrum, but there was something new about the emerging consensus, even among republicans and Socialists, that the status quo with regard to *laïcité* might have to change. For some, this new stance was strategic, but much of the center Left felt the Third Republic's uncompromising position on *laïcité* had fatally undermined French national unity and France's democracy. A lively world of organized youth, with vibrant confessional and secular movements coexisting side by side, gestured toward a totally different postwar democratic model based on religious pluralism instead of anticlericalism.

This wartime shift on the center Left converged with powerful currents in the Catholic world. Pluralism was a bedrock principle of social Catholicism, a transnational movement that appealed to a widening circle of left-leaning Catholics in interwar Europe. Some of social Catholicism's most prominent figures were French, and the movement spread in liberal Catholic milieus in France's empire as well. The emphasis on pluralism was part of a broader embrace of political modernity in social Catholic thought. As James Chappel has shown, social Catholics generally reconciled themselves to democracy and the modern secular state. As a result, their activism shifted from trying to capture the state to working with it to protect "religious freedoms" and support the spiritual life of the national community. But conceptions of pluralism and religious freedom varied widely. Social Catholics in Europe were deeply divided in their views on anti-Semitism, and those in France's empire who favored interfaith organizing with Muslims in French Africa and Algeria were in the minority.[1] Mainstream social Catholic discourse about pluralism in France and across Europe centered on the rapprochement between political secularism and European Christianity (Catholic and Protestant), part of a broader effort to transcend sectarian politics and re-center Christianity in European social and cultural life.

After 1945, the onset of the Cold War gave that rapprochement acute geopolitical significance as Christianity, democracy, *and* secularism became conjoined in a transatlantic anti-Communist front.[2] By 1950, French social Catholics like Jacques Maritain, who rejected the concept of "the West" or the idea that Europe was uniquely Christian, were marginalized by conservative anti-Communist Catholics in France like Robert Schuman and Georges Bidault, who explicitly championed European integration as the defense of "Christian Western civilization."[3] These Cold War shifts impacted French domestic policy. The 1950s

---

1. Chappel, *Catholic Modern*; Fontaine, *Decolonizing Christianity*.

2. Scott, *Sex and Secularism*; Moyn, "From Communist to Muslim." Moyn argues that the Cold War discourse of religious freedom and the equation of democracy and Christianity sought to marginalize secularism, whereas Scott, who I think makes the more persuasive case, argues that Christianity, democracy, *and* secularism became synonymous in Cold War rhetoric against Soviet *atheism*.

3. Chappel, *Catholic Modern*, 175–178.

were bookended by a pair of French laws that extended state support to parents who wanted to send their children to private religious schools (Marie and Barangé Laws, 1951) and another that provided state support to those schools directly (Debré Law, 1959).[4] All three laws were explicitly elaborated in the Cold War rhetoric of religious freedom and school choice.[5]

However, Cold War logics alone cannot account for the recalibration of French *laïcité* in debates about confessional youth movements, school policy, and philosophies of education across national-metropolitan, colonial African, and transnational European contexts over the course of the 1940s. The war opened new spaces and rationales for reassessing the anticlerical republic and the place of Christianity in whatever "civilization" France might belong to in the postwar order—Franco-African, European, Eurafrican, Western. As we have seen, wartime planners from London to Brazzaville considered overcoming France's historic *querelle scolaire* and providing young people with a more holistic formation as essential steps for the revitalization of French democracy. Planners' material support for Christian youth organizations and mission schools in Free French Africa made it easier for the Fourth Republic, which was officially secular, to fit in a postwar Europe whose unity was increasingly posed in Christian terms. In the late 1940s, French officials and educators debating the contours of *laïcité* in the new republic and postwar French Africa were also participating in transnational forums on "Europeanizing" youth and education policy to promote united Europe, where social Catholicism, Christian Democracy, and ecumenism flourished.[6] Those forums became important venues where shifts in French conceptions of *laïcité* that originated in metropole and colony were naturalized and reinforced by transnational processes of European integration.

Religious Pluralism, National Renewal, and Youth and Education Policy

During the war, state funding for confessional youth organizations found wide support from across the political spectrum, from Vichy to Free French London, Brazzaville, and Algiers. The different confessional branches of a single

---

4. In 1951, the *Loi Marie* provided scholarships to children attending private schools, and the *Loi Barangé* provided heads of household with a fixed sum for their children's education that could be used for private schools. In 1959, the *Loi Debré* formalized a system of state aid to private schools directly.

5. Chappel emphasizes the transnational European context of the Marie and Barangé Laws, which had analogues in both Germany and Austria. *Catholic Modern*, 215–216.

6. On the articulation of postwar ecumenism with the imperatives of decolonization and European integration, see Fontaine, *Decolonizing Christianity*; Greenberg, "Catholics, Protestants."

youth movement like the scouts seemed to offer an alternative democratic model based on pluralism instead of anticlericalism. For some, that pluralist model might include Jews and Muslims, but it was primarily envisioned for French Christians. The state's new stance toward confessional youth organizations changed the terms of the heated debate about *laïcité* and formal schooling. In the liminal years of the French provisional government (1944–1946), education reform commissions in Algiers and post-Liberation Paris failed to broker a compromise and implement lasting policy, but their proceedings reveal important conceptual shifts—even among champions of *laïcité*—about the relationship between Christianity, secularism, and French identity that had important ramifications from Brazzaville to Bruges.

All Eyes on Scouts

In the early war years, both Vichy and Free France singled out scouting as an exemplary form of organized leisure for young people. The Vichy regime brought the leaders of Christian scout movements into the state apparatus, effacing the barrier between public and private that had circumscribed state support for confessional scouting for decades. From their new posts in Vichy's Secretariat of Youth, the leaders of the Catholic Scouts de France and the Protestant Éclaireurs unionists joyfully proclaimed: "We are in power!" and "The hour of the Scouts has come!"[7] Incredibly, Vichy's first secretary of youth, Georges Lamirand, a social Catholic whose approach to youth policy emphasized pluralism and choice, recognized the Jewish Éclaireurs israélites de France and provided them with financial support. As late as May 1941, Jewish scout troops participated alongside their Christian counterparts in official May Day celebrations outside of Pétain's residence at the Hôtel du Parc. Lamirand and leaders of the Catholic and Protestant scout movements tried to protect the Éclaireurs israélites once the group became a target of the Commissariat for Jewish Questions later that year, but as Vichy's priorities shifted to focus on Jewish persecution, Lamirand's conception of pluralism proved untenable. He was forced to resign, and the Éclaireurs israélites were disbanded by his successor in January 1943.[8] Around this time, the leadership of the Catholic and Protestant scouts began to distance themselves from Vichy and established contacts with Free French officials in Algiers.[9]

---

7. Lionel Christien, "Une présence chrétienne au risque de la Révolution nationale? Jean Jousselin et le secrétariat général à la Jeunesse en zone occupée," in *Scoutisme entre guerre et paix*, ed. Baubérot and Duval, 72.

8. Daniel Lee, *Pétain's Jewish Children: French Jewish Youth and the Vichy Regime, 1940–1942* (Oxford: Oxford University Press, 2014).

9. Christien, "Une présence chrétienne," in *Scoutisme entre guerre et paix*, ed. Baubérot and Duval.

By then, "Free France" had maintained its own close ties with confessional scouting for several years. In fact, the Free French government-in-exile in London established its own scout movement for French émigré youth, the Éclaireurs français de Grande-Bretagne. Although the organization did not have an official religious affiliation, it was decidedly not laïc. Helmed by Catholic and Protestant troop leaders, the movement embraced an explicitly Christian, "interfaith" orientation, with its own Catholic and Protestant chaplains.[10] State support and intimate involvement with confessional youth organizations evidently proved equally attractive to Vichy and to de Gaulle's shadow government in London.

So too in Free French Africa, where the Catholic Scouts de France in the territories broke with the metropolitan leadership that supported Pétain. In November 1940, scouts marched alongside the Free French garrison in Brazzaville in a symbolic display of allegiance to de Gaulle.[11] State support soon followed. In October 1941, AEF Governor General Félix Éboué ordered a significant subsidy to scouting in the federation. Half went to develop the secular Éclaireurs de France—which at that time was virtually nonexistent in AEF—and half went to the Catholic Scouts de France. The latter had had a presence in the region since the late 1920s, but state support inaugurated a shift in the movement's orientation from serving French youth in the territories to developing local troops for Africans (to the dismay of many French in the region who did not want to see colonial hierarchies disturbed).[12] Funding for Catholic scouts was a harbinger of Éboué's important circular announcing AEF's new indigenous policy, which, a month later, guaranteed equal state support to public and mission schools.[13]

This proved a momentous precedent for youth policy in postwar French Africa. By the mid-1950s, Christian scout movements in the African federations had received millions in state subsidies, and the fact that this practice originated with a Free French regime gave the policy legitimacy and a specifically republican imprimatur.[14] Éboué's administration had specifically characterized its new stance toward mission schools and confessional scouting as epitomizing "Free French values." A report on Free French achievements in AEF, presented to the emerging governing structures in Algiers in early 1943, proudly

---

10. Jean-Jacques Gauthé, "La France Libre et le scoutisme," in *Pour une histoire de la France Libre*, ed. Patrick Harismendy and Erwin Le Gall (Rennes: Presses Universitaires de Rennes, 2010), 49–57.

11. Charles-Édouard Harang, "Les Scouts de France en Afrique équatoriale francaise, 1940–1945," in *Scoutisme entre guerre et paix*, ed. Baubérot and Duval, 200.

12. Harang, "Les Scouts de France," in *Scoutisme entre guerre et paix*, ed. Baubérot and Duval, 200, 195.

13. See chapter 1.

14. For AEF, see "Scoutisme en AEF," ANOM: AEF GGAEF 5D/219. For AOF, see "Scouts de France—subventions AOF—1950–1959" and "Éclaireurs Unionistes de France—subventions AOF—1946–1958," ANS: 18G/214 (160).

affirmed: "The preparation of the *indigènes* for the colonial administration, which implies schooling, and a progressive adaptation to an urban standard of living—*that* is the indigenous policy of Free France." Mission schools and public schools, Christian scout troops and secular ones, all worked in spreading "French civilization" in Africa, and therefore deserved the same institutional support.[15] This new stance in wartime AEF enabled Catholic leaders and colonial officials in AOF—which had been under Vichy control for almost three years—to deflect accusations by secularists after the war that continuing state support for confessional youth initiatives there was inherently *vichyste*. As Reverend Père Bertho, who oversaw Catholic education in AOF, relished pointing out, that the policy was spearheaded by Éboué proved that it was motivated solely by genuine "interest in the evolution of the *indigènes*," since Éboué of all people could not be "accused of having fallen under Vichy's spell."[16]

As a Black Frenchman of the Left, Éboué was a convenient symbol for this kind of argument, but Éboué's paternalistic view of Africans was in sync with the conservative colonial bureaucracy's attitude toward African youth. His administration attributed "a particular importance to the scout movements for the *éducation* of the youth of AEF today and for French youth tomorrow." Local officials were especially enthusiastic about scouting's beneficial effect on young Africans: "There is something particularly useful about [scouting] in our African territories, in that it will develop courage and the spirit of discipline—virtues that are all too rare."[17] As we saw in the chapter 1, the Free French in London had also thought that organized youth activities like scouting would provide a valuable, more holistic education for French young people, but the assertion here that scouting would redress a particular absence of discipline and courage among African youth signals how youth policy in Free French Africa, although very much in line with broader discussions about the development of French youth during the war, continued to be refracted through a prism of inherited racist ideas about Africans.

Colonial officials' emphasis on *éducation*, conceived as the formation of the whole person in contrast to the mere transmission of knowledge in formal schooling (*instruction* or *enseignement*), was otherwise identical to ongoing conversations about metropolitan youth and education reforms in Algiers and liberated Paris. René Capitant, who succeeded René Cassin as Free France's commissioner for public instruction and later became minister of education in the Provisional Government of the French Republic (1944–1946), based his

15. *Les Réalisations coloniales de la France Combattante en AEF, Rapport de la Délégation du Commissariat à l'Intérieur d'Alger à Londres,* January 5, 1943, 17–23, AN: F/1a/3731.

16. Letter from Père Bertho to Charles Cros, Dakar, November 7, 1944, ANS: O/11 (31).

17. *Les Réalisations coloniales de la France Combattante en AEF,* 52, AN: F/1a/3731.

proposals for postwar reforms on the idea of *éducation*. In his view, only *éducation*, not *enseignement*, could transmit "the ideal that is the basis of the French resurgence in the Resistance today and that will serve tomorrow as the basis of the French revival in the national reconstruction that must follow."[18] Echoing discussions in the Cathala Commission, Capitant's conception of *éducation* carved out a national role for confessional youth movements in young people's moral and civic development. Capitant felt that *enseignement* should remain *laïc*, while *éducation* should be "less statist" and "less strictly secular." He therefore proposed that the state should provide financial support to both secular and confessional youth groups. He was particularly enthusiastic about scouting, as it served secular and religious youngsters alike. Capitant's praise for confessional scout groups articulated a capacious vision of religious pluralism in an explicitly imperial framework:

> There is a secular movement: the Éclaireurs de France; a Catholic movement: the Scouts de France; a Protestant movement: the Unionistes; a Jewish movement: the Éclaireurs Israélites. And tomorrow, I deeply hope and believe, Muslim scouts. . . . Thus we have a complete range, and it seems to me that this has a very great symbolic value, even if the size of the scouting movements is not yet very large.

Capitant's invocation of Muslim scouting was not idle talk. There were a handful of Muslim scout troops in the region around Algiers, and Capitant personally met with their leaders over the course of 1944 to discuss expanding Muslim scouting and increasing Muslim scouts' interactions with the other scout movements.[19]

Capitant promoted his vision of robust religious pluralism through scouting in the CFLN's major planning body on education reform, the Capitant-Durry Commission, which met for much of 1944. Although Capitant instructed the commission to limit its deliberations to the metropolitan context, colonial questions came up frequently, often raised by Capitant himself.[20] Capitant encouraged planners to embrace "the unity of France and its empire, across the rich diversity of its territories" as the guiding principle for postwar youth and education policy.[21] Like Denis Saurat and René Cassin before him,

---

18. Procès-verbal de la Commission de l'Education Nationale et de la Jeunesse de la séance du 13 mai 1944 (Assemblée consultative provisioire-Alger), AN: C//15266.

19. Procès-verbal de la Commission de l'Education Nationale et de la Jeunesse de la séance du 13 mai 1944, AN: C//15266.

20. Procès-verbal de la Commission de la réforme de l'enseignement, Séance d'Ouverture, March 8, 1944, AN: F/17/13335.

21. Rapport au sujet du Centre d'Études et de Recherches sur l'Éducation, Alger 1943, AN: F/1a/3802.

Capitant had no prior colonial experience before the war, but his wartime "unity in diversity" rhetoric proved to be a long-lasting and deeply felt political commitment.[22] He became a passionate advocate for imperial federalism after the war, and in early 1946, he penned a substantial treatise that outlined what a federal constitution might look like.[23] However, his aspirations for both a federal French Union and for Muslim scouting were disappointed. Capitant's successors in liberated Paris retained many aspects of his ideas about *éducation* versus *enseignement* and the need for more flexibility regarding *laïcité*, but the conversation in the metropole narrowed to the state's relationship with Christian schools and youth groups. That narrow focus aligned well with policy in French Africa and would be further reinforced in transnational European forums by the decade's end.

School Policy and the Renovation of French Democracy

In the run-up to the Liberation, debates about *laïcité* and school policy within the CFLN and the internal Resistance were deeply intertwined with a desire to democratize French education more broadly. The Capitant-Durry Commission in Algiers characterized its work as reviving Jean Zay's interwar reforms and definitively ending France's *"enseignement de caste."* The commission's plan called for secondary education that would be free, obligatory, and the same for all French children, girls and boys, until at least age fifteen or sixteen. Students who wanted to pursue further study and prepare for the *baccalauréat* could do so, but everyone would continue with some kind of further training or apprenticeship; no one would be permitted to enter a profession until age eighteen. After announcing this proposal, the commission's president declared, "Today an ardent desire for renewal animates all Frenchmen, outside of France as well as in France," and those "aspirations for a vigorous rejuvenation" necessitated this "real revolution" in French education.[24]

---

22. A law professor at the University of Strasbourg, Capitant was a committed liberal and antifascist who wrote extensively on Nazi jurisprudence in the 1930s. Those writings have been published as René Capitant, *Face au Nazisme: Écrits, 1933–1938; Textes réunis par Olivier Beaud* (Strasbourg: Presses Universiatires de Strasbourg, 2004). When the University of Strasbourg relocated to Clermont-Ferrand after the defeat, Capitant set up an important Resistance network there. In 1941, he requested and was granted a transfer to the University of Algiers, where he continued his Resistance work and helped prepare for the allied landing in French North Africa in November 1942. Capitant was named the CFLN's commissioner of public instruction at the end of 1943.

23. René Capitant, *Pour une constitution fédérale* (Paris: Renaissances, 1946).

24. Marcel Durry, Rapport général des travaux de la Commission pour la reforme de l'enseignement, November 16, 1944, 1. Reprinted in *Bulletin officiel du Ministère de l'Éducation Nationale, numéro spécial*

That sentiment was indeed widely felt. As the Algiers commission began its work, the National Resistance Council (CNR)—an umbrella organization for the diverse networks that made up the internal Resistance—issued its own proposal for sweeping education reform in similar terms.[25] The CNR framed its reform program as the continuation of its "combat mission" after the Liberation. The program called for a battery of social policies that would form the bedrock of the French welfare state: the right to work, the right to leisure, social security, and unemployment insurance. Education reform was a central plank of this blueprint for postwar French social democracy.[26] "All French children," the CNR proclaimed, should "benefit from schooling and gain access to the most developed culture," regardless of the social position of their parents. This fairer system, "not of birth but of merit," would anchor a truly "unifying democracy" and "sweep away the reactionary regime instituted by Vichy."[27]

The CNR's education plan was loudly anti-Vichy, democratic, and socially inclusive, but it was silent on laïcité. This glaring omission presents a sharp contrast to the otherwise identical program the French Communist Party (PCF) presented to the CNR a few months earlier. That proposal was openly anti-clerical and affirmed in no uncertain terms that schooling would be secular. The PCF was a dominant faction within the internal Resistance, but the imperative for unity and consensus within the CNR coalition of Communists, Socialists, radicals, and Catholics evidently trumped the PCF's insistence on a staunchly laïc platform.[28] Much as the Cathala Commission had done in London the year before, the CNR kicked the can down the road.

The Capitant-Durry commission did not fare much better in setting parameters for postwar laïcité. Its final report affirmed that "the enseignement provided by the State will be laïc," but its members could not reach a consensus on how to translate that principle into actual school policy. They decided the issue was too divisive to be left to unelected officials like themselves and should be put to the people's representatives once parliament resumed in Paris. They also hedged on the question of state support for confessional youth organizations. The commission applauded the "educative character" of both secular and religious youth movements, and once again singled out scouts; it intimated that confessional youth organizations probably did deserve govern-

---

consacré aux travaux de la Commission . . . réunie à Alger du mars à septembre 1944 (Paris: Imprimerie Nationale, 1944), AN: F/60/427.

25. Programme du Conseil National de la Résistance, adopté dans la clandestinité, March 15, 1944, https://www.les-crises.fr/15-mars-1944-cnr/.

26. Programme du Conseil National de la Résistance, 2ème partie, art. 5b.

27. Programme du Conseil National de la Résistance, 2ème partie, art. 5d.

28. Esquisse d'une politique française de l'enseignment présentée par le PCF aux groupements de la Resistance, September 30, 1943, AN: BB/30/17333.

ment support but made no concrete proposals.[29] In the end, the Algiers commission left no clear policy recommendations for its successors in Paris.

Fearful that the old *querelle scolaire* would continue to derail comprehensive education reform, the provisional government's Ministry of National Education (MEN) formed two task forces once its Algiers operations relocated to Paris in November 1944: a commission on general education reform and another on relations between public and private schools. The former, known as the Langevin Commission, was made up of MEN officials and educators and charged with determining the technical details of education reform. The latter brought together politicians; educators and MEN officials; *and* representatives of the Church, Catholic and Protestant schools, and Christian youth organizations. This commission was placed under the stewardship of André Philip, a Socialist and Protestant leader who had himself been active in Protestant youth and student movements in the 1920s.

From the outset, Philip struggled to maintain a civil dialogue between the commission's secularist and clerical factions. At its opening session, Philip defined their overarching goal as the preservation of "the spiritual union achieved in the Resistance."[30] But the tenor of the conversation quickly turned combative. Catholic members protested that it was pointless for them to meet before the Langevin Commission issued its recommendations—rejecting the whole premise that the technical aspects of education reform could be detached from the political issue of *laïcité*. On the secularist side, MEN officials objected to the provisional government's stated intention to continue Vichy subsidies to Catholic schools for the 1945 school year. The continuation of that Vichy policy, Director-General of Education Jean Bayet declared, was a poor start to diffusing tensions.[31] The secularists in the Philip Commission ultimately agreed to the renewal of Vichy subsidies to Catholic schools on the condition that the subsidies would be suspended until a new policy was formally put in place.[32] The commission proved more conciliatory than the legislature, however, where continuation of the subsidies was voted down. The

---

29. Durry, Rapport général, 14–15, 31, AN: F/60/427.

30. Procès-verbal de la 1ère séance de la Commission Philip tenue le 6 novembre 1944, 1, AN: F/17/17539.

31. Procès-verbal de la 1ère séance de la Commission Philip tenue le 6 novembre 1944, 2–4, AN: F/17/17539. Vichy subsidies, which could amount to as much as 75 percent of schools' total budget, profoundly shifted the relative material situations of public and private schools. Before the war, most private schools had been in dire financial straits; by war's end, they were so flush with funding many were able to stop charging fees, whereas public schools, especially in deeply Catholic regions, were struggling. Nationally, between 1939 and 1945, private school attendance rose from 17 to 22.6 percent. Atkin, "Church and Teachers." Atkins suggests it is quite possible private confessional schooling might have died out if not for the Vichy interlude.

32. Procès-verbal de la séance de la Commission Philip tenue le 25 janvier 1945, 3–4, AN: F/17/17539.

Philip Commission's final recommendations suffered a similar fate. Seeking a compromise between the *école unique* and a hybrid system of public and private schools, the commission proposed all small communes would have one secular public school, but larger ones could also have state-subsidized private options. The secular teaching corps and the Catholic hierarchy alike found this proposal unacceptable, and even among those who had voted in favor, support was tepid.[33]

The Langevin Commission, meanwhile, unequivocally endorsed *laïcité* in its comprehensive proposal, the Langevin-Wallon Plan. However, by the time the plan was completed—after a staggering thirty-one months of deliberations—the political winds had shifted so dramatically it was dead on arrival. The plan had been the fruit of political *tripartisme*, a coalition of Socialists, Communists, and Christian Democrats (MRP) that had governed since 1944. That coalition collapsed in May 1947, when Communists were expelled from the government for voting against funding the war in Indochina. Never even presented before parliament, the stillborn Langevin-Wallon Plan was collateral damage of political infighting and the onset of the Cold War.[34] The plan would eventually serve as the basis of the sweeping education reforms that were finally realized under the Fifth Republic after 1968, but by then, the plan's position on *laïcité* was out of date.[35]

The Philip Commission's proceedings highlight how *laïcité* was being reconfigured in the postwar conjuncture. The fact that its secular majority could not arrive at a robust consensus points to a new unwillingness to forcibly impose *laïcité* on French Christians.[36] Most important, the commission provided a novel venue for dialogue—however hostile—between state officials, clergy, and Christian educators within the state apparatus itself, which became a model for na-

33. Arthur Plaza, "Paix ou guerre scolaire? Les divisions du Mouvement Républicain Populaire 1944–1960," in *Politiques de la laïcité au XXe siècle*, ed. Patrick Weil (Paris: Presses Universitaires de France, 2007), 481–504, 484–485.

34. Isabelle Clavel, "Réformer l'École après 1944: du consensus au *dissensus* entre la SFIO et le MRP," *Histoire@Politique: Politique, culture, société* 3, no. 18 (September–December 2012): 129–143, https://doi.org/10.3917/hp.018.0129.

35. See Claude Allègre, François Dubet, and Philippe Meirieu, eds., *Rapport Langevin-Wallon* (Paris: Mille et une nuits, 2002), 112–127; Jeremy Ahearne, *Intellectuals, Culture and Public Policy in France: Approaches from the Left* (Liverpool: Liverpool University Press, 2010), 128–138. The 1959 Debré Law reinstated state subsidies to confessional schools in the intervening years between the plan and 1968 student uprising. See Bruno Poucet, ed., *L'état et l'enseignement privé: L'application de la loi Debré* (Rennes: Presses Universitaires de Rennes, 2019).

36. In fact, this intense desire for reconciliation and consensus had already begun under Vichy. In 1941, fearful of alienating secular teachers, the regime rolled back its own policy of including invocations of God in school curricula, in favor of a curriculum emphasizing "Christian values and civilization." The regime also encouraged priests and secular teachers to work together in curriculum development. Atkin, "Church and Teachers," 13–15.

tional councils on youth and education for the duration of the Fourth Republic.[37] In those exchanges, even staunch secularists conceded that French culture and society—indeed, French civilization itself—were Christian at their core.

MEN officials in the commission frequently appealed to France's "Chrétieneté." They insisted on the neutrality of secular public schools and assured their clerical colleagues there was nothing antireligious about them. On the contrary, they argued, "one can find God by different paths," which they contended would be actively encouraged by secular public education. The only difference between secular and confessional schooling, the MEN officials reasoned, was that "the spirit of the *école laïque* is not to define the essential things from the outset."[38] When Catholic educators responded that they were not interested in mere neutrality and maintained their right to promote Catholic doctrine and faith to children whose parents desired it, defenders of the *école laïque* took a different tack. They argued that special Catholic instruction was unnecessary in light of the centrality of *Christianity* in French culture. A single school system dispensing a "humanist" education, they insisted, would unite all segments of French youth in a "common faith," precisely because "all of our culture is in fact impregnated with Christianity."[39] In this formulation then, even the secular morality that public schools would transmit to future generations was cast as thoroughly Christian.

Such arguments in favor of the *école unique* were countered by Catholics on the commission with a pluralist conception of what national unity ought to mean in modern democracies. Abbé Chéruel, a prominent figure in the Catholic Resistance in Brittany, declared that France was composed of "multiple and distinct spiritual families, woven together and communicating with one another," which gave France its "vital unity." France "is not their juxtaposition. It is their community." Referring explicitly to Catholics, Protestants, Communists, atheists, and even Jews, Chéruel continued, "in the great democracy our country wants to become again, and for the sake of national unity, there can be no question of refusing any one of these spiritual families the conditions they feel are necessary for them to thrive."[40] Chéruel's remarks are

---

37. Representatives of Catholic and Protestant schools and youth organizations were included as permanent members of official youth and education councils and committees, which served as central advisory and policymaking organs within the MEN. See Centre d'Archives Contemporaines—Fontainebleau, France (CAC): 19880437/24.

38. Procès-verbal de la séance de la Commission Philip tenue le 20 novembre 1944, 3–4, AN: F/17/17539.

39. Procès-verbal de la séance de la Commission Philip tenue le 20 novembre 1944, AN: F/17/17539.

40. Procès-verbal de la séance de la Commission Philip tenue le 4 décembre 1944, 3, AN: F/17/17539. On Chéruel, see Alain Lozac'h, *Visages de la résistance brétonne: réseau et mouvements de libération en Côtes-d'Armor* (Nancy: Coop Breizh, 2003), 300–301.

noteworthy not only because he insists the "right to difference" is essential for modern democracies to function—a notion pilloried as fundamentally *un-French* in mainstream French political discourse today—but also for his allusion to Jews.[41]

References to Jews in the commission's deliberations were infrequent and abstract; the question of funding Jewish schools was never posed. Consideration of Muslims' concerns and Islamic education was even more conspicuously absent. One exception came from an education official who had briefly served in Algeria during the war and who defended the compatibility of secular schooling and religious faith by using Algerian Muslims as an example. He stated that although "Islam defines and mixes God in all aspects of life, there has never been any difficulty and even the most pious Muslims have never hesitated to send their children to the *école laïque.*" No one directly responded to this point, however, and it was not made again.[42] Protestant schools were also seldom mentioned, but the mere *presence* of Protestants in the room was important, for it shifted the commission's focus onto the compatibility of French secularism and "Christianity" rather than the historic conflict between the Catholic Church and the republican state.

Recognition of Christian influences in French moral and civic life was even more pronounced in discussions about extracurricular youth activities, including among ardent champions of secular schooling. Catholics were wary of proposals to expand state support for confessional youth organizations, which both the Cathala and Capitant-Durry Commissions had considered a significant concession that would nonetheless maintain the "common formation" young people would receive in the classroom. Catholics were wise to this strategy. Chéruel viewed the distinction that wartime education reformers had been elaborating from London to Algiers between *enseignement* and *éducation* as nothing more than a rhetorical ploy to force Catholics to abandon their claims to operate their own schools. "Enseignement," Chéruel protested, was also "éducatif." If the state was prepared to acknowledge the role of confessional youth organizations in *éducation*, they were necessarily conceding the right to religious instruction as well.[43]

In response, MEN officials asserted once more that the general moral and cultural formation provided by secular schools was inspired by Christianity *insofar as it was French*. Bayet forcefully proclaimed, "The way in which *enseignement* [is] *éducatif,* is exactly the same in secular public schools and confessional

---

41. Pierre-André Taguieff, *La force du préjugé: Essai sur le racisme et ses doubles* (Paris: Gallimard, 1987).

42. Procès-verbal de la séance de la Commission Philip tenue le 20 novembre 1944, 2, AN: F/17/17539.

43. Procès-verbal de la séance de la Commission Philip tenue le 26 février 1945, 14, AN: F/17/17539.

private schools. We other French people, we are also necessarily immersed in a civilization that is Christian in its origins, Latin and Christian in its origins. It is absolutely impossible to detach ourselves from it." Bayet noted that even his "Jewish friends" recognized that as *French* Jews, they were "thoroughly Christianized, at least in mentality. That is to say in terms of civilization, or if you prefer, in terms of general culture and thus *éducation*." With this unambiguous characterization of French culture as Christian, Bayet categorically dismissed any difference between the way public secular and private Catholic schools transmitted cultural knowledge to their students. He concluded there was no difference in how Catholic and public schoolteachers would teach "the most Catholic parts of Bossuet" or "whatever page of Renan" if they "were to remain faithful to the tenor of French civilization."[44]

Such declarations could be read as nothing more than an attempt to appease Catholics on the commission without committing state resources to private Catholic schools. However, these same views were mobilized for the exact opposite ends in French Africa, where private Christian schooling began receiving state support in 1941—and, as we shall see, would continue to do so until African independence in 1960—precisely on the grounds that mission schools and public schools both advanced "French civilization" in Africa in much the same way. It is not surprising, then, that by the early 1950s, state support for Christian schooling would be offered in the metropole as well. Public opinion in favor of reestablishing subventions for Christian schools in the Hexagon doubled between 1946 to 1951, from 23 percent to 46 percent. That shift in popular views culminated in the 1951 Marie and Barangé Laws, which created public funds and state scholarships for parents to send their children to the school of their choice, including private confessional schools.[45] These laws brought school policy in metropolitan France closer in line with France's African territories as well as its European neighbors.[46] Indeed, Bayet's reasoning in the Philip Commission resurfaced in discussions with very different interlocutors about both African and European youth and education policy in the second half of the 1940s. Continuities across national-metropolitan, colonial African, and transnational European contexts suggests this was about more than political expediency—indeed, that this was a moment when French

---

44. Procès-verbal de la séance de la Commission Philip tenue le 26 février 1945, 15–16, AN: F/17/17539.

45. Plaza, "Paix ou guerre scolaire?," 493, 502–503. Interestingly, this shift in public opinion tracks with shifts in Christian Democratic political strategy. After the failed vote on private school subsidies in 1945, the MRP embraced *laïcité* as part of its official platform, detaching *laïcité* from the issue of "freedom of education" or "school choice," which clearly increasingly resonated with the French public.

46. West Germany and Austria implemented similar laws at this time. Chappel, *Catholic Modern*, 215–216.

politicians and educators could simultaneously endorse *laïcité* as an official policy framework *and* publicly embrace conceptions of "French civilization," even *laïcité* itself, as thoroughly Christian.

Christianity and the Civilizational Imaginary beyond the Hexagon

The many traumas of the war engendered acute feelings of temporal rupture in France and its empire and across Europe. Across these spheres, discussions about youth and education pivoted uncomfortably between the celebration of tradition and calls for sociopolitical transformation. Straddling these multiple temporalities, the architects of African and European youth and education initiatives conducted their planning discussions in a pronounced civilizational idiom; "civilization" provided a powerful framework linking past, present, and future in a unitary whole. Moreover, the scalar plane of civilization provided a comforting sense of continuity as postwar planners worked to effect meaningful generational change. The respective objectives of African and European youth and education initiatives were to implant "French civilization" in Africa and to locate France in "European civilization." The simultaneity of these efforts forced postwar education reformers to think about the substance and the contours of what it meant to be French, European, and African in new and sometimes contradictory ways, and, most important, rendered these identifications more intrinsically relational. Education officials' insistence that Christianity was a central feature of French civilization in the national debate about school policy and *laïcité* raised the stakes of how religious identity and secular values figured in the postwar French imaginary beyond the Hexagon.

As we saw in chapter 1, competing formulations of French and European civilization emerged in wartime discussions about youth and education policy in multiple venues from Free French London to Brazzaville. Mapping the continuation of those conversations into the later 1940s introduces important new sites, interlocutors, and points of reference. Contestation over the meaning and the contours of "French civilization" informed discussions about how to implement the Brazzaville Conference's recommendations on education reform, not just among French officials and educators on the ground in French Africa, but also in the French parliament and the Colonial and Education Ministries in Paris. While no Africans had been invited to participate in the formulation of those recommendations, the conversion of the empire into the French Union in 1946 extended the franchise to unprecedented numbers of Africans, and the dozens of representatives they sent to all three houses of

French Parliament made education reform their top priority.[47] From 1946 on, this first cohort of African deputies in Paris inserted themselves into the metropolitan policymaking process. Hundreds more francophone Africans entered local politics with the expansion of representative territorial and federal assemblies. Their interventions introduced different conceptions of what the expansion of education for Africans should entail and intensified pressure to enact meaningful reforms.

Meanwhile, the boundaries of "European civilization" continued to be debated in the Conference of Allied Ministers of Education. The CAME set for itself the paradoxical task of both affirming to the ministers themselves and to the world that a thing called "European civilization" did indeed exist and bringing that civilization into being through new kinds of transnational pedagogy, research, and cooperation in youth and education policy. That paradox signals the deep existential crisis driving early appeals for European unity. The CAME's quest to determine the "spiritual and intellectual factors" and the "manner of life" that made Europe a "single civilization"[48] was taken up by the vast network of transnational European movements that emerged immediately after the war.[49] In the 1948 Congress of Europe in The Hague, top French officials and European federalists joined more than seven hundred delegates from across Europe to work out the modalities of European cooperation and give the rhetorical figure "United Europe" institutional form. The congress is perhaps best remembered today for leading to the creation of the Council of Europe, but participants were no less concerned with promoting the "European idea" and fostering a European cultural identity, particularly among youth. Convinced that an activist cultural policy was a necessary corollary to political and economic European integration, the congress announced a second summit to deal exclusively with questions of culture and education, to be held in Lausanne the following year.

The Hague Congress ignited an explosion of pro-Europe activity. As Alain Peyrefitte wryly observed from his post in the French occupation authority in

---

47. For African representatives' concerns about youth and education, see transcripts of the Commission des territoires d'outre-mer in the National Assembly (AN: C//15293 for 1945–1946, C//15407 for 1947–1949, C//15408 for 1949–1951) and the Commission des affaires culturelles et de la civilisation d'outre-mer of the Assembly of the French Union (AN: C//16135, C//16236, C//16253, C//16274, C//16279).

48. Draft Minutes of the 22nd Meeting . . . 7 June 1944 at the offices of the British Council. Collected in the manuscript volume *CAME, London 1942–1945, vol III: Books and Periodicals Commission— History Committees and Subcommittees*, UNESCO Archives.

49. The largest and most significant was the European Movement (established 1946). Other significant players were the Socialist Movement for the United States of Europe (established 1946), which was first presided over by André Philip, and the Christian-Democratic Nouvelles Equipes Internationales (established 1947).

FIGURE 2.1. Attendees at the European Youth Congress in The Hague in spring 1953. The young man on the right is wearing a scout uniform. Courtesy of the Historical Archives of the European Union, AHUE: ME-43.

Bonn, committees for a united Europe were "sprouting like mushrooms."[50] So too did European youth and education initiatives (see figure 2.1). All the major pro-Europe movements created youth sections, which were appreciated by European organized youth. French, Belgian, and Dutch youth leaders assembled at a "European Study Day" in Lille in December 1948 applauded the European movements' commitment "to give youth a proper role in the construction of Europe."[51] Indeed, in the years that followed, the pro-Europe movements expanded their youth sections and created specialized transnational cultural institutions that focused on youth and education. Foremost among them was the College of Europe in Bruges, which reprised the CAME's mission to Europeanize education to mold future generations of pro-Europe elites.[52]

---

50. Alain Peyrefitte, Note sur la jeunesse allemande et la jeunesse européenne, Ambassade au Haut-Commissariat à Bonn, undated, AHUE: ME-1920.

51. Motion de la Commission de la Jeunesse des Journées d'Études Européennes, Lille December 17–19, 1948, AHUE: ME-1920. French signatories included Maurice René Simonet, leader of the Équipes Jeunes of the Christian-Democratic MRP party, and Jacques Boissieras, vice president of the Union nationale des étudiants français, the largest (secular) student federation in France.

52. Rapport sur la session preparatoire du Collège d'Europe tenue à Bruges du 20 septembre au 10 octobre 1949, par la Commission culturelle de la Section Belge du Mouvement Européen, presented to the Lausanne Conference on December 9, 1949, AHUE: ME-526.

Abstract meditations on the nature of the relationship between religion and civilization and the place of Christianity in France, Europe, and Africa represent recurring threads that unite this dizzying constellation of actors and institutions charged with devising postwar youth and education initiatives from Brazzaville to Bruges. In chapter 1, we saw how top education officials at the Brazzaville Conference mobilized essentialized portraits of *Europeans* to justify excluding Africans from metropolitan-style secondary education. The director of secondary education in AOF had declared unequivocally that everything about secondary education was a product of "classical culture" and "Mediterranean civilization" in his assertion that lycée was only suitable for "Europeans." These allusions conjure a certain vision of a "Latin" Europe that carries strong Christian overtones.[53] Those overtones became more explicit in discussions of how to enact Brazzaville's Education Plan in the late 1940s.

Christianity featured prominently in discussions about the Brazzaville resolution that French should be the exclusive language of instruction in primary schools in French Africa. Associations between language and religion were hardly new in the 1940s; there is a long French intellectual tradition linking language and religion (and race) that stretches back to nineteenth-century Romantic historiography and philology.[54] However, the intensity of that link in colonial education policy in Africa in the postwar conjuncture deepened the purchase of the culturalist conceptions of Christianity taking shape in metropolitan debates over *laïcité*.

In May 1944, the CFLN's Commissariat of Colonies in Algiers officially decreed the prohibition of African languages in primary education. In a missive announcing the new policy to colonial governors, Commissioner of Colonies René Pleven explained that *enseignement* was not only about learning but also constituted "a veritable 'socialization' of the child," in which children were imprinted with the ensemble of ways of thinking, behavior, and knowledge of their society so that they could become full participants in the community. French colonization, he went on, had already produced and would continue to produce such societal upheavals in "primitive societies that the educative action of the 'elders' of these societies is manifestly insufficient to ensure the adaptation of youth to their new modes of life. It is therefore necessary, at least provisionally, to substitute ourselves for those natural educators to promote the progressive integration of colonized peoples into the modern world." Pleven concluded that indigenous languages were ill-suited for this task; only

---

53. Edmond Cabrière, Rapport à M. le Directeur-Général de l'Instruction Publique sur l'Enseignement secondaire et la question indigène, undated (1943), ANS: O/171 (31).

54. Maurice Olender, *The Languages of Paradise. Race, Religion, and Philology in the Nineteenth Century* (Cambridge, MA: Harvard University Press, 1992); Edward Said, *Orientalism* (New York: Vintage, 1979).

French could serve as an appropriate vehicle to build "a new intellectual and moral civilization" in French Africa.[55]

When the central colonial authority returned to Paris in late 1944, it began publicizing the new language policy to organizations involved in colonial education. The head of the Colonial Ministry's education department, Delage, presented the Brazzaville Education Plan to one of the prominent colonial lobbies in France, which had its own "Education Commission."[56] He reprised much of Pleven's language on using French to socialize African children into what Pleven had called the "modern community," but Delage offered a thicker description of that term. The goal of French colonial education, Delage declared, was to promote the integration of colonized peoples into "the community of modern white nations of western and Christian civilization." The new policy, he argued, was a strong rejoinder to mounting African critiques, which were now coming from within various levels of representative government, that the colonial administration had strategically not taught Africans French to perpetuate colonial domination. Delage felt the new language policy proved "our generous desire to completely integrate African populations into the French community."[57] Thus, according to the director of colonial education policy, the "French community" was part of a broader community of "modern white nations," and that broader community was defined as fundamentally "Western" and "Christian"—indeed, the two terms appear synonymous. French was the conduit that would integrate Black Africans into the French national community, and by extension, into "modern white and Christian civilization."

French officials articulated strikingly similar reasoning in transnational European forums on youth and education policy. None other than the Philip Commission's Jean Bayet pronounced just such a view at the European Movement's Cultural Conference in Lausanne in 1949. The purpose of the meeting was to reawaken "the sentiment of our common belonging to a civilization to which we owe our *grandeur*." It also intended to show that "our cultural forces can contribute to European unification" just as only a "united Europe will preserve our cultures in their precious diversity." Subcommittees on exchanges, institutions, and education would all study the twinned objectives:

---

55. Circulaire a/s français langue véhiculaire unique de l'enseignement colonial, Alger, May 16, 1944, ANOM: 1AFFPOL/2256 dossier 3.

56. This group, the Comité de l'Empire français, had strong ties to the Church, financial institutions, and, during the war, to Vichy. Its Commission de l'Enseignement included a diverse group—from specialists in colonial history at the Collège de France to prominent heads of Franco-African investment banks. After 1946, in keeping with similar terminological changes, the group renamed itself the Comité Central de la France d'Outre-Mer.

57. Procès-verbal de la Commission de l'Enseignement du CEF du 4 décembre 1944, audition du M. Delage, Chef de Service—Direction Enseignement aux Ministère des Colonies, ANOM: 100/APOM/933.

"cultures in the service of Europe" and "Europe in the service of our cultures."[58] The French delegation comprised a cross section of French political and intellectual elites, including Michel Debré, Raoul Dautry, Raymond Aron, and Alexandre Marc, as well as education officials like Bayet and Jean Sarrailh, rector of the Academy of Paris.

Bayet gave a presentation on "Europeanizing" secondary and postsecondary education through dramatic changes in pedagogy, curricula, language study, and history textbooks.[59] However, he noted that this proposal would pose particular problems for countries with overseas colonies. "For the future and even the radiance of the European Union," he insisted, it behooved them to ensure that "that these diverse, faraway peoples have access to a culture that we know is imbued with fundamental values." Nevertheless, he felt European metropoles should not seek to impose "a superficial equality with cultured Europeans" on those populations. He therefore concluded that Europeanizing pedagogical and curricular reforms should not be implemented in colonial territories. And yet, Bayet, a classicist by training, confidently asserted that those "fundamental values" would be transmitted to colonial peoples in the language of the colonial power. "Happily," he declared, "the great European languages are carriers by their literatures and their very form, of the essential European values inherited from Greece, Rome, and Christianity."[60] In his view, then, overseas populations were essential to the "radiance" of united Europe but should not receive the same Europeanized education as their metropolitan counterparts. If we apply his logic to French Africa, Bayet was effectively suggesting that despite not receiving a proper European-style education, Africans would still learn core "European values"—here defined by classical antiquity and Christianity—by virtue of the fact that their education was in French.

As most of the largest European unity movements had ties to Christian Democratic parties or had their own confessional affiliation, appeals to Christianity as a core element of "European civilization" were common in venues like Lausanne. It may initially be surprising that a representative of ostensibly secular France, who himself had worked in the MEN, would espouse such a view. But the proceedings of the Philip Commission made clear that Bayet found no contradiction between ardently championing *laïcité* as a policy framework for the

---

58. Bureau d'Études pour un Centre européen de la culture: Conférence européenne de la culture à Lausanne 8–12 décembre 1949, undated, AHC: 1/DE/25.

59. His specific proposals included the provision of travel grants for secondary-school teachers to seek additional training at European institutes like the College of Europe in Bruges to infuse their teaching with a "Europeanist" outlook; making the study of a second European language mandatory; history textbook reform; and the equivalence of university diplomas across Europe. Bayet, Rapport à la Conference culturelle de l'Europe Unie sur l'Éducation, December 9, 1949, AHUE: ME-540.

60. Bayet, Rapport à la Conference culturelle, AHUE: ME-540.

metropolitan French education system and characterizing France as culturally Christian.

As new European educational institutions got off the ground in the late 1940s, tensions between rhetorical depictions of Europe as culturally Christian and competing conceptions of such institutions as religiously "neutral" bubbled to the surface. Debates at the founding of the College of Europe in Bruges, an elite postgraduate institution intended to provide "Europeanized" training for political, intellectual, and business leaders, provides a representative example. Before opening in late 1950, the college's transnational board organized a monthlong preparatory session, and leading members of the European movements, academics, and postgraduate students representing more than a dozen European nationalities were invited to participate. This mix of future administrators, faculty, and students of the college debated the role of Christianity in the political project of Europe as they discussed both the content of the college's curriculum and more practical matters such as whether or not the college would hold a common religious service. In the subcommittee on historical studies, most agreed that bringing Catholics, Protestants, and "others" together in a single religious service was impractical. The group voted against holding religious services, 6–2, to the consternation of the dissenting minority: an Austrian academic, who forcefully protested on the grounds that he "supported united Europe because of his Christian conscience," and Jean Bachelot, a French postgraduate student who later worked at the college. Bachelot said that while he recognized European unity as a "social and economic necessity," he was motivated by "his duty as a Christian" to work toward achieving it.[61]

A clearer picture of how this transnational European institution approached religious pluralism in Europe emerges in the preparatory session's seminar on "general culture." That seminar was led by a Frenchman, Henri van Effenterre, faculty at the University of Caen who became the college's first director of studies (1950–1952). The seminar sought to identify the communal European traditions that would be most effective in the formation of a "European spirit," and it concentrated on classical thought, Christianity, and state formation. In his summation of this work, Effenterre made four points about Christianity. First, he affirmed that Christianity had been one of the most important common factors of what he referred to as "the European tradition," and second, that the prevalence of Christians among all the European nationalities, "with the exception of Turkey," constituted an element of unity. His third and fourth points, however, stressed the limitations of Christianity as a unifying force in

---

61. Report on the History Study Group under the direction of John Bowle, undated, Collège d'Europe—Session préparatoire, Bruges, September 20–October 10, 1949, AHUE: ME-525.

two senses. He cautioned his colleagues should "not overestimate the current value of this element of unity, given the multiple forms and divisions in Christian thought." He then added, "Europe today comprises a quite large number of non-Christians, most of whom no longer even feel the historical link between their liberal or Marxist philosophies and any tradition whatsoever." These last two comments, and their juxtaposition with the passing reference to Turkey, indicate the narrowness of Effenterre's conception of European religious pluralism. His view of Europe was not as community of Christians and members of other faiths but rather as a collective of multiple Christian denominations and an ideologically diverse group of atheists, the latter of whom he associated historically, despite themselves, with Christian thought. It was with this vision of Europe in mind that Effenterre concluded, "it seems prudent to consider Christianity, *as a religion*, as an element of diversity in European unification rather than a real factor of unity."[62]

That conclusion still left open other modes of rooting European unity in Christianity—not as a religious tradition but explicitly as "culture." Effenterre thought he and his colleagues should "analyze, beyond the religious domain, the many Christian legacies from which the European idea may develop, such as the domains of the family, morality, social life, art and philosophy." In so doing, Effenterre proposed a culturalized and secularized conception of Christianity that could be linked to all of Europe's key sociocultural institutions. Drawing on an increasingly salient postwar discourse of Catholic familialism, Effenterre confidently asserted, "European unity rests on a family structure directly inherited from the Christian tradition." He added, "The encounter between Christian Revelation and classical antiquity was the source of the spiritual development of Europe"—an encounter that he saw continuing in the present in the "relations between Christian thinkers in the diverse countries of Europe and modern, scientific thought."[63]

The college's transnational board accepted this reasoning, which was duly reflected in the curriculum. All seminars in the college's inaugural year devoted considerable attention to the role of Christianity in European history, politics, and culture, despite the leadership's explicit characterization of the institution as "secular."[64] The college's first rector, Hendrik Brugmans, a Dutch professor of French literature, walked a fine line in negotiating these tendencies. Reflecting on the college's first year of programming, Brugmans noted that he

---

62. Compte-Rendu des sessions du Séminaire "Culture Générale," sous dir. de M. van Effenterre, undated, AHUE: ME-525.

63. Compte-Rendu des sessions du Séminaire "Culture Générale," AHUE: ME-525. On familialism in postwar Catholicism, see Chappel, *Catholic Modern*, 190–191.

64. Brochure du Collège d'Europe (1950), AHUE: ME-801.

had to turn down "a generous offer" from a Franco-Belgian Christian anti-Communist organization to endow a special chair in "Christian Civilization," since "that did not align with our conception of the college."[65] Nevertheless, Brugmans invited members of the group to deliver three lectures at the college every year, on such topics as "Christianity and Tolerance," "The Absolute," and "The Notion of '*Laïcité*.'"[66] Inviting guest lecturers from this deeply conservative Christian organization was not a radical move; it was in lockstep with the college's regular programming.

The College of Europe, like the Lausanne Conference, was a key venue where French officials and educators continued to develop the culturalist conceptions of Christianity that emerged in the Philip Commission that made explicit identification with Christianity compatible with republican *laïcité*. Philip himself, a committed European activist and first president of the Socialist postwar movement for European unity, lectured in the College of Europe's 1951 session.[67] In both the French and European arenas, *laïcité* was recalibrated to accommodate diverse Christian denominations and various "nonbelievers," most of whom, it was implied, came from Christian backgrounds and should still be considered culturally Christian. Furthermore, as Effenterre's argumentation also makes clear, as a secular morality anchoring "the spiritual development of Europe," *laïcité* itself was framed as a key part of the Christian tradition.[68]

Laïcité South of the Sahara

Culturalist conceptions of Christianity informed French colonial policy in postwar Africa, but debates about *laïcité* in the African federations also dovetailed with other local and international concerns. Ongoing state funding for Catholic and Protestant mission schools dominated conversations about *laïcité* in

---

65. Annexe par Hendrik Brugmans, Brochure du Collège d'Europe, AHUE: MFE-186. The organization in question was founded by French and Belgians in 1949 and styled itself as a "Christian Komintern." See Johannes Grossmann, "The Comité International de la Défense de la Civilisation Chrétienne and the Transnationalization of Anticommunist Propaganda in Western Europe after the Second World War," in *Transnational Anticommunism and the Cold War*, ed. Stéphanie Roulin, Giles Scott-Smith, and Luc van Dongen (London: Palgrave 2014), 251–62.

66. Letter from Hendrik Brugmans to Paul Lesourd, March 24, 1950, AHUE: ME-801.

67. Léonce Bekemens, Dieter Mahncke, and Robert Picht, *The College of Europe: Fifty Years of Service to Europe* (Bruge: Europacollege, 1999).

68. Some contemporary scholars continue to argue that secularization is a Christian social process, reifying the "civilizational" boundary between a secular-Christian West and the Islamic world. See René Rémond, *Religion and Society in Modern Europe* (Oxford: Blackwell, 1997); Christian Joppke, *The Secular State Under Siege: Religion and Politics in Europe and America* (Cambridge: Polity Press, 2015).

AEF, where the missionary presence—both French and foreign—long predated the French colonial state.[69] The missions operated a vast network of schools in AOF, but missionary education in West Africa often took a back seat to officials' growing preoccupation with Islam in this region with large, often majority, Muslim populations.[70] The colonial administration pursued a set of conflicting objectives regarding Muslim African youth: they simultaneously sought to integrate Muslim West Africans into French colonial society through formal schooling and youth programs, to control and limit new conversions to Islam, and to inoculate local Islam from political and theological currents rippling through the wider Muslim world. The situation in French Africa therefore entailed both continuities and contrasts with the civilizational discourses and reappraisals of *laïcité* in metropolitan French and transnational European forums. It is the particular arrangement of this new configuration of *laïcité* between metropole and colony that I aim to emphasize here.

The Brazzaville Conference had reaffirmed Christianity as a crucial vector of "French civilization" in Africa alongside the development of mass public schooling. In sessions devoted to "indigenous policy," Catholic clergy and French officials alike called for a new "Christian civil status" for African Christians in the hope of bringing African social organization—particularly relating to marriage, property, and inheritance—more closely in line with French social practice. Paul Biéchy, a top official in the Catholic hierarchy in the Congo, protested that "fetishist" converts to Islam obtained a "Muslim civil status," whereas African Christians received no legal recognition. He lamented, "In the current French colonial legislation, Islamism is king, fetishism less so, and Christianity nothing at all."[71] The AOF delegation responded to this reproach with a resounding endorsement of a special legal status for African Christians. They did so precisely because "our civilization is, in effect, essentially Christian. Consequently, any legal regime that is inspired by Christianity will constitute

---

69. Virginia Thompson and Richard Adloff, *The Emerging States of French Equatorial Africa* (Stanford, CA: Stanford University Press, 1960).

70. There were some notable exceptions: Dahomey, Ivory Coast, and Haute-Volta had majority Christian populations. Conversely, there were significant Muslim populations in parts of AEF, in Chad and Oubangui-Chari (today the Central African Republic), and in Cameroun (which was not technically part of AEF but tied to it administratively).

71. Mgr Paul Biéchy, Note sur le statut de la famille chrétienne, February 2, 1944, ANOM: 1AFFPOL/2201. Muslim civil status in French colonial law was part of a wider colonial practice that Saba Mahmood refers to as "suturing" minority/colonial identity to religion, despite state claims of religious neutrality. She argues this should not be read as "colonial hypocrisy" but rather as a "diagnostic of the dual impetus internal to political secularism—the modern state's disavowal of religion in its political calculus *and* its simultaneous reliance on religious categories to structure and regulate social life." Mahmood, *Religious Difference in a Secular Age: A Minority Report* (Princeton, NJ: Princeton University Press, 2015), 25.

for the *indigène* a step towards a civilization closer to ours." The delegation offered a hypothetical Christian Baga couple living in Conakry (Guinée) as an example: "The household lives, if not *à l'européenne*, at least, *'à la chrétienne.'*" Without Christian legal status, if the husband died, the widow, her children, and their property would be drawn back into "the patriarchal community."[72] The emphasis here on the fate of women and children is key. For most Catholic leaders in Africa, it did not much matter whether African communities were Muslim or animist; both, they believed, treated women and children as "slaves" of their male relatives and the larger clan. They therefore considered Christian marriage one of the surest ways for African women to escape a life of "slavery."[73] An official Christian legal status could ensure that that escape would be permanent. The status was not codified, but similar criteria determined voting eligibility and the fate of Africans' applications for full citizenship for years to come.[74]

The equation of "European" and "Christian" in the discussion about the ideal typical African convert couple at the Brazzaville Conference anticipated transnational European discourses of familialism after the war and the rhetorical moves of a figure like Effenterre who coded European family structures as essentially Christian. The triadic opposition between Christianity, Islam, and "fetishism" in French Africa deepened the purchase of the culturalization of Christianity in metropolitan France and transnational European milieus. The social, political, and religious local landscape also helped shape a set of conflicting institutional approaches to *laïcité* in the French African federations.

While the specificity of the colonial context may seem to align with a long scholarly tradition of considering the empire as the exception to the rule of republican *laïcité*, the postwar conjuncture recast what made the colonial context unique. J. P. Daughton has shown that Third Republican colonial policy underwent a profound shift around the turn of the century from a platform of "anticlericalism is not for export" that accommodated state funding for Catholic missions to increasingly restrictive policies on missionary work and mission schools in particular prior to World War I. This change in turn precipitated a shift within the missions from evangelizing to "civilizing" and "colonizing," which more closely aligned the missions with republican goals and rhetoric. Daughton underscores this history of conflict and rapprochement

---

72. Opportunité d'un statut chrétien—Rapport de l'administration [AOF], undated, ANOM: 1AFFPOL/2201.

73. Foster, *African Catholic*, 240–246.

74. Emily Lord Fransee, "'I May Vote Like All Women': Protest, Gender, and Suffrage in French Senegal," *French Colonial History* 20 (2021): 119–44, https://doi.org/10.14321/frencolohist.20.2021 .0119; Cooper, *Citizenship between Empire and Nation*.

between secular republicans and Catholics in the empire to argue that French colonial ideology and practice cannot be defined as exclusively republican or Catholic but rather combined the two.[75]

As the discussion about Christian civil status makes clear, this was very much still the case moving into the postwar period, but with a crucial difference: in the late 1940s, this "colonial" blend of republican and Christian civilizational discourses no longer looked so different from conversations about *laïcité*, civilization, and education reform in either the national-metropolitan or transnational European arenas. Nor did "colonial" accommodations toward confessional private schools. On the contrary, the issue of public versus private schooling in AEF was often posed in exactly the same terms as in the metropole. As the inspector-general for education in AEF put it in 1946, the colonial administration must absolutely avoid "the danger, given the delicate political conjuncture we are experiencing, of letting the schools become once more the field of political battles."[76] The postwar imperatives of national unity and reconciliation that had precipitated a turn away from militant *laïcité* in the metropole reframed policy decisions in AEF as well.

Of course, this was not the only consideration underwriting postwar financial support for mission schools in AEF. Material conditions on the ground and the precedent set by Éboué's and Laurentie's "indigenous policy" in the early war years also played important roles. During the transition from provisional government to Fourth Republic (1944–1946), the question of state funding for confessional schooling in AEF, as in the metropole, became a matter of deciding whether to continue subsidies that had been introduced during the war. But unlike in the metropole or AOF, where the practice originated with Vichy, the wartime extension of subsidies to mission schools in AEF had been enacted by Free France. When AEF rallied to de Gaulle, the missions in the federation were cut off from their traditional sources of funding in the metropole and Rome. The administration feared the schools would be forced to close without state aid.[77] This circumstantial need was quickly transformed into a substantive policy reorientation by Éboué and Laurentie. Éboué's dictum that as "public schools and Christian schools have similar goals and methods, they both should receive equal support from the government" was often cited in administrative correspondence in the late 1940s.[78]

---

75. Daughton, *An Empire Divided*, 17–24.

76. Rapport de l'Inspecteur-Général de l'Enseignement au sujet de l'ouverture d'une école des cadres par la Société de Marie, Brazzaville, October 1, 1946, ANOM: GGAEF 5D/219.

77. V. Fournier, Note pour le gouverneur-général, May 3, 1946, ANOM: AEF GGAEF 5D/219.

78. Christian Merlo, Note pour le directeur du cabinet au sujet de la subvention à l'enseignement privé, May 9, 1946, ANOM: AEF GGAEF 5D/219.

Some officials and educators protested this retreat from a strict interpretation of *laïcité*, but the subsidies introduced by Éboué remained in full effect
until the dissolution of the federation a decade later.[79] Many considered the
policy a sheer necessity: AEF simply did not have the resources or personnel
to make schooling available to significant numbers of African children without the missions' help. In 1946, of the mere thirty thousand *aéfiens* who had
been to primary school—which represented a scandalous 1 percent of the total population—fully half attended mission schools.[80] Some local officials lamented the situation, but the reason was usually the inferior quality of mission
schooling, not a principled commitment to *laïcité*. Although student enrollment in AEF was split evenly between public and mission schools, 455 of the
657 students who obtained the coveted *certificat d'études* attended public ones.
Still, the administration remained optimistic about the value of mission schooling as a key means of integrating Africans into the French community, noting
that seven of the eight *aéfiens* standing for election to the French Constituent
Assembly in Paris had attended mission schools.[81]

As subsidies to mission schools became regularized, the administration
made its support conditional on the missions' acceptance of administrative
oversight of curricula, pedagogy, exams, teacher certification, and new school
construction.[82] Indeed, the new consensus that "here private education constitutes a significant part of the work of educating the country and supports the
work of the public schools" led colonial officials in the late 1940s to explicitly
characterize private Christian education as a "public service."[83] With the distinction between public and private formally effaced, colonial officials described the relationship between the two types of schools in terms of "unity"
rather than cooperation, affirming "both are French and both provide an education exclusively in French that follows the official curriculum."[84]

---

79. The rare protest from metropolitan secular organizations were dismissed by top colonial officials. See, for instance, a letter from Paul Coste-Floret (then Minister of Overseas France) to the Ligue
Française pour la Défense des Droits de l'homme et du Citoyen, 10 juin 1948, ANOM: 1AFFPOL/238.

80. Enquête sur les Missions Religieuses en AEF, undated (c. 1946), ANOM: 1AFFPOL/3349.

81. Enquête sur les Missions Religieuses, ANOM: 1AFFPOL/3349. Two of the *aéfiens* ultimately
elected to the Constituent Assembly, Abbé Barthélémy Boganda (Oubangui-Chari) and J.-H. Aubame
(Gabon), had attended mission schools. Both men continued to serve in the National Assembly and
pushed for robust colonial reform for the remainder of the Fourth Republic.

82. Compte-Rendu du Conseil Supérieur de l'Enseignement—session 1947, undated, ANOM: AEF
GGAEF 5D/217; Letter from Haut Commissaire AEF to Gouverneurs, Chefs de Territoire a/s formali-
tés d'ouverture des etablissements privés d'enseignement, June 22, 1949, ANOM: AEF GGAEF 5D/27.

83. H. Cormary (Inspecteur-Général de l'Enseignement), Note pour M. le directeur AFFPOL,
Brazzaville, January 22, 1949, ANOM: AEF GGAEF 5D/27.

84. Christian Merlo, Note a/s la politique scolaire en AEF, March 13, 1948, ANOM: AEF GGAEF
5D/219.

Mission personnel were accordingly brought into the policymaking process and given permanent seats in AEF's top education policymaking body.[85] While this would have been inconceivable under the Third Republic—in either metropole or colony—from the Philip Commission onward, this became standard practice in the metropole as well. Moreover, francophone Africans in the new territorial assemblies of AEF, who were disproportionately Christian and mission-educated, did not object. On the contrary, the assembly of Gabon, where the state paid for 80 percent of mission schools' total costs, made direct, urgent appeals to the administration *and* the missions in late 1947 to open more schools in six counties where the dearth of schools meant that most children there received no formal education whatsoever.[86]

The changing international landscape of the postwar conjuncture further encouraged the administration in AEF to support mission schools. Africans' entry into national and local government was a response not only to African demands but also to mounting international pressure to democratize the empire.[87] As we saw in chapter 1, a "world is watching" attitude was already in full force during the Brazzaville Conference, and colonial education became an even more important barometer of France's commitment to meaningful colonial reform after the war. As Christian Merlo, head of mission affairs in AEF, argued in favor of the subsidies, if the French did not take advantage of every resource at their disposal, including mission schools, "the African citizen and the international powers will not hesitate to give us grief about the shortcomings of our school policy."[88]

At the end of the war, French observers looked on with trepidation as the United States stepped up its anticolonial rhetoric in its global competition with the Soviet Union for colonized hearts and minds, and the creation of the United Nations raised the alarming prospect of the "internationalization" of France's African colonies.[89] Significantly, many French colonial officials believed growing US interest in French Africa stemmed primarily from US religious

85. Compte-Rendu du Conseil Supérieur de l'Enseignement—session 1947, ANOM: AEF GGAEF 5D/217.

86. Voeu no. 15 du Conseil Representatif du Gabon s/d (1947); Christian Merlo, Note pour M. le Chef du Cabinet a/s réponse à Conseiller Durand-Reville, 27 septembre 1947, ANOM: AEF GGAEF 5D/219.

87. Gamble also connects the drive to democratize education in postwar Africa to parallel debates in the internal Resistance and links the Brazzaville Conference's focus on education to contemporaneous metropolitan projects like the Langevin-Wallon plan. *Contesting French West Africa,* 203–204.

88. Merlo, Note pour M. le Chef du Cabinet, ANOM: AEF GGAEF 5D/219.

89. French leaders were particularly disturbed by the creation of the United Nations' Trusteeship Council in 1945 as an international supervisory body overseeing the administration of France's African League of Nations mandates, Togo and Cameroun, which France persisted in considering an integral part of the French Union contrary to mandatory agreements.

congregations. AEF officials obsessively monitored American missionary incursions in the federation and US press coverage of the problem of mass education in French Africa more generally.[90] On the heels of the 1945 San Francisco Conference and the founding of the United Nations, Minister of Colonies Paul Giacobbi sent a secret missive to the colonial leadership in the African federations to actively support French missionary activity to stave off the "internationalist" and "anticolonial" assault of US missions. He declared that the French would have to harness this "great religious movement" by developing their own "proactive religious policy."[91] This became a common refrain in AEF for years to come. As the governor general of AEF declared in a 1947 request for more funds for French missions, "in Black Africa where all foreign influences converge (Arab League, North American anticolonialism, Soviet propaganda), each French missionary, by his very presence in the bush and his ministry of education, maintains our prestige."[92]

Competition between Anglo-American and French missionaries had always been an important factor in imperial rivalries in sub-Saharan Africa, in AEF especially.[93] However, the postwar imperative to democratize France's African empire assigned a new, urgent role to mission schools: preparing Africans for increased political participation in the Fourth Republic and French Union. As the head of education in AEF proclaimed to a room full of public schoolteachers and missionaries at the opening session of AEF's education council in 1947: "For two years a prodigious juridical revolution has occurred in the French Union. We are passing from a regime based on authority to a regime of democracy. Democracy is incompatible with illiteracy and superstition." He continued, "By the massive extension of rights and all the forms of democracy to the overseas territories, [our country] is also undertaking a massive transformation of the nature of those societies, that is, by *instruction*, which, in truth, if we had had the time, should have come first." He concluded that the administration and the missions had to work together to accelerate the opening of more schools to "reestablish the harmonious order of things" and

---

90. In *African Catholic*, Foster argues that fears of US Protestant missionary designs on French Africa trumped French anxieties both about Soviet Communism and Islam in the immediate war years (41–46). This may have been true among Catholic missionaries, but this is less clear among officials in the administration.

91. Paul Giacobbi, Circulaire à MM les Gouverneurs Généraux et Gouverneurs des Colonies a/s Missions Religieuses, November 7, 1945, ANOM: 1AFFPOL/3349.

92. Gougal-AEF à MFOM-AFFPOL a/s voyages des missionaires et "politique religieuse positive," undated (c. 1947), ANOM: AEF GGAEF 5D/219.

93. See Owen White and J. P. Daughton, eds., *In God's Empire: French Missionaries and the Modern World* (Oxford: Oxford University Press, 2012). Concern over US missionaries, and Protestant missionaries generally, reflected French officials' belief that both would favor the British in sub-Saharan Africa.

"adjust realities to rights."[94] This rhetoric featured prominently in subsequent defenses of state support for private Christian education in AEF. "Illiteracy," Merlo declared the following year, was a "social evil that encourages superstition and fetishism and is incompatible with the exercise of a real democracy and French citizenship extended to all."[95]

By 1948, state subsidies to mission schools had indeed effectively transformed private Christian schooling in AEF into a "public service," formalizing the equation of Christianity and "French civilization" in postwar colonial policy. Indeed, it was the very real incorporation of mission schools into public education in AEF that enabled administrators to dismiss the most common criticism of the subsidies policy: that funding mission schools would force the administration to fund Muslim schools as well.[96] To this charge, defenders of the policy repeatedly insisted that only private institutions that teach "the official curriculum, in French" were subsidized, which excluded Qur'anic schools a priori.[97] Thus as the opposition between public education and private, Christian education was rendered moot in French Equatorial Africa, only Islamic education would be excluded by the strictures of republican *laïcité*.

In AOF, with its substantial Muslim populations, discussions about *laïcité* after the Brazzaville Conference centered squarely on Islam. The cause was a potent combination of international developments, emboldened demands from Muslim Africans for access to Islamic education, and French perceptions of African Islam. Confrontations between Catholics and secularists over subsidies to mission schools in AOF—even seemingly abstract, principled arguments for or against *laïcité*—were often filtered through one or more of these concerns. As Catholic educators and secularists in the administration sparred publicly in the local press over continuing subsidies to mission schools in 1944–1945, they accused one another of seeking to "incite" local Muslims.[98] For both camps, state support for Islamic education, either by subsidizing Qur'anic

94. Compte-Rendu du Conseil Supérieur de l'Enseignement—session 1947, ANOM: AEF GGAEF 5D/217.

95. Merlo, Note a/s la politique scolaire en AEF, ANOM: AEF GGAEF 5D/219. Despite his assertion that "French citizenship" had been extended to all in 1946, Africans continued to be deprived of equal civil *and* political rights.

96. See, for instance, Fournier, Note a/s répartition des subventions à l'enseignement privé pour le 1er sémestre 1948, Brazzaville, March 9, 1948, ANOM: AEF GGAEF 5D/219.

97. Fournier, Note a/s répartition, ANOM: AEF GGAEF 5D/219. The substance of traditional African Qur'anic schooling is discussed in chapter 5.

98. See the exchanges of Père Bertho, directeur-général des Écoles Catholiques de l'AOF, and Charles Cros, inspecteur des Ecoles du Sénégal in 1944–1945, ANS: O/11 (31); and between Bertho and Lucien Paye, directeur de l'enseignement at the central colonial ministry, ANS: O/9 (31). Significantly, in one letter (November 7, 1944), Bertho compared militant *laïcité* to Nazism: "French people, those who knew how to die for their Patrie, want Catholic schools. How can you suppress Christian schools if you want France to be a liberal and just Republic, and not a dictatorship along the Nazi model?" This

schools or by authorizing Muslim clerics to provide religious instruction in public schools outside of regular school hours—a privilege enjoyed by Catholics—was to be avoided at all costs.

State support for Muslim youth organizations in AOF was likewise deemed inappropriate and potentially dangerous. Though such concerns were most often couched in universalist language that framed all confessional youth groups as a "factor of division" that threatened "national cohesion," Muslim groups were understood to be more divisive and more threatening than others. In a 1945 policy note on subsidies to confessional scout movements in AOF, Charles Brun, head of the social affairs service, first posed the issue as an opposition between a positive secular morality and "Catholic, Protestant, Muslim and Jewish morality" that taught "young French" to identify with their faith more than their *patrie*. However, when Brun arrived at his actual policy recommendation, the problem was framed differently. He insisted that if they were to fund Catholic and Protestant scout movements in AOF, they would have to authorize Muslim scout troops, lest "we be accused of bias and all the incidents that would cause." He therefore concluded that since it was absolutely "necessary to restrict Muslim scouting in AOF," they should adopt a firm policy against funding any confessional scout organizations whatsoever.[99]

Such resolute opposition to Muslim scouting in late 1945 was rooted in political concerns as much as religious ones. We have seen that just a year earlier, Free French Commissioner of Education René Capitant had wanted to provide financial and material support to develop Muslim scouting in the empire.[100] Things changed, however, in May 1945, when the Scouts musulmans algériens participated in nationalist demonstrations in Sétif, Guelma, and elsewhere in Algeria. French officials believed that Salafi ulemas and other foreign provocateurs had turned the organization into a nationalist training ground.[101] This was a turning point in official views on the potential benefits of Muslim scouting not just for Algerians but for all Muslims in the empire. The Colonial Ministry urged territorial governors in AEF and AOF to put any Muslim scout organizations in their jurisdictions under surveillance and disband

---

rhetoric strikingly parallels Abbé Chéruel's "religious freedom" discourse in the deliberations of the Philip Commission, which was convening in the metropole precisely at this time.

99. Charles Brun, Note a/s scoutisme, October 26, 1945, ANS: O/2 (31).

100. Procès-verbal de la Commission de l'Education Nationale et de la Jeunesse de la séance du 13 mai 1944 (Assemblée consultative provisioire-Alger), AN: C//15266.

101. See Jean-Jacques Gauthé, "Quant le Scoutisme prépare à la guerre . . . Les Scouts musulmans algériens vus par l'armée française," in *Le scoutisme entre guerre et paix*, ed. Baubérot and Duval. Scout movements in British Africa would also be involved in anticolonial resistance after the war. See Timothy H. Parsons, *Race, Resistance, and the Boy Scout Movement in British Africa* (Athens: Ohio University Press, 2004).

them if they engaged in any political activity.[102] Governors in both federations reported back that happily there were no Muslim scout movements in their territories and that they would not authorize any in future.[103]

A formal ban on Muslim scouting was not put in place, but by withholding state aid to develop local Muslim scouting, the colonial administration all but guaranteed there would be no Muslim scouts in French Africa. After all, secular and Christian scout movements created local troops for Africans only after receiving generous subsidies from Éboué, a policy continued by the postwar administration in AEF. In the end, it proved much easier to be inconsistent in this matter than Brun had feared. The administration in AOF began providing financial support to the Catholic Scouts de France and the Protestant Éclaireurs unionistes in 1946; by the mid-1950s, Christian scout movements in AOF had received tens of millions of francs CFA, whereas no funding was allocated to develop Muslim scouting in the federation.[104] Indeed, officials in AOF not only were hostile to creating Muslim scout troops but feared introducing scouting to young Muslims at all. In 1946, the head of public education in AOF insisted that scouting in Muslim countries was so dangerous that "the only territories in AOF where scouting would have a chance of fulfilling its educative and moral role, are those in which Christianity can take root: Dahomey and Côte d'Ivoire." Invoking the incidents with Muslim scouts in Algeria, he concluded they must do everything in their power to limit scouting to "Christian territories" and prevent it from "spread[ing] among populations steeped in Islamism."[105] Clearly, Muslim scouting was officially discouraged insofar as it was *Muslim,* whether officials' rationales referred to *laïcité* or not.

In 1947, the federal administration in AOF funded a delegation of scouts to represent the federation in the sixth annual International Scout Jamboree, which that year happened to be held in Moisson, France. Of the 112 members of the delegation, just under half were secular Éclaireurs de France, a third were Catholic Scouts de France, and the rest were Protestant Éclaireurs unionistes.[106] Some Muslim West African youth did attend the jamboree as part of the secular contingent, but their participation was predicated on the subsumption of their

---

102. See correspondence from 1947–1948 between the MFOM, the AEF governor-general, and territorial governors in Oubangui-Chari, Congo, Chad, and Gabon in dossier on scouts and nationalism, ANOM: AEF GGAEF 5D/219.

103. Correspondence in ANOM: AEF GGAEF 5D/219; Charles F. Brun, Note a/s scoutisme, October 26, 1945, ANS: O/2 (31).

104. See folders, "Scouts de France—subventions AOF—1950–1959" and "Éclaireurs Unionistes de France—subventions AOF—1946–1958," ANS: 18G/214 (160).

105. Letter from Berlan [DG-APAS] to DG-Instruction Publique, May 14, 1946, ANS: O/2 (31).

106. R. Braem (commissaire de province, *Eclaireurs de France* en AOF), "Le Jamboree de 1947," undated, ANS: O/2 (31).

Muslim-ness in an explicitly secular movement, since secular and Christian were the only permissible options. Despite the small Muslim presence in its ranks, the delegation—which was intended to "represent" the youth of AOF, close to 50 percent of whom were Muslim, to metropolitan France and the world— officially comprised only Christians and laïcs. African Christians were recognized and included in the Franco-African community as such, while African Muslims were uniquely denied such recognition.

That said, around this time officials in AOF were beginning, albeit reluctantly, to contemplate a more proactive Muslim youth and education policy. As Muslim West Africans became more involved in the policymaking process, and African elites' expectations for democratic reform rose, the colonial administration received increasingly aggressive petitions for state support for Qur'anic schools, the inclusion of Islamic instruction in public schooling, and language instruction in Arabic. In March 1947, Ibrahima M'Bodj of the Grande Mosquée of Saint Louis appealed directly to Vincent Auriol, president of the Fourth Republic, demanding Arabic instruction in public schools in Senegal. M'Bodj must have been cruelly disappointed to receive a response from a low-level administrator in Dakar, who replied that he understood Arabic's importance to the Muslim faithful but nonetheless insisted that Arabic instruction would have to come from the community "in light of the very principles at the heart of the republican regime which interdicts any state intrusion in matters of religion."[107] Similarly, when the federal assembly of AOF demanded state support for Islamic religious education in Muslim-majority regions, the governor general himself declared: "It is impossible for us given the principles of laïcité . . . to promote Qur'anic education and notably to introduce it into the curriculum." He continued that it was crucial "not to consider Islam an official religion, thereby breaking the traditional position of republican and secular France."[108] Considered alongside state aid to Christian schooling and youth organizations in the African federations and increasing support for similar policies in metropolitan France, such rhetorical depictions of laïcité as a nonnegotiable, bedrock republican value with regard to schooling were clearly no longer in step with actual practice in either French Africa or the metropole. Rather, laïcité was selectively applied to a single faith: Islam.

And yet, the sheer volume of protest, coupled with growing concerns to insulate West African Muslims from broader currents rippling through the Islamic world, led officials in AOF to contemplate their own "Franco-Muslim"

---

107. Letter from Mérat to Prof. Ibrihima M'Bodj [of the Grande Mosquée de Saint Louis], March 28, 1947, ANOM: 1AFFPOL/2131.

108. Letter from the Governor General AOF to the MFOM—Inspection-Générale—Enseignment et Jeunesse, November 25, 1949, ANOM: 1AFFPOL/2131.

school policy in the late 1940s. Subsequent debates on what Franco-Muslim education in Africa should entail hinged on racialized understandings of Islam in West Africa, which most French colonial officials tellingly referred to as *Islam noir*. Many French officials considered African Muslims more "African" than "Muslim"—a belief that was duly registered in the terminology they used to refer to Muslim-majority regions and populations: *islamisé·e·s* as opposed to *musulman·e·s*. In this sense, Muslim Africans were figured as still "in play"— as potentially more receptive and open to French social and cultural practices than Muslim Arabs, perhaps even convertible to Christianity.[109] The framework of *Islam noir* simultaneously justified the colonial administration assuming responsibility for Muslim religious instruction—if *Islam noir* was as pliable as administrators and educators thought, they could mold it to suit their own purposes—and aggressively curtailing the opening of new Qur'anic schools and Arabic language instruction, which were often framed as "foreign imports" lacking deep roots in African spiritual, social, or cultural life. As AOF's governor-general put it in 1949, "The juridical customs of the Islamized populations really do not derive from the precepts of the Qur'an and Arab culture." Those customs, he continued, have had a "destructive influence on Negro-African civilizations," which "have become bastardized and even disappeared in certain regions."[110] It was their job, he therefore concluded, to protect Black Africans *from* Islam.

French education officials moved away from a version of *laïcité* that dissociated French national identity from Christianity at the very moment that France was trying to build a more democratic Franco-African community. The equation of Christianity, French culture, and "European civilization" turned non-Christian religious difference into a starker boundary between European and African France. That boundary was both conceptual and institutional. As French leaders, educators, and activists considered to what extent France and Europe's "Christian inheritance" should guide education reform across metropolitan, colonial, and European space, they developed substantively different approaches to youth and education policy *depending on the religion*, even though they continued to articulate those policies in an undifferentiated rhetorical framework of "republican *laïcité*."

That discursive continuity obscures the cleavages created in this period, and belie contemporary constructions of *laïcité* as a totalizing, unitary principle

---

109. Robert Coquereaux, École Franco-Arabe ou École Franco-Musulmane dans le Nord du Cameroun? Mémoire présenté à M. le Directeur du Centre des Hautes Etudes d'Administration Musulmane, undated (c. 1950), ANOM: 1AFFPOL/2256.

110. Letter from the Governor General AOF to the MFOM, ANOM: 1AFFPOL/2131.

of French political culture and republican practice since World War II, let alone since 1905, the 1880s, or 1789. While recent work has emphasized the structurally "unsettled" nature of *laïcité*, the postwar conjuncture was a particularly turbulent time for the concept and the practice.[111] The novel contours of postwar *laïcité* emerged at the crossroads of national reconstruction, postwar colonialism, and European integration. The critical interplay between the culturalization of Christianity, racist ideas about African Islam, and institutional arrangements across metropolitan, colonial, and transnational space in the late 1940s located France more firmly in a Europe that was understood to be *both* secular and Christian, which created new patterns of inequality and exclusion in the French Union.

---

111. Fernando, *The Republic Unsettled*, 11–12.

CHAPTER 3

Reconstructing Race in French Africa and Liberated Europe

As a student in the mid-1940s in French schools in Senegal, Marie Louise Potin Gueye had a wildly diverse set of classroom experiences. The daughter of *métis* parents from royal Serer lineages, Potin Gueye was born into the small francophone elite in Saint Louis and was part of an even smaller subset of African girls pursuing formal education in the middle decades of the twentieth century.[1] In a 2010 interview with the French leftist magazine *Libération*, Potin Gueye, then seventy-eight, recalled how during the war, she and her classmates were forced to pay homage to Pétain at the start of their lessons. Just a few years later, she was part of the first African cohort to desegregate the Lycée Van Vollenhoven, the lone French high school in Dakar. She recounted how her teachers there "explained to us who we are: we are not white, we are not French. We are Africans."[2] She singled out one particular teacher in this regard, Jean Suret-Canale. A radical Communist, Suret-Canale taught history at "Van Vo" from 1946 to 1949, when he was expelled from AOF

---

1. Barthélémy, *Africaines et diplômées*.

2. The audio recording of the full interview is available here: "Interview de Marie Louise Potin Gueye," *Libelabo*, July 3, 2010, audio, 6:51, https://soundcloud.com/libelabo/interview-de-marie-louise-potin-gueye. For the accompanying article, see Sandrine Pacitto-Mathou, "Reportage: Génération construction," *Libération*, July 10, 2010, https://www.liberation.fr/planete/2010/07/10/generation-construction_665143.

for helping to coordinate a debilitating wave of railway worker strikes.[3] Potin Gueye associated Suret-Canale's arrival in Dakar in 1946 with the founding of the first pan-African political party—the Rassemblement Démocratique Afric-ain (RDA)—in Bamako later that year, which she characterized as a turning point when Africans finally came together to say "Basta!" to French colonial-ism. In making this connection, Potin Gueye was not alone. Many of Suret-Canale's African students in Dakar have written about the formative role he played in their political evolution and their embrace of an African identity.[4]

If Jean Suret-Canale's influence and role in radicalizing a rising generation of African students and syndicalists have long been recognized, less attention has been paid to local white reactions to his activities in Dakar. Suret-Canale certainly attracted the attention of the colonial security forces that eventually had him deported, but he also made an impression on his white students and their parents, who complained to school officials and the federal administra-tion that the version of French history Suret-Canale was teaching in his classes was *racist* insofar as it was "anti-white."[5] That response reflects a wider trend, for it is precisely at this time that we first begin to see virulent accusations of "anti-white racism" in the face of mounting African demands for equal rights that were explicitly framed in the language of racial justice.[6]

Perceptions of what or who was "racist" and what "racism" was and how it worked were in flux in the postwar conjuncture. Edmond Cabrière, who argued so forcefully against secondary education for Africans at the Brazza-ville Conference, was appointed principal of Van Vo in October 1943, almost

---

3. Suret-Canale would later become one of the pioneers of modern African history. For a short personal and intellectual biography, see R. W. Johnson, "Forever on the Wrong Side," *London Review of Books* 34, no. 28, September 27, 2012, https://www.lrb.co.uk/the-paper/v34/n18/r.w.-johnson/forever -on-the-wrong-side. See also Catherine Cocquery-Vidrovitch's tribute, "Jean Suret-Canale, 1921–2007," *Outre-mers: Revue d'histoire*, no. 358–359 (2008): 395–397, https://www.persee.fr/doc/outre_16310438 _2008_num_95_358_4806.

4. Amadou Booker Sadji, *Le rôle de la génération charnière ouest-africaine—indépendance et développe-ment* (Paris: L'Harmattan, 2006), 112–122.

5. Johnson, "Forever on the Wrong Side."

6. Significantly, this discursive strategy is not specific to the francophone sphere. According to a Google Books Ngram Viewer search, "anti-white racism" first appears in English in 1947. A search for "racisme anti-blanc" dates the first usage to 1951, much later than the instance described here and others that I have written about in parliamentary debates from the late 1940s. See my "Obscuring Race"; "Anti-white racism, 1800–2000," Google Books Ngram Viewer, accessed April 12, 2021, https://books.google .com/ngrams/graph?content=anti-white+racism&year_start=1800&year_end=2000&corpus =15&smoothing=3&share=&direct_url=t1%3B%2Canti%20-%20white%20racism%3B%2Cc0#; "Rac-isme anti-blanc, 1800–2000," Google Books Ngram Viewer, accessed April 12, 2021, https://books.google .com/ngrams/graph?content=racisme+anti-blanc&year_start=1800&year_end=2000&corpus =19&smoothing=3&share=&direct_url=t1%3B%2Cracisme%20anti%20-%20blanc%3B%2Cc0 #t1%3B%2Cracisme%20anti%20-%20blanc%3B%2Cc0.

a year after the collapse of Vichy rule in AOF (1940–1942). His racist policies had nothing to do with that ignoble regime; his segregationist stance was widely shared in the colonial bureaucracy. And yet, just two years later in late 1945, the Colonial Ministry forced him out of his post for refusing to reconsider his race-based admissions policy. Cabrière's removal paved the way for Marie Louise Potin, her future husband Doudou Gueye, and a handful of other young Africans to enroll in that historically white institution the following year.

The desegregation of the Lycée Van Vollenhoven was certainly a necessary first step toward African empowerment. However, as Harry Gamble has emphasized, Cabrière's colleagues in Dakar deeply regretted and fought against his ouster (including AOF's top education official Yves Aubineau and Governor-General Pierre Cournarie). More important, Cabrière's removal did not in fact derail his career in postwar colonial education. On the contrary, shortly thereafter he was appointed director of education in Madagascar, which basically amounted to a promotion.[7] Africans' demands for racial equality might yield reluctant concessions and piecemeal gains, but they constantly hit up against systemic inertia and active resistance. The constitutional reforms of 1946 amplified Africans' voices, but their activism created new patterns of evasion and racial resentment that proved to be powerful countervailing forces in shaping postwar education policy and institution building in French Africa.

The conflict over school desegregation in Dakar in the postwar conjuncture is one node in a larger constellation of struggles over race and education reform in postwar French Africa and liberated Europe. I suggest those struggles helped consolidate a new, specifically postwar kind of racial common sense, in which a newfound sense of European racelessness helped cast African antiracism and claim-making as the central driver of ongoing racial tension.[8] As we shall see, this new set of assumptions had powerful reracializing effects. Postwar racial common sense reproduced itself in the mutually reinforcing interplay between new ways of thinking and talking about race and racism and the concrete policies and institutional arrangements to which they gave rise.[9] From the mid-1940s on, African educators, activists, and students found themselves caught in this toxic feedback loop of political ambivalence, racial resentment, and new modes of racialization.

---

7. Gamble, *Contesting French West Africa*, 210.

8. For a more theoretical reflection on postwar European racelessness, see David Theo Goldberg, *The Threat of Race: Reflections on Racial Neoliberalism* (Oxford: Wiley-Blackwell, 2009).

9. My formulation of racial common sense and its institutional, structural basis builds on Michael Omi and Howard Winant's theory of "racial formation" in their *Racial Formation in the United States*.

Education and the Problem of Race at the End of World War II

The ideological battle between the Allies and the Axis called into question long-standing and widely held assumptions about the meaning of race. As Allied victory in the fight against Nazism loomed on the horizon in late 1944, European leaders and francophone Africans alike articulated hopes for a postwar order in which racism would be eliminated. The postwar conjuncture was not the first time that francophone Africans in France's colonies made explicit appeals for racial equality, but Allied rhetoric against Nazi racism raised African expectations that those appeals might no longer fall on deaf ears. There had also been a European antiracist tradition before the war, but it was not until the Nazi regime took racial logics and racial violence to such extremes that most postwar European leaders felt compelled to publicly condemn racism and distance themselves from the concept of race altogether. However, African and European conceptions of what a postwar world without racism would look like differed markedly. Postwar racial common sense was first forged in that divergence.

African Postwar Expectations: Education Reform for Racial Justice

"The man who wrote that blacks are monkeys is dead." This is how Léopold Kaziendé, a schoolteacher who would later serve as a top government minister in independent Niger, remembers feeling upon hearing the news of Hitler's suicide, huddled around a radio with a group of friends and fellow teachers in Niamey in spring 1945.[10] Like so many French-educated Africans, Kaziendé understood Hitler's death not only as signaling the end of Nazism in Europe, but also as a devastating blow to anti-Black racism the world over, with real consequences for Africans' everyday lives in postwar Greater France. Africans in AOF had, after all, experienced the ideological dimensions of the war first-hand during three years of repressive, openly racist Vichy rule.[11] As Abdourahmane Konaté, a student in Senegal during the war, later recalled, "we were

---

10. Léopold Kaziendé, *Souvenirs d'un enfant de la colonisation*, vol. 4 (Porto Novo: Editions Assouli, 1998), 45–46. Kaziendé was born in 1912 in the Kaya region of Upper Volta, which was later folded into the French colonial territory of Niger. A Catholic of Mossi background, he attended the École Primaire Supérieure in Ougadougou and then the École Normale William Ponty in Gorée (Senegal). He held a number of school director posts across Niger in the 1930s, 1940s, and 1950s before entering the Nigerian government in the independence era.

11. Ginio, *French Colonialism Unmasked*.

living through the great contest between the Allies and the Axis powers, which here took the form of the Gaullists and the *Vichystes*. We Africans were deeply embroiled in these grave conflicts." Konaté described the daily racist indignities he suffered during the Vichy interlude, even as he and his schoolmates were forced to sing the Pétainist hymn "Maréchal, nous voilà" on holidays and special occasions in school.[12]

Indeed, French-educated Africans interpreted the Allied victory as one in a series of promising internal and international developments heralding the coming of a new era of racial equality in French Africa. In January 1944, the Brazzaville Conference and the colonial administration's promise to end forced labor had presaged the "equality of whites and blacks before French law" to Kaziendé and his friends.[13] Expectations in francophone milieus rose further still in late 1945 as Africans were elected to the constituent assembly charged with drafting a new constitution for what would become the Fourth Republic and French Union. Two of these newly minted African deputies lent their names to the bills that finally abolished forced labor (*Loi Houphouët-Boigny*) and the invidious distinction between French citizens and colonial subjects (*Loi Lamine-Guèye*) in spring 1946.[14]

Kaziendé describes how the passage of these laws inspired joyous celebration in both city and countryside, as young people organized "neighborhood dances to the sound of tam-tams to celebrate the new era." Moreover, he notes that these laws prompted a real change in how francophone Africans, most of whom were either low-level functionaries or teachers like himself, carried themselves and expected to be treated by white French in the territories. No longer excluded from the category, "man and citizen," these men—and they were virtually all men—would no longer accept being "conspicuously *tutoyer*-ed the whole length of the day" by their white colleagues.[15] On the contrary, with their new status as "freedmen" (*affranchis*), "they reacted vigorously to all

---

12. Abdourahmane Konaté, *Le cri du mange-mil: Mémoires d'un préfet sénégalais* (L'Harmattan, 1990), 57. Konaté was born in 1931 in Saint Louis, Senegal. A prominent figure in syndicalist youth movements in Dakar in the 1950s, he also worked during that time in the financial and administrative services division of the federal administration for AOF, where he developed close ties with some of the leading figures in higher education in AOF. He remained in government administration after independence.

13. Konaté, *Le cri du mange-mil*, 31.

14. On the first cohort of African deputies to the Constituent Assembly and the passage of these laws, see Cooper, *Citizenship between Empire and Nation*, chaps. 1–3.

15. In French, *tutoyer* means to address someone with the informal "tu" as opposed to the polite "vous" form. "Tu" is typically only used between close friends, or by adults speaking to children, but it was used by whites in the colonies to assert their authority over Africans (even educated African adults working within the colonial administration or the corps of teachers). We have seen in chapter 1 that Éboué and Laurentie had bucked the trend when they led AEF in 1940–1944, but the practice remained the norm among their colleagues as well as their successors.

acts of disrespect in their offices, in the street, in public places," and demanded equal pay for equal work for Africans in the colonial bureaucracy and teaching corps. Kaziendé was quick to stress that they were not "provocateurs." They simply considered themselves as equals and were eager for colonial society, not just the law, to follow suit. On the heels of the Allied victory, in what so many Africans understood to be an ideological battle against Nazi racism, this did not seem too much to expect.[16]

Crucially, Kaziendé hoped that racial equality would be realized within the framework of a renovated Franco-African community, not by way of national independence. While Kaziendé and his circle closely followed and welcomed the news that France officially recognized Syrian sovereignty (January 1944) and the growing international support for self-determination coming out of the San Francisco Conference, which founded the United Nations (spring 1945), none of them saw total separation from France as a viable or attractive option for French Africa at that time.[17] Recent work by Frederick Cooper and Gary Wilder has shown that this view was far from marginal: many franco-phone Africans at the close of the war and in the early postwar years ardently sought decolonization *without* independence. In this alternative path out of empire, the deep structures of colonial domination in French Africa would be dismantled, and Africans would obtain full citizenship and greater political autonomy for their territories, but they would nonetheless remain within a nonimperial and democratic Franco-African polity.[18]

To proponents of this other form of decolonization—from local teachers like Kaziendé to the most prominent African leaders of the time like Senghor, as well as lesser-known Africans in the French government—legal measures such as the new constitution or the Houphouet-Boigny and Lamine-Guèye laws were not sufficient to achieve these goals; only robust social reforms and a new kind of cultural politics, particularly the expansion and improvement of African education, could actually decolonize the empire.[19] After the war Senghor, who, like Kaziendé, was a teacher by training, became convinced that "association in interdependence" required both increasing Africans' access to educational opportunities as well as inventing a fundamentally new kind of education for Africans rooted in "cultural *métissage* and symbiosis."[20] Such an education would be nei-

---

16. Kaziendé, *Souvenirs*, 49–50.

17. Kaziendé, *Souvenirs*, 31.

18. Cooper, *Citizenship* between Empire and Nation; Wilder, *Freedom Time*.

19. As Harry Gamble has argued, the centrality of education reform in Senghor's postwar politics has been consistently underappreciated in the literature on decolonization. Senghor's very first speech before the Constituent Assembly was almost entirely about education. *Contesting French West Africa*, 213.

20. Gamble also underscores how deeply Senghor's wartime experience as a prisoner of war affected the evolution of his thought on this issue. Senghor wrote about how his direct experience of Nazi

ther a sterile copy nor a watered-down version of education in the metropole, Senghor argued, for it would both "ground the student in the values of Negro-African civilization" and "initiate him in French values, to produce an indigenous elite *equal* to the French."[21] Only then, he insisted, would colonialism truly end and a new era of egalitarian Franco-African relations begin in earnest. Jeanne Vialle, senator of Oubangui-Chari and the first African woman to serve in the French parliament, similarly envisioned decolonization as a revolution in African education. For her, decolonization meant the obsolescence of the very category of the *évolué* through mass education and the uplift of the entire population. Reaching that outcome, in turn, necessarily entailed educating African women and girls, Vialle insisted, since they were ultimately the ones who would raise future African generations.[22]

Senghor and Vialle were not alone in these views. With each passing year, African politicians, educators, and students looked to concrete realizations (or the lack thereof) in the domain of education as a benchmark of the progress of colonial reform and racial justice in postwar Greater France more generally. Their demands centered on the expansion of primary education, the development of secondary education, the creation of African universities, and, in the interim, more scholarships for African students to pursue their secondary and postsecondary education in France. They also deeply resented that schooling for Africans remained under the jurisdiction of the central colonial ministry. A 1947 bill Senghor coauthored with Yacine Diallo (Guinée) and Lamine Guèye (Senegal) called for the Ministry of National Education (MEN) to assume full control of all levels of education in the territories to ensure parity with the educational system in France. Their proposed legislation explicitly framed the issue as "liberating education" from colonial domination and securing Africans' "educational rights."[23] Despite this powerful rhetoric, the bill did not pass.

By the end of the 1940s, faltering education reforms had become a lightning rod in wider African campaigns to get the French to make good on the promise of an egalitarian French Union that had been so triumphantly announced in the preamble of the 1946 constitution, in which all inhabitants of the French Union were supposed to be equal "without distinction of race, religion or creed."[24] In

racism in captivity taught him the dangers of any kind of cultural and racial essentialism and the importance of bringing people together across racial-cultural divides. Senghor reported that after his release in 1942, he had been "cured of the ghetto of Negritude." Gamble, *Contesting French West Africa*, 233.

21. Léopold Sédar Senghor, "Préface," in Jean Capelle, *L'éducation en Afrique noire à la veille des Indépendances (1946–1958)* (Paris: Editions Karthala, 1990), 7–9 (my emphasis).

22. Joseph-Gabriel, *Reimagining Liberation*, 107–108.

23. Gamble, *Contesting West Africa*, 229–230.

24. Preamble to the Constitution of October 27, 1946, art. 1. The constitution became an important rhetorical tool for African deputies in the National Assembly as they relentlessly pressed their

a rousing speech decrying stalled colonial reform before a gathering of youth leaders in Montpellier in 1949, Congolese teacher Jean Dadet characterized the abysmal education statistics for French Equatorial Africa as a deliberate "racial politics" on the part of the French to "maintain the black man in an animal state."[25] How else, he asked, could one explain that after six decades of French rule, in his federation of more than four million people, only *five* Africans obtain the *baccalauréat* each year?[26] Dadet lambasted the colonial administration for both the scandalously low rates of schooling for Africans and the poor quality of the education they received. He declared that the paucity of schools in France's African territories amounted to a "politics of illiteracy," while he derided the schools that did exist as mere "caricatures," built reluctantly and in bad faith. He did not mince words in his overall assessment of this situation: the current state of colonial education, he argued, was at the root of the *racism* Africans continued to experience every day in the French Union.[27]

French educators in the African federations, colonial officials, and politicians in the metropole usually dismissed such accusations of racial discrimination out of hand, at best as deeply misguided or, worse, as political grandstanding. Even the most liberal and otherwise sympathetic French observers were provoked by this rhetoric. Jean Capelle, head of education in AOF from 1946 to 1949, offers a case in point. Capelle was a lifelong metropolitan educator and bureaucrat; both before and after his stint in AOF, he served as rector of the University of Nancy. Like René Cassin and René Capitant, who had unexpectedly found themselves in charge of colonial education during the war, Capelle brought a different set of sensibilities to colonial problems. As Harry Gamble has noted, his very appointment signaled a commitment to more integrationist reforms during the brief tenure of Socialist Marius Moutet as minister of Overseas France in 1946–1947.[28]

---

metropolitan counterparts on these issues in the Assembly's special commission on overseas territories in the late 1940s. I write about this at greater length in "Obscuring Race."

25. Note d'Information a/s la "Journée Mondiale Contre le Colonialisme," Service de Liaison avec les Originaires des Territoires d'Outre-Mer, February 22, 1949, ANOM: 1AFFPOL/2400. This event was organized by a Communist international youth organization (the World Federation of Democratic Youth, which will be discussed in chapter 5), but Dadet's "anticolonialism" did not call for an abrupt rupture with France; rather, Dadet's "anticolonialism" closely resembled that of Senghor. For biographical background on Dadet, see Claude-Ernest Kiamba, "Construction de l'état et politiques de l'enseignement au Congo du 1911 à 1997: Contribution à l'analyse de l'Action Publique en Afrique Noire" (PhD diss., Université Montesquieu-Bordeaux IV, 2008), 44, 93.

26. According to statistics compiled by the French central colonial authority, in 1946, six inhabitants of AEF obtained the *baccalauréat*; by 1949, that number had risen to twenty-nine. I have not been able to verify how many of these *bacheliers* were African. *Bulletin de l'Inspection-Générale de l'Enseignement et de la Jeunesse du Ministère de la France d'Outre-Mer* (December 1950): 40, ANOM: BIB AOM/20205/1950.

27. Note d'Information a/s la "Journée Mondiale Contre le Colonialisme," ANOM: 1AFFPOL/2400.

28. Gamble, *Contesting French West Africa*, 223. Moutet first tried to more closely align colonial education with norms and standards in the metropole as minister of colonies during the Popular Front. In

Indeed, Senghor considered Capelle one of his closest allies in the struggle for education reform. Nevertheless, in an administrative memoir about his efforts to restructure education in postwar AOF, Capelle derisively recalled that many Africans "accused us of a Machiavellian plot to reestablish a system based on racial discrimination."[29] His allusion to a "Machiavellian plot" construes this position as paranoid and delusional. Moreover, the term "reestablish" implies that systemic racial discrimination in the territories had been effectively dismantled before he assumed his position, even though Capelle's own struggle to effect meaningful education reform in the face of what he himself considered to be a recalcitrant colonial administration suggests quite the contrary.[30]

Though French officials refused to accept African characterizations of the sorry state of colonial education as "racist," they were nevertheless well aware that they had to build more schools in the African Federations. In 1946, the French government allocated billions of francs for social and economic development in the overseas territories, and a portion of those funds, known as FIDES, was devoted to new school construction and expanding the capacity of existing schools in French Africa (including mission schools).[31] With the help of the FIDES program, the prewar rate of primary school attendance in both federations effectively doubled by the end of the 1940s, but since the rate in 1939 had been infinitesimal, overall percentages remained extremely low. In 1950, only 5.7 percent of the 2.25 million school-age African children in AOF attended school; in AEF, the rate was 7.57 percent for a school-age population of just under a million. In both federations, the percentage of the total population who had any formal schooling whatsoever still hovered around 1 percent.[32]

1947, he was ousted from his post as the top colonial official in Paris with the collapse of tripartism and replaced by the much more conservative Christian Democrat Paul Coste-Floret, who encouraged local colonial administrations to resist integrationist reforms. Gamble, *Contesting French West Africa*, 235.

29. Capelle, *L'éducation en Afrique noire*, 49.

30. Capelle, *L'éducation en Afrique noire*. More on this topic follows.

31. Rachel Kantrowitz, "'So That Tomorrow Would Be Better for Us': Developing French-Funded Catholic Schools in Dahomey and Senegal, 1945–1975" (PhD diss., New York University, 2015). The majority of FIDES funds went to the African federations, but allocations for education made up just a fraction. In the 1949 FIDES budget for AOF, education spending totaled 8 percent, less than half of the funding for roads and bridges.

32. Eléments de rapport sur le développement de l'Enseignement dans les TOM, April 7, 1950, ANOM: 1AFFPOL/1015. Capelle provides slightly different figures in his memoir: 4.2 percent for AOF and 8.5 percent for AEF. See his *L'éducation en Afrique noire*, 56. Higher school attendance in AEF was largely attributable to the older presence and higher volume of mission schools (which FIDES helped fund). In 1950, there were 889 public schools and 237 private schools in AOF; in AEF, the figures were much closer: 327 public schools compared with 275 private ones. Rates of school attendance in French-controlled Togo and Cameroon, which were under international supervision as UN Trust Territories, were noticeably higher—20 percent and 22.9 percent, respectively—a strong indication of how important international pressure was in determining educational outcomes in the French Union.

While most French and African observers attributed this situation in part to the sheer lack of schools, they disagreed considerably as to why Africans who did have the opportunity to go to school might actively choose not to. Their divergent interpretations reflect how differently metropolitan French and francophone Africans conceived the problem at hand. Capelle understood African hostility to French schools as a holdover from the early days of the *indigénat*, when the colonial administration employed traditional chiefs to both conscript local people for the *corvées* and forcibly send a small number of children to colonial schools to provide the administration with clerks and translators. Capelle believed that because this schooling had been compulsory, sending children to French schools assumed an indelible social stigma.[33]

The legacy of forced schooling may have been a contributing factor to some African parents' wariness of French education, but Africans who had attended colonial schools framed African ambivalence to French schooling quite differently. Their explanations hark back to Senghor's critique of the spirit of colonial education. Abdourahmane Konaté recounts in his memoir how his father reacted when the local teacher in his village in rural Senegal proposed that Konaté come to his school: his father said, "I must admit, I am not thrilled with colonial education. It produces strangers in our midst, supplanting the education the child has received from his parents and above all, attachment to the land and to our way of seeing the world."[34] Konaté insists that this view was widely shared and that weak attendance figures for French schools in the late 1940s were due to "popular resistance to the alienating content in these schools." For Konaté, what made this content "alienating" was not just the cultural deracination that his father (and so many colonial officials and ethnologists) feared. Rather, it was the anti-African bias built into the curriculum itself, particularly in history instruction, which Konaté characterized as an instrument of racial domination. He lamented that the official curriculum in the late 1940s was still marked by "the derisory treatment of ancient African history," which "does its best to paint African chiefs of the resistance as 'savage and bloody tyrants.'" Konaté argued that this view of African history produced a racial inferiority complex in African schoolchildren that helped maintain the colonial status quo of racial inequality. Curricular reforms were therefore a fundamental prerequisite, and would indeed be the foundation, for the broader "cultural, political, and social revolution" he and his compatriots sought for postwar French Africa.[35]

---

33. Capelle, *L'éducation en Afrique noire*, 79.
34. Konaté, *Le cri du mange-mil*, 53.
35. Konaté, *Le cri du mange-mil*, 67–68.

Bringing the views of Senghor, Vialle, Kaziendé, Konaté, and Dadet together reveals that a broad swath of Africans who had firsthand experience with colonial schooling emerged from the war convinced that decolonization had to begin with education. They demanded not just more schools or better schools but fundamentally different kinds of schools, with wholly different objectives. Colonial education had been designed to produce a colonial elite to uphold the colonial order.[36] If the empire was to be "decolonized," African education would have to provide young Africans with cultural confidence to match that of their French peers.[37] Only this could empower and prepare rising generations of Africans to formulate their own priorities for the development of African societies and Africa's future relations with France.

The circumstances of the war and its aftermath emboldened francophone Africans to demand racial equality and created a new climate, both within the francosphere and abroad, in which those demands carried newfound currency. French-educated Africans expected that the racial scaffolding of the old empire would be rapidly dismantled and that equality would soon be a lived reality for all Africans in the new French Union. The kind of equality these Africans sought—social and cultural as well as legal and political—focused their efforts on education, and they framed their demands for substantive education reform explicitly as a racial justice issue: if true equality depended on successful education reforms, failure to enact such reforms amounted to racial discrimination.

The postwar conjuncture heightened the power of this rhetoric as more Africans began to participate in the policymaking process in both French parliamentary bodies in the metropole and local representative assemblies in the territories. As teacher-training institutes constituted one of the few opportunities for Africans to obtain a postelementary education before the war, a significant proportion of Africans who ran for office in the immediate postwar years were themselves teachers and intimately familiar with colonial schooling and the education bureaucracy.[38] Henceforth, French lawmakers, administrators, and educators would have to reckon with African insistence that colonial education reform was about racial justice, whether most French figures

---

36. For a similar argument in the Algerian context, see Fanny Colonna, "Educating Conformity in Colonial Algeria," trans. Barbara Harshay, in *Tensions of Empire: Colonial Cultures in a Bourgeois World*, ed. Frederick Cooper and Ann Laura Stoler (Berkeley: University of California Press, 1997), 346–370.

37. Liz Foster has shown the same basic ideas circulating in francophone African Catholic milieus during this period regarding the training of African clergy. She highlights how African priests like Robert Sastre (Dahomey) and Robert Dosseh (Togo) outlined a vision of African missionary training for African empowerment. *African Catholic*, 187.

38. Seven of eight African deputies in the National Assembly's commission on overseas territories came from the teaching corps, a point the deputies themselves made when pushing for the urgency of education reform.

agreed with that characterization or not, as well as Africans' conceptions of racial equality, racial discrimination, and what a truly egalitarian French Union would look like. For every action, however, there is a reaction. African politicians and reformers ultimately found themselves in a double bind: their unwelcome insistence on racial justice produced new iterations of older racist stereotypes about Africans that became an important part of postwar racial common sense.

European Postwar Expectations: Racial Reeducation for European Unity

African formulations of robust equality and racial justice were not the only racial expectations with which the French had to contend. The prospect of an Allied victory over Nazi Germany produced a different set of priorities among European elites, whose prewar conceptions of race were challenged by the close association of racism and Nazism during the war. To those on the Allied side—whether in the resistance on the continent or in exile elsewhere—opposition to Nazi racism had proved a powerful rallying cry and potential unifying force for greater European cooperation once the war was won. Nazism's mixture of racism and authoritarianism was framed as intrinsically anti-European, a frontal assault on supposedly fundamental European values of democracy, universalism, and individualism.[39] And yet, postwar planners knew that state racism had become part of everyday life for most Europeans living under Nazi rule, and they feared that many Europeans, especially the young, were indoctrinated with Nazi race theory. Thus, as the war started drawing to a close, the denazification of occupied Europe put questions of race and education front and center in transnational European discussions about postwar reconstruction.

Gathered in the London-based Conference of Allied Ministers of Education, European political elites, intellectuals, and educators contemplated the "racial reeducation" of an entire generation of European youth who had come of age under Nazi occupation. Members of the CAME were quick to characterize the "Nazi doctrine of Man" as "rubbish," "pseudo-scientific" and "insane."[40] How-

---

39. Conway, *Western Europe's Democratic Age.*

40. For "rubbish," see Dr. Alf Sommerfelt, "Education and Racial Tolerance," London, February 12, 1945, UNESCO Archives: CAME/Correspondence/I/12623; for "insane," see K. Eydziatowicz, "Notes on Educational and School Broadcasting," London, February 15, 1945, UNESCO Archives: CAME/Correspondence/I/12623. For "pseudo-scientific," see "Notes on the Draft Resolution on the Enquiry into the Theory of Race," appendix I, London, March 19, 1945, UNESCO Archives: CAME, London, 1942–1945, vol. III: General Series Documents II.

ever, these discussions remained remarkably abstract: no one made explicit references to Nazi eugenics, racial anti-Semitism, the Final Solution, or anti-Black Nazi racism, nor did the members of the CAME seriously consider the extent to which race theory and racism in Europe were not unique to Nazi Germany.[41] What discussions about race and education within the CAME in 1944–1945 did do was to inaugurate a broader international effort to debunk scientific racism after the war, which culminated in a pair of influential "Statements on Race" issued by the CAME's successor organization, UNESCO, in the early 1950s. The statements both reflected and enshrined new international norms about the need to combat "race prejudice."[42]

While the authors, audience, and scope of the UNESCO Race Statements were international, the CAME's deliberations were conducted primarily by Europeans who were working within a European framework. For Norwegian delegate Alf Sommerfelt, a prominent linguist who trained and worked largely in France before the war, the basic problem was that after so many years of exposure to "Nazi" race theory, most Europeans—even those in unoccupied lands—were utterly misinformed about what race really was, all too often confusing what he called "anthropological type" with national and linguistic groups. Sommerfelt recounted with dismay how he had recently encountered a British couple who, having adopted an orphaned French infant, began teaching themselves French so that they could communicate with the child when the child grew up. The CAME's main task, he argued, should be to develop pedagogical tools and curricular reforms for all levels of European education to combat such gross misconceptions about the nature of race. Sommerfelt tied this imperative to the CAME's projects to produce a handbook for European schoolteachers and a new European history textbook to be distributed across the continent after the war. He insisted that these and whatever other efforts the CAME might pursue in the future to retrain teachers and redesign

---

41. Indeed, it is worth noting that after combing through the transcripts of the CAME, I encountered almost no references to Jews. Two exceptions were a reference to Jewish children as a distinct subset of children in a list of youth populations in liberated Europe who would need special "education 'treatment'" after the war, and discussion of removing all "Jewish books" to Jerusalem. In the case of the former, Jewish children were listed alongside "children of quislings," "backwards children," and "children and young people who have been deliberately perverted by the enemy," in light of the "the effects of race persecution [and] statelessness" (see the unsigned, undated report, "Human Rehabilitation of Children and Young People," UNESCO Archives: CAME, London 1942–1945, vol II: General Series Documents I).

42. On the particular contribution of French anthropologists to the UNESCO Race Statements, see the epilogue in Alice Conklin, *In the Museum of Man: Race, Empire and Anthropology in France, 1850–1950* (Ithaca, NY: Cornell University Press, 2013). On the transformation of the CAME into UNESCO, see Mylonas, *La genèse de l'Unesco*. For a critical reading of the Race Statements and the specific UNESCO tradition of postwar European antiracism, see Alana Lentin, *Racism and Antiracism in Europe* (London: Pluto Press, 2004).

school and university curricula had to provide teachers and students with the "basic facts" about race. He listed those as the following:

> The difference between race, language and nation, an elementary survey of the different anthropological types (in Europe and the countries of European civilization with a summary treatment of the rest of the world), the problems of the inter-relations between civilization and "race" and the question of "racial superiority," some notions of the European languages and the "origin" of the European peoples.[43]

As the passing remark about "the rest of the world" indicates, to Sommerfelt, the primary objective of the CAME's educational initiatives was not to refute racial thinking *tout court* but rather to correct spurious notions of racial divisions *within Europe.*

This view predominated within the CAME. The representative for the education ministry of the Polish government-in-exile affirmed that to counteract Nazi racial theories, the CAME had to "establish fundamental theses of education common to all the peoples of the continent," so as to instill them with the consciousness "that they all belong to the same European civilization."[44] Several British academics involved in the textbook project likewise stressed that they had to downplay the "principle of race" as a significant factor in Europe's past in order to produce an historical narrative that clearly portrayed Europe as a "single civilization."[45] The CAME was a unique venue where such views converged and flourished, an incubator for an emergent postwar consensus that the diversity of European peoples and cultures was, in fact, not a question of race at all.[46]

That race would no longer be considered an appropriate category for interpreting intra-European difference was a significant departure from the elaborate racial frameworks undergirding so much political and social-scientific discourse and public policy in the interwar period.[47] It was also a departure from interwar European treatises refuting Nazi racism, which sported such titles as *The Equality of the European Races and the Ways to Improve Them.*[48] The

---

43. Sommerfelt, "Education and Racial Tolerance," UNESCO Archives: CAME/Correspondence/I/12623.

44. Eydziatowicz, "Notes on Educational and School Broadcasting," UNESCO Archives: CAME/Correspondence/I/12623.

45. Draft Minutes of the 22nd Meeting of the History Committee, June 7, 1944, UNESCO Archives: CAME, London 1942–1945, vol III: Books and Periodicals Commission, History Committees and Subcommittees.

46. On "racelessness" in postwar Europe, see Goldberg, *The Threat of Race,* chap. 5.

47. On racial hierarchies of Europeans in the 1920s and 1930s, see Camiscioli, *Reproducing the French Race.*

48. This was the title of the findings of a group of scientists at the Academy of Science in Prague whom Masaryk commissioned to refute Nazi racial theory in the early 1930s. Edited by K. Weigner,

proceedings of the CAME suggest that championing "racial equality" among Europeans was fast becoming moot in the postwar conjuncture; as conceptual registers shifted, there no longer seemed to be multiple, if equal, "European races" but rather one unitary "European civilization."

The evolution of the CAME's history textbook provides an illustrative example. Though the CAME officially withdrew its sponsorship of the project in late 1945 to ensure the academic integrity and the "independence" of the scholarship, all three editors of the three-volume work sat on the CAME's History Committee, including Frenchman Paul Vaucher. The title of the work, published in 1954, aptly captures the conceptual shift away from race: *The European Inheritance: A History of European Civilization.*[49] This is not to say that long-held notions about the distinctiveness of northern versus southern Europeans, east versus west, or racial-religious categories such as "Slavs," "Latins," "Anglo-Saxons," and "Germanics" disappeared from the postwar European imaginary, for they most certainly did not. Indeed, *The European Inheritance* used this terminology, but its authors made a special point to dissociate these terms from race: "Each of these names is linguistic, and not a name or term of race. None of them signifies breed or blood, or any of the physical facts which are studied by anthropologists: each of them indicates a language, and the culture contained in and carried by that vehicle."[50]

This racial erasure among Europeans made it possible to actively celebrate and valorize Europe's cultural and linguistic diversity in a new way, not only as a cultural asset or abstract moral value, but as a defining feature of Europe and "European civilization" itself. By the end of the 1940s, European cultural diversity had become a major theme for pro-Europe activists and, indeed, was figured as both a means and a motivation for European integration. This sentiment became a fixture of the era, both in France and elsewhere in Western Europe. As the European Movement had put it in the promotional materials

---

the volume was published (in Czech) in 1935. Though members of the CAME cited this work, as I show later, their own language struck an entirely different note. See "Notes on the Draft Resolution on the Enquiry into the Theory of Race," appendix I, London, March 19, 1945, UNESCO Archives: CAME, London, 1942–1945, vol III: General Series Documents II.

CAME member (and future president of UNESCO) Julian Huxley coauthored an important work in 1937, *We Europeans*, debunking Nazi racial policy and scientific racism more generally, though the work also did not unequivocally disavow racial categories.

49. Ernest Barker, George Clark, and Paul Vaucher, *The European Inheritance: A History of European Civilization*, 3 vols. (Oxford: Clarendon Press, 1954). I have found no evidence that the work was translated into all major European languages and used across the continent as originally intended.

50. Barker, Clark, and Vaucher, *The European Inheritance*, vol. III, 311. The very term "inheritance" points to the deep ambiguity of such assertions and evokes the "culturalization" of race in postwar discourse. Alana Lentin identifies UNESCO as the key agent of this process in her *Race and Antiracism in Postwar Europe*, chap. 2.

for its first major cultural summit in Lausanne in 1949, the variety and breadth of Europe's cultural resources could be mobilized to help achieve European unity, just as "only a united Europe could preserve our cultures in their precious diversity."[51] A few months earlier, the French-led Union of European Federalists promoted its first youth congress, proudly declaring, "Europe is a mediating force of 280 million people formed by a common culture and belonging to a single civilization, rich in its diversity and in its unity."[52]

Despite its veneer of inclusivity, there was an implicit racial oneness underpinning this rhetoric that can be clearly traced to more explicit declarations of Europe's "civilizational" unity within the CAME in 1945.[53] Civilization talk was clearly beginning to replace the discredited language of race, but precisely for that reason, the postwar civilizational idiom both absorbed many of the assumptions of older racial paradigms and produced new racial meanings.[54] Members of the CAME made a clear distinction between correcting racial misconceptions about Europeans and race beyond Europe's borders; the very way that they framed the issue constituted the problem of race differently across this presumed "civilizational" divide. As Sommerfelt noted at the end of his proposal for racial reeducation in liberated Europe, "the instruction envisaged in this memorandum will be of importance not only in combating Fascist and Nazi ideas but also in furthering a more tolerant and comprehending attitude toward people of non-European civilization." He then added, "With the growing industrialization of Asiatic and African countries and the poisonous effects of Japanese propaganda it is of the utmost importance to exterminate racial prejudice."[55]

---

51. Announcement for the Conférence Européenne de la Culture (Lausanne, December 8–12, 1949), undated, Bureau d'études pour un Centre européen de la Culture, AHC: 1/DE/25. I discuss this event at length in chapter 2 and will return to this topic later. The Lausanne Conference was the first major European conference devoted exclusively to cultural and educational issues.

52. Gilbert Giraudon, Jeunesse Européenne Circulaire C, May 19, 1949, AHUE: UEF-178.

53. This racial undercurrent is obscured in the literature on early European integration and European identity, which does not critically interrogate the explosion of European civilizational discourse in the postwar conjuncture. This is especially true in the French scholarship on these questions. See, among others, Girault, ed., *Identité et conscience européennes*; Jean-Michel Guieu et al., *Penser et construire Europe*; Robert Frank, ed., *Les identités européennes au XXe siècle: Diversités, convergences et solidarités* (Paris: Sorbonne, 2004); Gérard Bossuat, "Des lieux de mémoire pour l'Europe unie," *Vingtième siècle: Revue d'histoire* 61 (January–March, 1999): 56–69, https://www.jstor.org/stable/3771459.

54. I do not mean to suggest that race had not been connected to the notion of "European civilization" previously—it surely had. But there were also important countertrends—that is, the concept of civilization was mobilized *against* "German" notions of racial community. As race was purged from postwar discourse, however, I propose this opposition faded away as race and civilization became tacitly intertwined in both transnational European and French imaginaries—which was something new.

55. Sommerfelt, "Education and Racial Tolerance," UNESCO Archives: CAME/Correspondence/I/12623.

There are several assumptions in this brief comment that are worth considering in some detail, as they were widely shared by Sommerfelt's colleagues in the CAME and informed transnational efforts to craft European education policies in the years that followed. First, Sommerfelt doubly externalized the phenomenon of "racial prejudice" as a "Fascist and Nazi" imposition in Europe and a Japanese import elsewhere, effectively absolving Europe—the good, *true* Europe—of complicity in the development of modern racism. Contrary to the claims of some modern historians that the experience of the war shattered Europe's "civilizational confidence" or its "superiority complex,"[56] formulations such as these implied that Europe possessed vast moral and intellectual resources that could be mobilized to fight prejudice throughout the world, which, not incidentally, would provide Europe with a new global vocation as colonial empires seemed to teeter on the brink. More important, Sommerfelt's reference to "people of non-European civilization" carried racial overtones that go beyond the common postwar practice of European policymakers developing coded language to avoid increasingly taboo racial terminology; Sommerfelt was helping to infuse this phrase with new content.

Having dismissed the application of racial categories to differentiate Europeans from one another, Sommerfelt recast race as existing somewhere else beyond Europe's borders. In so doing, he effectively produced a new boundary between Europeans and non-Europeans: race itself. His suggestion that the pedagogical and curricular reforms he was proposing would foster a "more tolerant and comprehending attitude" among Europeans toward non-Europeans accentuates, rather than diminishes, the chasm between them, further reinforcing and naturalizing that boundary as common sense.

It may not be surprising that a transnational group of elite Europeans tasked with the postwar reconstruction of education on the continent would insist on the racial unity of Europeans but only racial *tolerance* for non-Europeans.[57] However, this conceptual framework would be woefully ill-suited to satisfy francophone Africans' expectations for an egalitarian French Union. Senghor, Vialle, Konaté, Kaziendé, Dadet, and so many others were not interested in "tolerance" and "mutual understanding"; they were demanding equality between whites and Blacks, Africans and French, and Europeans and Africans—the same equality that members of the CAME and European unity activists now took for granted as occurring naturally among Europeans. In the colonial

56. Judt, *Postwar*, 5; Helmut Kaelble, "L'Europe 'vécue' et l'Europe 'pensée' au XXe siècle," in Girault, ed., *Identité et conscience européennes*, 39.

57. For an interesting comparison, see Heide Fehrenbach's discussion of the limitations of the notion of tolerance in what she calls West German "postwar racial liberalism" in her *Race after Hitler: Black Occupation Children in Postwar Germany and America* (Princeton, NJ: Princeton University Press, 2005).

African context, that kind of equality could not be achieved solely by changing young people's outlook or knowledge of the "basic facts about race." Rather, that equality required deep structural changes to the entire edifice of colonial education.

Educating Africans in Postwar French Africa

In the special circumstances of the late war years, French leaders, officials, and educators seemed to acknowledge as much. The architects of French colonial education reform, in addition to negotiating African and European expectations, were also confronted with a new international climate that was, at least rhetorically, hostile to colonialism and racism. The overhaul of colonial education in French Africa was first laid out in de Gaulle's landmark summit on colonial reform in Brazzaville in January 1944, an event that was a tool of political propaganda as much as it was an occasion for rigorous policymaking. The summit's key goal was to justify continued French rule in Africa to an international, primarily US audience. Minister of Colonies Paul Giacobbi reminded the governor-general of AOF regarding the implementation of the Brazzaville recommendations in 1945:

> If the head of the government takes pains to repeat that our colonial policy has definitely taken a new orientation, it is because it is indispensable to affirm our position vis-à-vis international opinion. The Hot Springs Conference clearly showed American interest in colonial territories. . . . We are no longer in 1939, when we could regulate our own affairs among ourselves without the international observer casting his glance over the wall into our backyard.[58]

French planners also hoped that the Brazzaville Conference would shore up morale in elite African milieus. Although no Africans were invited to participate in the conference, its convocation was publicized widely on local African radio. That Kaziendé had interpreted news of the conference as a turning point in the march toward racial equality in French Africa was no accident—this was exactly the message the French had hoped to convey to Africans just like him. And yet, ideas about African racial difference, old and new, suffused the general outlook of the conference's organizers, which were duly reflected in their proposals for education reform and subsequent education policy and

---

58. Ministre des Colonies à GOUGAL-AOF a/s application recommandations Brazzaville, undated (c. 1945), ANOM: 1AFFPOL/2201, dossier 5.

practice in French Africa. The kind of equality men and women like Kaziendé, Senghor, and Vialle hoped for was never envisioned at Brazzaville. Given that as late as 1948 the minister of Overseas France (Paul Coste-Floret) was still invoking the Brazzaville recommendations as France's "charter" for "the development of Africa in the interests of Africans" in heated exchanges with African deputies on the parliament floor, those recommendations merit further attention here.[59]

The conference's dual imperatives to justify continued French rule in Africa and to dissociate that rule from unsavory practices of colonial domination created a rhetorical predicament for conference participants. Though racial categories and racial logics continued to guide participants' conversations and proposals, they were more sensitive to the impropriety of *appearing* racist in light of the historical conjuncture. Many participants (though by no means all) tried to shed explicitly racial terminology from their discourse, and they relied on the rhetoric of "civilization" to do so just as the members of the CAME were doing back in London at this time. Crucially, policymakers and colonial officials at Brazzaville used "European civilization" to articulate the differences and the distance separating Africans from the French. If the racial underpinnings of this concept were somewhat ambiguous in the proceedings of the CAME, they were laid bare in the colonial context of the Brazzaville Conference. "European civilization" emerged as a key conceptual referent in a new racially coded language that took shape at Brazzaville and that subsequently became the medium through which postwar colonial education reform was instituted.

The point of departure of the conference was to outline a new colonial doctrine and give the empire a political form that would be "constitutional, republican and democratic." While Senghor and Konaté might have appreciated the implicit acknowledgment that existing colonial arrangements did not meet these standards, colonial administrators' understanding of the standards' shortcomings surely would have proved less palatable. As Louis Delmas, an official in Guinée and one of the conference organizers put it,

Why, we ask ourselves, did what worked for the Romans not work for us? The barbarians surrounding Rome, including our ancestors the Gaulois, as the old saying goes, were much closer to the Roman than

---

59. Procès-verbal de la Commission des territoires d'outre-mer (Assemblée Nationale), Audition de Paul Coste-Floret, March 3, 1948, AN: C/ / 15407. It is worth noting that African deputies also continued to cite the Brazzaville Conference in parliamentary debates into the 1950s as the framework for colonial reform and a standard, however modest, to which French officials did not even hold themselves. See, for instance, the argumentation of Jean-Hilaire Aubame (Gabon) in a tense exchange about unequal pay for African *fonctionnaires* in the colonial bureaucracy in Procès-verbal de la Commission des territoires d'outre-mer, January 4, 1950, AN C/ / 15408.

the Frenchman is to the savage of the black continent. There were greater racial affinities between them. . . . The formula for the assimilation of the barbarian is not the same as the formula for the assimilation of the savage. And it should go without saying that I do not mean to be offensive with this word, which, in seventeenth-century parlance, had a connotation of being pleasant.[60]

The disclaimer at the end of the passage is significant, indicating that even colonial administrators who used inflammatory racial language were not wholly unaware of the dissonance between the practical and the propagandistic goals of the conference. The analogy with Rome is also not incidental—this was another way of highlighting the racial unity of Europeans in contrast to the gulf separating Africans and the French, here represented by the well-worn figure of the "the savage." The task at Brazzaville was to specify what the appropriate formula for assimilating "the savage" would entail.

This mindset informed discussions at Brazzaville about education reform, even when explicit racial language such as this was replaced with a civilizational idiom. According to the representatives of the education service of French Soudan (contemporary Mali), the challenge of colonial education was to find a way to balance the two "educative forces" operating on African society, African "tradition" and "European civilization." These forces were understood not only to be different but diametrically opposed, as Africans' customs, family structure, and traditional authorities were thought to constitute a seemingly "insurmountable barrier against the aspirations our civilization naturally awakens [in Africans]." The officials cautioned against overestimating the extent to which they could contain the interplay between these forces through education policy alone, since so much of the "civilization" the French brought with them was transmitted to the local population unconsciously—for instance, in "the tidal wave of hopes and dreams inspired by the sight of a passing truck."[61] In a similar vein, other officials warned of the unintended consequences of the French presence on African society, urging "Europeans" to behave self-consciously around "indigènes," who were all too often inclined to "imitate" them: "The *indigène* observes the European . . . the smallest gesture of the white man is watched, commented on, and retold to others and interpreted according to some logic that escapes us. The European should be on his guard against this continual observation by the *autochtone*."[62] In this

---

60. Louis Delmas, "Contribution à une doctrine de politique impériale" (1944): 15–16, ANOM: 1AFFPOL/2201 dossier 6.

61. Rapport a/s enseignement, Colonie du Soudan, undated, ANOM: 1AFFPOL/2201, dossier 6.

62. Rapport a/s relations métropole-colonies, undated, ANOM: 1AFFPOL/2201, dossier 6.

statement, European and "white" are unambiguously synonymous, and Africans' performance of Europeans' whiteness is construed as a racial threat.

The belief that Africans had an innate proclivity for imitation carried over into discussions about how Africans *learn* and shaped how administrators and educators interpreted African aptitudes for academic subjects and extracurricular activities in the late 1940s and 1950s. Sometimes this belief could take a positive form: for instance, in 1949 the head of the education service in Bobo-Dioulasso (the second-largest city in contemporary Burkina Faso) wrote, "endowed with a keen sense of observation and imitation, the Black instinctively detects the smallest particularities of human comportment." This official therefore suggested that Africans had unique "theatrical aptitudes" that the colonial administration should actively develop by funding local theater troupes and acting programs.[63] More often, however, especially with regard to formal schooling, such characterizations were tied to negative assessments of Africans' intellectual abilities. Colonial officials frequently remarked on Africans' supposed "capacity for assimilation by simple memorization," which, they stressed, "did not forcibly imply comprehension."[64] The supposedly acute African ability to learn by rote, officials believed, explained why so many African students excelled in languages and literature and, once more Africans began entering higher education in the 1950s, why so many of them studied the law. Colonial observers clung tenaciously to this stereotype. A 1952 article in one of the outlets of the Colonial Lobby regretted that so many Africans obtained the *baccalauréat* by sheer force of memory, when "so few of them really have the capacity to pursue higher study and keep up with their European peers." As a result, "they become bitter in their bush, which they had quitted so enthusiastically in the hopes of becoming bureaucrats."[65]

This scenario was precisely what everyone gathered at Brazzaville had wanted to avoid. The conference resolutions on education began with a question: "What are *our* needs?" The answer was, unsurprisingly, the same as it had been before the war: low-level functionaries and technicians on the one hand and rural artisans on the other. Thus, the Brazzaville Education Plan

---

63. Gaston Piolet, "Dans l'Union Française: créations de foyers de culture et d'amitié franco-africaine," *L'Information Pédagogique*, no. 4 (September-October 1949): 163, AN: F/17/17539.

64. Rapport des deuxième et troisième trimestres, Affaires Politiques Musulmanes-AOF (1948), ANOM: 1AFFPOL/2259. This understanding particularly colored how French officials perceived traditional Qur'anic schools in West Africa, where instruction focused on the memorization of the Qur'an. As we shall see in chapter 5, despite the fact that this was the traditional method of Qur'anic schooling across the Muslim world, French observers interpreted the practice as further evidence of the shallowness of West Africans' "Muslim-ness." See Ware, *The Walking Qur'an*.

65. Excerpt from *Climats*, reprinted in the Catholic African student journal *Tam-Tam*, deuxième année, no. 1 (November–December 1952).

stipulated that schools in the territories should teach Africans French, but otherwise, the curriculum should be devoted to handicrafts, agricultural techniques, household training, and physical education—in sum, it should be "the least literary possible."[66] Indeed, the consensus among those gathered at Brazzaville was that Africans were ill-suited for metropolitan-style secondary and university education. Cabrière, who, as we have seen, was one of the fiercest opponents of secondary schooling for Africans, claimed to speak from experience when he declared that Africans were unfit for this kind of schooling. He noted that though he had seen several Africans obtain the *baccalauréat* "with great discipline and memory," he insisted that "few give the impression of having truly internalized this culture or of being able to pursue further studies."[67] His report on educating Africans was widely circulated among the regional education services of AOF and at the Brazzaville Conference, which spread the notion that secondary education was made for "Europeans" only.[68]

This opinion endured among education officials on the ground, even as political expediency encouraged the central colonial authority back in Paris to actively solicit African candidates for more advanced study in France. In late 1944, the provisional government's minister of colonies, René Pleven, sent several missives to the governors-general of AOF and AEF announcing the availability of a handful of scholarships for Africans to study in the metropole. He was disturbed to receive a steady stream of negative responses informing him that there were no "suitable" African candidates in the territories. One response reported that the entire federation of AEF did not have any candidates at the time: three "Europeans" who might have benefited from the offer were still mobilized, and the eight best "indigènes" had been sent to the École Normale William Ponty.[69] This teacher training school had been the main institution of higher education open to African men in the interwar period; both Kaziendé and Senghor, and many other elites of their generation, were alumni. A year later, Pleven's successor, Paul Giacobbi, was still receiving the same excuses, which he found "highly regrettable." Giacobbi took pains to remind Pierre Cournarie, governor-general of AOF, that "the entirety of our current colo-

66. Conférence Africaine de Brazzaville, Plan d'Enseignement, undated, ANOM: 1AFFPOL/2201, dossier 6.

67. Edmond Cabrière (Chef de la section de l'enseignement secondaire, AOF), Rapport à M. Directeur-Général Instruction Publique sur l'enseignement secondaire et la question indigène, undated, ANOM: 1AFFPOL/2201, dossier 6.

68. Yves Aubineau (Directeur-Général de l'Instruction Publique), Rapport a/s de la Conférence de Brazzaville, January 10, 1944, ANOM: 1AFFPOL/2201, dossier 6.

69. Telegram from René Pleven to GOUGAL Dakar, Brazzaville, Madagascar et al., November 18, 1944; telegram received November 23, 1944, from Dakar (Digo); telegram received December 28, 1944, from Brazzaville (Bayardelle), ANOM: 1AFFPOL/3408. Similar responses were received from Togo.

nial policy consists in strengthening the French community by putting its different members on the same level." He continued, "The first step is to elevate the intellectual level of our overseas populations and thereby bring them closer to the population in the metropole. Secondary education plays a vital role in this and will help identify an indigenous elite from the general population of schoolchildren."[70]

Cournarie was unmoved. He was deeply suspicious of educated Africans, especially those who were studying in the metropole. Shortly after Giacobbi chided him for not promoting more Africans in secondary education, Cournarie wrote a panicked missive back to the colonial ministry in Paris about a letter his surveillance service in Dakar had intercepted from an African medical student in Montpellier. In the letter, Emmanuel Franklein described his life in France to a friend back in Senegal. *"Les toubabesses abondent à gogo,"*[71] he wrote, "all you have to do is go outside and you can pick them up in the street." He went on to say that regrettably, he had been too busy with coursework to think about the "toubabesses" of late, but he reassured his correspondent: "Don't worry, I will have them during the break, and then: vengeance."[72]

Here was the quintessential colonial nightmare coming home to roost: angry Black men coming to the metropole and pursuing sexual relations with white women. The AOF security service had informed Cournarie that Franklein wrote often to a wide circle of friends and that all his letters were of the same genre, always returning to the theme of "vengeance." Cournarie urged Giacobbi to not only put Franklein under strict surveillance but to closely monitor the behavior of *all* students from AOF in the metropole. Indeed, the incident convinced Cournarie of the need for separate dorms for African students. That, he argued, would be "the only way to ensure that they do not become perverted by contact with a civilization that they do not understand, of which they are always prone to take up the worst parts."[73]

Colonial officials in Paris, however, were not terribly alarmed by Franklein's aggressive rhetoric. In their internal correspondence, they suggested his letter should probably be chalked up to the general "impetuousness of youth." They did recommend writing to the head of Franklein's residence hall for more information on him, as well as a general assessment of the mood among other African students in Montpellier. But they rejected the idea of creating special

70. Letter from Ministre des Colonies to GOUGAL-AOF, May 12, 1945, ANOM: 1AFFPOL/3408.

71. This is a playful way of saying "white women are everywhere." The term *toubabesse* combines a West African slang term for foreign white person with a French feminine ending.

72. Letter from Emmanuel R. Franklein to unknown recipient, April 3, 1945, ANOM: 1AFFPOL/3408.

73. Letter from Cournarie to Ministre des Colonies, May 17, 1945, ANOM: 1AFFPOL/3408.

dormitories for African students. Such a move, they worried, would further isolate young Africans from their metropolitan peers and French ways of life.[74]

It ultimately fell to Henri Laurentie, who stayed on at the Colonial Ministry after it relocated from Algiers back to Paris, to respond to Cournarie. Laurentie reiterated his staff's position that Franklein's remarks seemed to reflect a brashness common to all youth that was not a particularly African problem. However, he did see something specifically African in Franklein's allusion to "vengeance," though not in Cournarie's sense. Laurentie did not think the sentiment stemmed from any "perversion" provoked by culture shock; the sheer fact that Franklein was pursuing advanced study, one of just a handful of Africans to do so at the time, signaled to Laurentie that he must have been well acquainted with "French civilization." Rather, Laurentie interpreted it as "that resentment that *évolués* often feel from not always being treated by us, in the colonies, as social equals."[75] Laurentie was no radical, but this was an unusually candid admission for its time (or later, as the 1952 article cited earlier suggests). Taken to its logical conclusion, Laurentie's response implies that it was precisely educated Africans' *intimacy* with French values that enabled them to perceive the incongruence of French republican ideals on the one hand and Africans' social reality at the bottom of the colonial hierarchy on the other. This reasoning comes shockingly close to confronting the central contradictions of a system of French colonial rule rooted in racial domination that was resistant to change at a time when the French were trying to rebrand their empire as democratic, inclusive, and egalitarian. Little wonder that Laurentie would be pushed out of his post two years later, with the rightward turn in colonial leadership after the collapse of *tripartisme* in 1947.

With that shift in political winds, Christian Democrat Paul Coste-Floret was installed at the helm of the central colonial authority. As Dadet's admonition that only five Africans obtained the *baccalauréat* in AEF in 1949 indicates, Africans' access to secondary and postsecondary education, whether in the territories or the metropole, did not dramatically expand under Coste-Floret's tenure (1947–1949). Considering the consensus at Brazzaville that metropolitan-style secondary education was suitable for "Europeans" only, and that Coste-Floret still viewed the Brazzaville recommendations as his overarching policy framework in 1948, this is not surprising. If not in European France, educational models for French Africans would have to be found elsewhere. Tellingly, French officials looked instead to the United States and the Jim Crow South.

---

74. Note a/s interception postale de Franklein, June 8, 1945, ANOM: 1AFFPOL/3408.
75. Letter from Laurentie to Cournarie, June 29, 1945, ANOM: 1AFFPOL/3408.

AEF's inspector-general of education Vincent Fournier cited Booker T. Washington as the inspiration for the renovation of the École des Cadres in Brazzaville in 1946, which was supposed to be the premier institution of higher education for all of AEF. This was the only major initiative in secondary education in the entire federation that came directly out of the Brazzaville Conference.[76] The "soul" of the renovated École, Fournier wrote, "should be the laboratory. The era of exclusively literary and discursive education is outdated, just as theological and dogmatic education became outmoded during the Renaissance." Fournier then paraphrased the words of another Black American who shared Washington's educational philosophy, George Washington Carver, about how white teachers needed to be "patient" with their Black pupils. Fournier added in his own words that what was needed for the École to succeed was "much docility on the part of our *autochtone* students, [and] much devotion on the part of their white teachers."[77]

Despite Fournier's clear endorsement of a Tuskegee-style education for Africans in postwar AEF, he nonetheless insisted that the overarching goal was certainly not to produce "technicians without culture." That would not be in keeping with the "great French humanist tradition." Some study of the French language and French literature would teach African students "how to think well." But that would be only one part of young Africans' broader development, which would also include physical education "to harden their will and form their characters" and participation in youth movements like the scouts to "endow them with a simple but solid moral code." In this way, he continued, France would "contribute to the formation of an African citizen worthy of the Great French Union, fraternal and just," and—he could not resist adding—"possibly the ultimate realization of the ideals of the Revolution which have been transforming the world since 1789." This grand rhetoric aside, Fournier remained committed to his pragmatic vision for the École des Cadres, which he hoped would soon be valued more than a traditional lycée education and the *baccalauréat*. In his view, neither corresponded to the real needs of "Black Africa." The practical education the École des Cadres would dispense

---

76. For an earlier instance of the cross-fertilization between the politics of race and education in colonial Africa and the US South, see Andrew Zimmerman, *Alabama in Africa: Booker T. Washington, the German Empire and the Globalization of the New South* (Princeton, NJ: Princeton University Press, 2012); and Anton Tarradellas, "La formation des étudiants africains aux Etats-Unis: 'Mission civilisatrice,' connexions panafricanistes, et aide au développement (1880–1980)," in *Repenser la "mission civilisatrice." L'éducation dans le monde colonial et postcolonial au XXe siècle*, ed. Damiano Matasci, Miguel Bandeira Jéronimo, and Hugo Gonçalves Dores (Rennes: Presses Universitaires de Rennes, 2021).

77. Vincent Fournier, "L'Enseignement en AEF en 1947," *Nos Écoles: Bulletin de l'Enseignement de l'AEF*, no. 20 (October 1947), ANOM: 1AFFPOL/2135 dossier 5.

was specifically designed to avoid the disquieting prospect of increasing numbers of "overeducated" Africans, whom Fournier referred to as "those monsters that carry around overly ambitious brains atop restless and malnourished bodies."[78] Perhaps this is how he would have characterized Jean Dadet, the Congolese schoolteacher who would accuse Fournier's administration of a deliberate "racial politics" to "maintain the black man in an animal state."[79]

Fournier's discussion of what the formation of the whole African person would entail helps reconstruct what many French colonial officials really thought about Africans and the qualities they were perceived to naturally *lack*: rational thinking, physical fortitude, and a strong moral compass. These were crucial failings indeed, as indicated by Fournier's subsequent comment that these qualities were necessary for Africans to be "worthy" citizens of the French Union. Moreover, according to Fournier, these supposed deficiencies were precisely what made educating Africans uniquely difficult; the challenges of education in Africa, he argued, were unknown in the metropole and other "countries of old civilization." This reference was to Europe. "In Europe," he continued, "each nation has its own school tradition; the culture has deep roots that plunge into the past," whereas in Africa, the situation was entirely different. There, educators' task was one of "wholesale creation."[80] In Fournier's estimation, then, metropolitan France and the rest of Europe had diverse educational traditions, but they all shared the same fundamental relationship to the past that ensured an enriching cultural continuity across generations. They were, in short, part of a single civilization. Africans, on the other hand, not only lacked key personal qualities as individuals; their societies seemed devoid of historicity and deep cultural roots.[81] They were effectively civilizationless. What they did have, as the references to Booker T. Washington, George Washington Carver, and the promotion of a Tuskegee-style education make clear, was *race*.

Fournier's depiction of the "overeducated" African as a grotesque was a common representation of francophone Africans in the late 1940s. This caricature became more frequent as more Africans were admitted to modern middle schools (*collèges*), lycées, and universities in the 1950s. The "uppity" educated African became a recurrent trope for colonial education officials as well as French leaders in the metropole, who, after 1946, found themselves face-to-face with a significant number of Africans making claims as their ostensible equals

---

78. Fournier, "L'Enseignement en AEF," ANOM: 1AFFPOL/2135 dossier 5.

79. Note d'Information a/s la "Journée Mondiale Contre le Colonialisme," ANOM: 1AFFPOL/2400.

80. Fournier, "L'Enseignement en AEF," ANOM: 1AFFPOL/2135 dossier 5.

81. This was of course an old colonial trope. For a classic analysis, see Eric Wolf, *Europe and the People without History* (Berkeley: University of California Press, 1982).

for the first time. As African politicians, educators, and student and youth leaders became more aggressive in their campaigns for meaningful reform and racial justice, the image of the "arrogant" educated African prone to verbal demagoguery became a powerful weapon to delegitimize and dismiss African demands for reform in general and African accusations regarding the persistence of systemic racism in the French Union in particular.

Indeed, Fournier's views were widely shared by his counterparts in AOF and in the central colonial authority back in Paris. Even as the number of Africans in secondary education started to rise ever so slightly over the course of the 1940s, French officials began to worry that *too many* young Africans were being admitted into secondary schools.[82] These concerns were exacerbated by the fact that centralized directives to orient secondary school curricula in the direction outlined at Brazzaville were not always followed by individual school directors and teachers. In a presentation to the education committee of a colonial interest group in 1949, the colonial authority's inspector-general of education, Gaston, recounted how he had recently learned of a class of seventeen young Africans who were receiving a classical education in a "modest middle school" in some unspecified corner of "Black Africa." While he was "certainly moved" by the thought that the study of Latin and Greek was perhaps enjoying a renaissance in Africa even as it was dying out in France, he nonetheless questioned the utility of such an education for Africans:

> Our young black Hellenists are learning French, Latin and Greek in French schools! I would prefer, for my part, less languages and more math, physics and natural sciences. The immense landscapes of Africa, where man has yet to make his mark—it is not with eloquent speeches that we will transform them; great rhetoricians are not needed for this task, but men who have received a practical education.[83]

The key challenge they now faced, Gaston continued, was that Africans were demanding *more* metropolitan-style education, not less, which would only exacerbate the supposed overproduction of *bacheliers* when what Africa really needed were *techniciens*.[84] Framed in this way, Africans' preoccupation with

---

82. According to figures compiled by the central colonial ministry, there were 3,951 students in secondary schools (which included *collèges* [middle schools] as well as lycées) in AOF and another 623 in AEF in 1946. Those figures rose to 5,480 and 1,161, respectively, by 1949. It is, however, unclear what percentage of these students were African. *Bulletin de l'Inspection-Générale de l'Enseignement et de la Jeunesse du Ministère de la France d'Outre-Mer* (December 1950): 38, ANOM: BIB AOM/20205/1950.

83. Procès-verbal de la Commission de l'Enseignement du Comité Central de la France d'Outre-Mer, June 8, 1949, ANOM: 100APOM/933.

84. Procès-verbal de la Commission de l'Enseignement du Comité Central de la France d'Outre-Mer, June 8, 1949, ANOM: 100APOM/933.

racial equality was itself an impediment to African development and "racial progress."

To put all of this in perspective, it is worth noting that in the same year that Gaston delivered these remarks only a few dozen African students obtained the *bac* in AOF and AEF combined.[85] The overreaction verging on panic that these paltry figures produced underscores not only the intensity of French hostility toward educated Africans but a deeper ambivalence toward African equality more generally. As one member of the audience put it in response to Gaston's presentation, "Liberty, Equality, Fraternity—that signifies for [Africans] the freedom to do whatever they want and equality with those who know better than they do. There is nothing wrong with having *indigènes* who will make their own way, participate in businesses and be our associates, our friends; but what are we seeing now? *Évolués* who are our rivals, who are not even grateful for the education they have received and who speak badly of France, their benefactor and educator."[86]

This blatant paternalism did not go unchallenged in the session. Algeria-born Émile Moussat, an academic (of mixed French and Italian ancestry) on the committee, generalized the problem, noting that the pursuit of certain kinds of studies for social advancement was not a uniquely African phenomenon. In France too, he asserted, "the desire to socially reclassify oneself is identical. We are in the process of becoming a nation of *cadres*." They should therefore not be surprised to find that they have transmitted this sense of social ascension through a particular course of education to colonial populations.[87] Also present was Guinean youth leader Antoine Lawrence, who objected on rather different grounds. He focused on the suggestion of African ingratitude, which he characterized as a particular colonial problem rooted in a longer history of French racism. He declared, "To this I respond that the initial fault lies with certain metropolitan French who imported their opinions and doctrines to the overseas territories." Though Lawrence defended Africans' behavior as a reasonable response to white racism in the territories, he nevertheless insisted that Africans who possessed such a "disagreeable attitude"

85. *Bulletin de l'Inspection-Générale de l'Enseignement et de la Jeunesse du Ministère de la France d'Outre-Mer* (December 1950): 40, ANOM: BIB AOM/20205/1950.

86. Procès-verbal de la Commission de l'Enseignement du Comité Central de la France d'Outre-Mer, 8 June 8, 1949, ANOM: 100APOM/933.

87. Procès-verbal de la Commission de l'Enseignement du Comité Central de la France d'Outre-Mer, June 8, 1949, ANOM: 100APOM/933. Moussat was not the only one to make this analogy. Fournier also characterized the overvaluation of the *baccalauréat* as an obstacle for France and cited Édouard Herriot—a key figure in the interwar critique of the overly intellectual and elitist nature of French education—on this subject at length. Fournier, "L'Enseignement en AEF," ANOM: 1AFFPOL/2135 dossier 5.

were exceptions to the rule. The majority of Africans, he reassured everyone, thought as he did: "We do not hate France, we love her."[88]

In the late 1940s, assurances such as these did little to lessen French hostility, suspicion, and paranoia as African nationalist movements gained momentum in the face of the slow pace of colonial reform, and the specter of armed, and possibly Soviet-backed, anticolonial uprisings loomed larger in the minds of French officials.[89] From this perspective, the trope of the bitter and ungrateful educated African became entwined with the trope of the overly "political" African. Jean Capelle noted after one of his many "tours of the bush" during his tenure as head of education in AOF at this time:

> Mid-level positions are filled by Africans who have attended upper primary school or teacher training institutes; they are, in general, devoted and good at their jobs. However, some are embittered by a damaging feeling of inferiority, which gives rise to *expressions of vanity and irritability and vicious criticism of Europeans*. . . . They feel themselves to be stuck on the margins of two societies—the black and the white. Political extremism finds in them an ideal group of followers for blind and sometimes violent opposition.[90]

By linking criticisms of "Europeans" to Africans' purported vanity and irritability, Capelle construed that criticism as emotional and irrational, as a form of *prejudice* rather than as a legitimate political grievance. Capelle's concluding remark extended this motive to undesirable African political engagements in general, which channeled older stereotypes of African irrationality and hotheadedness into depictions of the swelling ranks of francophone African university students and politicians.

This logic resonated strongly in the ranks of colonial officials and political elites in the metropole and colored how they perceived the most vocal African politicians and activists. Indeed, around this time we find the first instances of French officials accusing African leaders and activists of "anti-white racism."[91] Such accusations proved a powerful and enduring rhetorical strategy for French policymakers and colonial administrators to dismiss African demands

---

88. Procès-verbal de la Commission de l'Enseignement du Comité Central de la France d'Outre-Mer, June 8, 1949, ANOM: 100APOM/933.

89. On the Cold War in francophone Africa, see Elizabeth Schmidt, *Cold War and Decolonization in Guinea, 1946–1958* (Columbus: Ohio University Press, 2007). I return to the impact of Cold War anxieties on colonial education policy in chapter 5.

90. Capelle, *L'éducation en Afrique noire*, 100 (my emphasis).

91. Rapport du Procureur-Général AEF à M. le Ministre de la France d'Outre-Mer, March 24, 1951, ANOM: 1AFFPOL/2254.

for more meaningful reform. This proved especially true with regard to Africans' calls for more secondary schools; a proper university in the territories that would grant the same degrees offered in the metropole; and, until those eventualities actually came to pass, more scholarships to send Africans to France to obtain a decent education. The ease with which those demands could be dispensed with by invoking "anti-white racism" became another key component of postwar racial common sense.[92]

French-educated Africans were keenly aware of this new constellation of feelings and resentments toward them, which they identified as part of the reason racial tensions after the war seemed to be mounting rather than abating. To cite one much-discussed example at the time, relations between white and Black teachers in Côte d'Ivoire deteriorated in 1945–1946 when African teachers started to protest unequal lodgings provided to them and their white counterparts. In the midst of the dispute, Nazi Bony, an *école normale* graduate who had taught in Abidjan, wrote to a (white) fellow teacher that the tensions there were so vicious because "the white educator sees his black colleague as a big child who does not understand the subtlety of his words and gestures, and as a rival rather than a partner." After homing in so precisely on the tropes we have seen circulating in French circles in both the territories and the metropole, he added, "the white teacher is refusing to evolve in a country that is evolving." Bony recalled one particularly upsetting remark he overheard one of his white colleagues make to a group of fellow teachers: "Don't believe the Black [*le Noir*] understands chemistry—he doesn't understand it like we do." Clearly exasperated, Bony wrote in response: "The Black [*Le Nègre*]—do I really have to say it?—possesses the full range of human qualities, and the laws that govern the human spirit change neither with the degrees of latitude nor with the skin."[93]

When reports of the kind of unabashed racism encountered by Bony reached the higher echelons of the colonial administration, officials were quick to condemn the individuals involved for their "retrograde" attitude but seldom considered a substantive shift in discriminatory policies. Bony's letter was forwarded to colonial officials in Paris, who affirmed that the practice of providing unequal lodgings "formally contradicts the principles of our colonial policy, which will only provoke terrible resentment." But the officials also character-

---

92. Liz Foster has identified this same rhetoric in the Franco-African Catholic world around this time. She cites one French missionary referring to African priests' calls for the Africanization of the local clergy as "antiwhite racism" in 1952. *African Catholic*, 169. The term began cropping up several years earlier in parliamentary debates between white French and African deputies in the late 1940s. See my "Obscuring Race."

93. Letter from Nazi Bony to Joseph Eyraud, Tenkodogo, December 2, 1945, ANOM: 1AFFPOL/3408.

ized Bony and his eloquent letter as exceptional, evidence of "a singular level of culture and clarity of mind."[94] Bony's antiracist protest perversely reinforced, rather than dislodged, stereotypes about African intelligence and aptitudes.

That same year, when the federal administration in AEF proposed providing scholarships to a mere eight African students to attend a middle school class in Brazzaville that had previously been reserved for "Europeans," several white parents threatened to withdraw their children from the school. As a result, local officials decided to send the African students to schools in other territories.[95] Minister of Colonies Giacobbi reproached the parents: "We can only regret this kind of thinking and the hostility of certain Europeans—a minority, I can only hope—who seem unable to appreciate the political consequences of their attitude." In Giacobbi's view, those "consequences" had less to do with local African reactions than with how the affair would play out in the international press. It was with that international audience in mind that he urged the governor general of AEF to personally intervene, to bring "the interested parties to a clearer understanding of the interests of the colony and their duty as Frenchmen." Giacobbi had found it particularly deplorable that this incident occurred in Brazzaville, which was the site, less than a year earlier, of the great African conference announcing to the world France's "new," ostensibly more progressive approach to colonial policy. But the proceedings of the Brazzaville Conference make clear that French colonial officials emerged from the war at best ambivalent about and often openly opposed to providing young Africans with the same secondary education offered to metropolitan French students in the territories. In the end, Giacobbi did not forcibly desegregate the school.[96]

That ambivalence stymied efforts to establish a proper university in French sub-Saharan Africa in the late 1940s. Despite the overwhelming consensus against advanced schooling for Africans, the Brazzaville Education Plan had in fact called for the immediate creation of an "African university" in Dakar. However, the plan did not offer any guidelines for this massive undertaking.[97] In 1945, the Colonial Ministry sent instructions to the federal administration in AOF that an African university should open its doors by the fall of 1946. French officials in both Dakar and Paris urged that the administration should wait until the Langevin Commission made its official recommendations for metropolitan education reform so that the institution would be in line with the new regime the

---

94. Note pour le Directeur AFFPOL, February 19, 1946, ANOM: 1AFFPOL/3408.
95. Extrait du rapport no. 514 I.G.E. du 26 juin 1945 sur la situation de l'enseignement secondaire en AEF, ANOM: 1AFFPOL/2136.
96. Letter from Giacobbi to GOUGAL-AEF a/s admission d'élèves indigènes en classe de 6ème des établissements secondaires, September 27, 1945, ANOM: 1AFFPOL/2136.
97. Conférence Africaine de Brazzaville, Plan d'Enseignement, ANOM1AFFPOL/2201, dossier 6.

officials expected to be instituted in France.[98] As concrete preparations for the university stalled in this bureaucratic limbo, colonial officials in Paris nevertheless began publicizing the "African University of Dakar" on African radio, which they proudly announced would open its doors in October 1946. This publicity campaign struck Cournarie, then still governor-general of AOF, as dangerously premature. He feared the risks of raising Africans' expectations were far greater than a long delay. He was fully aware that African students would no longer accept special "African diplomas." They wanted diplomas "that would give them absolute parity with Europeans," which Cournarie, who was as we have seen a long-standing skeptic of African higher education, claimed to find "perfectly legitimate." He therefore considered making the "African university" a *real* university "vitally important."[99] Internal as well as external pressures often pushed conservative colonial officials into contradictory and inconsistent positions.

In the end, the opening was indeed postponed, and the colonial bureaucracy did everything in its power to infuse the new institution with old colonial logics. For the next three years, colonial officials, French educators, and African representatives in Paris and Dakar debated the organization of the Dakar institution. The colonial administration wanted to retain full control of the school, but most French educators supported African politicians' demands that the new institution be integrated into the metropolitan education system and placed under the jurisdiction of the Ministry of National Education (MEN).[100] This campaign was led by Léopold Senghor and supported by Jean Capelle. In impassioned speeches on the subject before both the French parliament in Paris and the Grand Conseil in Dakar, Senghor explicitly linked race, education, and generational change. Affiliation with the MEN, he argued, "by facilitating the formation of state workers and elites worthy of the name, would lay the foundations of a Negro-French culture." At the same time, Senghor insisted that the Dakar institution should emphasize African issues and African needs. The new African university should not "produce 'average French people' [*des français moyens*] but rather black French people [*des négro-français*], modern men."[101]

---

98. Letter from Cournarie to Direction Enseignement et Jeunesse, MFOM, undated; Dépêche 6.900/EJ, November, 5 1945; Telegram 125/EJ, January 10, 1946, ANS: O/574 (31). See chapter 2 for a longer discussion of the Langevin Commission's work.

99. Letter from Cournarie to Direction Enseignement et Jeunesse, MFOM, March 30, 1946, ANS: O/574 (31).

100. On the intense jurisdiction battle between colonial and MEN officials, see Harry Gamble, "La crise de l'enseignement en Afrique occidentale française (1944–1950)," *Histoire de l'éducation* 128 (October–December 2011): 129–162, https://doi.org/10.4000/histoire-education.2278.

101. Rapport de Senghor a/s Projet du Décret portant création d'une Académie de l'AOF; Projet du Décret portant création d'un Institut Universitaire à Dakar, Commission des Affaires Sociales, Grand Conseil de l'AOF, Séance plénière du 3 juin 1949, AN: F17/17641.

Despite Senghor's and Capelle's efforts, the colonial administration jealously guarded its jurisdiction over every order of colonial education, including the proposed university in Dakar. Ultimately, increasing international pressures forced colonial officials to relent at least partially. In 1946, UNESCO launched its fundamental education program that targeted sub-Saharan Africa, and French colonial officials were desperate to keep the organization out of France's African territories. That same year, the United Nations started to demand reporting on education not just in the trust territories under its supervision but all colonial possessions, which French officials recognized could be potentially embarrassing for the administration.[102] The UN Trusteeship Council, which formally oversaw French governance in Togo and Cameroon, had already been fiercely critical of France for failing to develop higher education in its African territories. In 1947, the first tripartite Franco-Belgo-British Colonial Conference met in Paris in 1947 to set up an "intercolonial front" against this onslaught of international oversight in the colonial education sector. The tripartite conference met again in early 1949 in response to the inclusion of the right to education in the Universal Declaration of Human Rights (1948) and recommendations out of the UN General Assembly to guarantee equal rights to equal education and a proposal to create a common university for the trust territories.[103] French officials hoped that moving forward quickly with the university in Dakar would help stave off that latter possibility. Those international considerations, combined with the campaign of the African deputies, eventually pushed the French colonial administration to make some concessions. It agreed to share responsibility for the Dakar institution with the MEN and ensure that classes would be open for the 1949–1950 school year.[104]

The terms of joint jurisdiction stipulated that the Dakar institution would be affiliated with a university in the metropole, where students would complete the full cycle of their studies until capacity was built up in Dakar. Colonial

---

102. The British had gotten a jump on the French in that regard. The Asquith Commission (1943) led to the creation of the first university colleges in British Africa immediately after the war. The British also had a more robust response to UN pressure on education in the trust territories. In 1947, the British issued a ten-year plan for education in its trust territory in Tanganyika and infused an extra one million pounds into the education system there. Clive Whitehead, "The Impact of the Second World War on Education in Britain's Colonial Empire," in Roy Lowe, ed., *Education and the Second World War: Studies in Schooling and Social Change* (London: Routledge, 1992), 152–153.

103. Matasci, "Une 'UNESCO africaine'?" I discuss this at greater length in chapter 5.

104. Letter from Gaston, MFOM Inspection-Générale de l'Enseignement et de la Jeunesse, to Donzelot, MEN, dir-Enseignement Sup, August, 18 1949: AN F17/17641. Jessica Pearson has detailed a similar French colonial response during this period to pressure from the UN family of organizations in the health sector in her *The Colonial Politics of Global Health: France and the United Nations in Postwar Africa* (Cambridge, MA: Harvard University Press, 2018).

officials, who were wary of a concentration of African students in Paris, lobbied hard for that affiliation to be with the University of Bordeaux. Senghor adamantly opposed the choice of Bordeaux, a city that had a long history of profiting from slavery and colonial exploitation.[105] Capelle, who had by this time resigned his post as education director in AOF in protest over the general obstructionist attitude of the colonial administration, lobbied the MEN to respect Senghor's position and affiliate the Dakar institution either with the University of Paris system or with Capelle's own institution, the University of Nancy. However, Capelle's personal view of Senghor's opposition betrays the same paternalist and resentful attitude we have seen throughout this chapter. In a letter urging Jean Sarrailh, rector of the University of Paris, to support Senghor's bid for an affiliation with Paris or Nancy, Capelle explained: "The city of Bordeaux represents for African *autochtones* the logic of the Colonial Pact," a view he characterized as "both sentimental and unjust." Nevertheless, Capelle reported that that argument had made an impression on the Grand Conseil in Dakar, and so the administration ought to take it into consideration.[106]

The outcome of all this bureaucratic wrangling mirrored Capelle's ambivalent effort to take African positions seriously. When the Institut des Hautes Études de Dakar (IHED) officially opened its doors in 1950, it was formally affiliated with both the University of Paris *and* the University of Bordeaux. The IHED did not grant the same degrees as those delivered in the metropole, and the curriculum remained under the partial discretion of the colonial authorities.[107] These half measures failed to deliver on the promise of robust equality and racial justice that Senghor held so dear. They also reflected a potent combination of older habits of racial paternalism and new racial resentments in the face of postwar pressures to end racism. That toxic mixture of ambivalent feelings and unequal institutions is the essence of postwar racial common sense.

The first cohort of African students who enrolled in the IHED was painfully aware of these dynamics. They did not leave it to their elders to contest colonial intransigence and the ongoing structural inequality they felt the slip-

---

105. In the same speech before the Grand Conseil cited earlier, Senghor exhorted: "In every case, we must refuse the tutelage of Bordeaux. It is enough that economically, this city continues the tradition of the old Colonial Pact." Projet du Décret portant création d'un Institut Universitaire à Dakar, Séance plénière du 3 juin 1949, AN: F17/17641.

106. Letter from Capelle, recteur de l'Université de Nancy, to Sarrailh, Recteur de l'Académie de Paris, October 3, 1949, AN: F17/17641.

107. The IHED finally become a proper French university that was fully integrated into the MEN's national system on the eve of Senegalese independence. On the neocolonial logics of that institutional arrangement, see Hendrickson, *Decolonizing 1968*; Tony Chafer, *The End of Empire in French West Africa: France's Successful Decolonization?* (New York: Berg, 2002).

shod IHED patently embodied. In November 1953, Moustapha Diallo, president of the main student association in Dakar (AGED), sent a formal letter of complaint to AOF's governor-general protesting conditions at the IHED. Diallo denounced the second-rate faculty hired to teach there and relayed his and fellow students' particular outrage that the administration seemed to think it was appropriate for high school teachers to lead university-level classes for Africans in law and letters and regular doctors without any pedagogical training to teach them medicine. Diallo sent copies of this letter to the ministers of education and Overseas France in Paris, the rector of Bordeaux, and the African leadership of the Grand Conseil and the territorial assemblies in the federation. He also published his letter in the December issue of the student newspaper, *Dakar-Étudiant*.[108]

In early January, the rector of University of Bordeaux issued a scathing non-response, in which he categorically refused to acknowledge Diallo's letter with its "gross falsehoods" and "insulting tone." He scolded Diallo and the AGED that they would do well to remind themselves of the "elementary rules of respect due to their masters" and, in a final condescending, paternalist flourish, concluded: "I can only assume that inexperience, due to the absence of a long-standing student tradition, can account, at least in part, for such recklessness." This remark not only dismissed African student grievances out of hand; it questioned Africans' understanding of what being a student entailed and implicitly undercut young Africans' claims for their right to higher education. Indeed, the rector closed his letter with a threat that any students who "persist in this attitude that misunderstands the traditional rules of the French University" would not be admitted to metropolitan institutions to complete their studies.[109]

This acrimonious back-and-forth continued for the next several months not only in private correspondence between African student leaders and French education officials but also in the pages of *Dakar-Étudiant*. In a June 1954 special issue entitled "Those Who Fight," the journal's editors, Thierno Diop and Samba Diarra, penned a blistering editorial that laid bare the underlying logics of postwar racial common sense. They wrote, "The great men of today are the students of yesterday. Those of tomorrow will be, God willing, the students of today. To misunderstand this is to go against history, the history of the promotion of peoples. And that attitude fatally leads to hate, whether

---

108. The full text of this letter, the subsequent back-and-forth with the colonial administration, and published editorials about those exchanges are reprinted in Sadji, *Le rôle de la génération charnière*, 175–184.

109. Sadji, *Le rôle de la génération charnière*, 176.

we like it or not." Then, citing Diallo's exchange with the rector of Bordeaux specifically, they declared: "The time to speak the truth has come. Messieurs of Bordeaux and Paris, be serious and do not play a game in bad faith that risks costing us dearly, perhaps in the very near future." African students would no longer accept acts of bad faith and "hollow words," and they urged their "supposed tutors" to recall Gandhi's caution to his own "betters" to mind the will of the youth and the danger of crossing them.[110]

The clash between African students and French colonial *and* metropolitan education officials over the IHED created new nodes of conflict between Black African students in Dakar and white French students in both metropole and colony. In 1954, the AGED withdrew from the National Union of French Students (UNEF) over the latter's refusal to support African students' battles with the French education authorities. That rift also escalated tensions between white and Black students enrolled at the IHED, which culminated in the dissolution of the AGED into two separate student associations, the General Union of Students of West Africa (UGEAO) and the General Association of French Students in Black Africa (AGEFAN). The AGEFAN, which quickly rejoined the UNEF, was exclusively white, but it was the UGEAO—which was majority Black but *not* exclusively so—that had to defend itself against charges of "racism." In a 1956 editorial in *Dakar-Étudiant*, UGEAO president Tidiane Baïdy Ly wrote, "African students are not racist. We want to loyally collaborate with our *European* comrades" (emphasis added). Ly continued that if the African students were racist, they would not have appointed Christian Lamaury, a *European*, to a leadership position in their organization. Ly quickly explained that this was not mere tokenism; rather, Lamaury "earned the trust of the Assembly" by being a true accomplice[111] in the fight for African equality and the fact that "he couldn't give a damn about the vicious slander unleashed on him by his compatriots."[112] While French observers doggedly sought to cast African student protest and politics as being all about *race*, Ly powerfully located the real roots of the

---

110. Sadji, *Le rôle de la génération charnière*, 182–183.

111. I use "accomplice" here instead of "ally" deliberately, inspired by the 2014 manifesto "Accomplices Not Allies: Abolishing the Ally Industrial Complex—an Indigenous Perspective." As the manifesto puts it, "the risks of an ally who provides support or solidarity (usually on a temporary basis) in a fight are much different than that of an accomplice. When we fight back or forward, together, becoming complicit in a struggle towards liberation, we are accomplices." With this distinction in mind, I find that Ly depicts Lamaury more as an accomplice than an ally. "Accomplices Not Allies," version 2, *Indigenous Action Media*, May 2, 2014, http://www.indigenousaction.org/wp-content/uploads/Accomplices-Not-Allies-print.pdf.

112. Sadji, *Le rôle de la génération charnière*, 184.

conflict between African and "European" students in Dakar in their opposing stances on racism.[113]

Toward the end of World War II, many Europeans and francophone Africans
began to hope for a postwar order free of racism. However, their aspirations
took on radically different forms. European intellectual and political elites in
organizations like the CAME approached race as if it were a primarily discursive and conceptual problem rather than a social and political one. They concentrated their efforts on expunging race as a category from the European
political lexicon and cultural repertoire, even though their hierarchical views
about the world's peoples and cultures did not necessarily change. Francophone Africans both young and old had a very different view of the matter.
Their focus on robust education reform in France's African territories grew
out of a conception of race as a relation of power that was deeply woven into
the social fabric and institutional arrangements of postwar Greater France. As
Europeans' turn away from racial language and conceptual categories seemed
to make race disappear in Europe, francophone Africans' tireless campaign for
racial justice was a constant, unwelcome reminder that racism remained a potent force shaping everyday lives and life trajectories in the postwar republic
and French Union.

   This foundational tension between European and francophone African understandings of race and racism contributed to the consolidation of a new
kind of postwar racial common sense. Associating race with non-Europeans
only in venues like the CAME turned race itself into a boundary between Europe and Africa. This hardened racial binary between Europeans and Africans
surfaced at the Brazzaville Conference and influenced how French officials
thought about African intellectual aptitudes and the suitability of Africans for
higher education. Such views then became part of the institutional framework
the French put in place for postwar colonial education reform, as is clearly reflected in the limited scope of French financial investments in expanding and
enhancing Africans' educational opportunities after the war. What is more,
francophone Africans' rhetorical strategy to frame their demands as a racial
justice issue struck a particularly discordant note at a time when Europeans
were trying to avoid any and all references to race. This tonal clash reinforced
an older repertoire of racist stereotypes about Africans as presumptuous and
irrational, which further strengthened the notion that Africans were naturally

---

113. For an excellent discussion of this distinction, see Karen E. Fields and Barbara Fields, *Race-craft: The Soul of Inequality in American Life* (New York: Verso, 2014).

unfit for advanced study. Dadet had accused the French of purposely pursuing a "politics of illiteracy" that reproduced structural inequality in France and French Africa. Postwar racial common sense encouraged French officials to attribute the abysmal state of colonial education to natural incompatibilities between Africans and "European" education rather than to French administrative practice, material investments, and policy choices. Acutely aware of these dynamics, young Africans at the Institut des Hautes Études de Dakar became increasingly isolated from their "European" peers in Dakar and in the student syndicalist movement in France, thus pitting Africans and Europeans, Blacks and whites, against one another. The growing number of African students in the metropole in the 1950s would experience the pernicious feedback loop of postwar racial common sense even more keenly.

CHAPTER 4

Encountering Diversity in France and "Eurafrica"

Between the founding of the French Union in 1946 and the 1949–1950 academic year, rates of schooling slowly but steadily rose in French Africa. By 1950, 100,000 more Africans in AOF and AEF were enrolled in some kind of school. Most of those gains were at the primary level, but Africans in secondary and higher education also increased from 5,819 in 1946 to 8,414 in 1950. Of those, 1,200 were studying in France on state scholarships.[1] State support for mission schools during and after the war ensured that a disproportionate number of students on scholarships, known as *boursiers,* were Catholic; in 1951, half of the African students in France were Catholic, even though Catholics then made up just under 6 percent of French Africans overall.[2] The number of *boursiers* continued to climb in the 1950s and reached more than four thousand by decade's end.

More African students also went to France in the 1950s without state aid. French officials assiduously tried to discourage the practice, but the constitution of 1946 guaranteed French Africans the right to seek employment and education in the metropole. Therefore, the administration had no legal recourse to prevent young Africans from enrolling themselves in any French

---

1. Tableaux statistiques, Première Partie, *Enseignement Outre-Mer: Bulletin de l'Inspection-Générale de l'enseignement et de la jeunesse du Ministère de la France d'Outre-Mer* (December 1950): 37–41, ANOM: BIB AOM 20505/1950.

2. Foster, *African Catholic,* 128.

school that would have them. *Non-boursiers* were sometimes able to secure state aid after their arrival, incentivizing parents and students to try their luck. The danger for these students was not just the possibility of academic failure; the cost of living in France was always higher than expected, and young Africans' uncertain access to food, clothing, and shelter jeopardized their health. Death became such a regular occurrence that African students organized an annual memorial service for their comrades who died pursuing their studies in France each year.[3] Nonetheless, the prospect of social advancement encouraged thousands to take the risk. By the end of the 1950s, *non-boursiers* almost equaled their state-funded counterparts, bringing the total number of African students in European France to more than eight thousand.[4]

Despite its modest size, the African student population in France in the 1950s has generated considerable scholarly interest. The extant literature focuses on how African students and youth leaders inserted themselves in the process of decolonization by founding their own networks of associations, publications, and syndicalist movements. Politically organized and passionately committed to playing their part in shaping Africa's future, this cohort of African students pursued a more radical anticolonial politics than the older generation of francophone African elites who were working for colonial reform from within the French government. African students grouped themselves along multiple axes, including territory and religion, but they also transcended those divisions in a federated Black African student union, the Fédération des étudiants d'Afrique noire en France (FEANF). Scholars have stressed the pan-African ethos of the FEANF and its increasingly militant advocacy for independence. The literature also details French responses to African student mobilizations, particularly the surveillance of African youth and censorship of their journals, and presents those tactics as overt political repression in a highly charged Cold War context in which African political organizing and protest were often blamed on foreign Communist provocateurs.[5]

---

3. For a description of this practice, see "Premier Novembre," *Bulletin Mensuel de l'Association des Étudiants Congolais,* no. 7 (December 1954), ANOM: AEF GGAEF 5D/280.

4. Fabienne Guimont, *Les étudiants africains en France, 1950–1965* (L'Harmattan, 1997), chap. 2.

5. Michel Sot, ed., *Étudiants africains en France, 1951–2001: Cinquante ans de relations France-Afrique, quel avenir?* (Paris: Karthala, 2002); Françoise Blum, "Transfers of Knowledge, Multiple Identities: The Example of Students from the FEANF (Fédération des Étudiants d'Afrique Noire en France)," *African Identities* 16, no. 2 (2018): 130–145, https://doi.org/10.1080/14725843.2018.1449719; Blum, "L'indépendance sera révolutionnaire ou ne sera pas: Étudiants africains en France contre l'ordre colonial," *Cahiers d'histoire: Revue d'histoire critique* 126 (2015): 119–238, https://doi.org/10.4000/chrhc.4165; Louisa Rice, "Between Empire and Nation: Francophone West African Students and Decolonization," *Atlantic Studies* 10, no. 1 (2013), https://doi.org/10.1080/14788810.2013.764106; Amady Aly Dieng, *Les premiers pas de la Fédération des Étudiants d'Afrique noire en France (1950–1955): De l'Union française à Bandoung* (Paris: L'Harmattan,

Encounters between French officials and African students in France in the 1950s can also be read as a struggle over those students' entry into conversations about youth, pluralism, and global transformation that French, African, and European political leaders had been having since the middle war years. African students were not equal participants in those discussions, and their actions did not achieve their intended effects. Nevertheless, the presence of a vocal francophone student population moving back and forth between French Africa and metropolitan France—a population that was, in a way, bringing into being the Franco-African polity that French and African politicians hoped for in the postwar conjuncture—changed the terms of debate. As they navigated the tortuous path to obtaining a decent education and professional credentials in France's postwar empire, young Africans formed their own views about multiracial democracy and the viability of a Franco-African community. African students' critiques of ongoing colonial injustice and French racism, and French reactions to those critiques, were a key part of the toxic feedback loop of postwar racial common sense. Security services certainly monitored young Africans' political activity, but administrative surveillance carried out by educators and youth workers themselves was more of an ethnographic enterprise. And like so many midcentury ethnographers, the colonial bureaucracy's informants had a blinkered view of Africans' social attitudes, comportment, and interactions with their French peers. Their "findings" produced new patterns of racialization that renaturalized structural inequality and race prejudice.

These high-stakes Franco-African encounters took place in a French Union trying to integrate itself into an expanding network of European institutions. The core institutions of today's European Union were all founded in the 1950s; first came the creation of the European Coal and Steel Community (1952), whose governing bodies formed the basis of the European Commission, the European Parliament, and the European Court of Justice; then the 1957 Rome Treaty established the Common Market (EEC) and the European Atomic Energy Agency (EURATOM). In addition, the Council of Europe was also developing its own parallel and complementary institutions in Strasbourg: the European Parliamentary Assembly (1949), made up of members of the national parliaments of member-states; the European Convention on Human Rights (1950); and ultimately, the European Court of Human Rights (1959).

This European institution building reframed the urgency of educating Africans in the 1950s—whether in France or French Africa—as a crucial building block in the construction of the modernist, technocratic project of "Eurafrica."

2003); Pierre Nkwengue, *L'union nationale des étudiants du Kamerun: Ou la contribution des étudiants africains à l'émancipation de l'Afrique* (Paris: L'Harmattan, 2005).

For many French officials, the success of colonial youth and education initiatives was no longer just a question of France's relationships with its African colonies. As the leaders of tomorrow, francophone African youth, along with their metropolitan French and west European counterparts, now seemed to hold the future of Europe-Africa relations in their hands. Moreover, European efforts to elevate pluralism as a bedrock value of united Europe and dissociate the new Europe from its colonial, racist past further raised the stakes of democratizing France's empire and including young Africans in quintessentially republican institutions like schools. Some African politicians, most famously but not only Léopold Senghor, saw European integration as an opportunity to force France to make good on its postwar promises: Senghor and others ardently championed Eurafrica from the late 1940s on.[6] African students in France in the 1950s, on the other hand, overwhelmingly opposed Eurafrica. In a 1957 editorial in response to the signing of the Treaty of Rome, Samba Ndiaye, editor-in-chief of the FEANF's main publication, *L'Étudiant d'Afrique Noire*, denounced Eurafrica as a form of "colonial reconquest" and the Common Market as a road map for the "superexploitation" of African resources. He concluded bitterly: "So much for the 'Spirit of '46.'"[7] Many important political and geopolitical shifts occurred in the intervening decade, but Ndiaye's position cannot be fully understood without considering his generation's experience of enduring structural inequality combined with new forms of racial resentment and everyday racism as they tried to complete their educations in postwar France.

French Strategies of "Managing" Diversity: From *Brassage* to Race Relations

Throughout the late colonial period, Africans seeking middle school, high school, and university educations came to France because local opportunities for postprimary schooling were exceedingly rare and advanced degrees virtually nonexistent. As colonial officials scrambled to build more schools in the territories in the late 1940s, sending African students to the metropole was a necessary stopgap measure. But to young Africans' great consternation, travel to France remained the surest way for them to pursue advanced study throughout the 1950s. In a 1957 group interview in the French press, one African student did not mince words: "We come to France because the education here

---

6. I discuss Senghor and Eurafrica in the introduction.

7. Samba Ndiaye, "Nouvelle mesure arbitraire," *L'Étudiant d'Afrique Noire*, no. 11 (April 1957), reprinted in Sadji, *Le rôle de la génération charnière*, 207.

is much more complete than in the overseas territories. France, it is often said, does a lot for its territories. In reality, it has not done all that it could do. Period." He continued, "By coming to France, the African student is asserting himself. For him, it's an initial victory, that of moving from third-rate circumstances to a universal situation."[8]

Such feelings were precisely what French reformers wanted to avoid by providing education of higher quality to Africans in the territories, but the requisite resources and political will to make that happen never materialized. French officials tried to put a positive spin on the fact that African students were coming to France out of necessity by emphasizing that their sojourns in France opened up new opportunities for metropolitan French and African young people to get to know one another better. They hoped African students would learn to mix and mingle with their French peers and that the rising generation of French and African youth would develop genuine admiration and mutual respect across racial lines. French officials and African politicians alike referred to that process as *brassage,* a term that can mean either intermixing or incorporation. In the early 1950s, French and African leaders championed *brassage* as a way to overcome the legacies of racism and colonialism. However, celebrating *brassage* served different purposes for French and African leaders. For the French, commitment to *brassage* was offered up as proof of France's goodwill toward its African citizens and an unequivocal rejection of racism. For Africans, *brassage* justified more financial and material support for young Africans to study and train in France.[9]

African students were quick to note that such support was in short supply. However much French rhetoric celebrated African and French students mixing and mingling in the metropole, French policies denied most Africans the opportunity. Age limits kept anyone over twenty-five from obtaining a scholarship for higher education in the metropole, even though most African schoolchildren started later and took longer than their French peers because of the dismal state of primary education for Africans in the territories. The number of African *boursiers* in France was also kept low because the colonial administration summarily rejected scholarship applications for courses of study in France that could be pursued in Africa. In a 1953 "Plea for the African Student" in the Catholic student journal *Tam-Tam,* Antoine Yaméogo denounced both maneuvers as patently racist. The age limits perpetuated structural racism because Africans

---

8. Lena de Faramond, "De Jeunes Africains Parlent," *Pensée française-fédération,* special issue, "Jeunesses d'Afrique Noire," no. 3 (January 15, 1957): 27, ANOM: BIB SOM C/BR/3324.

9. *Brassage* was a recurrent theme in Houphouët-Boigny's successful campaign to expand exchange programs for Africans in France during school breaks. See, for instance, his letter to the minister of national education, December 7, 1956, AN: F17/15727.

were not given "equal chances" from the outset, he argued, while the rejection of applications on the grounds of a viable local alternative was racially discriminatory because it applied only to Africans. "Time in France is necessary for a complete formation," he wrote. "The French know this well, for the obstruction of student *boursiers* in Africa does not apply to white *boursiers!*"[10]

Significantly, Yaméogo, who went on to serve as economics minister in postindependence Upper Volta (later Burkina Faso), further exposed French hypocrisy toward African students in relation to European students. He wrote, "European countries have grasped the full importance of university exchanges: English, Germans, etc., study in France; and French study in England, in Germany." If they all recognize that cultural exchange and the experience of being abroad expands young people's horizons, "why refuse to Africans what is good for Europeans?" Yaméogo also considered the broader societal benefit of Africans studying and training in France in a comparative perspective: "The gains made by Africans in France will combine with Africa's own assets, and thus an original, African civilization will be born! Other so-called civilized countries did not develop otherwise."[11] For Yaméogo, there was nothing particularly African about culturally enriching exchanges driving social and civilizational progress; that Africa suffered from a particular lack in that regard was just another racist fallacy.

However disingenuous French discourse about *brassage* may have been, it had real consequences. As a stated policy goal, it encouraged bureaucrats in both the colonial and education ministries to monitor how French and African students interacted. That entailed fastidious surveillance of and endless commentary on African students' activities, behavior, and overall comportment, in France and back home in the territories. State officials obtained this information from various sources, soliciting reports from a vast network of educators and youth workers.[12] In the late 1950s, French officials even commissioned the national polling agency (IFOP) to survey African students about their experiences in France.[13] This administrative scrutiny was consistently inflected with ideas about "the African personality" that proved incredibly difficult to dislodge. Colonial

10. Antoine Yaméogo, "Plaidoyer pour l'Étudiant Africain," *Tam-Tam,* deuxième année, no. 4 (April 1953), Bibliothèque Nationale de France (BNF). Yaméogo's reflections on Europe and racism in the 1950s may have proved formative later in his career. He represented Upper Volta in the negotiations with the EEC that led to the Yaoundé Accords (1963) and, in the late 1970s, was a key figure in the campaign to get the International Monetary Fund (IMF) to stop lending to apartheid South Africa.

11. Yaméogo, "Plaidoyer pour l'Étudiant Africain," *Tam-Tam,* BNF, 10.

12. Présidence du Conseil, Haut Comité de la Jeunesse de France et d'Outre-Mer, Groupe de travail "Contacts entre jeunes de France et d'Outre-Mer," January 1957, AN: F17/15727.

13. See, for instance, "Les Étudiants d'Outre-Mer en France," IFOP, November 1960, CAC: 19771 275/28.

tropes and racist stereotypes—especially about African sexuality, intelligence, and temperament—withstood evidence to the contrary again and again.

A common trope among French officials was that African students had an irrational penchant for studying the law rather than pursuing more "useful" professions tailored to Africa's particular needs. This perception was rehearsed year after year, even though it was not true. In the 1950s, the vast majority of African postsecondary students in France were enrolled in programs in the sciences, medicine, pharmacy, dentistry, and engineering.[14] The racist discourse about Africans' course of study was widely commented on by their French peers. In 1958, the largest metropolitan French student union weighed in on the issue, noting that the pervasive stereotype that African students flocked to the law "out of their love of controversy and endless debate" was false. However, they did not dispute that Africans were disproportionately going into law. That distortion was left unchallenged.[15]

Of course, some young Africans did want to study law or other fields French officials found pointless—not in general, just for Africans. Those students were often hamstrung by school administrators who refused to let them choose their courses for themselves. After completing the *bac* at the Lycée Van Vollenhoven in Dakar in 1955, Amadou Booker Sadji, son of the prominent Senegalese writer Abdoulaye Sadji, sought a scholarship to study German at a university in France. Despite France's deepening institutional relationship with West Germany in European institutions at precisely that time, the official reviewing Sadji's application saw no benefit in Africans studying German language and culture. He refused Sadji's request and pushed him to pursue geography at the Institut des Hautes Études de Dakar instead. Sadji continued to press his case and ultimately prevailed, but when he finally arrived at the University of Toulouse, he was a full year behind his peers. He recalls how he constantly feared having to abandon his beloved German and resign himself to studying geography, a field "arbitrarily decided for me" by the French colonial authorities.[16]

The provision of scholarships produced new nodes of conflict and racialization. State aid to the *boursiers* bred palpable and widespread resentment. French officials and the colonial press complained that the state should not financially support students who were openly critical of France. Rather than engaging with the substance of critiques like Yaméogo's and Sadji's about

---

14. Tableaux Statistiques in the *Bulletin de l'Inspection-Générale de l'Enseignement et de la Jeunesse du Ministère de la France d'Outre-Mer*, ANOM: BIB AOM/20505/1950-1958.

15. See "Le Logement des Étudiants d'Outre-Mer," in *UNEF Informations—Outre-Mer* (1958), BNF.

16. Sadji, *Le rôle de la génération charnière*, 191–196. I return to Sadji's tortuous path to study German in chapter 5.

insufficient resources, coercive measures, and unfair treatment, administrators and commentators dismissed African student demands as intolerable "ingratitude" that reflected a misplaced sense of entitlement, a set of qualities that became increasingly common in postwar characterizations of francophone African elites. Yaméogo's piece in *Tam-Tam* inspired a vitriolic tirade in a weekly satirical magazine in Dakar, *Les Échos de l'Afrique Noire*, that was usually fiercely critical of the colonial administration. (The publisher and author of the rant, Maurice Voisin, was sued by the local authorities for defamation and even served jail time for his incessant invectives against colonial abuses of authority.) Voisin attacked Yaméogo personally as a "petit gourmand" for suggesting that African students' stipends were so low they often went hungry. Voisin then declared that all Africans needed to be made to understand that "they are not owed everything." Indeed, he suggested that African students got more support from the government than their French peers. He concluded his screed by mockingly anticipating the accusations of racism that were sure to follow: "Why should we sacrifice our metropolitan students . . . and replace them with black students? Where is the racism there? Where is the demagoguery?"[17]

Metropolitan commentators were no more sympathetic. In a series of articles for the pro-empire magazine *Climats* in 1952, Annie Gacon offered scathing critiques of African *boursiers*, many of whom she refused to recognize as "real students." As part of her research, Gacon wrote to officials in the education ministry for information about the funding structure of African students' scholarships, statistics on "mixed" marriages, and African students' relations with French women more generally. She was particularly keen to learn more about other "distractions" affecting their studies and, sarcastically, "this famous *'brassage'* we hear so much about." She inquired about what happened when they returned to Africa, a question she posed in both sociocultural and political terms: Did they bring "our European habits" back with them? Were they "our advocates" before the local population or "the opposite"?[18]

Gacon received a full report that focused on demographics and details about student aid packages. Shortly thereafter, Gacon decided to go to Senegal to see for herself how the *boursiers* spent their time back home. In another piece for *Climats* later that fall (1952), she relayed her outrage at what she had seen. She affirmed, "We are here *FOR* the real overseas students, those who work and live loyally among us by trying to assimilate the habits and culture of our country;

17. Maurice Voisin, "Si Nous Parlions un peu de la Situation des Étudiants Africains," *Les Échos de l'Afrique Noire*, June 29, 1953. Reprinted in *Tam-Tam*, troisième année, no. 1 (November–December 1953), 15–18, BNF.

18. Letter from Annie Gacon to M. le Chef de Cabinet de M. le ministre de l'Éducation Nationale, May 14, 1952, AN: F/17/17768.

we are resolutely *AGAINST* the agitators and troublemakers, against those African bums who deceitfully call themselves students but who are not." She was particularly incensed by the tone and tenor of a gathering at a movie theater in Saint Louis. Gacon was incredulous that virtually all the students in attendance, whom she accused of peddling "lies and hypocrisy" against France, were on paid leave from their studies in the metropole. She closed by distinguishing between the "unruly" *boursiers*, whose diatribes she found laden with "all the clichés of communist dialectics," and the older generation of francophone elites whom she praised for their moderate views and steady character.[19] Her depiction of *boursiers* was entirely one-dimensional: they were ungrateful, unrefined, and dangerous.

Housing was another node of bitter conflict. African students struggled to find suitable lodging among the general student population, both on account of the expense and because many landlords refused to rent to them. African organizations, prominent individuals, and eventually, territorial governments sometimes felt they had to take matters into their own hands. Already in 1947, Jeanne Vialle, senator for Oubangui-Chari, had personally purchased two hostels, including a fifty-room building in Paris, to house female students who could not afford suitable housing on their meager and often delayed government stipends.[20] French officials were torn over whether they should encourage such special dormitories for Africans in France. Officials in Paris were especially concerned that doing so would fatally undermine *brassage*.

Despite those reservations, special student centers and dormitories for Africans were created not only in Paris but at all provincial universities with large contingents of African students in the early 1950s.[21] Most notably, a special pavilion for students from "overseas France" was created at the Cité Universitaire Internationale in Paris in 1951, and the lion's share of beds there were reserved for Africans. The Cité U, as it is commonly called, had been founded in the early 1930s as a residential village for international students in the spirit of promoting international intellectual and cultural cooperation, primarily among Europeans.[22] The Maison de la France d'Outre-Mer broadened the Cité U's purview by including students from the empire. That inclusion gave

---

19. Annie Gacon, "La Propagande communiste en Afrique Noire: Choses vues et entendues à un meeting 'd'étudiants' à Saint-Louis-du-Sénégal," *Climats* (October 30–November 5, 1952), ANOM: 1AFFPOL/2199.

20. Joseph-Gabriel, *Reimagining Liberation*, 90–91.

21. For the founding documents of the Maison, see ANOM: 1AFFPOL/2265. On local *foyers des étudiants africains*, see ANS: 18G/211 (160). For heated exchanges between the colonial and education ministries on the creation of the *foyers* in the early 1950s, see AN: F/17/17768.

22. Akira Iriye links the founding of the Cité U to the League of Nation's Eurocentric initiatives in interwar international intellectual cooperation. See Iriye, *Cultural Internationalism*. The vast majority of

the project a progressive veneer, but the idea for the Maison was first proposed in response to unambiguous perceptions of racial threat shortly after the Liberation. As we saw in chapter 3, in 1945 the governor general of AOF, Pierre Cournarie, was so provoked by the angry tone of the correspondence of a single African medical student in Montpellier that Cournarie called on the central colonial authority in Paris to steer all African students into segregated dormitories and put them under rigorous surveillance. At the time, Cournarie's concerns were dismissed by more moderate officials in the metropole like Henri Laurentie; and yet, Cournarie's calls for extensive surveillance of African students and special housing were heeded.[23]

By the mid-1950s, bureaucrats in both the colonial and education ministries had grown more anxious that African students were becoming ghettoized in the Maison de la France d'Outre-Mer and its provincial analogues. As more African students arrived in France, they seemed to mix with metropolitan students less. The centers continued to receive substantial funding from the education ministry as well as from the overtaxed budgets of the territories. The passage of the *Loi Cadre* in 1956, which devolved more authority to local governments in the territories, made it more difficult for French officials in the metropole to change course. Once the territories were in control of their own budgets, they were free to purchase special residences for their students at their discretion. When the territorial assembly of Côte d'Ivoire decided to buy a building in Paris for its students in 1956, officials' hands were tied, though they complained bitterly. Just before the passage of the *Loi Cadre*, education officials wrote to Gaston Defferre, minister of Overseas France and author of the law, protesting the Ivorian assembly's plan. Both the rector of the Academy of Paris and the head of the Office of Overseas Students insisted that African students should be dispersed throughout the country to be "mixed [*brassé*] with metropolitan students, and not grouped together in a center that is more or less closed, where particularisms grow stronger." Defferre agreed that it would be preferable to promote "*brassage* with metropolitan students," but since the purchase was authorized by the territorial assembly, there was nothing he could do. His opposition, he hastened to add, would be particularly inopportune "at the very moment when I am trying so hard to get the *Loi Cadre* passed to give more autonomy to the territories."[24] Ultimately, the centers outlasted

---

pavilions from the interwar period were European, though the United States and Latin America were also well represented.

23. On the extensive surveillance of students from AOF, both during their time in France and when they returned home, see multiple dossiers: ANS: 17G/269 (111), 17G/604 (152), O/666, O/668 and O/669 (31), 21G/210 (178); and ANOM: 1/AFFPOL/2265, 1/AFFPOL/2395, 1/AFFPOL/2398.

24. Billères-Defferre correspondence, March 20 and April 5, 1956, AN: F17/15727.

the end of empire and became an important part of the educational infrastructure for receiving African students in the postcolonial era.[25]

Concerns about housing and the behavior of the *boursiers* were key parts of the rationale for extensive administrative surveillance of African students in the 1950s. That surveillance offers a worm's-eye view of the evolution of French views about francophone Africans in a rapidly changing domestic and geopolitical context. Cournarie's move from thinking about one individual student to the African study body writ large became standard practice by the 1950s. The resulting portraits of African students were then reproduced and circulated not only among French officials but also among educators, youth organizers, and other nonstate actors who worked directly with young Africans studying or training in France.

The issue of interracial sex and marriage highlights the stickiness of colonial tropes and racist stereotypes. According to an IFOP poll commissioned by French officials, by the end of the 1950s, only a tiny fraction (4 percent) of African young men living in France had married French women.[26] Interviews with African students reveal they had their own diverse views on interracial marriage; most seemed to feel it was not a good idea. As several male students put it in 1957, "since they are duly rejected by European society and African society, such unions are best avoided at all costs."[27] Moreover, African students criticized French dating practices and lax sexual mores in their journals, memoirs, and other writings from the period.[28] Nevertheless, reports from French officials and local educators assumed that African young men pursued relationships with French women relentlessly, so much so that observers frequently registered their surprise at the "propriety" of African male students' behavior toward French girls.[29] Even though this was repeatedly proved to be a nonissue, this commentary did not go away.

The tenacity of such stereotypes may be explained at least in part by the fact that African students in France were written about as an anonymous mass rather than as individuals. As the ranks of African students in France swelled from a few dozen in 1945 to several thousand by the mid-1950s, administrative correspondence rarely identified African students by name. This depersonalization

25. For correspondence, administrative reports, and budgets, see the dossier "Maison de la France d'Outre-Mer—subventions AOF—1953–1958," ANS: 18G/211 (160). For the postcolonial era, see dossiers on the Office de Coopération et d'Accueil Universitaire, successor of the Office des Étudiants d'Outre-Mer, in CAC: 19780596/42. See also Sot, *Étudiants africains en France.*

26. "Les Étudiants d'Outre-Mer en France," IFOP, November 1960, CAC: 19771275/28. None of the female African students polled had married French men.

27. Faramond, "De Jeunes Africains Parlent," 30, ANOM: BIB SOM C/BR/3324.

28. Bernard Dadié, *Un nègre à Paris* (Paris: Éditions Présence Africaine, 1959), 183.

29. Rapport de M. Lamy Roger sur les stages ruraux, undated (c. 1957), CAC: 19860445/2.

was reproduced in the media, even in articles whose express purpose was to better acquaint the French public with the African student population. In a 1957 feature entitled "Young Africans Speak," the author-interviewer never identified her student interlocutors by name. Instead, the reader learns only their territory of origin and course of study: a Togolese and a Dahomean studying law, two Guineans interning as radio technicians, and another Guinean studying gynecology. The anonymity of the interviewees is particularly jarring in light of the thrust of the piece: "For most metropolitans, the young Africans they cross in the street or stare at distractedly in the metro or on the bus remain rather foreign. Why?" She attributed this to most French people's willful indifference to the historic changes underway in French Africa, although she conceded many French continued to hold political, social, and racial prejudices of which they themselves were only dimly aware.[30] By not naming her subjects, the author, who hoped to redress this situation, missed an obvious opportunity to demystify African students for the French public.

More egregious, however, is the sole image accompanying the piece (see figure 4.1). The article's subjects are postgraduate students living in Paris, but the image on the title page is of an African child in traditional dress, naked from the waist up, with a bicycle in a desolate field. The profound contrast between this stock colonial imagery and the objective of the article is all the more remarkable given the author's own description of the everyday exoticization African students endured in France: "All it takes is to listen to the amused reflections of pedestrians when they pass an African in the street to realize that a good number of French people still view a 'black' as an object of curiosity, a 'savage,' a 'big child' taken straight out of the exotic imagery in which the call of the tam-tam blends into the mysterious sounds of the bush at night." She added that such views had real consequences: "One can also cite an incalculable number of cases in which a landlord refuses to house an African student because of prejudice and retrograde ideas." She then reflected, "What most offends the young African who arrives in France, is to be seen as someone who has everything to gain and nothing to give."[31]

The French public's general indifference to and ignorance of colonial youth stands in stark contrast with a general preoccupation and desire to understand young people at precisely this time in French popular culture. "Young Africans Speak" was published the same year as Françoise Giroud's landmark exposé on French youth in *L'Express* (October 1957), in which she dubbed the young postwar generation "the New Wave." She quickly followed up that piece with

---

30. Faramond, "De Jeunes Africains Parlent," 25, ANOM: BIB SOM C/BR/3324.
31. Faramond, "De Jeunes Africains Parlent," 29, ANOM: BIB SOM C/BR/3324.

Figure 4.1. Title image of the article "De Jeunes Africains parlent." Courtesy of the Archives Nationales d'Outre-Mer, ANOM: BIB SOM c/br/3324.

a massive survey of millions of young French that was published in several mainstream news outlets to showcase young people's opinions across boundaries of class, gender, education, and region. As Richard Ivan Jobs has shown, Giroud's work helped "define a social group by intentionally homogenizing and generalizing the young."[32] Thus, young Africans were being reified as a group apart at the very moment that "youth" was crystallizing in the French imagination as a vital and cohesive national category.

"Young Africans Speak" ended with a set of deeply ambivalent reflections on African difference. The interviewer drew two conclusions from her conversations with African students. The first speaks directly to stereotypes about African intelligence and ability to reason. She affirmed, "The positions of these young Africans can sometimes seem unnuanced, brutal, and impassioned, but they are resolute, stable, and coherent." To further drive home the point, she added, "none of them contradicted themselves at any point in the discussion. And when they gave an opinion, they justified it straightaway." Her second impression spoke more to why *brassage* did not seem to be working. Unlike many administrators, she did not put the blame solely on young Africans' shoulders. She acknowledged their distrust of metropolitan French was strong, but she did not think it was based on any kind of inherent "bias." With people they trust, she reassured her readers, they are quite capable of warm and thoughtful exchanges of views. The difficulty for them, she concluded, was in finding "true interlocutors."[33]

The "reserve" of African students was a common refrain among local educators and youth workers throughout the decade. On the eve of African independence in 1960, officials in the education ministry urged rectors of universities across France with large contingents of African students to designate special faculty mentors to work with them more closely. Responses to this missive varied widely: some insisted there was no need since their African students did not seem to have any issues; some opposed the idea on principle, arguing that integration should proceed "naturally" without signaling anyone out for special treatment; others replied curtly that they had more important priorities.[34] Several reported that their faculty had already taken it upon themselves to reach out to African students—that they had been inviting them to dinner or to their summer homes for years.[35] The rector in Bordeaux forwarded several letters

---

32. Jobs, *Riding the New Wave*, 32–33.

33. Faramond, "De Jeunes Africains Parlent," 30, ANOM: BIB SOM C/BR/3324.

34. Dossier "Réponses à la circulaire ministérielle du 15 janvier 1960," CAC: 19770181/6; Letter from Recteur Clermont-Ferrand to HJCS, May 9, 1960, CAC: 19860445/6.

35. Letter from Doyen de la Faculté de Médecine to the Recteur de l'Académie de Bordeaux, February 19, 1960, CAC: 19860445/6. See also the response from the rector at the University of Nancy in the Dossier "Réponses," CAC: 19860445/6.

from faculty detailing activities already undertaken and impressions of the students. One law professor wrote that in his ten years of experience, African students were initially intimidated and withdrawn, but he found that "they open up very quickly and are glad to have personal contacts with French families."[36] Another similarly commented that in the students' reserve, "one could detect a kind of fear," but that once students realize "we do not have a segregationist attitude, they open up and bloom and offer a lot of trust, deference, and attachment." He concluded, "I believe it is a duty—a duty of charity in the good sense of the word—to try to liberate them from their fearful reserve which certainly causes them pain."[37] By portraying African students as suffering from debilitating inferiority complexes without serious consideration of how that might be tied to their lived experience, such accounts naturalized those dispositions as intrinsically African.

These portraits of African students informed how French officials structured exchange programs that brought African youth to France. Planning documents often referred to "what we know of the African temperament" or warned that program organizers must "beware of the well-known distrust of the students."[38] Those observations often led program organizers to focus even more on fostering personal contacts between young Africans and the local French population and scrutinizing those interactions ever more minutely. *Brassage* was the raison d'être of these initiatives, even as the myopic monitoring of African students hardened conceptions of African difference, reshaped policy in counterproductive ways, and made *brassage* more difficult in practice.

Throughout the decade, French officials invoked *brassage* as a distinctly French approach to managing diversity. However, administrative discourses about the African student population were laying the groundwork for the "race relations" model of postwar liberalism that scholars have typically associated with Britain, Germany, and the United States to take root in France.[39] That model places the onus on minoritized populations to integrate into the dominant society without expecting society or individual members of the dominant group to change from the encounter. It does not address the deep structural roots of continuing inequalities. French officials hoped that racial identifications would simply fade away through *brassage*, but African students in France kept

---

36. Letter from Jean Brethe de la Gressaye to Doyen Garrigou-Lagrange, February 27, 1960, CAC: 19860445/6.

37. Letter from Lucien Martin to Doyen Garrigou-Lagrange, February 15, 1960, CAC: 19860445/6.

38. Note à l'attention de M. le HCJS a/s projet d'établissement de contacts entre des étudiants africains et la population de Villefranche de Rouergue (Aveyron), undated; Directeur de l'Office des Étudiants d'Outre-Mer à Délégué Académique, Dir-BUS, May 3, 1960, CAC: 19860445/5.

39. See Fehrenbach, *Race after Hitler;* Paul Gilroy, *"There Ain't No Black in the Union Jack": The Cultural Politics of Race and Nation* (Chicago: University of Chicago Press, 1991).

forcing their French interlocutors to think about race and confront the realities of structural racism. Young Africans' reactions to French society and their vocal protests about the racism they experienced in France and French Africa encouraged officials to frame hostile Franco-African encounters as an inevitable, intractable "race relations" problem.

Africans in monthlong *stages* had different impressions of France than those who became long-term student residents, but the former also addressed racism head-on. Unlike the student population in the metropole who spoke out about racism *in France,* participants in short-term youth exchanges focused on racism in the territories. An evaluation of youth exchanges in 1956 cited one young Mauritanian teacher who completed a *stage* with the secular youth group Francs et Franches Camarades, on the stark contrast between his experience in France and life at home. He declared:

> We leave filled with emotion . . . from the open friendship we found among the metropolitan French. And before such personal contact, that sincere fraternity, we cannot help but ask ourselves: why don't the Whites in Africa work together with the Blacks? What must we do to breach that barrier of hate and contempt that spreads day by day between the two races?[40]

French youth workers were distressed to learn of this situation in the territories. Lamy Roger, president of the Fédération Départementale des Foyers Ruraux de la Côte d'Or, which hosted a few dozen African *stagiaires* in the summer of 1957, reported to the education ministry that the African trainees were stunned that the local population was not "racist, for the only reason (and I am only quoting them) that 'the French here are not like the French there.'" He continued, "For us metropolitan French, it's a disconcerting report."[41]

The *stagiaires* expressed these sentiments in their own words to the population in the region in a letter that was published by several local news outlets. Addressing their "Burgundian friends," the African trainees professed profound shock at the warm welcome they received. They assured their readers they would tell everyone back home how surprised they were to find that France is a country of "humanism and civilization." With rhetorical flourish, they continued that they had "heard and seen the beating of the French heart, so little and poorly understood in the overseas territories." In that same spirit of mutual comprehension, they entreated the local population to be patient with them:

---

40. Présidence du Conseil, Haut Comité de la Jeunesse de France et d'Outre-Mer, Groupe de travail "Contacts entre jeunes de France et d'Outre-Mer," January 1957, AN: F17/15727.

41. Rapport de M. Lamy Roger sur les stages ruraux, undated (c. 1957), CAC: 19860445/2.

"If, on our side, one day by accident we offended one of you or made a mistake, some blunder, please forgive us, because though we are animated by similar souls as you, it is undeniable that we have different customs and a different way of life."[42]

African students' uncomfortable insistence that racism remained an intractable part of their everyday lives did occasionally compel some French officials to acknowledge enduring institutional inequality—in the second-rate education Africans received prior to coming to France and in housing discrimination once they got there—but most French officials reacted defensively. Often this entailed shifting the blame back onto Africans' supposedly "irrational" hostility toward the French and their distinctly African "inferiority complexes." Henri Laurentie's modest candor about racism in the territories in the postwar conjuncture (see chapter 3) did not survive long under the crushing weight of the contradictions of postwar empire and the rightward turn in the colonial administration in 1947–1948. Unwilling to confront those contradictions, the more conservative, often Christian Democrat administrators who came to dominate colonial affairs in the 1950s devised an array of rhetorical strategies to deflect African criticisms of stalled youth and education reforms. By mid-decade, the tactic of attributing the persistence of "racial prejudice" to a handful of misfits and bad apples to sidestep the issue altogether had become the norm.[43]

Such deflections are crucial for understanding how French officials interpreted and evaluated African students' experiences in France. Convinced that *brassage* was the solution to their troubles, French officials and others who worked with African students were baffled and dismayed that racial tension did not in fact wither away in light of their efforts. These ostensible "failures" reified African difference and young Africans' seemingly intractable inability to integrate into French social and cultural life. Little wonder, then, that young Africans were completely excluded from the French national discourse of rejuvenation in the 1950s and Françoise Giroud's limited portrait of *white* French youth as the "New Wave."[44]

African Perspectives: "This Is Truly a White Country"

Subjected to extensive surveillance and stereotyping, young Africans turned the "colonial gaze" back on their surveillants as they took stock of French

---

42. Annexe II: Les Stagiaires d'Afrique Noire disent au revoir à leurs Amis Bourguignons, signed Bagouro Noumansana, undated, CAC: 19860445 / 2. Noumansana became a top agricultural engineer in independent Mali. The exchanges did indeed produce a new African elite.

43. See my "Obscuring Race."

44. Jobs, *Riding the New Wave.*

people, culture, and society during their time in France. They judged their surroundings in light of their own cultural values, social norms, and lifestyle preferences. In student journals, personal correspondence, and literature, African youth in France critiqued stalled colonial reforms, French racism, the lack of material support for them to pursue their studies, and French ways of life more generally.

Responding directly to French caricatures of Africans as "ungrateful," African students refuted the notion that they were "anti-French." In a 1956 editorial in the FEANF journal, *L'Étudiant d'Afrique Noire*, R. Mawlawé turned this accusation on its head: "Logic, truth, justice—we have been taught that these are quintessentially French qualities. Why when we avail ourselves of them do you find us anti-French? A surprising truth!" He continued, "As paradoxical as it seems, it is the colonized who are reviving the authentic tradition of France, of the true France whose vocation surely is not to stifle black consciousness, but to arouse their initiative, to help them realize their freedom as men."[45] As Laurentie had feared a decade earlier, francophone Africans had indeed become well acquainted with French values, which they mobilized as a powerful rhetorical weapon in their fight for racial equality and social justice.[46]

In the same issue, Isabelle Tévoedjrè, a literature student at the University of Toulouse from Dahomey (contemporary Benin), framed African students' contacts with their French peers in a charged political and racial context in a piece entitled "'Metropolitan' Students and Us." She found that France's colonial wars, first in Indochina and then Algeria, seemed to have pushed some of their French peers to open themselves up to and learn about African students' concerns, while others distanced themselves even more. In describing her daily experiences at her provincial university, she detailed a constant stream of what we would recognize today as microaggressions.[47] In the lecture hall, she wrote, it is easy to read the faces of French students and to slot them in one camp or the other: "By instinct, we can perceive straightaway the hostility that animates

---

45. R. Mawlawé, "Sommes-nous anti-Français?," *L'Étudiant d'Afrique Noire*, nouvelle série, no 3 (April 1956), ANS: 21G/209 (178).

46. Laurent Dubois has long observed that it was people in France's colonies that concretized the promise of French revolutionary values in their most radical and egalitarian forms. See his *Colony of Citizens: Revolution and Slave Emancipation in the French Caribbean, 1794–1804* (Chapel Hill: University of North Carolina Press, 2004).

47. For a lucid analysis of these dynamics today, see Derald Wing Sue, *Microaggressions in Everyday Life: Race, Gender and Sexual Orientation* (Hoboken, NJ: Wiley, 2010). I discuss African students' keen and prescient perceptions of how racism actually worked in France's postwar empire based on their lived experience in France at greater length elsewhere. See Emily Marker, "African Youth on the Move in Postwar Greater France: Experiential Knowledge and Decolonial Politics at the End of Empire," *Know: A Journal on the Formation of Knowledge* 3, no. 2 (Fall 2019), 283–303, https://doi.org/10.1086/704620.

their looks, gestures, vocal inflections. That hostility affects us so profoundly that we also suffer when our comrades are nothing more than indifferent, cruelly indifferent." Even on the streets of Paris, she continued, "that supposedly cosmopolitan city—I could not ignore those stares looking me up and down, those glances that would follow me, inquisitive, ironic, disdainful, distrustful, scared."[48]

For Isabelle, the most frustrating part of those encounters was how woefully ignorant her French peers were of the full spectrum of racial discrimination she and other African students faced on a daily basis, which took different forms in France and in the territories. She lamented that metropolitan French have no idea that "still now, in certain cities like Brazzaville, for a Black to enter the 'White' quarter would be a sacrilege," just as they also do not know that when African students are sent to organizations that find students housing, they are presented with listings "that carry that atrocious line, unworthy of the French who are supposed to be against racial discrimination: 'No Blacks, No Arabs!'" Given this situation, she found it especially intolerable that African students were, as a group, constantly accused of "ingratitude." She was unsparing in connecting accusations of disloyalty to old colonial stereotypes of "docile, sycophantic blacks." Here was further proof that Africans remained inferior in French eyes: Africans were denied the right to protest inequality and discrimination, and when they did, they were perceived as a dangerous threat, as radical anticolonial nationalists or Communist provocateurs, rather than loyal defenders of French values. "They claim to know us," she concluded, "but could not be more mistaken."[49]

Isabelle's husband, Albert Tévoedjrè, also sought to *educate* his French peers about the realities of Africans' social experience in his writing, and he too emphasized the different forms racism took in French Africa and the metropole. His 1958 *cri de coeur*, *L'Afrique révoltée*, painted a bleak picture of "Black France" and unsparingly catalogued the ways that the "spiritual revolution" so jubilantly announced for French Africa in the postwar conjuncture had not come to pass. Albert used photography to convey this to powerful effect. The book's insert presents images of racial hierarchy and everyday racism

---

48. Isabelle Tévoedjrè, "Les étudiants 'métropolitains' et nous," *L'Étudiant d'Afrique Noire,* nouvelle série, no 3 (April 1956), ANS: 21G/209 (178).

49. Such critiques often proved too much for French officials, who seized multiple editions of *L'Étudiant d'Afrique Noire* that year. African students aggressively protested to their political representatives in Paris and made appeals to international youth organizations, which eventually led to the journal's reinstatement. Lettre ouverte à Guy Mollet du Bureau exécutif du Bloc Populaire Sénégalais: "Laissez Paraître *L'Étudiant d'Afrique Noire*," March 18, 1957, ANS: 17G/596 (152). I return to this in chapter 5.

in his home territory of Dahomey alongside others that highlight structural racism throughout AOF. A photograph titled "July 1957: Cotonou (Dahomey), return from the market," shows a young white mother pushing a baby carriage down the street, followed by a Black man, in a military uniform, carrying her bags (see figure 4.2). The caption reads, "A European woman elegantly walks with her baby. Behind her, her Mamadou, in this case, a *tirailleur 'sénégalais,'* carrying her purchases. The African in military service can live in the barracks, participate in the repression of some Arabs in revolt . . . or serve as an unpaid domestic in the household of a European." The indignity of that scenario was then juxtaposed with an image that homes in on the root of structural inequality: a photograph of a dozen scantily clad, primary-school-age children, milling about on the steps of a building in Saint Louis (see figure 4.3). The caption reads, "After three hundred years of French presence in Saint-Louis-du-Sénégal, one child in six can go to school. And the rest? Well . . . they hang out in the streets!"[50] For Albert Tévoedjrè, Africans' unequal access to education in the territories was the foundation of the larger edifice of racial domination in postwar French Africa.

Albert focused more on racism in France in his writing in student publications. In addition to serving as an editor of *L'Étudiant d'Afrique Noire,* he was also a frequent contributor to the journal of the Association of Catholic Students in Dakar. In a 1955 piece in that publication, he framed his experience of racism in Toulouse in explicitly Christian terms. African Catholic students, he wrote, found their isolation in metropolitan France especially painful. Like so many African students, Albert was stung by the trauma of trying to find lodging: "We have all felt the pathological distrust that certain sons of France harbor towards people of color." But he was devastated to find that a ready welcome in French congregations could prove equally challenging. He relayed with relief and excitement that the Catholic Institute in Toulouse recently created a special parish for overseas students. If they were not welcome in French churches, they would form their own.[51]

Religion could have been a factor of internal division among African students, but they developed their own kind of religious pluralism. As Catholic Senegalese student Thomas Diop wrote in 1957, African youth included Christians, Muslims, Communists, and "traditionalists," but they all shared a commitment to Africa's future. Indeed, he emphasized that African Christians and

---

50. Albert Tévoedjrè, *L'Afrique révoltée* (Paris: Présence Africaine, 1958).

51. Albert Tévoedjrè, "Un écho des étudiants africains catholiques de France: Discours adressé à son excellence Mgr. Garronne, Archevêque-Co-Adjuteur de Toulouse au nom des Étudiants d'Outre-Mer," *Jeunesse d'Afrique: Organe mensuel de l'Association des Étudiants catholiques de Dakar,* no. 3 (June–July 1955): 8, ANOM: BIB SOM POM/b/275.

Figure 4.2. Photographic insert in Albert Tévoedjrè's *L'Afrique révoltée* (Paris: Présence Africaine, 1958).

Figure 4.3. Photographic insert in Albert Tévoedjrè's *L'Afrique révoltée* (Paris: Présence Africaine, 1958).

Muslims in particular shared common views and spiritual principles. Diop defended African Muslims who traveled to Cairo to pursue higher Islamic study—students the colonial administration maligned as "Wahhabi" fanatics.[52] Indeed, intra-African diversity, as well as the very real differences separating Africans from their French counterparts, led Diop to think more expansively about building solidarity in the globalizing postwar world. He urged that "to think globally," young people should root their identities in *goals* and *objectives* rather than religion or ideology. He concluded, "Identity of goals would promote tolerance, not only between diverse groups of young Blacks, but also between black youth and metropolitan youth."[53]

The everyday racism that African students detailed in their periodicals was also a recurrent theme in francophone African literature of the period. In his moving fictional memoir *Un nègre à Paris* (1959), Ivorian writer Bernard Dadié subversively turned the colonial-administrative gaze on its head. Set in 1956, the narrator keenly observes everything around him, at one point declaring forcefully, "This is truly a white man's country."[54] Dadié's narrator channels the tone and mood of the colonial travelogue as he meticulously scrutinizes France and the French: "What we share with this people makes us more sympathetic towards them. I even found here fairytales just like ours." He continues, "And when I see a French father take his child by the hand, smiling at him and telling him stories, I say to myself, 'but they act just like blacks—they are just like us!' They too love their children."[55]

Despite those surprising ironic flashes of connection, Dadié's narrator dwells on the isolation he feels in Paris, the fast pace of city life, and the lax moral behavior of French youth. These observations lead to extended reflections on the prospect of a nonracist multiracial society: "I watch the people come and go. I am aware of my color that distinguishes me at a distance, day and night. And I ask myself: didn't God create men of different colors so that we would have to study each other? Is color the only barrier that men free themselves from with such difficulty?" He continues, "We speak of different customs, colors, countries, cultures, but aren't men all the same?" And yet, the book's take on Franco-African relations is ultimately deeply ambivalent. The

---

52. Thomas Diop, "Problèmes philosophiques et religieux," *Pensée française-fédération* no. 3, special issue, "Jeunesses d'Afrique Noire" (January 15, 1957): 20–21, ANOM: BIB SOM C/BR/3324. I discuss this topic at length in chapter 5.

53. Diop, "Problèmes philosophiques et religieux," 23, ANOM: BIB SOM C/BR/3324.

54. Dadié, *Un nègre à Paris*, 25.

55. Dadié, *Un nègre à Paris*, 30. My interpretation draws on an excellent master's thesis by Nicole Cesare, "An African in Paris . . . and New York and Rome: Bernard Dadié and the Postcolonial Travel Narrative" (master's thesis, Villanova University, 2007).

narrator not only notes that Africans are exoticized in France but also detects a new, *performative* aspect to French behavior toward Africans:

> These Parisians still have that affection that their ancestors had for us back in the days when everyone had their own little Negro [*Négrillon*]. It's truly a pleasure for them to have us. What's more, those who [in the territories] would never dare invite us to their table, here they are the first to do so. They want to publicly prove their generosity of spirit and dupe everyone.[56]

Significantly, the narrator explicitly frames these reflections about racial diversity in France in the context of European integration. He marvels at the prospect of European unity and admires its universal aspirations. As the narrator recounts his rambling walks through Paris, he pauses for a moment's reflection at the Place de l'Europe in the eighth arrondissement. He muses, "The Parisian believes that men will be able to unite themselves. . . . The Place de l'Europe imagines that each nation, with its history and its monuments will let go of its victories which were defeats for others. History will no longer be the history of killing fields, but rather of man *tout court*."[57]

Youth and Eurafrica

Dadié's narrator may have been moved by the idealism of the European project, but pro-Europe activists struggled to generate popular enthusiasm for European integration in the 1950s. That was not for want of effort. The decade-spanning (and CIA-funded) European Youth Campaign focused on educating young people about European integration and how European institutions work. Head-quartered in Paris, the campaign's leadership was largely French. The campaign's outreach efforts added a pronounced European dimension to the way French colonial education officials thought about African youth and *brassage*. Indeed, some came to promote an explicitly "Eurafrican" vision that pointed beyond the French Union to the grander, intercontinental scale of Europe-Africa relations.

African leaders' qualified support for Eurafrica lent credibility to this Eurafrican turn in colonial policy. As colonial reform stalled in the late 1940s, many African leaders sought to leverage the upsurge in European institution building in the early 1950s to get the French to recommit to the democratization of the empire. As the French delegate to the European Parliamentary Assembly in

---

56. Dadié, *Un nègre à Paris*, 182–183.
57. Dadié, *Un nègre à Paris*, 206.

Strasbourg in 1950, Ousmane Socé Diop (senator for Senegal) voiced his and his constituents' support for both the proposed European Coal and Steel Community (ECSC) and the "third continent" such an institution would bring into being. However, he forcefully declared that this support was conditional on real social and economic progress in Africa, "at the European level." Then and only then, Diop insisted, would Africans give their consent to the construction of Eurafrica.[58] In the end, French Africa was not included in the ECSC, but subsequent plans for a European Defense Community (EDC) and a European Political Community (EPC) re-posed the question of Eurafrica even more pointedly. Most African leaders also embraced this more political form of European integration, but only if French Africa was included on equal terms with the rest of France. At the peak of the EDC/EPC debate in 1953, Sourou Migan Apithy (deputy for Dahomey) warned that "to admit France into Europe without its territories would be to foreclose the possibility of a French *grand ensemble* integrated from the Rhine to the Congo, by definitively giving the impression to the African public that we refuse to exit the colonial regime."[59] With the prospect of political European integration looming on the horizon, it became vitally important to bring the generational projects of Franco-African and European integration together.

Eurafricanism and French Colonial Education Policy

Eurafrica figured prominently in the rhetoric of Louis-Paul Aujoulat, the top education official in the colonial ministry from 1949 to 1953. A missionary doctor and Christian Democrat who represented the white population of Cameroon in the French National Assembly for the first postwar decade, Aujoulat also chaired the coordinating committee for FIDES in 1950 that disbursed French development funds to youth and education initiatives in French Africa. He was instrumental in creating one of the earliest training programs for young Africans, a summer *stage* at the national teacher training institute at Saint-Cloud. From 1951 on, this program provided pedagogical training for both African and metropolitan schoolteachers assigned to posts in Africa. Aujoulat celebrated the inaugural program at Saint-Cloud as one of the admin-

---

58. Ousmane Socé Diop, Intervention faite à Strasbourg par M. Ousmane Socé Diop, Sénateur du Sénégal, Délégué de la France au Conseil de l'Europe a/s le Plan Schuman, August 22, 1950, AMAE: K-Afrique, 1944-1952-Généralités, 53.

59. Cited in Supplément a/s la Communauté politique européenne, unsigned, *Perspectives*, November 14, 1953, 7, AN: C//15913.

istration's shining achievements of the year, alongside the ostensibly more significant opening of the Institut des Hautes Études de Dakar and the Maison de la France d'Outre-Mer in Paris.[60]

Aujoulat promoted his Eurafrican vision for Franco-African relations at the second Saint-Cloud *stage* in 1952. In a long presentation to the *stagiaires*, he articulated the administration's goals for colonial education in a new spirit and vocabulary. First, he proudly declared, "it is time for us to listen to what Africa and Madagascar want."[61] Second, he called on the *stagiaires* to build "a new Eurafrican civilization." Aujoulat alluded to Senghor's well-known support for Eurafrica and stressed that he was not the only Black intellectual to champion Eurafricanism. Aujoulat expressed the challenge of reaching a Eurafrican symbiosis in temporal metaphors: "It concerns the inevitable conflict between two conceptions of life and world, the instability between the old equilibrium of yesterday and the new equilibrium of tomorrow." Crucially, he insisted Africans could not be forced to choose between "Europe" and "Africa"; rather they must achieve a synthesis:

> Even if the African elite demonstrates a remarkable receptivity to Latin culture and European values, they are well aware that they should not renounce their origins nor lose touch with their ancestral patrimony for any price. [The African elite] shares the aspirations of all non-European countries that hope to benefit from the West's technical secrets without losing their own personalities, to assimilate [those techniques] into their values in pursuit of a human universal.[62]

Aujoulat then concluded by associating his stance with several prominent Africans in the campaign for robust education reform: "We must reject both the cultural imperialism that presumes Africa is a blank slate and a systematic filtering of the kinds of knowledge and disciplines offered to black children: that seems to me to be the position of African teachers and thinkers like Senghor, Hazouné or Alioune Diop."[63]

Aujoulat distilled his "Eurafrican symbiosis" into three action items: (1) develop elite and mass education at the same time and stop treating this as an

---

60. Louis-Paul Aujoulat, "Avant-Propos," *Bulletin de l'Inspection-Générale de l'Enseignement et de la Jeunesse du Ministère de la France d'Outre-Mer*, no. 3 (April 1952), ANOM: BIB AOM/20505/1952.

61. "Conférence donnée le 8 juillet 1952 devant les Stagiaires de Saint Cloud par Dr. Aujoulat," reprinted in *Bulletin de l'Inspection-Générale de l'Enseignement et de la Jeunesse du Ministère de la France d'Outre-Mer*, no. 4 (December 1952) (emphasis in original), ANOM: BIB AOM/20505/1952.

62. "Conférence donnée le 8 juillet 1952 . . . par Dr. Aujoulat," ANOM: BIB AOM/20505/1952.

63. "Conférence donnée le 8 juillet 1952 . . . par Dr. Aujoulat," ANOM: BIB AOM/20505/1952.

either-or proposition; (2) stop fearing Africans obtaining advanced degrees; and (3) overcome the false opposition between *"l'esprit"* and *"la technique."* On this last point, he added, "Africans are the first to declare that we are living in a technical age, and that countries cannot thrive or modernize without technicians." He continued, "If Blacks reject assimilation by force, they are nevertheless eager to participate in the great advances of modern civilizations."[64]

Aujoulat mobilized the framework of "Eurafrica" as a new way to think about the function and design of education for Africans in a French Union that was deepening its ties to its European neighbors and trying to modernize in the process. Not only was Eurafrica therefore gaining currency as a way of thinking about institutional arrangements between united Europe and European-controlled parts of Africa; Eurafrica was also becoming a new scalar frame for considering the social and cultural work of educating Africans in France's African territories. Aujoulat's insistence that Africans must be consulted about their own goals and aspirations also had a European dimension. As we have seen, African leaders had made this consultation the sine qua non for African participation in the European project. But the importance of African consent could also be tied to pro-Europe propaganda of the period—especially in youth and education initiatives—that aggressively proclaimed the new Europe's liberal, tolerant, and pluralist values. That added pressure for France to make the French Union a genuinely inclusive, democratic entity: a noncolonialist France within a larger nonimperialist Europe.

This was a new register in the cultural repertoire of France's historic civilizing mission.[65] In prewar colonial parlance, "Eurafrican" designated mixed-race people *(métis)*.[66] Eurafrican discourse was not a common feature of either "assimilationist" or "associationist" colonial education policies. But in the 1950s, the geopolitical situation reframed the problem of difference in France and French Africa and sometimes turned conventional identifications on their head. In this era of rapid political change, many French officials were wary of *overidentifying* with Europe. Just a few months after the *stage* at Saint-Cloud, as the French parliament began to debate the European Political Community, officials in the French Foreign Affairs Ministry warned: "France is not a European power. . . . Her interests, her aspirations and her destiny have long ex-

---

64. "Conférence donnée le 8 juillet 1952 . . . par Dr. Aujoulat," ANOM: BIB AOM/20505/1952.

65. Conklin, *A Mission to Civilize*; Bryant, *Education as Politics*; Wilder, *The French Imperial Nation-State*. Wilder emphasizes the newness of Senghor's postwar vision of Eurafrica in a contribution to the edited volume *Black France/France Noire*.

66. Saada, *Les enfants de la colonie*; Owen White, *Children of the French Empire: Miscegenation and Colonial Society in French West Africa* (Oxford: Oxford University Press, 1999); Rachel Jean-Baptiste, "Miss Eurafrica: Men, Women's Sexuality, and Métis Identity in Late Colonial French Africa," *Journal of the History of Sexuality* 20, no. 3 (September 2011): 568–593, https://www.jstor.org/stable/41305885.

tended beyond the continent." The officials insisted, "A great future may yet await her in Africa."[67]

At the same time, African politicians who continued to try to leverage their support for the European project to secure more robust reform in the French Union proudly declared themselves committed "Europeans"—not ethnically, but politically. They found a ready welcome in the pro-Europe movements, whose interest in Eurafrica peaked in the second half of the decade. By the mid-1950s, virtually all the European movements had created special committees on Europe-Africa relations. In 1958, Hamani Diori, a former schoolmaster in Niamey, deputy and vice president of the French National Assembly, and later first president of independent Niger, delivered a speech to the European Movement's Europe-Africa Commission. He affirmed, "We are Europeans, because we are facing the same problems," but he quickly qualified that support: "I am telling you that we are resolutely Europeans on the strict condition that the juridical and political reform of the Franco-African Community precedes our definitive entry into the construction of Europe. European nations and the French African territories have arrived together at the same idea of a communal association at the appropriate scale for the modern world: Eurafrica." After a long reflection on the importance of fostering mutual understanding among European and African youth, Hamani Diori concluded, "we are not presenting ourselves to European Nations as beggars, whatever our social needs may be. We come to Europe with France and through France in the hope of becoming what you have taught us to want to be: free citizens." These remarks resonated with the French leaders of the European Youth Campaign (EYC); they reprinted Hamani Diori's speech in its entirety in the EYC's main publication, whose print run was in the tens of thousands.[68] Thus, as global pressures made linking Africa, through France, to the new Europe-in-the-making more appealing to some French and African leaders, long-standing questions about cultural *métissage* and cultural pluralism in colonial African youth and education policy took on an added "Eurafrican" valence. "Eurafrica" became an important framework for reimagining African difference in the context of an emergent modern, technical, and interconnected society.

Roland Pré, another Christian Democrat in the upper ranks of the colonial bureaucracy in the mid-1950s, also embraced this conceptual repertoire. Pré's career perfectly captures how entangled colonial and European concerns

---

67. Direction Générale-Affaires Politiques, Direction-Afrique, "Note sur la position des territoires français d'outre-mer dans la question de l'intégration européenne," October 14, 1952, AMAE: K-Afrique, 1944-1952-Généralités, 53.

68. Hamani Diori, "Le Pari du Siècle: France—Europe—Afrique," *Les Cahiers de Jeune Europe*, no. 4 (Supplément à *Jeune Europe* no. 7, March 1, 1958): 13–16, BNF.

had become. A former governor of both Gabon and Guinée, Pré was a found-ing member of the Union of European Federalists' study group for "over-seas" issues in Paris in 1953. Moreover, the following year, he oversaw the allocation of the second installment of FIDES, which financed youth and ed-ucation initiatives in Africa. In late 1954, Pré returned to French Africa as chief administrator in Cameroon.[69] Like the European Movement, the Union of European Federalists was a transnational European political action group with its own youth wing. At the first session of its Europe-Overseas Commission, Pré urged that the group should promote more than narrowly technical and economic cooperation between Europe and Africa. He forcefully argued that they must pursue "political integration" as well if they were going to get Af-ricans to accept the idea of Eurafrica:

> African opinion will soon be torn between two poles: Eurafricanism (the integration of Africa into Europe by way of technical arrangements) and Pan-Africanism (the integration of African countries amongst themselves by way of political arrangements). In this way, the victory of Eurafrican-ism risks being compromised if the issue is solely approached from a technical perspective without consideration of political questions.[70]

This argument did not convince everyone. Cornelius Van Rij, a Dutchman on the commission, rejected Pré's vision of political integration for Europe and Africa for religious reasons. The Netherlands, he declared, did not envision in-tegrating any overseas territories into united Europe precisely because "reli-gious issues will accentuate the many difficulties" such integration raised.[71]

Religion was also deeply important to Pré, but he viewed it as a potential connector rather than a divider. Christianity occupied a central place in the deliberations of Pré and his colleagues in charge of deciding how to allocate FIDES money to expand education in French Africa. Under Pré's leadership, the FIDES board characterized Eurafrica as a "civilizational choice" in favor of the Christian West over the Islamic world.[72] Ignoring Aujoulat's entreaty

---

69. In Cameroon, Pré acquired a reputation as a fanatical crusader against African nationalists. The "massacre of May" 1955 in Cameroon occurred during his tenure. See Martin Atangana, *The End of French Rule in Cameroon* (Lanham, MD: University Press of America, 2010), 53.

70. Procès-verbal des débats de la Commission Europe-Outre-Mer, UEF, Paris, July 3–4, 1953, ANOM: 1AFFPOL/2314.

71. Procès-verbal des débats de la Commission Europe-Outre-Mer, UEF, Paris, July 3–4, 1953, ANOM: 1AFFPOL/2314.

72. James Chappel argues that by 1950, the more open, pluralist strand of social Catholicism associ-ated with Jacques Maritain and his associates had been thoroughly eclipsed by the "Defenders of the West" in Catholic federalist circles, including the Union of European Federalists. Chappel, *Catholic Mod-ern*, chap. 4.

to stop regarding Africa as a blank slate, Pré and the FIDES planners framed that choice in a vacuum:

> Unlike the populations of the Middle East and Asia, our populations in French Africa cannot claim a civilization of their own. Rather, they are looking to fill the void with external elements that they can adapt to their own tendencies. *This is a unique opportunity we must seize,* for the Eurafrican bloc, the cornerstone of this "great entity *Metropole-Outre-Mer*" that we are so intently trying to build, can be realized by a solid foundation: a common civilization, which is to say, Western civilization, which is nothing other than French civilization *tout court.*[73]

In their view, millions of sub-Saharan Africans were awaiting "an orientation toward new forms of civilization." Crucially, Pré and the FIDES planners believed that *Islam noir* had not yet taken on the "totalitarian forms that are incompatible with our civilization"—unlike in the Arab world. Indeed, they considered conditions in Africa favorable to westernization and African Islam as not posing an obstacle to that evolution. As we shall see in chapter 5, this attitude was widespread and had profound implications for colonial education policies in Muslim-majority regions in both AOF and AEF.

Africa and the European Youth Campaign

The European Youth Campaign initially focused on promoting the European Defense Community and the European Political Community. The collapse of those projects in 1954 was not only a devastating blow to more robust European political integration: it also raised doubts about the efficacy of the EYC's tactics and strategy. In its early years, the EYC organized small-scale educational programming for young people who were already involved in organized youth movements. By 1955, a showier display of young people's support for European integration seemed urgently needed and would require transforming the EYC from an elite movement of young *cadres* to a mass movement for all. To reach a wider audience, the EYC concentrated on regional and local activities "to reach out to young people where they live, work, and learn."[74]

At the same time that the EYC was pivoting to more grassroots organizing, it was also trying to redefine its objectives in light of the rapidly changing international situation. French officials in the EYC felt the upheavals wrought

---

73. Commission Roland Pré, "L'Afrique à la recherche d'une civilisation: Orient ou occident?," February 1954, ANOM: 1AFFPOL/2260.

74. "Note sur les objectifs et méthodes des 'États-Généraux de la Jeunesse d'Europe' 1957," January 19, 1955, 1, AHUE: ME-1458.

by decolonization in Asia and the failure of the EDC and EPC put European youth in a double bind. EYC officials feared that young people, confronted with a "heritage of failure," were resigning themselves to withdraw from the international arena. According to Jacques Eugene, one of the French leaders of the EYC, the campaign needed to get young people involved in finding a role for Europe in world affairs, to encourage direct civic participation in the process of European integration, and to clearly outline young Europeans' responsibilities toward "under-developed countries and the associated territories."[75]

In pursuit of that latter goal, the French section of the EYC created its own "Overseas Group," which was presided over by Antoine Lawrence, a Guinean youth leader who was involved with a number of French youth organizations and served as the president of the US-backed World Association of Youth for most of the 1950s.[76] The founding of the group was a key step in converting the French section of the EYC to the Eurafrican cause. By 1957, the section's official program identified its core objectives as creating a European representative assembly elected by universal suffrage and formally instituting a "Europe-Africa Community."[77] Subsequently, Eurafrica was a recurring theme in the EYC's journal *Young Europe*, which published studies on the *Loi Cadre* and a steady stream of reflections on the political, economic, and "ethnic" issues raised by the prospect of forging closer ties between Europe and Africa.[78]

The EYC's "Eurafrican" turn was not just rhetorical. The French section fought hard to get African students in France involved in EYC initiatives in neighboring European countries. By the end of the decade, a quarter of state-funded summer *stages* and exchange programs had added a European dimension to their initiatives for Africans. For example, in 1959, the Confédération Nationale de la Famille Rurale designated five places for African trainees to attend its study sessions in the Netherlands and Germany; the Fédération française des maisons de jeunes et de la culture reserved five spots for Africans in a study mission on rural life in Italy and another ten spaces for Africans to attend a six-month training session for directors of youth clubs in France, Italy, and

---

75. Jacques Eugene, "Déclaration-Programme," January 19, 1955, AHUE: ME-1458.

76. Lawrence was sharply criticized by more radical African youth leaders as a lackey of the colonial regime and the Americans. It is surely not a coincidence that he was involved with the WAY and the EYC, which were both sponsored by the United States. On the eve of independence, Kane Ali Bokar, president of the Federal Council of Youth of AOF, described Lawrence's position as president of the WAY as "pure demagoguery. . . . It was just necessary to hire a *nègre* to prove that the WAY was not racist." Extraits du Rapport moral de Kane Ali Bokar concernant le Conseil de Jeunesse de l'Union Française, *UNEF Informations—Outre-Mer* 1958, Annexe II, 73, BNF.

77. Jacques Eugene, "Rapport Général," Comité National d'Action Jeune du Mouvement Européen, Secrétariat Français de la Campagne Européenne de la Jeunesse, June 28, 1957, 60, AHUE: EN-2703.

78. Eugene, "Rapport Général," 55–56, AHUE: EN-2703.

Germany; the Organisation centrale des camps et activités de jeunesse arranged for several Africans to go to Italy for a cultural enrichment program on "Roman Civilization" and pledged to reserve spots for young Africans upon request in its network of 180 camps and youth centers across Western Europe.[79]

Like the gathering at Brest that opened this book, European youth initiatives in the early 1950s had focused on getting French and European youth to envision French Africa as part of Europe. Political developments like the *Loi Cadre* refocused EYC officials' attention on making sure young Africans participated in these efforts directly.[80] Jacques Eugene admitted,

> It is distressing to note that until now these projects [of associating Europe and Africa] have practically only been studied by metropolitan French, or at best, by Africans of the preceding generation who have been thoroughly Frenchified [*francisés*]. The reactions of the younger generations, of more modest cultural development, remain to be properly studied. If this work is not done, we should fear Eurafrican projects will appear to them as a *hypocritical new form of colonization*. In that case, it would be a total failure.[81]

Henceforth, Eugene concluded, engaging African youth would be a priority.

The French section of the EYC attempted to do just that at a three-day conference in Troyes in November 1957 on the theme, "The Responsibility of Youth Toward Europe."[82] In a notable departure from past practice, Africans were invited to participate in the proceedings. Nabi Ibrahima Youla, a Guinean former teacher, past education director for the Rassemblement Démocratique Africain (the largest African political party at the time), and member of the Social and Economic Council of the EEC, gave an impassioned speech on the role of youth in building Eurafrica. He declared that for Eurafrica to succeed, African youth must first be truly welcomed in metropolitan France—that is, they must finally achieve *brassage*. Summer *stages* and exchange programs were a step in the right direction, but Nabi Youla cautioned that organized programming would go only so far. *Brassage* required metropolitan French to really get to know young Africans. He exhorted his audience that it was wholly up to *them* to take on this

---

79. See the folder "Dossier Échanges France Outre-Mer, 1959," CAC: 19860445/2.

80. The EEC created its own "Bureau Liaison France-Afrique-Europe," which was also headquartered in Paris. See AHUE: BAC003/1965-28. Some of the faculty mentors discussed earlier in the chapter got funding from the bureau to take their African mentees on educational trips to EEC countries. For instance, one of the Bordelais law professors received support to take students to Berlin. Letter from Lucien Martin to the HCJS, May 31, 1960, CAC: 19860445/6.

81. Eugene, "Rapport Général," 26 (emphasis in original), AHUE: EN-2703.

82. Rapport d'orientation, "Éléments pour une nouvelle étape," *Les cahiers de Jeune Europe*, no. 1 (supplément au *Jeune Europe*, no. 1, nouvelle série, December 1957), BNF.

responsibility: "*You* can do it," he urged, "reach out to them, create contacts, overcome the difficulties." He concluded that if his talk inspired even just one person in the audience to make the effort, it would be a real turning point. "By multiplying contacts," he concluded, "we will create new horizons."[83]

Nabi Youla's views were folded into the final recommendations of the Overseas Group. Its top two priorities were to dispel the impression that France wanted to substitute a new European "supracolonialism" for the old French model and to develop more contacts with African students in the metropole. The group's observations and proposals on the latter point reprised many of the French bureaucrats' tropes and tactics. The main challenge would be what the group referred to as the "psychological difficulties" of working with African youth, which the group identified as the particular African "mentality" and also the "appeal of communism." The group posited that Africans were instinctually drawn to Communism because it resembled the "structure of the African world, with its hierarchy, taboos, and the disappearance of the individual in the collective," rather than any reasoned ideological, political, or genuine social commitments. In light of these African qualities, group members concluded they would have to be extremely careful in how they managed their exchanges with African youth.[84]

Over the course of the following year, the group organized regular conferences and "dinner-debates" on Eurafrica across France. According to one of its leaders, Louis Planchais, the group's priority was to facilitate contacts between young Africans and metropolitan French as well as youth from the other member-states of the new EEC.[85] Planchais was quite candid about the difficulties they encountered at these events, which included a two-day "Franco-African Colloquium" in Noisy-sur-Oise with more than fifty participants. Planchais reflected at length about the challenges of frank exchanges between "young people who come from the most diverse political and religious backgrounds," which he published as a "Letter to an African Friend" in one of the EYC's monthly publications. The conversations at Noisy-sur-Oise, he wrote, were useful and important but quite "painful" for the young Europeans. Their African comrades were wary of Europeans, he wrote, and it was difficult for them to break through that barrier of distrust.[86]

---

83. Nabi Ibrahima Youla, "L'Eurafrique, une communauté librement consentie," *Les cahiers de Jeune Europe*, no. 1 (December 1957): 13, BNF.

84. "Rapport de la commission 'outre-mer,'" *Les cahiers de Jeune Europe*, no. 1 (December 1957): 14, BNF.

85. Louis Planchais, "Bilan des activités de la CEJ," undated, AHUE: ME-185.

86. Louis Planchais, "Lettre à un ami africain," *Les Cahiers de Jeune Europe*, no. 3, "L'espace Europe-Afrique" (supplément au *Jeune Europe*, no. 5, nouvelle série, February 1, 1958): 13–14, BNF.

Like Laurentie a decade earlier, Planchais acknowledged that that distrust stemmed from legitimate grievances. "We know that French action in Africa has not always been positive," he admitted. Writing in 1958, Planchais had witnessed thirteen more years of stalled reform, "endlessly postponed and distorted in application." Nevertheless, he still launched into a vigorous defense of French colonial policy, citing the *Loi Cadre* and France's "generous scholarships" as evidence. He insisted, "We believe that your very presence in metropolitan universities and the *Grandes Écoles*, the scholarships you receive, which are often much higher than those of French students, and the freedom of expression that you enjoy that allows you to openly criticize the action of the metropole, can be considered as so much proof that French actions in the overseas territories are not entirely negative." Planchais admitted these remarks were tinged with "bitterness," but he entreated his African audience not to see that as a reproach, but rather as a symptom of the "painful shock" of the encounter. He recognized it was now time for Africans to decide Africa's fate, but he still hoped they would choose a Franco-African community and eventually a "Eurafrican" one as well.[87]

In this hope, Planchais would be intensely disappointed. African students in France overwhelmingly opposed Eurafrica and passionately denounced their own politicians for entertaining the prospect. Togolese vice president of the FEANF Noé Kutuklui not only rejected the idea of Eurafrica but also incisively juxtaposed French support for European integration and the "balkanization" of Africa with the *Loi Cadre*. In a 1957 essay, "The Fear of the Truth," Kutuklui called out this shocking hypocrisy in no uncertain terms: "It is no surprise that [the *Loi Cadre*] will lead to the formation of 13 *Républiquettes*. At the very moment that [the French] commit themselves to working toward European unity, they are doing everything in their power to make African unity impossible by cementing artificially imposed divisions. Vigilant youth," Kutuklui forcefully concluded, "cannot but denounce this new form of colonialism," whatever their elected representatives may say.[88]

Some of Kutuklui's comrades, like Samba Ndiaye, whom we met at the beginning of this chapter, focused more on the neocolonial economic relations Eurafrica would surely entail. For Ndiaye, Eurafrica amounted to nothing more than the machinations of "European capitalists."[89] Communist militant and FEANF press secretary Joseph van den Reysen, a Congolese student with roots in both the French and Belgian Congo, agreed. His opposition to Eurafrica

---

87. Planchais, "Lettre à un ami africain," 13–14.

88. Noé Kutuklui, "La peur de la vérité," *L'Étudiant d'Afrique Noire*, nouvelle série, no. 10 (March 1957), partially reprinted in Sadji, *Le rôle de la génération charnière*, 203–204.

89. Ndiaye, "Nouvelle mesure arbitraire," reprinted in Sadji, *Le rôle de la génération charnière*.

looked beyond the French sphere to transnational Europe. He attacked "Monsieur Europe" Paul-Henri Spaak, then serving as Belgium's foreign minister, in the pages of the *L'Étudiant d'Afrique Noire*. Van den Reysen questioned Spaak's Socialism and called him out for never consulting the Congolese about whether they were interested in Eurafrica. He also compared German chancellor Konrad Adenauer to Portuguese dictator Antonio Salazar and highlighted Britain's tacit support for apartheid in South Africa.[90] For young pro-Europe activists who saw united Europe as a beacon of democracy and pluralism, such views must have been a "painful shock" indeed.

African and European Youth and Globalization

African student leaders like Ndiaye, Kutuklui, and van den Reysen vociferously denounced Eurafrica as a political and economic project. And yet, by inserting themselves in conversations about youth, development, and global transformation that were unfolding across France, Europe, and Africa, these young Africans were in many ways helping to create an Afro-European public sphere and a shared conceptual repertoire about youth, agency, pluralism, and global change. A central anchor of that repertoire was Daniel Halévy's widely read 1948 treatise, *Essay on the Acceleration of History*. Halévy's *Essai* was a meditation on modernity and what we would now call globalization—but it was also an aperçu of "Europe" and what distinguished Europe and Europeans from other "peoples" and civilizations. Laden with orientalist tropes about the immobility of Eastern societies, the *Essai* defined Europe as a fundamentally "youthful" civilization that grows, invents, and innovates: "It was in Europe that the idea to change the world originated."[91]

Halévy's tone and style are reminiscent of the Romantic historiography of the nineteenth century. In fact, the *Essai* begins with an extended quotation from Michelet: "The pace of time has totally changed," Michelet wrote in 1872. "In the average man's lifespan (typically 72 years), I have witnessed two great revolutions, which in the past, would have likely been separated by a thousand years' interval." This reflection, Halévy argues, was worth revisiting in 1948, a time when "the ground has disappeared beneath our feet; in fact there is no more history, just an obscure movement of peoples."[92] Halévy's *Essai* bridges a very nineteenth-century way of thinking about historical acceleration and late-twentieth-century theories of the shifting terrains of temporal-

---

90. Joseph van den Reysen, "L'Eurafrique, le Marché Commun et quelques autres projets," *L'Étudiant d'Afrique Noire*, nouvelle série, no. 8 (January 1957), reprinted in Sadji, *Le rôle de la génération charnière*, 211.

91. Daniel Halévy, *Essai sur l'accélération de l'histoire* (Paris: Editions Self, 1948), 45, 60.

92. Halévy, *Essai*, 1, 12.

ity and the diffuse and impersonal "forces" associated with globalization.[93] The *Essai* asks how people could regain the reins of those forces, but Halévy did not propose a clear course of action. Nevertheless, he did provide a new vocabulary that resonated strongly with those concerned with education and the formation of youth, as well as with young people themselves.

The theme of the "acceleration of history" cut across African and European meditations on the role of youth in charting a new future for Europe and Africa in the 1950s. The quickening pace of historical change meant that the young generations would henceforth be the main drivers of history—the generation upon whose shoulders it fell to remake a changing world. In 1950, Catholic African intellectual Alioune Diop organized a conference on this theme in Saint Louis, Senegal. Diop was then representing Senegal in the French Senate, but he remained close to African student and youth milieus in both Paris and AOF. In Paris, where he had founded the influential journal and imprint *Présence Africaine* in 1947, Diop regularly participated in student mobilizations and, after 1951, the cultural life at the Maison de la France d'Outre-Mer. In his talk in Saint Louis, Diop ruminated on Franco-African relations in the French Union. He framed those relations in racial terms and located the problem of race in the context of a worldwide "acceleration of history," citing Halévy's *Essai* explicitly.[94]

Diop opened his presentation with an extended reflection on what separates "Blacks and Whites." He asserted, "Whites and Blacks do not understand one another" for two main reasons—one economic, the other psychological. Diop's characterization of "the European" echoed Halévy's: "For the European, the universe is an equation of forces endlessly put in play by the militant and constituent will of man." Diop continued, "the European" seeks a permanent revolution in given institutions and constantly strives to transcend them. Whereas "for the Black," the purpose of life is to prosper within and through extant institutions, religion, natural laws, and "the heritage of our ancestors." And so, Diop went on, "our aspirations are not constituted in the same way, or in the same style. What can remedy this incomprehension?"[95]

---

93. "The acceleration of history" is the opening line of Pierre Nora's "Between Memory and History: *Les Lieux de Mémoire*," *Representations* 26 (Spring 1989): 7–24, https://doi.org/10.2307/2928520. François Hartog acknowledges the provenance of the phrase in his *Regimes of Historicity: Presentism and the Experience of Time* (New York: Columbia University Press, 2015), 123–124. Reinhardt Koselleck also took up this issue in a 1976 essay translated and republished in *High-Speed Society: Social Acceleration, Power, and Modernity*, ed. Harmut Rosa and William E. Sheuerman (University Park: Pennsylvania State University Press, 2009).

94. Alioune Diop, "Pour que Noirs et Blancs se comprennent," résumé d'une conférence organisée à Saint-Louis par la Ligue des Droits de l'Homme, December 23, 1950, ANS: 21G/172 (144). On Diop's politics and activities in this period, see Foster, *African Catholic*, chap. 2.

95. Diop, "Pour que Noirs et Blancs se comprennent," ANS: 21G/172 (144).

Diop then exclaimed, "Pluralism, is what they propose to us!" But in that very concept, Diop found yet another layer of "misunderstanding" between whites and Blacks. "In fact, there has never been pluralism without assimilation," and it was always Africans who were expected to assimilate, not the other way around. Rather than reject genuine pluralism as a pipe dream, Diop insisted it was imperative to find a new balance, precisely considering the seemingly inevitable future of global integration. He declared, "This pluralist association concerns the equilibrium of the world. History, in its turbulent trail, demands and awakens urgent reflection in both groups. For history is moving fast." Diop's concluding exhortation was for Africans to confront this reality and liberate themselves from older, colonial ways of thinking about preparing Africans to take control of their own destinies. Africans must be "equipped" (*équipé*)—rather than "educated" (*éduqué*)—with the same acuity and frenetic energy as that cultivated in young Europeans. Diop was optimistic that African youth could make this happen, and he ended by cheering on young Africans and their aspirations.[96]

African students in Diop's orbit in Paris embraced this message. The same theme and vocabulary were picked up by Joseph Ki-Zerbo, a prominent Catholic student leader in France from Dahomey who frequently published in *Tam-Tam*. In a 1955 piece entitled, "Pioneers or Mandarins?" Ki-Zerbo reflected on the crucial role African students in France would play in building Africa's future, not only by returning home to contribute to the development of the local economy but also in forging links between Africa and the rest of the world. Ki-Zerbo anchored the recent history of "encounters between Europe and Africa" in the mobilization of African troops in World War II, when "black heroes went to die on the 'front of liberty' to defend the world, all of the world, against a Racism elevated to a state religion." He continued, "Then crowds of young blacks were given access to Universities and Schools in the metropole—a second encounter, and those who find themselves in that position have a special responsibility."[97] Ki-Zerbo stressed that since the tax dollars of their compatriots back in Africa sent them to France and subsidized their studies, African students in France owed it to their fellow Africans—not the French—to master a profession that would be "useful" for Africa.

Ki-Zerbo had a broad view of the significance of growing numbers of African students in France. He declared, "It is up to us to make this influx of African students to Europe a historic phenomenon, that is, a turning point in

---

96. Diop, "Pour que Noirs et Blancs se comprennent," ANS: 21G/172 (144).

97. Joseph Ki-Zerbo, "Pionniers ou Mandarins?," *Tam-Tam*, deuxième année, no. 5 (May 1955): 5, BNF. Ki-Zerbo also features prominently in Foster's work. See *African Catholic*, chap. 4.

the development of the black world, rather than a random bit of miscellany." According to him, that would depend on whether they chose to be "pioneers" or "mandarins," that is, what they chose to do with their new educations. Ki-Zerbo framed the urgency of that choice specifically in the context of historical acceleration. He wrote, "In an era when airplanes allow the colonizers to streamline their commercial operations and to gain ever more time, can we convince the colonized that this 'acceleration' is made for them? Technology is a shortcut that we too can seize." However, Ki-Zerbo warned that technological prowess also threatened to annihilate "all that remains of black culture." On this point, he added, "Human progress has accelerated also for moral, ideological and spiritual discoveries that we must also draw inspiration from. . . . We cannot build Africa if we bring the virus eating away at western civilization back with us." In a prescient critique of technocracy and overspecialization, Ki-Zerbo continued: "Whoever today proposes a five-year plan for African development will be handicapped tomorrow by the blinkers of his 'specialty' . . . . We must be vigilant in opposing the spirit of profit and egotistical individualism that is already infecting Africa." He concluded with an appeal to Africans of his generation to imagine, invent, and create. The task of his generation, he exhorted, was not to continue "to ruminate in the abstract on theories about Négritude" but rather "to get to work, without delay."[98]

The sense that there was no time to lose also inspired reflections about youth in pro-Europe circles. Writing in the main publication of the Union of European Federalists' youth wing in 1954, the leader of the movement, Max Richard, invoked Halévy and the acceleration of history in a meditation on the distinctiveness of European culture and European conceptions of democracy and freedom. For Richard, youth had to steel themselves against not only Soviet Communism and Islamism but also US hegemony. He called on young Europeans to resist the mounting forces of Americanization: "It is out of the question to adopt an *American way of life*, to become American colonies. We will conserve, we will elaborate our own European way of life if we learn to unite as Europeans."[99] The preservation of a "European way of life" in the face of historical acceleration and global integration was an important part of the rationale for creating properly transnational European universities. A year after Richard's *cri d'alarme,* Michel Mouskhély, French delegate to the Council of

---

98. Ki-Zerbo, "Pionniers ou Mandarins?," *Tam-Tam,* BNF. This piece was widely read among African students in France and the territories. It was cited at length in a similar reflection by Senegalese student Pape Soulaye Ndiaye, "L'étudiant africain et la notion d'élite," which was published in *Dakar-Étudiant* shortly thereafter and reprinted in full in Sadji, *Le rôle de la génération charnère,* 186–188.

99. Max Richard, "Justice et réconciliation dans la transformation de la société," *Jeunesses européennes fédéralistes* (September 15, 1954), AHUE: UEF-176.

Europe, elaborated on this theme in a special session of the European Parliamentary Assembly in Strasbourg. Mouskhély suggested that European universities would prepare rising generations of Europeans to tackle new situations as they arose. He declared, "With the acceleration of the rhythm of history, every day we will be confronted with unexpected challenges." He lamented an "intellectual laziness" that looked to "nineteenth-century solutions" to address twentieth-century problems. That laziness held them hostage to the nation-state, "even though current realities are brutally pushing us toward international and supranational entities." European universities, Mouskhély concluded, would provide Europe with the "spiritual infrastructure" to forge ahead into an uncertain future.[100]

Proposals to create a European university stalled in the mid-1950s. When the project was revived a decade later, the theme of historical acceleration was even more pronounced. In a widely circulated Council of Europe report, French youth specialist Jean Jousselin (who, as it happens, had represented the Protestant scouts in Vichy's Secretariat of Youth during the war) identified the acceleration of history as *the* determinant factor that produced "youth" as a distinct social category and turned young people into a new social and political force, both domestically and on the world stage.[101] He wrote, "Technical civilization is a civilization of youth and it will be so ever more with each passing day. Henceforth, the young person knows and even understands more . . . than his elder." In this sense, "the effect of the acceleration of history is the source of a rupture in the dialogue between adults and young people, and consequently, a radical transformation of youth." This "new" youth required different institutions and the structural transformation of society. That assessment was borne out just a few years later in the May 1968 student uprisings across Europe *and* ex-French Africa that led to the massive overhaul of higher education on both continents.[102]

The generational conflict between youth and their elders in Europe ignited by historical acceleration was not quite the same as that between French-educated African youth and the traditional African gerontocracy, but French colonial officials stressed the similarities. In a 1957 article entitled "From the

---

100. Michel Mouskhély, "Les Universités et la communauté spirituelle de l'Europe," Rapport présenté à la 2ème réunion spéciale a/s universités européennes, Assemblée consultative du Conseil de l'Europe, Commission des Questions Culturelles et Scientifiques, June 11–13, 1955, AN: 70/AJ/27.

101. Jean Jousselin, Comité de l'Education Extrascolaire, Conseil de l'Europe, "L'Organisation de la Jeunesse en Europe," Tome 1, Strasbourg, January 12, 1965, CAC: 19780596/66.

102. For a transnational Franco-African perspective on May 1968, see Hendrickson, *Decolonizing 1968*. The "acceleration of history" became a common refrain in the Association of European Teacher's meeting to draft a "Charter of European Education," which was held in Brussels just weeks before the May 1968 uprisings. AHUE: AEDE-23.

Africa of Yesterday to That of Tomorrow," veteran colonial official Robert Delavignette pinned Africa's prospects on an alliance between French and African youth. He wrote, "Eight and a half million children and adolescents are returning to class in European France. . . . It is banal to say that this youth constitutes France's great hope." He continued:

> [That youth] is charged with building a less inhuman world. . . . Who doubts that [that youth] is already interdependent with another youth, which does not always have schools, and yet has its own ways of being and its own aspirations. Who doesn't dream of that beautiful and necessary common future of which metropolitan youth and the youth of black Africa, both carriers of hope, are the key elements?

Like Ki-Zerbo, Delavignette opposed an obsession with Negritude and the precolonial African past with a more future-oriented outlook. It was important to celebrate Africa's rich history, but he hoped that would not "lock African youth in an impasse, in which it would *lose time,* at a moment when *there is no time to lose* if men of all colors and all races want to learn to live together."[103] Delavignette ended his piece with a forceful affirmation that Africans themselves had to deal with Africa's problems, but he also insisted those problems were also *French and European* problems. Indeed, he declared, "these are problems of human relations within a universal civilization that is more and more mechanized, these are problems of psychological equilibrium amidst disruptive technologies." He concluded, "We are all *equal* before the unknowns [these problems] bring. We all must study them and free ourselves of old superiority and inferiority complexes. Neither Europe nor Africa holds the solutions. But the youth of Europe and the youth of Africa must work together to humanize the atomic age that has descended on us."[104] With these words, Delavignette acknowledged—albeit obliquely—the need to overcome the ongoing legacies of colonial domination based on racial hierarchies if not just French but also *European* and African youth were to build a future together under the conditions of historical acceleration.

Over the course of the 1950s, the promise of pluralism and *brassage* waned, leaving in its wake a toxic stew of disappointed hopes, political resentment, and new patterns of racialization and institutional inequality. This set the stage for a more radical conceptual shift with African independence and deepening

---

103. Robert Delavignette, "De l'Afrique d'hier à celle de demain," *Pensée française-fédération,* special issue: "Jeunesses d'Afrique Noire," no. 3 (January 15, 1957): 4–8 (emphasis added), ANOM: BIB SOM C/BR/3324.

104. Robert Delavignette, "De l'Afrique d'hier," 8, ANOM: BIB SOM C/BR/3324.

European integration in the 1960s. These two world-historical developments became entwined in more ambitious European cultural policy with the launching of the Council of Europe's European Cultural Fund in 1960. A successor to the EYC, which by then was defunct, the European Cultural Fund homed in on education and youth development as crucial vehicles for further European cooperation. The fund identified the "presentation of Europe to non-Europeans" as one of its key mandates. Its executive board affirmed, "One of our main tasks must be to make quite clear the part Europe must play in a world in which its former supremacy is giving way to cultural pluralism." This global pluralism was characterized by "the great difficulties that arise from the inevitable conflict between our liberal and technical culture and the traditional cultures of Asia, Africa and the Middle East." In this formulation, there was a singular "Europe," and there was the rest of the world: "European civilization should be presented to the outside world as a single unit embodying national variations. There can be no point of contact between French, English or Italian national culture and a completely different civilization such as that of India or Mexico. Europe as a whole must be presented as a single entity to the rest of the world."[105]

Africa was of particular concern because France had locked European institutions into providing technical aid to its former African colonies.[106] The board asserted in no uncertain terms its view that those countries had acquired "premature and perhaps somewhat precarious independence." Nevertheless, the fund would not renege on its commitments and would continue training European technicians to send to Africa. The fund would also publicize European unity to African students and trainees in Europe:

> Although Great Britain and France have long been aware of the problems raised by the presence of temporary residents from distant countries, the general situation has changed considerably in recent years, and responsibility towards these visitors is no longer national but European; they no longer come to France, Germany, or Italy, but to Europe, and they must be given an opportunity to gain a true picture of Europe as a whole.

It was hoped this kind of pan-European education campaign directed at students from former colonies would overcome the legacies of colonialism. Since

---

105. Consultative Assembly of the Council of Europe, 12th Ordinary Session, Resolution 186 (1960) in reply to the First Report of the Administrative Board of the Cultural Fund, CAC: 19770181/1.

106. Véronique Dimier, "Bringing the Neo-patrimonial State Back to Europe: French Decolonization and the Making of European Development Aid Policy," *Archiv für Sozialgeschichte* 48 (2008): 433–457, https://www.fes.de/index.php?eID=dumpFile&t=f&f=46875&token=b7cbf72149fd16efd96 7b632d62d31d4914fb944.

the "overseas peoples" had obtained independence, "they tend[ed] to hold hostile prejudices to their former masters. Only by encouraging the peoples of the new states to consider Europe as a whole will this uneasiness be dispelled."[107] Thus already in 1960, the year of African independence, institutions like the European Cultural Fund were actively reframing the issue of receiving African students from France's former empire in a transnational European perspective.

That process continued to unfold in a series of colloquia organized by the Council of Europe over the next several years. At a session held in Paris in January 1964, French delegates stressed the need for shifting French thinking about students from France's former empire into a transnational European frame: "A Senegalese, a Cambodian, a Moroccan, an Algerian—they are all foreigners, even though the French are reluctant to apply that label because they all speak French." In this formulation, language is singled out as the only reason for this "reluctance," erasing not just the postwar experiment of Franco-African integration but all of France's colonial history. The delegates further pressed the issue by noting that Tunisians or Vietnamese might speak French even though they have their own national languages, while French was the national language everywhere in sub-Saharan Africa, confusing matters further still. "Despite these nuances," the delegates insisted, "it is necessary to speak of 'foreign' students and trainees for francophone Africans, as for Americans or Latin Americans."[108]

Participants at the colloquium also drew attention to the percentages of foreign students in different European countries. In Britain and France, approximately two-thirds of all "foreign students" came from former colonies. In France, most of those students were North African and sub-Saharan African: 45 percent of all "foreign students" in France were listed as coming from Africa, whereas only 21 percent were listed as coming from Western Europe. These statistics raised concerns that there was a decline in the percentage of European students "in favor of Africans." Commentary on those students' attitudes and social milieus noted a latent hostility among former colonial students toward their ex-metropoles. Consequently, participants suggested that countries without colonies like Germany were attracting more students from developing countries precisely because they were not a (recent) colonial power.[109] In their concluding report, participants noted that Africans in France, "despite a

107. First Report of the Administrative Board of the Cultural Fund, CAC: 19770181/1.

108. Accueil et Séjour en Europe des Étudiants et Stagiaires Étrangers: Étude comparative sur leur accueil et leur orientation du point de vue social, linguistique, pédagogique et technique dans les pays membres du Conseil de l'Europe," undated, CAC: 19771275/28.

109. On ex-colonial students in Germany, see Quinn Slobodian, *Foreign Front: Third World Politics in Sixties West Germany* (Durham and Oxford: Duke University Press, 2012).

certain reluctance," had been welcomed in France and "only very rarely" showed real hostility toward the French. And yet, the report also acknowledged that racism among host populations was real. This phenomenon was both externalized as a particularly acute problem in Germany and totally naturalized—as if the mere presence of Africans explained hostility or aversion toward them in and of itself. The authors suggested that since there were few students of color in Germany before 1950, the "reserve" but also the "curiosity" that these students inspired in the German population was an "obvious, natural reaction."[110] As Heide Fehrenbach has shown, the naturalization of racial conflict anchored a particular strand of racial liberalism that took root in postwar Germany under US occupation.[111] Shifting the register of the now decades-long discussion about youth, race, and pluralism from a Franco-African imperial context to the transnational European plane further encouraged the eclipse of *brassage* and the ascendancy of that "race relations" model in late twentieth-century France. The transformation of African student-citizens of the French Union to "foreign students in Europe" was complete.

---

110. Accueil et Séjour en Europe des Étudiants et Stagiaires Étrangers: Étude comparative sur leur accueil et leur orientation du point de vue social, linguistique, pédagogique et technique dans les pays membres du Conseil de l'Europe," undated, CAC: 19771275/28.

111. Fehrenbach, *Race after Hitler.*

CHAPTER 5

Forging Global Connections

When Amadou Booker Sadji graduated from the Lycée Van Vollenhoven in Dakar in 1955, he intended to study German at a university in France. That same year, French, German, and other Western European leaders committed themselves to a "European relaunch" after the French parliament voted against the European Defense Community and European Political Community in 1954. Pro-Europe activists successfully pivoted to narrower forms of economic and technical cooperation, which led to the creation of the European Economic Community and the European Atomic Energy Community in 1957.[1] As we have seen, excitement about the new European Communities stoked a surge in Eurafricanism among colonial policymakers and educators in metropolitan France in the mid-1950s.[2] Local officials in Dakar, however, evidently deemed deepening Western European integration irrelevant to the rising generation of francophone African elites like Sadji; they viewed his ambition to study German in European France as

---

1. Enrico Serra, ed., *The Relaunching of Europe and the Treaties of Rome: Actes du Colloque de Rome 25–28 Mars 1987* (Brussels: Bruylant, 1989).

2. See chapter 4. On the European Communities and Eurafricanism beyond the education sphere, see Brown, *The Seventh Member State*; Pierre Guillen, "L'avenir de l'Union française dans la négociation des traités de Rome," *Relations internationales* 57 (Spring 1989): 103–112, https://www.jstor.org/stable/45344281; Rik Schreurs, "L'Eurafrique dans les négociations du Traité de Rome, 1956–1957," *Politique africaine* 49 (1993): 82–92, http://www.politique-africaine.com/numeros/pdf/049082.pdf.

a foolish waste of time and pushed him to study geography at the Institut des Hautes Études in Dakar instead. But Sadji did not relent. The following year he secured a *bourse* to study German at the University of Toulouse, where he found himself facing new hurdles. His year as a geography student in Dakar had not prepared him well for intensive German-language study, and Sadji quickly fell behind his French classmates. He decided he would have to study German in Germany to catch up and was crestfallen to learn that he could not use his scholarship to study abroad, even if his intended destination was France's most important European partner.[3]

There was another Europe, though, and another Germany, where Sadji's ambitions fared much better. In spring 1957, Sadji traveled to Moscow as part of the FEANF delegation to the Sixth World Festival of Youth and Students, a major international event sponsored by two Soviet-backed movements, the Union of International Students and the World Federation of Democratic Youth. In Moscow, Sadji relayed his situation to the Czech president of the student movement, Jiří Pelikán, who was able to arrange a scholarship for Sadji to pursue his studies in the German Democratic Republic (GDR) the following fall. Thwarted at multiple turns in the West's "Eurafrica," Sadji completed his German degree at the Universität Karl Marx in Leipzig. By the time he returned home in 1964, both the French Union and its successor, the French Community, had collapsed; the political dream of Eurafrica had been scaled back to little more than a development framework; and Senegal had become an independent nation-state under the presidency of Léopold Sédar Senghor.[4]

Sadji was one of a few hundred francophone Africans who made their way behind the Iron Curtain in the late 1950s to earn advanced degrees or obtain professional training.[5] Soviet outreach and propaganda actively targeted colonial youth around the globe as part of the "Cold War youth race" with the United States for young hearts and minds, African and European alike.[6] The superpower confrontation broadened the world of youth and student exchanges beyond the France-Europe-Africa nexus that has been the focal point of this book. So too did the rise of complex webs of Third Worldist coalitional politics that promoted South-South cultural and educational exchange, espe-

3. Sadji, *Le rôle de la génération charnière*, 191–196.

4. Sadji, *Le rôle de la génération charnière*, 250–254.

5. Many more would do so after independence. See Monique de Saint Martin, Grazia Scarfò Ghellab, and Kamal Mellakh, eds., *Étudier à l'Est: Expériences de diplômés africains* (Paris: Karthala, 2015); Constantin Katsakioris, "The Soviet-South Encounter: Tensions in the Friendship with Afro-Asian Partners, 1945–1965," in *Cold War Crossings: International Travel and Exchange across the Soviet Bloc, 1940s–1960s*, ed. Patryk Babiracki and Kenyon Zimmer (College Station: Texas A&M University Press, 2014): 134–165.

6. Christopher Sutton, "Britain, Empire and the Origins of the Cold War Youth Race," *Contemporary British History* 30, no. 2 (2016): 224–241, https://doi.org/10.1080/13619462.2015.1079489.

cially in the Muslim world, which offered alternative poles of attraction to young African Muslims. As youth were simultaneously recruited to serve on the front lines of the Cold War and the global movement for decolonization, student exchanges and international youth forums became crucial staging grounds for these interconnected, "multiaxial" global conflicts.[7]

Still, Franco-African solidarity and European unity remained important nodes of aspiration and contestation within those broader global constellations. In the immediate postwar years, international Socialism attempted to fuse anticolonialism and Europeanism to position Europe and its colonies as a "Third Force" between Soviet Communism and US capitalism. French Socialists were especially enthusiastic and played a key role in that effort. In the summer of 1946, they formed the Movement for the Socialist United States of Europe under the presidency of André Philip; shortly thereafter, the French group joined forces with other European Socialists to form the transnational Socialist Movement for the United States of Europe (MSEUE). The French continued to dominate within the wider movement; the MSEUE's first major initiative was to convene a "Congress of European, African and Asian Peoples" in the Parisian suburb of Puteaux the following spring (1948).[8]

The Puteaux Congress brought together more than 200 members of the non-Communist European Left, including Socialist members of the other European federalist movements, along with dozens of African and Asian politicians, syndicalists, and youth leaders, a large proportion of whom were from the French Union.[9] The congress's goal was to find common ground between Europeanist Socialist internationalism and indigenous movements for colonial emancipation in the face of the looming Cold War. The congress's final resolution insisted on the interconnectedness and complementarity of those political projects: "A Socialist United States of Europe and the liberation of dependent peoples are two stages toward the reordering of the global economy within the framework of political, economic, and social democracy." The resolution concluded with a particular appeal to and from youth: "We, the

---

7. Connelly, *A Diplomatic Revolution*; Westad, *The Global Cold War*.

8. Anne-Isabelle Richard, "The Limits of Solidarity: Europeanism, Anticolonialism, and Socialism at the Congress of the Peoples of Europe, Asia and Africa in Puteaux, 1948," *European History Review* 21, no. 4 (2014): 519–537, https://doi.org/10.1080/13507486.2014.933187.

9. Congrès des Peuples d'Europe, d'Asie, et d'Afrique, Puteaux 16–21 juin 1948: Liste des délégués et des observateurs, AHUE: ME-704. Notable participants included Guy Mollet, Alain Savary, Émile Zinsou, and Léopold Senghor (French parliamentary delegation), Frenchmen Alexandre Marc and Henri Frenay and Belgian Hendrik Brugmans (Union of European Federalists), and diverse delegations from Algeria, Néo-Destour, UGT-Tunisia, Istiqlal, Cameroon, and Madagascar, as well as observers from the West African Student Union (the primary association of students from British West Africa) and the Pan-African Congress.

youth, must be the vanguard of this action. . . . We appeal to the conscience of all young people to resist the stultifying indoctrination of which they are the first victims. We must rise up against chauvinism, imperialism, racism, and sectarianism."[10]

While this declaration would seem to align with the stated mission of the congress, the proceedings left its French organizers profoundly disillusioned. The organizing committee lamented that the "European" and "indigenous" delegations had arrived with "diametrically opposed dispositions" and that what had begun as a gathering to promote international Socialism had ended under the banner of national liberation. The committee was particularly disappointed that the *"indigènes* with a European education" had not acted as mediators as the French had hoped and expected and instead allowed the discussions to be overtaken by "demagoguery" and a "primitive political consciousness." Henri Frenay, French president of the transnational Union of European Federalists (UEF) and one of the chief promoters of the congress, relayed with utter dismay that he could not even support most of the motions passed. Frenay and the other organizers concluded that the proceedings proved to be more about "the colonial education of the French delegates than addressing the questions at hand."[11] In other words, the organizers' main takeaway was that the *temperament* of the rising class of colonial leaders foreclosed meaningful dialogue with their European counterparts; French expectations about Franco-African or Euro-African partnership would have to change.[12]

This dispirited postmortem transposed the repertoire of racist stereotypes about francophone Africans and growing pessimism about *brassage* that we have seen developing across European and African France into a transnational European register. The disappointment at Puteaux inaugurated a decisive move within the MSEUE toward a more centrist Europeanism and a retreat from anticolonial politics within the Socialist Left, not just in France but across Europe, though the consequences were felt most profoundly in the French context.[13] To French observers, the colonial delegates at the Congress ap-

---

10. Rapport Politique, Congrès des Peuples d'Europe, d'Asie, et d'Afrique, Puteaux 16–21 juin 1948, AHUE: ME-704.

11. Comité d'Études et d'Action pour les États-Unis Socialistes d'Europe, Rapport sur le Congrès des Peuples, undated, AHUE: ME-704.

12. French Communists did not fare much better in this regard. They experienced similar disappointment and disillusionment with their African comrades at the 1952 Congress of Peoples for Peace in Vienna, organized by two French Communists, Frédéric Joliot-Curie and Jean Lafitte. Two francophone African participants, Jacques N'Gom and Latyr Camara, denounced US imperialism and racism—the main objective of the gathering—but had no less vitriol for the imperialist French Union and called for independence for colonial territories. See Katsakioris, "The Soviet-South Encounter," 139.

13. Richard, "The Limits of Solidarity"; Shaev, "The Algerian War."

peared to be turning away from France and Europe in favor of a larger "Third World" bloc, and their behavior in doing so was deemed *un-French*. Frenay and his colleagues may have regretted what they saw as a kind of emergent global identity politics, but they actively contributed to it in their refusal to recognize their colonial interlocutors as true equals, entitled to their own opinions and free to set their own priorities.

The tension between French recognition of the need for African participation in these kinds of forums and dismissal of what Africans had to say came to operate on a broader scale in the 1950s. French officials grew increasingly alarmed as the onset of the Cold War and the rise of Third Worldism dramatically multiplied the venues and opportunities for African youth to participate in the global debate about what the postwar world should look like. The outbreak of the Algerian Revolution (1954–1962), and Algerian militants' extensive and largely successful international public relations campaign to win sympathy for their cause, intensified French paranoia about international meddling in France's colonial affairs and heightened French concerns about Islam.[14] This final chapter considers how fears about international youth mobilizations in that broader global context collided and converged with more particular anxieties about Franco-African and European integration, further deepening the purchase of postwar racial common sense and the culturalization of Christianity. Those entwined historical processes, whose unfolding this book has traced over the course of the 1940s and 1950s, both contributed to and helped naturalize the astonishingly rapid disaggregation of African and European France in the early 1960s.

Youth Internationalism during the Early Cold War

Toward the end of World War II, French policymakers and educators hailed youth internationalism as a crucial means of securing a peaceful postwar global order. In mid-1944, the Free French commission on education reform in Algiers confidently predicted that international youth exchanges would foster "mutual comprehension of peoples based on familiarity and respect. Union of peoples through youth, through the elites of the future, is the surest guarantee of peace between nations."[15] Such sweeping optimism did not last long, as tensions

---

14. Jeffrey James Byrne, *Mecca of the Revolution: Algeria, Decolonization, and the Third World Order* (Oxford: Oxford University Press, 2016); Shepard, *The Invention of Decolonization*; Connelly, *A Diplomatic Revolution*.

15. Robert Prigent, Rapport au nom de la Commission de l'Éducation nationale, annexe au procès-verbal du 17 mai 1944, AN: C//15255.

between the United States and the Soviet Union escalated at the war's end. Shortly after its founding in London in 1945, the World Federation of Democratic Youth aligned itself with the Soviet Union. Four years later, the United States promoted the World Association of Youth as an anti-Communist alternative for international youth mobilization. These rival forums anchored sprawling networks of youth and student movements and a seemingly endless stream of conferences, congresses, and youth festivals in the 1950s that were attended by tens of thousands of young people in the United States and the Soviet Union, in Western and Eastern Europe, and in Africa and Asia.

Both forums aggressively courted European youth. The Cold War contest for young Europeans' allegiance added an extra impetus for French officials and pro-Europe activists to quickly establish their own youth movements and educational exchanges that would support not just European integration but also Europe's independence in the postwar order. These Cold War dynamics were laid bare in divided Germany. In the French occupation zone, Europe-minded youth and education officials found themselves in possession of a captive audience to promote their vision of united Europe. By the time Amadou Sadji Booker and several dozen other francophone Africans found their way to the GDR in the late 1950s, tens of thousands of young metropolitan French had traveled to West Germany through state-sponsored youth exchanges that sought to achieve Franco-German reconciliation within an explicit transnational European framework.

Youth and European Unity in French-Occupied Germany and the Early Federal Republic

As the Western Allied military governments began transferring authority to the Federal Republic in the fall of 1949, the French ambassador to Britain sent a celebratory note to Raymond Schmittlein, the outgoing head of public education in the French occupation zone. A military man who rallied early to de Gaulle, Schmittlein first started working on education issues in mid-1944 as a member of the Algiers commission on education reform; he assumed his post as education director in the French military government in Germany the following year. The missive from London congratulated him for the praise his work was receiving in the British press.[16] Enclosed was the full text of an article in the foreign

---

16. Ambassadeur de France en Grande Bretagne to Raymond Schmittlein, Baden-Baden a/s appréciation britannique sur notre politique culturelle en Allemagne, September 21, 1949, AMAE: Série HCRFA, Affaires Culturelles, Cabinet: 1AC/168/3.

affairs publication *Time and Tide,* entitled "Hitler's Lost Generation." The piece commended the French occupation authority for its "imaginative realism" in its approach toward German youth. Its author, a British peer and writer for the BBC, effusively lauded French efforts to forge personal contacts with German students, educators, and youth leaders. Significantly, he characterized the French approach as distinctly "European." He mused, "The Russians think as Asiatics, the Americans as Americans, the British, in their more enlightened moments, as citizens of the world. Only the French think as Europeans. And, not unnaturally, it is this European approach that has the most appeal for young Germans."[17]

All the Western occupying powers agreed on the need for German reeducation, but the French occupation strategy stood apart from that of the British and the Americans. The French focused on culture and specifically targeted German youth, whereas the Anglo-American approach centered on the German leadership.[18] As Richard Ivan Jobs has shown, the French authorities were the first to institute a policy of youth travel on a mass scale as a means of reconciliation and intentionally promoted a policy of "fraternization." As early as 1946, more than a thousand French youth had visited the French zone; by 1948, some fifty thousand French children had attended summer camps in the Black Forest region near the French border.[19] Schmittlein's department acted quickly in the realm of formal education as well; the occupation authority brought in hundreds of French-language instructors and set up French Institutes in all the major cities in the French zone. The French authorities also maintained their oversight over education the longest, until the very end of the occupation (whereas the British handed control over education back to the Germans in 1947). As Jobs emphasizes, all these initiatives demonstrate an "ideological commitment to using interpersonal contact as a tool of foreign policy."[20] In this, the French approach in postwar Germany was not all that different from the promotion of *brassage* as the basis of France-Africa relations.

---

17. Sir Basil Bartlett, "Hitler's Lost Generation," *Time and Tide,* September 10, 1949.

18. That said, both the British and the US occupation authorities did promote active pedagogical methods in education as part of their broader democratization project. In general, the French authorities emphasized democracy much less, but Sonja Levsen characterizes Schmittlein as an exception in this regard, for he did consider renovated pedagogical methods as a democratizing tool. Sonja Levsen, "Authority and Democracy in Postwar France and West Germany, 1945–1968," *Journal of Modern History* 89 (December 2017): 812–850, https://doi.org/10.1086/694614.

19. Significantly, these *colonies de vacances* had an explicit Christian orientation; Jewish children, many of whom had been orphaned during the war, were sent to separate *colonies israélites,* which were privately organized and sponsored by Jewish charities. See Karen Adler, "Children as a Tool of Occupation in the French Zone of Occupation of Germany, from 1945 to 1949," *Nottingham French Studies* 59, no. 2 (2020): 191–205, https://doi.org/10.3366/nfs.2020.0284.

20. Jobs, *Backpack Ambassadors,* 62–65.

However, for Schmittlein, the broader context for Franco-German reconcilia-tion was not the French Union but rather a robust and independent united Eu-rope. Under his stewardship, the French occupation zone became a crucial site for the articulation of a vision of Europe and European values in explicit con-tradistinction not only to Soviet Communism, but also to Anglo-Americanism within the larger frame of "the West." During his tenure, Schmittlein helped found several European institutions that continue to operate today, including a school to train interpreters in European languages in Germersheim and the In-stitute for European History in Mainz.[21] Generally, though, he prioritized pro-gramming that went beyond pedagogical and curricular reform in the classroom to forge lasting personal bonds between French and German young people. To that end, he developed a series of regular *rencontres* and exchange programs for French and German students, youth leaders, and teachers.

Franco-German youth programs in the late 1940s were not mass events—they typically brought together no more than one hundred participants who were already active in organized youth movements. Prominent pro-Europe leaders were brought in to make the case for European federalism, including André Philip and Hendrik Brugmans (who helped organize the Puteaux Con-gress and served as the rector of the College of Europe from 1950–1972). Most participants' time was spent in small breakout sessions over the course of a week, sometimes even a month, discussing such topics as the historical bases of European unity, Europe's role in international affairs, and "the responsibil-ity of youth in remaking the world." Young Germans sat for presentations on "French civilization and religion" and "the evolution of secular rationalism," alongside the occasional lecture on the French Union. Race and racism, how-ever, were conspicuously absent topics from the programs year after year, re-inforcing the construction of postwar European racelessness that we saw unfolding in organizations like the Conference of Allied Ministers of Educa-tion at the end of the war.[22]

---

21. His other achievements included the founding of several modern middle schools, Johannes Gutenberg University in Mainz, and what is today the Deutsche Universität für Verwaltungswissen-schaften Speyer. On Schmittlein and French youth and education policy in occupied Germany more generally, see Jérôme Valliant, ed., *La Dénazification par les vainqueurs: la politique culturelle des occupants en Allemagne 1945–1949* (Lille: Université de Lille, 1981); Stefan Zauner, *Erziehung und Kulturmission: Fransreichs Bildungs-Politik in Deutschland, 1945–1949* (Munich: R. Oldenbourg Verlag, 1994).

22. For a typical program of the Franco-German *rencontres* of the period, see the schedule of the Centre d'Action Culturelle de Spire, Session d'études du 16 août–16 septembre 1949: "L'Europe à la re-cherche de l'unité: Ses éléments constitutifs dans l'Histoire, Perspectives d'avenir," AHUE: ME-1920. On Brugmans's involvement, see André Decamps, Consul de France à Francfort, to M. Tarbe de Saint Har-douin, Ambassadeur de France à Berlin, May 26, 1948, a/s Commémoration des événements de 1848, AMAE: Série HCRFA, Affaires Culturelles, Cabinet: 1AC/168/3.

Rather than tackle Nazi racism head-on, Schmittlein deliberately excised the vocabulary of race from his efforts to dismantle "German nationalism." Schmittlein saw his essential mission as convincing young Germans to stop believing that conflict with France was "something natural that they inherited from their fathers, their grandfathers, and even their oldest ancestors. It is essential that they stop believing this, first because it simply is not true, and second, because even if it was once true, it can no longer be so." Schmittlein construed the racial undertones of this line of thought as a relic of the past, and he invoked his own youth initiatives as proof. Unlike the preceding generation, he insisted, French and German youth were now, "in their real desire to get to know one another," becoming conscious of their "common origin and common civilization." For Schmittlein, a "United States of Europe" would further strengthen those bonds if the groundwork were properly laid, which was precisely what his Franco-German youth gatherings sought to do. As the CAME had done in London in 1945, Schmittlein also identified new approaches to history instruction as another important and related step in that process. Thus, Schmittlein instituted extensive programs for German schoolteachers to attend *écoles normales* in France in addition to exchanges for French and German high school and university students.[23]

The French High Command in Bonn lauded the spirit of these efforts but criticized their limited reach. Alain Peyrefitte, a young attaché in Bonn (who would later have the misfortune to serve as education minister during the 1968 uprisings), lamented in 1950 that most young Germans had not had the opportunity to participate in Schmittlein's exchanges and consequently remained "lost at sea." Peyrefitte saw similar hopelessness and indifference among youth across Europe. He urged that what both German and European youth needed was a higher ideal to inspire them at a time when nations and nationalisms seemed increasingly "outdated" and the war itself had "broadened young people's mental horizons." He was especially worried that if European youth were left to themselves, they would get swept up in the movements aligned

---

23. Raymond Schmittlein, Note pour M. le Général d'Armée, Commandant en Chef Français en Allemagne, December 24, 1948, AMAE: Série HCRFA, Affaires Culturelles, Cabinet: 1AC/168/2. The textbook reform project continued and expanded after the end of the French occupation with the 1951 Franco-German Historians Agreement, which Mona Siegal and Kirsten Harjes describe as "one of the most successful models of cultural diplomacy and peace education worldwide." Although they acknowledge its significance as a "lynchpin of the New Europe" and a powerful symbol of "postnationalist Europe," they also emphasize that the success of the venture was rooted in a longer, specifically Franco-German history of conflict and reconciliation going back to World War I. See Mona Siegal and Kirsten Harjes, "Disarming Hatred: History Education, National Memories, and Franco-German Reconciliation from World War I to the Cold War," *History of Education Quarterly* 57, no. 3 (August 2012): 371–372, https://doi.org/10.1111/j.1748–5959.2012.00404.x.

with the opposing Cold War blocs and lose their sense of self. He insisted that only the idea of Europe itself could truly energize European youth in a productive direction. Consequently, he proposed a European mass youth movement for boys and girls from all class backgrounds, ages 15–25, to rival the Soviet- and US-backed networks of youth and student organizations.[24]

Christina Norwig has argued that the "myth of youth" encouraged early pro-Europe activists to approach European integration as a generational project.[25] Peyrefitte's reports from Bonn reveal just how deliberate and self-consciously that myth was mobilized. In his plea for a European youth movement, he declared: "Europe—a cultural, historical, artistic, and spiritual entity as well as a political one—appears to be becoming the 'myth' of the twentieth century, just as nationalities were the myth of the nineteenth: if the seeds of Liberty were planted in the name of national independence in 1848 . . . in 1950, they are being planted in the name of European independence."[26] This sentiment was widely shared by the West German leadership. As Konrad Adenauer, the Federal Republic's first president and an ardent partisan of European integration, bluntly put it: "European ideology" would be the solution to German youth's troubles. German youth leaders in Bonn expressed similar opinions in the local press.[27]

Adenauer (b. 1876) and Peyrefitte (b. 1925) were of different generations and social milieus, but they shared a Christian conception of Europe. Adenauer came from a conservative Catholic family, had been active in Catholic student associations in his youth, and was a cofounder and the first leader of Germany's Christian Democratic Union. His Europeanism, unsurprisingly, was unabashedly Christian. Peyrefitte, on the other hand, came from a strong

---

24. Alain Peyrefitte, Note a/s jeunesse allemande et jeunesse européenne, undated (c. 1950), AHUE: ME-1920.

25. Norwig, "A First European Generation?"

26. Peyrefitte's clear articulation of this conceptual shift demonstrates that it was not just elder statesmen and established politicians who were framing European unity as a generational project, but elite European youth themselves. (Peyrefitte was only twenty-five when he penned this position, which, according to his own rubric, slotted him in the category of youth.)

27. Cited in Jobs, *Backpack Ambassadors*, 36. Jobs also cites a 1946 article by twenty-one-year-old Dieter Danckwortt, blaming Germany's situation on the older generation and proposing identification with Europe and a new kind of camaraderie for "young Europe" as a way forward for German youth (34). Danckwortt remained committed to this political ideal more than a decade later. He became a specialist and researcher of youth exchanges and intercultural contact and frequently worked on projects for European entities. Notably, he conducted a major study on African and Asian students in Europe, one of the first big projects commissioned by the Foundation of European Culture shortly after its founding in 1959, which preempted many of the conceptual shifts discussed at the end of chapter 4. See his *Une jeune élite de l'Asie et de l'Afrique comme hôtes et élèves en Europe (problèmes de la communication d'une image de la culture européenne aux étudiants et stagiaires en Europe, venus de pays en voie de développement de l'Asie et de l'Afrique): Une étude sociologique sur l'ordre de la Fondation Européenne de la Culture* (Institut Psychologique de Hambourg, August 1959).

secular-republican background, the son of two public schoolteachers and a graduate of the École Normale Supérieure and the first class of the new École Nationale d'Administration. Nevertheless, Peyrefitte also framed his vision for European youth in explicitly Christian terms. Only a properly European youth movement, he argued, would "mobilize the energy and enthusiasm of [European youth] according to the values of Western, democratic, and Christian civilization."[28]

The Christian aspect of Peyrefitte's pro-Europe rhetoric is less surprising given the significant recalibrations of postwar *laïcité* that we saw taking place across France, French Africa, and transnational European institutions in the late 1940s. To those processes, we may also add French management of the reconfessionalization of German schooling in the French occupation zone. The Nazi regime had closed religious schools when it nationalized education in 1937. Consequently, reinstating the long-standing right of German parents to send their children to the *Konfessionsshule* of their choice was understood as part of the larger process of democratization and bringing postwar Germany back into the European fold. In post-Holocaust Germany, in practical terms, that meant reopening Protestant and Catholic schools.[29] What was really at issue, then, was the right of Christian parents to provide their children with a Christian education. The process was essentially inverted in post-Vichy France; the Vichy regime had inaugurated state support for confessional schools, and the postwar republic stayed the course. Thus, it was not empty rhetoric when French and German youth in Schmittlein's *rencontres* were taught that they belonged to a common European civilization that was *both* Christian and secular. That vision was institutionally instantiated in the postwar educational landscape across France and West Germany.

Peyrefitte's aspirations for the mobilization of European youth on a grander scale were realized with the founding of the European Youth Campaign (EYC) in late 1951. The EYC was a transnational European organization, but it grew out of the European youth programs developed in the French occupation zone. In the summer of 1949, with the French occupation authority's full support, the organization Juventus, which soon after became the Young European

---

28. Peyrefitte, Note a/s jeunesse allemande, AHUE: ME-1920.

29. Travail de synthèse sur les questions de reconfessionalisation des écoles primaires allemandes dans la Province du Palatinat, December 8, 1949, AMAE: Série HCRFA, Affaires Culturelles: 1AC/198/2a. In 1933 in Rhineland-Palatinate, there were 305 Catholic schools, 421 Protestant schools, six Jewish schools, and 74 "simultaneous schools" (where religious instruction was offered in multiple faiths). The government's proposal to reopen confessional schools in 1949 called for the establishment of 273 Catholic schools, 401 Protestant schools, 103 simultaneous schools, and no Jewish schools.

Federalists, organized a European Youth Camp for about one hundred participants on the banks of the Rhine at the Lorelei rock formation.[30] This small gathering was deemed such a success that it was dramatically expanded two years
later. The summer-long European Youth Rally in 1951 brought more than
thirty-five thousand young Europeans to the Lorelei camp grounds for one- to
ten-day sessions. Sixty percent of the participants were German; 20 percent
were French; 10 percent were British; and the rest mainly hailed from the Netherlands, Belgium, and Italy. (Participants of all nationalities were overwhelming
male; just a third were young women and girls.) This meeting of "Europe on the
Rhine" was officially sponsored by the West German Bundesjugendring, but the
idea and the lion's share of the planning originated with the French occupation
authorities on the eve of their departure. Jean Moreau, head of the department
of international meetings in the French military government, saw the Lorelei
Rally as the culmination of his work in occupied Germany.[31] Shortly thereafter,
he assumed the first presidency of the EYC, which used the Lorelei Rally as a
model for its large-scale events over the next several years.[32]

The timing of the 1951 Lorelei Rally aligned with the internal process of
European integration as well as the escalating Cold War youth race. The rally
took place amid public debate about the European Coal and Steel Community (ECSC), the first major institutional breakthrough in early European integration. French Christian Democrat Robert Schuman had unveiled his plan
for the ECSC the year before; the Schuman Plan, as it was known, was rati-
fied by the parliaments of "the Six" the following summer.[33] The ECSC was
a recurring subject of dinner-debates and plenaries at Lorelei. The organizers
hoped that the massive scale and press coverage of the event would promote
the ECSC to the wider public. At the same time, the Lorelei Rally was also
intended as a counterweight to the Third World Festival of Youth and Students
that was held in East Berlin that same summer, which similarly drew tens of
thousands of young people, not just from Europe but from more than one
hundred countries around the world.[34] The anti-Communist rationale for the

---

30. See the dossier "Jeunesses européennes fédéralistes, création et activités, 1950–1951," AHUE:
UEF-175.

31. Jobs, *Backpack Ambassadors*, 68–81.

32. See the dossier "Campagne européenne de la jeunesse—projets de rallye ou rassemblement
européen de la jeunesse, 1951–1954, Correspondance et notes," AHUE: ME-134. The EYC continued
to organize smaller-scale events along the model of Schmittlein's *rencontres* as well, like the 1953 European Youth Gathering in Brest discussed at the beginning of this book.

33. The six original members of the ECSC, as well as the EEC and EURATOM, were France,
West Germany, Italy, Belgium, the Netherlands, and Luxembourg.

34. Nick Rutter, "The Western Wall: The Iron Curtain Recast in Summer 1951," in *Cold War Crossings*, ed. Babiracki and Zimmer, 78–107.

Lorelei Rally was also a driving force behind the creation of the EYC, which was secretly funded by the US Central Intelligence Agency (CIA).[35]

And yet, despite those incontrovertible Cold War dimensions, neither the European Youth Rally at Lorelei nor the EYC that grew out of it should be reduced to Cold War imperatives alone. Both were intended to achieve broad social and cultural processes of European integration through interpersonal contact and connection—that is, to make young people in Europe *feel* "European." That goal was perhaps the most important factor in determining the actual content of pro-Europe programming in postwar West Germany and beyond. Schmittlein's *rencontres,* the Lorelei Rally, and subsequent EYC events all emphasized specifically European forms of solidarity and belonging. Such cultural particularism distinguished European youth initiatives from the more global orientation of Cold War internationalism. That distinction also had important repercussions with regard to race. European youth mobilizations doubly avoided any serious discussion of race and racism, first by reframing histories of conflict and division within Europe as the result of unbridled nationalism, and second by either sanitizing or ignoring European colonialism in both the past and the present. The rival Cold War youth forums, on the other hand, locked in a fierce battle for the allegiance of colonial youth, openly championed self-determination and racial equality.[36] However disingenuous those commitments may have been, the vast scope of US- and Soviet-backed youth and student movements, in which hundreds of thousands of young people from around the world participated over the course of the 1950s, elevated those principles to powerful international norms.[37]

While European youth events in the late 1940s and early 1950s were generally exclusive spaces, the Cold War youth forums actively cultivated participation from the colonial world. As both physical venues and moral arbiters, those forums dramatically expanded opportunities for francophone African youth to

---

35. This has come to light in recent years with a newly declassified cache of documents, referenced in both Norwig, "A First European Generation?," and McKenzie, "The European Youth Campaign in Ireland." This obviously compromised the EYC's ostensible independence, but in my research, I have found that many, if not most, of the people who volunteered with the EYC were genuinely committed to an independent Europe and were unaware of the CIA connection.

36. On the evolution of the Soviet side of this campaign, from the late 1940s into the postindependence period, see Nick Rutter, "Unity and Conflict in the Socialist Scramble for Africa," in *The Global 1960s: Convention, Contest, Counterculture,* ed. Tamara Chaplin and Jadwiga E. Pieper Mooney (New York: Routledge, 2018): 33–51.

37. Metropolitan French and French Africans were fully aware of US hypocrisy in this regard, but Francophone Africans' experience of racism, including racist violence, in the Soviet Union and elsewhere in the Eastern bloc was a painful shock, as was Soviet suspicion and derision when African visitors tested Soviet claims of religious liberty by seeking out Catholic churches or mosques. See Katsakioris, "The Soviet-South Encounter," 135–141. For personal and eyewitness accounts, see Sadji, *Le rôle de la génération charnière,* 250–276.

make claims for particular rights, to protest ongoing discrimination and new forms of oppression, and to embarrass France in the court of international opinion at a time when French leaders were trying to project an image of the French Union as a model multiracial democracy to the world. At the same time, French anxieties about Communist and US influence on African youth reinforced French stereotypes about African susceptibility to foreign manipulation, which also informed French concerns about pan-Arabism and Islam in "Black Africa." French officials monitored with equal vehemence African participation in the Cold War youth forums and the itineraries of young African Muslims who pursued Islamic religious study and Arabic-language instruction elsewhere in the Muslim world. Surveillance of African youth in the international arena both reflected and intensified the culturalization of Christianity and postwar racial common sense across European and African France in the 1950s.

African Youth on the World Stage

French officials entered the postwar era convinced that the most serious threats to French rule in the region came from forces from *outside* rather than from *within* African societies. Just two months after the German surrender that ended the war in Europe, the French provisional government meditated on the fragility of France's position in sub-Saharan Africa. As one national security briefing put it, Africa had been "folded in on itself, morally separate from the rest of the planet . . . for millennia" but now found itself, "in one sudden stroke, integrated into the rest of world." That sentiment reflected a long-standing repertoire of colonialist tropes that depicted Africa as both a blank slate and a world apart. Given Africa's "extreme permeability" to "new ideas and the great spiritual movements of the age," the briefing continued, it was no longer clear whether the old colonial powers could retain control of the social transformation and "spiritual progression" of the continent. The gravest threats, the briefing concluded, were Soviet and US anticolonialism and "Islamism."[38] A decade later, French officials were even more distraught by the prospect that young Africans would heed "the call from Cairo, Bandung, New York, or Moscow."[39]

From 1945 on, French colonial education officials were keenly attuned to anticolonial international opinion, and they were not alone. British and Belgian colonial officials were also deeply alarmed by postwar international interest in the state of colonial education in their African colonies. Schooling for Africans in

---

38. "Bulletin de renseignements: Étude a/s Islam et Afrique Noire; Les grands courants politiques dans le monde islamique et en Afrique Noire," July 25, 1945, ANOM: 1AFFPOL/2260.

39. Letter from Paul Chauvet [Gougal AEF] to the Directeur-Affaires Politiques, MFOM, June 6, 1955, ANOM: AEF GGAEF 5D/269.

the Belgian Congo remained extremely limited, but the British had recognized the urgency of investing more in African education during the early war years, slightly before the French. The British Colonial Office sent metropolitan bureaucrats on educational missions to wartime British Africa beginning in 1940, and in 1943—a year before the Brazzaville Conference—the British formed a Colonial Higher Education Commission that explicitly called for "radical" reforms. The Colonial Welfare and Development Acts (1940, 1945), like the French FIDES program (1946), made unprecedented volumes of British public funds available for African social programs and educational development. In contrast to the French case, though, in 1947, Britain's African colonial governors jointly committed to prioritizing African higher education, rather than universal primary schooling, in anticipation of an eventual transfer of power and African self-rule. They quickly established a first round of university colleges in Makerere (Uganda), Ibadan (Nigeria), and Legon (Gold Coast), with more following soon after.[40] Britain was, therefore, in a much better position than France to stave off international oversight and intervention at the university level after the war, but Britain was similarly vulnerable regarding the lower orders of education.

When UNESCO announced that guaranteeing basic education would be one of its first priorities, French, British, and Belgian colonial education authorities banded together to prevent UNESCO's basic education programs from making inroads in colonial Africa. After a series of tripartite conferences to "coordinate" their colonial education efforts in the late 1940s, France, Britain, and Belgium formed a more extensive intercolonial front, the Commission for Technical Cooperation in Africa (CCTA, 1950–1965), with the other remaining African colonial powers. Despite an ostensible emphasis on coordination, the CCTA's intercolonial conferences were purely comparative and informational; they were not intended to create common policies or new standards for African education. As director of education in Madagascar, Edmond Cabrière forcefully drove that point home in his opening remarks as the host of the CCTA "inter-African" conference on primary education in Tananarive in 1954. A decade after he lost his post as director of the Lycée Van Vollenhollen in Dakar for refusing to desegregate the school, Cabrière was still in the upper echelons of the French colonial education bureaucracy, and he found like-minded colleagues in the deeply conservative and defensive CCTA. The CCTA's obstructionism was wildly successful over the next decade; prior to 1961, UNESCO was able to get a real foothold only in US-allied Liberia.[41]

---

40. Whitehead, "The Impact of the Second World War."
41. Matasci, "Une 'UNESCO africaine'?" See also Hugo Gonçalves Dores and Miguel Bandeira Jéronimo, "Un 'développement' éclairé? La question de l'éducation coloniale en Afrique et les organisations interimpériales (1945–1957)," in Repenser la mission civilisatrice, ed. Matasci et al., 85–103.

The colonial powers were suspicious of UNESCO as an arm of US Cold War cultural diplomacy. They read UNESCO's interest in Africa as a reflection of both US and Soviet influence on international opinion and growing anticolonial sentiment worldwide.[42] At a Franco-British session on colonial education at Oxford in 1946, French official Paul Henry characterized that influence as the most significant factor—more than pressure coming from the colonies themselves or metropolitan public opinion—that was "accelerating the rhythm of political evolution" in colonial Africa. As we saw in chapter 4, the perception of the increasing pace of change encouraged observers to think in generational terms. Henry underscored the "profound rift in the thinking of administrators who have been pursuing a more traditional approach for the past ten years and those who are developing new colonial policies in response to the pressures of global opinion."[43] For Henry, that rearguard older generation, which included men like Cabrière, was a real impediment to achieving more lasting and meaningful reform.

The political consequences of the generation gap in colonial officials' mentalities were perceived in almost the exact opposite sense as generational divides in colonial African society. In the late 1940s, metropolitan French leaders self-consciously included African politicians in French delegations to the UN and other international bodies as proof of the French Union's democratic bona fides.[44] French colonial officials deployed this strategy because they were comfortable with the older generation of French-educated African elites, the évolués. French officialdom felt very differently about the rising generation of Africans who were participating in the continuous cycle of congresses, conferences, and festivals associated with the Cold War youth forums in the 1950s on their own terms. Colonial officials recognized that they could not ban African participation outright with the democratic legitimacy of the French Union on the line, but they were intensely suspicious that the forums were hotbeds of anticolonial propaganda that would radicalize African youth.[45] As a result, young Africans with connections to the Soviet- or US-backed movements were put under rigorous surveillance, their every move and every contact closely monitored and recorded.

---

42. For a Cold War perspective on the UNESCO campaign for universal education, see Dorn and Ghodsee, "The Cold War Politicization of Literacy."

43. Paul Henry, Note sur les Sessions d'études coloniales, Oxford, April 17, 1946, ANOM: 1AFFPOL/1296.

44. On this strategy of tokenism in the international arena, see Marker, "Obscuring Race."

45. Young Africans themselves possessed a strong generational identity. Sadji's memoir, *Le rôle de la génération charnière*, is also a collective biography of African youth and student activists in the 1940s–1960s; "la génération charnière" translates as "the hinge generation."

From their inception, the World Federation of Democratic Youth (WFDY) and its sister organization, the International Union of Students (IUS), championed the rights of colonial peoples to self-determination. Thus, they posed an unambiguous threat to France's ambition to hold on to its African empire after the war.[46] The organizations took outspoken positions against global racism and used multiracial imagery in their posters, journals, and pamphlets to appeal to colonial youth. Despite French efforts to deter African participation in these movements, young francophone Africans began finding their way to their festivals behind the Iron Curtain in the early 1950s.[47] That participation exploded once the youth wing of the largest African political party in AOF, the Rassemblement de Jeunesse Démocratique Africaine (RJDA), became a WFDY member.[48] From then on, WFDY- and IUS-sponsored events became a key part of the political and international formation of many future postcolonial African elites. The French security apparatus in AOF took note when Abdoulaye Wade (future president of Senegal) and Ousmane Sembène (celebrated Senegalese filmmaker), as well as lesser-known student activists like Sadji, headed to the World Festival of Youth and Students in Moscow in 1957. They were part of a delegation of close to 350 young francophone African men and women who marched under the banner of "Black Africa under French domination."[49] The 1957 festival was a milestone of the post-Stalinist Thaw and a major accelerator of Soviet outreach to young Africans; it led to the creation of the Soviet-African Friendship Society (1959) and the People's Friendship University (1960), renamed Patrice Lumumba University shortly after Lumumba's CIA-assisted assassination in early 1961.[50]

The Soviet-backed forums also served as key venues for Africans to protest the extraordinary surveillance they were subjected to, both at home and abroad. Shortly after the Moscow festival, a delegation from the FEANF traveled to Prague to denounce French efforts to stymie their movement before Jiří Pelikán and the executive board of the IUS.[51] The delegation decried the

---

46. Rutter, "Unity and Conflict in the Socialist Scramble for Africa," 35.

47. Odile Goerg notes that a young Sékou Touré attended the 1951 Festival in Berlin. See her "Les mouvements de jeunesse en Guinée de la colonisation à la constitution de la JRDA, 1890–1959," in *Le mouvement associatif des jeunes*, ed. d'Almeida-Topor and Goerg, 35.

48. The evolution of the group's stance can be traced in their publication *La Voix des Jeunes: Bulletin officiel du RJDA*, ANOM: BIB SOM POM/d/174. On the RJDA and Cold War politics, see Schmidt, *Cold War and Decolonization in Guinea*.

49. Bulletin de renseignement, SDECE, November 30, 1957, ANS: 17G/604 (152). French security services also tracked French Communist youth who traveled to the African Federations. See multiple dossiers in ANOM: 1AFFPOL/2265.

50. Katsakioris, "The Soviet-South Encounter," 145.

51. Pelikán found asylum in Italy after the Prague Spring (1968) and served in the European Parliament on behalf of the Italian Sociality Party from 1979 to 1989.

withdrawal of the colonial administration's financial support and multiple seizures of the FEANF's journal, *L'Étudiant d'Afrique Noire*. The trip was successful: the IUS issued a resounding condemnation of France's "flagrant violation of the most basic democratic freedoms of African students in France" and affirmed "unflinching support for the FEANF in the anticolonial struggle."[52] The colonial administration resumed its financial support of the FEANF the following month.[53]

While the conflict between French interests and the ideological stance of the Communist youth and student movements was clear, the French position toward the US-backed World Association of Youth (WAY) was more complex and changed significantly over the course of the 1950s. French officials initially viewed the organization favorably, as another potential platform to shore up France's international prestige. In 1950, the French member council of the WAY requested millions of additional francs from the French Foreign Affairs Ministry to provide its delegations with more polished printed materials to bring to international meetings, and the council urged that France should try to host a WAY summit somewhere in southern France. "The arrival in France of some 400 foreign delegates," the council argued, "would be a unique occasion to impress upon them the cultural radiance of our country."[54]

One way to bolster the French position within the WAY was to bring in France's African territories. The colonial administration established the Youth Council of the French Union in 1950 as an umbrella organization to align local African youth groups with the WAY.[55] By 1952, the French national council had fifty delegates and the council of the French Union had another fifty. The metropolitan council cheered that the sizable delegation from the French Union "enabled the French perspective to maintain the preponderant place it has always occupied in the international arena regarding questions relating to youth."[56] Indeed, the doubling of the French delegation advanced the French bid to host one of the WAY's international congresses later that year. However, it was ultimately Dakar, rather than some southern metropolitan town, that French officials decided to showcase. Hosting the WAY in Dakar served dual purposes for the French. The decision sought to celebrate all that France had achieved in French Africa and promote the French Union, but it was also a com

52. Letter from Dir-Services de Sécurité AOF to Chefs des Services de Police a/s Résolution sur la FEANF par le Comité Exécutif de l'UIE, July 23, 1957, ANS: 21G/210 (178).

53. Haut-Commissaire AOF—Décision du 27 août 1957, ANS: 18G/210 (160).

54. Budget du Conseil Français pour l'Assemblée mondiale de la jeunesse, 1950, CAC: 19880437/24.

55. For a longer discussion, see Hélène d'Almeida-Topor, "Les associations de jeunesse en AOF (1946–1960): Évolution d'ensemble et particularités locales," in *Le mouvement associatif des jeunes*, ed. d'Almeida-Topor and Goerg, 61–62.

56. Conseil Français pour le WAY, Exposé des motifs (1952), CAC: 19880437/24.

petitive response to Britain's bid to host the next WAY conference in the Gold Coast (contemporary Ghana).[57] Some French Africans also saw the public relations value of the opportunity. Jean Marc Ekoh, a mission-educated youth leader from Gabon, was immensely proud to see Dakar, "a French city, an African city," host the WAY. Ekoh was especially keen for an international audience to see that students at the lycée were Black, that the mayor was Black (Lamine Guèye), and that Blacks occupied other important positions in the French Union.[58]

The central topic at the 1952 WAY meeting in Dakar was the role of youth in the fight against racial, religious, and gender discrimination. This was, in fact, a continuation of the theme of the previous WAY conference the year before, in Ithaca, New York, where two representatives from French Africa, Étienne Nouafo of Cameroun and Émile Zinsou of Dahomey, coauthored the conference's final resolution on racial discrimination with a US delegate from the National Association for the Advancement of Colored People (NAACP).[59] The resolution called for curricular changes and youth exchanges to combat racial prejudice—particularly new textbooks and "interracial summer camps." The resolution also championed the social promotion of racial minorities and autochtones and called on public administrations around the world to hire more young people from those backgrounds.[60]

French colonial officials found the WAY's early emphasis on racial discrimination less threatening than the more overtly anticolonial position the movement increasingly espoused in the mid-1950s. That racial discrimination and colonialism could be construed as totally separate issues in the French official mind speaks volumes about what French politicians and policymakers thought colonial reform actually entailed. Indeed, many French observers felt that France had nothing to be ashamed of with regard to racial discrimination, especially when compared to the United States. French delegates were incredulous when Americans at the Ithaca conference tried to convince their francophone African interlocutors that reports about the dreadful state of race relations in the United States in the foreign press were merely part of a Communist conspiracy to make the United States look bad.[61]

57. Conseil Français pour le WAY, Exposé des motifs (1953), CAC: 19880437/24.

58. Jean Marc Ekoh, "La Jeunesse de tous les coins du monde découvre l'Afrique française," undated (enclosed in a missive from Gougal-AEF to MFOM, September 26, 1952), ANOM 1AFFPOL/2265.

59. Zinsou was also a participant at the Congress of Peoples in Puteaux in 1948.

60. Atelier 1: Discrimination Raciale, Texte Définitif, Congrès de la WAY, Ithaca, August 1951, ANOM: 1AFFPOL/2265. This reflected francophone African demands for the Africanization of the colonial bureaucracy, which became a key point of contention in the broader project of colonial reform. See Cooper, Citizenship between Empire and Nation.

61. Note d'Information a/s reunion de la WAY, January 16, 1952, ANOM: 1AFFPOL/2265.

The tables turned, however, once the WAY's focus on combating racism shifted to ending colonialism. French officials then became as suspicious of the WAY as they were of the Soviet-backed youth and student movements. By 1958, the French security service concluded: "The WAY is thoroughly anticolonialist in two senses—as much by the natural vocation of its sponsors on the other side of the Atlantic, as out of concern to not leave the field open to the World Federation of Democratic Youth with regard to the dependent peoples. It has consequently pursued a politics of one-upmanship and interference towards the youth of those peoples."[62] Odile Goerg, an historian of African youth politics in this period, proposes a different interpretation of the WAY's anticolonial politics. She argues that the movement's growing anticolonial militancy in the late 1950s was a response to francophone African youth leaders' decision to withdraw their associations from the WAY and the Youth Council of the French Union in 1955 in protest of both entities' close ties with the French colonial administration.[63]

In this light, African activism, as much as the Cold War youth race, shaped the global politics of the WAY. Put another way, the collective and individual actions and politics of young people themselves mattered. This was true for both francophone African and US activists. It was likely not merely a coincidence that the increasingly militant anticolonialism of the WAY coincided with Immanuel Wallerstein's tenure as vice president of the movement from 1954 to 1958, when he was still just a promising doctoral student. His incendiary speeches at youth rallies during his frequent visits to French Africa in the late 1950s attracted the attention of the French security services, which labeled him "a systematically anti-French anticolonialist" and "intransigent enemy" of France.[64] Wallerstein spoke on behalf of the WAY at a festival independently organized by francophone West African youth in Bamako in 1958 that was attended by more than three thousand people. According to one French witness, Wallerstein roused the crowd, proclaiming: "The WAY ardently hopes that the mobilization of African youth will lead to the ultimate goal—the independence of the continent." The observer noted that even Communists were more discreet.[65]

Fearful of both Soviet and US anticolonialism, French colonial authorities tried to discourage African students from traveling to the United States or behind the Iron Curtain for university throughout the period. For most of the

---

62. SDECE, Notice d'Information—La WAY, August 18, 1958, ANOM: 1AFFPOL/2398.

63. Goerg, "Les movements de jeunesse," in *Le mouvement associatif des jeunes*, ed. d'Almeida-Topor and Goerg, 27. For a scathing critique of the WAY and its conference in Dakar alongside a withering resume of stalled education reform, see Alioune Paye, "Rapport Moral du RJDA," undated (transmitted from the Gougal AOF to MFOM, February 22, 1956), ANOM: 1AFFPOL/2265.

64. SDECE, Notice d'Information—La WAY, August 18, 1958.

65. De la Fournière, Note a/s Festival de la Jeunesse d'Afrique, Bamako, 6–12 septembre 1958 (September 16, 1958), ANOM: 1AFFPOL/2189, dossier 2.

late colonial period, the number of Africans going in either direction remained quite small.[66] Sadji was one of the first francophone Africans to study in the GDR; few others ultimately joined him there, with the notable exception of students from Guinée. Young Guineans actively sought out educational opportunities in the East earlier than most after Guinée's historic vote to not join the French Community in September 1958 abruptly ended state support for Guineans to pursue advanced study in Dakar or metropolitan France.[67]

However, as the French provisional government had already anticipated in 1945, the United States and the Soviet bloc were not the only foreign poles of attraction for African students in the postwar decades. Young Africans were also considering new opportunities in the emerging "Third World." The Afro-Asian Conference in Bandung, Indonesia, in April 1955 is typically considered a watershed in that regard.[68] The Conference's Final Communiqué condemned European colonial powers' efforts to deny "their dependent peoples basic rights in the sphere of education and culture" and explicitly called for independent Asian and African countries with more advanced educational facilities to provide admission for students and trainees from colonial territories in Africa where access to higher education had been denied.[69]

The Bandung Conference helped Gamal Nasser, president of the newly formed Egyptian Republic, consolidate his domestic power and elevate his international stature. Nasser's nationalization of the Suez Canal the following year further emboldened him to pursue a more aggressive foreign policy, in which he sought to make Egypt the dominant regional power on the African continent.[70] That had significant consequences for France's African Empire

---

66. On the United States, see the dossier "Envoi d'étudiants camerounais et africains aux USA," ANOM: 1AFFPOL/2199; see also Anton Tarradellas, "La formation des étudiants africains aux Etats-Unis: 'Mission civilisatrice,' connexions panafricanistes, et aide au développement (1880–1980)," in *Repenser la mission civilisatrice*, ed. Matasci et al., 157–170; and Louisa Rice, "Cowboys and Communists: Cultural Diplomacy, Decolonization and the Cold War in French West Africa," *Journal of Colonialism and Colonialism History* 11, no. 3 (Winter 2010): 1–23, https://doi.org/10.1353/cch.2010.0023. On the Soviet Union, see Saint Martin et al., *Étudier à l'Est*.

67. Sadji, *Le rôle de la génération charnière*, 250–276. Guinée became a prime destination for Soviet-backed youth and student movement events. In 1960 alone, Conakry (capital of Guinée) hosted a meeting of the Soviet-backed International Teacher's Federation, an executive committee meeting of the WFDY, and the WFDY-sponsored All African Youth Conference. That Soviet-linked activity raised Guinée's profile in South-South organizing as well. Conakry also hosted the second conference of the Afro-Asian Peoples Solidarity Organization later that year. Rutter, "Unity and Conflict in the Socialist Scramble for Africa," 36.

68. Lee, *Making a World after Empire*.

69. Final Communiqué of the Asian-African Conference, Bandung (24 April 1955), part B, 2 and 4, https://www.cvce.eu/en/obj/final_communique_of_the_asian_african_conference_of_bandung_24_april_1955-en-676237bd-72f7-471f-949a-88b6ae513585.html.

70. Nasser's push for dominance in Africa may be read as one aspect of the conflict between Nasser's Egypt and Saudi Arabia c. 1957–1962, which Reinhard Schulze has called "an inter-Arab Cold War."

both north and south of the Sahara. Nasser's financial, material, and moral support for independence movements in French North Africa, especially his ties to the Algerian National Liberation Front (FLN), have been well studied, as have French and American reactions to that support.[71] Less attention has been paid, however, to Egypt's bid for influence in sub-Saharan Africa from the mid-1950s onward and French responses to that campaign.

Nasser's Africa policy focused on youth and education on several fronts. In 1956, he convened a "Conference of African Youth" in Cairo, which was attended by representatives of almost all of the African student associations in France.[72] Soon after, he founded the Afro-Asian Peoples' Solidarity Organization (AAPSO), which concentrated on reaching out to sub-Saharan African youth associations and hosted regular conferences from 1958 to 1965.[73] Nasser also intensified the activities of the Islamic Congress, which he had cofounded in 1954 with King Saud and Pakistani premier Ghulan Mohammed, whose platform included strengthening cultural relations and educational cooperation in the Muslim world. After Bandung, the Islamic Congress began awarding a significant number of scholarships to foreign students to come to al-Azhar University in Cairo, a prestigious center of Muslim learning that dates to the tenth century.

Despite Nasser's secularism, al-Azhar, as a venerable Islamic institution, provided him with an effective tool to reach out to Muslim youth in general and sub-Saharan African youth in particular.[74] By the mid-1960s, the Egyptian state increased the number of stipends for foreign students to come to al-Azhar from 400 to more than 2,500. Al-Azhar's student rolls swelled with Africans from

---

See his "La *da'wa* saoudienne en Afrique de l'Ouest," in *Le radicalisme islamique au sud du Sahara: Da'wa, arabisation et critique de l'Occident,* ed. René Otayek (Paris: Karthala, 1993). On Suez, see William Roger Louis and Roger Owen, eds., *Suez 1956: The Crisis and Its Consequences* (Oxford: Clarendon Press, 1989).

71. See Fathi Al Dib, *Abd El Nasser et la révolution algérienne* (Paris: L'Harmattan, 1985); Connelly, *A Diplomatic Revolution.*

72. Note a/s la "Conférence de la jeunesse africaine," January 11, 1956, ANOM: 1AFFPOL/2265.

73. Christopher J. Lee, "Introduction: Between a Moment and an Era: The Origins and Afterlives of Bandung," and James R. Brennan, "Radio Cairo and the Decolonization of East Africa, 1954–64," in *Making a World after Empire,* ed. Lee, 12–15, 65. Katsakioris notes that the preliminary 1957 conference that led to the founding of AAPSO was sponsored by the Soviets. However, subsequent Soviet Afro-Asian organizing accentuated, rather than overcame, rifts between Soviet and Afro-Asian intellectuals. Arabs boycotted the Soviet Solidarity Committee's Afro-Asian writers conference in Tashkent in 1958 over its weak stance on the Algerian question; and the Société Africaine de la Culture, led by Alioune Diop, withdrew in the conference's preparatory stages over its Soviet organizers' refusal to let the group select its own delegates. Katsakioris, "The Soviet-South Encounter," 147.

74. Tareq Y. Ismael, "Religion and UAR African Policy," *Journal of Modern African Studies* 6, no. 1 (1968): 52–53. See also Ali A. Mazrui, "Africa and the Egyptian's Four Circles," *African Affairs* 63, no. 251 (April 1964): 129–141. On Nasser's nationalization of Al-Azhar in the early 1960s and the position of the university in modern Egyptian religious politics, see Malika Zeghal, "Religion and Politics in Egypt: The Ulema of al-Azhar, Radical Islam, and the State (1952–1994)," *International Journal of Middle East Studies* 31, no. 3 (August 1999): 371–399, https://doi.org/10.1017/S0020743800055483.

thirty-two countries, and it placed more than two hundred religious scholars around the world, many of them on the continent.[75] This outreach campaign made its mark in francophone Africa. As one Nigerien historian has noted, in postcolonial Niger, everyone who studied at an Arab university, whether at al-Azhar or elsewhere, came to be known colloquially as "graduates of Cairo" (*les licenciés du Caire*).[76] Nevertheless, the number of African Muslims from the French African Federations who went to al-Azhar in the 1940s and 1950s remained small. French colonial officials at the time, however, painted a radically different picture.

Islamic Education in French Africa

The French colonial archive contains a stream of frenzied missives, reports, and administrative correspondence from the 1950s on the "exodus" and "flood" of African Muslims to al-Azhar, primarily from Muslim-majority regions in AOF and Chad.[77] The prospect of al-Azhar alumni bringing back pan-Islamism, Salafism, or other supposedly "anti-French" Muslim currents to their home territories put colonial officials in a perpetual state of panic. Indeed, many of them viewed political Islam and the theological reform movements as detrimental to French interests in Africa—worse even than Communism. French anxieties about Islam in Africa, reflected in the mythic depiction of African enrollment at al-Azhar, became a dominant frame for French interpretations of South-South connections and Third Worldism more broadly. On the eve of the Bandung Conference, Minister of Overseas France Pierre-Henri Teitgen, a leading Christian Democrat and an ardent partisan of European integration, alluded to Africans at al-Azhar when he characterized Bandung as a specifically *Muslim* threat to French rule south of the Sahara.[78]

Muslims in France's African colonies had been drawn to al-Azhar long before Bandung and Nasser's Africa policy, for the same reason some were drawn to it afterward: a desire to pursue advanced Islamic study and the increased social status that would bring. Prior to World War II, African Muslims who had the means or opportunity to embark on the hajj would sometimes stop

---

75. Ismael, "Religion and UAR African Policy," 56; Brennan, "Radio Cairo," in *Making a World after Empire*, ed. Lee, 187.

76. Abdoulaye Niandou Souley, "Les 'licenciés du Caire' et l'État au Niger," in *Le radicalisme islamique*, ed. Otayek.

77. For some of the most concentrated documentation with such references, see ANOM: 1AFFPOL/2256 and 1AFFPOL/2260 for AOF; and ANOM: AEF/GGAEF 5D/269 for AEF.

78. Letter from Pierre-Henri Teitgen to Governor-General of AEF a/s des affaires musulmanes et Bandoeng, April 8, 1955, ANOM: AEF GGAEF 5D/269.

in Cairo on their way back to study at al-Azhar, in some cases for many years.[79] After the war, French colonial and military officials consciously attempted to manage the pilgrimage to Mecca, providing African pilgrims with financial and logistical support in order to propagate an image of the French Union that was favorable to Muslim interests and open to at least certain forms of Muslim religious practice.[80] As more African pilgrims went to Mecca, more passed through Cairo, some of whom also ended up at al-Azhar.

Still, contrary to the overheated rhetoric conjuring up images of floods and tidal waves, the number of Africans who actually went to al-Azhar in the late 1940s and early 1950s, though perhaps more significant than in years past, nonetheless remained quite small. Even by French accounts, the figures were modest: colonial officials claimed that by 1952, there were 105 West Africans at al-Azhar (out of AOF's total population of some 16 million), and another 90 "non-Arab" Africans from Chad.[81] Oral interviews with al-Azhar alumni conducted by Lansiné Kaba in Mali in the 1960s indicate that even those paltry figures may have been exaggerated. Kaba's informants recalled that there were around 20 students from AOF at al-Azhar in the late 1940s.[82]

The French colonial regime's obsession with African enrollment at al-Azhar reflects the postwar administration's ambivalent, often deeply confused stance toward Islam in Africa generally and toward traditional Qur'anic schooling in particular. In precolonial West Africa, access to Islamic knowledge was limited to people of status: high castes, the wealthy, and the freeborn. Colonization in the late nineteenth century destroyed the old social order—dissolving the martial monarchies, upending local hierarchies, and abolishing slavery—but French rule put little in its place. Access to Islamic knowledge increasingly came to fill that void. By the 1910s, Sufism had become a mass movement offering personal dignity and Muslim identity to previously excluded populations, and its chief vehicle for doing so was the Qur'an school. As Butch Ware has argued, French officials doubly misread the success of Sufism around the turn of the century as

---

79. Lansiné Kaba, *The Wahhabiyya: Islamic Reform and Politics in French West Africa* (Evanston, IL: Northwestern University Press, 1974), chap. 3; Christopher Harrison, *France and Islam in West Africa, 1860–1960* (Cambridge: Cambridge University Press, 1988), epilogue.

80. Gregory Mann and Jean Sébastien Lecocq, "Between Empire, Umma, and the Muslim Third World: The French Union and African Pilgrims to Mecca, 1946–1958," *Comparative Studies of South Asia, Africa and the Middle East* 27, no. 2 (2007): 367–383, https://www.muse.jhu.edu/article/220772.

81. "L'Islam en Afrique Noire," April 27, 1954, ANOM: 1AFFPOL/2260; G. Medina, "Les Étudiants tchadiens de l'Azhar ou contribution à l'étude de l'enseignement franco-arabe au Tchad," Fort-Lamy, January 1953, ANOM: AEF GGAEF 5D/269. Of the 150 Chadians the administration counted at al-Azhar, 60 were described as "Arabs."

82. Kaba, *The Wahhabiyya*, 77n13.

the "conversion" of previously non-Muslim populations on the one hand and as a political reaction to French conquest on the other, whereas the "Sufi revolution" was really about the democratization of religious knowledge in post-slavery societies.[83]

During the conquest, colonial officials promoted French schools in direct opposition to Qur'an schools and considered French schooling essential to legitimizing French colonial rule and supremacy in the region. The French position on Qur'anic schooling changed in the early twentieth century from a stance of competition and hostility to benign neglect. Qur'an schools, faithful to traditional Islamic education methods, transmitted embodied forms of Islamic knowledge to their pupils through corporeal discipline and practices like drinking the ink that students had used to write out Qur'anic verses in their lessons—literally ingesting God's word. The French interpreted the emphasis on embodiment in Qur'anic schooling through "the dual lenses of race and Orientalism . . . which equated Islam with texts and Africans with idolatry and ancestor worship."[84] As a result, colonial observers saw local Islam, which they referred to as *Islam noir*, as syncretic, heterodox, and ultimately less threatening than its Arab variants. In this view, the key to maintaining the colonial order was to isolate this "harmless" form of African Islam from currents in the wider Muslim world. Thus, in the early 1900s, the French administration cultivated increasingly close relationships with the leaders of the Sufi brotherhoods, whom the French called *marabouts,* as a means of securing French control and social stability in the region.[85]

French understandings of African Islam changed again in the postwar era, when colonial officials like Marcel Cardaire began to argue that *Islam noir* was a colonial delusion that had bred dangerous administrative complacency that outside agitators could now exploit.[86] The French colonial "quarantine" of *Islam noir* had indeed coincided with dramatic changes in Islamic education and Arabic-language instruction elsewhere in the Muslim world.[87] For a small minority of French observers, including some progressive priests, a fortified and purified local Islam could potentially serve as a bulwark against the spread of Communism in Africa. They consequently advocated for the reform and

83. Ware, *The Walking Qur'an*, 163–165, 170–171, 185–186.

84. Ware, *The Walking Qur'an*, 191–196.

85. David Robinson, *Paths of Accommodation: Muslim Societies and French Colonial Authorities in Senegal and Mauritania, 1880–1920* (Athens: Ohio University Press, 2000); Cheikh Anta Babou, *Fighting the Greater Jihad: Amadu Bamba and the Founding of the Muridiyya of Senegal, 1853–1913* (Athens: Ohio University Press, 2007).

86. Marcel Cardaire, *L'Islam et le terroir africain* (Dakar: Institut français d'Afrique Noire, 1954).

87. Ware, *The Walking Qur'an*, 38.

modernization of Islamic education in French Africa, making common cause with reformist milieus within African Muslim communities.[88]

The Salafi and Wahhabi theological reform movements then spreading across the Middle East were exactly the kinds of "spiritual movements of the age" the provisional government had feared so intensely in 1945. French colonial officials viewed those movements—which they tended to indiscriminately lump together under the label "Wahhabism"—as fanatical, "xenophobic," and fundamentally incompatible with French culture and values.[89] Because most colonial officials still retained a sense of *Islam noir* in the exact opposite terms, as distinctively pliable and tolerant, they tended to read all reformist impulses among African Muslims as necessarily "based on Middle Eastern ideas."[90] Here again was a fundamental misreading of the complex dynamics and the dynamism of African Muslim communities. Some local Muslim reformers had indeed been exposed to Salafi and Wahhabi conceptions of Islam, which saw the Sufi orders as corruptions of the Sunna, but others were French-educated reformers who viewed Sufi leaders as neo-feudal figures who were holding back African progress and development.[91] It was precisely the convergence of these two groups of reformers that led to the opening of a spate of new Muslim schools in French Africa in the immediate postwar years (c. 1945–1950).

In 1951, the colonial administration in French Soudan (contemporary Mali) shut down a private Muslim school that four al-Azhar graduates had established in the capital, Bamako, the year before. The Azharists' vision for the school was to teach Arabic and the Qur'an in addition to the French secular curriculum. The administration rejected the Azharists' proposal to hire French-educated personnel to teach French and other subjects, which would have obliged the administration to provide the institution with the same financial support it provided to mission schools. Despite this setback, the Azharists' school was a smashing success during its brief existence. When it opened, it welcomed sixty pupils from the Bamako area; when it was shuttered the following year, officially for exceeding the maximum number of hours of Arabic instruction the French administration had agreed to, the school had more than *four hundred* pupils from across AOF. The Azharists' syncretic École Cor-

---

88. Foster, *African Catholic*, chap. 6, esp. 201–202, 217, 220–221.

89. "Wahhabism" refers to the religious doctrines attributed to Muhammad Ibn Abd al-Wahhab, (1703–1792). This form of Islam was officially adopted by the kingdom of Saudi Arabia in 1932. Crucially, most African Islamic reformers did not self-identify as "Wahhabi," and many were not familiar with the teachings of al-Wahhab; rather this label was leveled at them by both the French and traditional Sufi leaders as an epithet to discredit their projects of reform.

90. Haut-Commissaire AOF Cornut-Gentille au MFOM, *Rapport confidentiel*, February 1, 1954, ANOM: 1AFFPOL/1014.

91. Ware, *The Walking Qur'an*, 212.

anique Supérieure de Bamako clearly appealed to a large segment of the urban West African Muslim bourgeoisie who wanted their children to be raised
in their faith but also to acquire the skills they would need to participate in
the modern colonial economy.[92]

Al-Azhar alumni were not the only West Africans seeking to open new Muslim schools with more modern pedagogical methods and curricula after the
war. Others, like Saada Oumar Touré, who opened a Qur'an school in 1946 in
Ségou (also in French Soudan), had never left their home territories. Rather,
these reformers were motivated by their own educational experiences in
French schools to modernize Islamic education.[93] As Ware has shown, this
impetus had already begun to take hold in the interwar period. When asked
to reflect on their prior religious schooling, students at the École William Ponty
in the early 1930s clearly conveyed that they had internalized French rational-
ist epistemology and the opposition between the embodied practices and rote
memorization in traditional Qur'an schools, which they referred to as "indoctrination," and the intelligent and thoughtful teaching they encountered in
their French education.[94] After the war, Senegalese writer Cheick Hamidou
Kane poignantly depicted the stark opposition between the Qur'an school and
French education in his classic coming-of-age novel, L'aventure ambiguë (1961).
In that autobiographical novel, which Kane had begun writing in 1952 while
pursuing his studies in Paris, the protagonist Samba Diallo experiences French
schooling as an existential crisis; detached from his culture and Islamic faith,
he feels that he belongs nowhere.[95] Such feelings of cultural deracination and
specifically religious alienation are precisely what the endogenous postwar experiments with new kinds of Franco-Muslim schools in the Sahel and Chad
sought to avoid.

The École Coranique de Bamako appears to have been the only school
opened by local Muslims trained at al-Azhar after the war, but it was the
Azharists' school that became the ultimate cautionary tale for French colonial
officials and eventually prompted a major shift in French colonial Islamic education policy. The colonial administration made sure that no more such schools
were opened and went a step further. Under Cardaire's leadership, the federal
administration in AOF launched its own "counter-reform movement" in

92. Louis Brenner, *Controlling Knowledge: Religion, Power, and Schooling in a West African Muslim Society* (Bloomington: Indiana University Press, 2001), 55–59.

93. Touré's school proved equally attractive to local parents—by the early 1950s, it had more than three hundred pupils. Brenner, *Controlling Knowledge*.

94. Ware, *The Walking Qur'an*, 194–195.

95. Cheikh Hamidou Kane, *L'aventure ambiguë* (Paris: Julliard, 1961). See also Samba Gadjigo, *École blanche, Afrique noire: L'école coloniale dans le roman d'Afrique noire francophone* (Paris: L'Harmattan, 1990).

Qur'anic schooling. The colonial state opened its own Qur'an schools that would conduct lessons in African vernacular languages, as opposed to Arabic, in urban centers where pedagogical innovation or reformist tendencies seemed to be on the rise.

As local Muslims gained greater access to postelementary education in the early 1950s, they inserted themselves into the debate about Islamic education in AOF and vocally condemned the administration's Islamic school policy. In the summer of 1956, the reformist-leaning Association Musulmane des Étudiants d'Afrique Noire (AMEAN) brought together African Muslim students studying locally in AOF and in France for a five-day conference in Dakar. In their manifesto, they denounced French efforts "to isolate us from the Muslim world by all means necessary." They also called out their representatives in the local assemblies and in the national government in Paris for supporting subsidies to mission schools while refusing to defend local Muslims' right to Islamic education, either because the representatives themselves were not Muslim or because they were acquiescing to French pressure.[96] Most important, the conference participants passionately protested the way French officials construed Islam as a foreign import in the region and offered a stinging refutation of the French fiction of *Islam noir*:

> Looking back at history, we Muslim students attest that the diffusion of Islam in Black Africa goes back a millennium, and that black writers expressed themselves exclusively in Arabic until the last century. Our Congress denounces as particularly pernicious and offensive all publications in European languages by Africans or others that neglect, obscure, or willfully ignore Islamic culture and the fact that Islam represents an important common sociological and political influence in Black Africa.[97]

In this spirit, the AMEAN's formal resolutions called on the administration to reverse course on virtually every aspect of its policies toward Islamic education, and thereby dismantle the infrastructure that had been built on the premise of *Islam noir*. AMEAN's five motions stipulated (1) the inclusion of Arabic instruction in the official French curriculum in primary schools; (2) that young Africans be taught "the true history of African pioneers"; (3) the inclusion of some religious instruction in public secondary schools; (4) support for high school graduates to attend universities elsewhere in the Muslim world; and (5) an end to the prohibition on teaching Arabic in Qur'an schools.[98] The non-

---

96. A disproportionate number of Catholics figured among the first cohort of African political leaders, a direct consequence of policies that had long relied on and actively promoted mission schooling.

97. AMEAN, Manifeste, July 1956, ANOM: 1AFFPOL/2256, dossier 3.

98. AMEAN, Motions, July 15, 1956, Dakar, ANOM: 1AFFPOL/2256, dossier 4.

confessional Rassemblement de Jeunesse Démocratique Africain, which was aligned with the Soviet-backed WFDY, publicly and aggressively called for similar measures in solidarity with Muslim African youth.[99]

Those demands were also a cornerstone of the platform of the Muslim Cultural Union, an organization of reformist Muslim Senegalese founded by Cheikh Touré in Dakar in 1953, largely in response to the French administration's Islamic education policies.[100] Two weeks after the AMEAN conference in Dakar, the Muslim Cultural Union held an assembly in Thiès that was attended by some three hundred people. In its final resolution, the union called for the creation of modern Arabic-language schools that would teach a secular curriculum—precisely the kind of school the Azharists had tried to open in Bamako. Such schools, the writers of the resolution argued, would not be "religious schools" and, therefore, would be perfectly in line with *laïcité*, providing the population with a "valuable, modern education." The union then called on all Africans in the French parliament, local religious leaders, and syndicalist organizations to join the union in denouncing "the maneuvers taken by the administration in Senegal that aim to curb the right of African citizens to educate themselves in the language of their religion."[101] Though the members of both the Muslim Cultural Union and the AMEAN were primarily francophone elites, the Muslim population at large evidently shared these sentiments. The "counter-reform" Qur'an schools never attracted much local interest, and most had closed by independence.[102]

Arabic-language instruction also dominated the debate about Islamic education in AEF. Most of the Muslim population in AEF resided in northern Chad, where large communities of Arab merchants had been established for centuries and Arabic was used as a vernacular language.[103] There were also Muslim communities in the southern regions of the territory, but most people in the south were Christian or animist. After Bandung, AEF governor general Paul Chauvet urged Chad's territorial governor, Ignace Colombani, to fund new mission schools in the southern regions specifically to prevent new conversions to Islam.

99. "Appel à la jeunesse d'AOF," unsigned editorial, *La Voix des Jeunes: Bulletin officiel du RJDA*, no. 12, August 1954, ANOM: BIB SOM POM/d/174.

100. On the Muslim Cultural Union, see Ousman Kobo, *Unveiling Modernity in Twentieth-Century West African Islamic Reforms* (Leiden: Brill Academic Publishing, 2012), 123.

101. Motion des membres de l'UCM réunis en Assemblée générale le 28 juillet 1956, Thiès, ANS: 17G/596.

102. Brenner, *Controlling Knowledge*.

103. The debate over "Franco-Muslim" or "Franco-Arabic" schooling also took place in Cameroon, where the population was similarly divided between a largely Muslim north and Christian south. See, for instance, Robert Coquereaux, "Ecole franco-arabe ou École franco-musulmane dans le nord du Cameroun?" Mémoire de thèse, CHEAM, Received by the Dir-AFFPOL 15 February 1950 and stamped "confidential," ANOM: 1AFFPOL/2256, dossier 1.

Colombani replied that he did not think it mattered whether they opened new public schools or private Christian ones. For Colombani, the spread of Islam was not really about religion. Conversions to Islam, he argued, were not the result of some "metaphysical anguish." Rather, it was the spread of Arabic that held such great appeal, and attached to the language, "the seduction of rules for everyday life, a way of dressing, certain attitudes—a form of dogmatic thought that is more concerned with the preoccupations of this earth than those of the heavens." This clear reformulation of Islam as culture led Colombani to a corresponding culturalization of Christianity: "To this seduction, we are continually countering with the use of French, and, without always realizing it ourselves, a form of Cartesian thought that rests on a Christian substratum, a material way of life that extends from what we eat to how we dress, which is the same in public schools and private ones."[104] Much as Chad's most famous governor, Félix Éboué, had done fifteen years earlier, Colombani completely equated the student experience in French schools and mission schools—but this equation led him to a different conclusion. Facing a recent burst of pressure from the teachers' corps to uphold *laïcité*, Colombani felt that expanding the network of public schools in Chad would be the most politically expedient course of action.[105]

Chauvet dismissed opposition to his proposal on the grounds of *laïcité* out of hand. He fired back, "To be concerned with passive neutrality in religious matters, at a time when Islam is bringing anti-French political propaganda to our door—and has already brought it among us—would only further work to its favor." Chauvet elaborated on why he thought Christianization was the most effective weapon in their arsenal: "Whether we intended it or not, in animist regions, western influence is wearing away at traditional beliefs that are linked to a social and political system that is disintegrating. If he is not tormented by 'a certain metaphysical anguish,' the Black nevertheless has religious needs . . . elementary needs, which, in their very simplicity, Islam can satisfy." Chauvet concluded by reiterating his firm conviction that the active Christianization of the population was the only viable path to stanch the spread of what he considered an increasingly "political and aggressive" Islam.[106]

If Chauvet and Colombani disagreed on how to stop the spread of Islam in Chad's southern regions, they nonetheless shared the same racist repertoire for thinking about young Africans' spiritual and intellectual needs. Just as Chauvet had emphasized Africans' innate simplicity in his exposition on why

---

104. Report from Ignace Colombani to Paul Chauvet, June 24, 1955, ANOM: AEF GGAEF 5D/269.

105. On the opposition of the French teaching corps to the ongoing funding of mission schools in AEF in the mid-1950s, see Adolphe Baillet, "L'école libératrice: La législation scolaire français bafouée en AEF," May 7, 1954, ANOM: AEF GGAEF 5D/234.

106. Response from Chauvet to Colombani, August 12, 1955, ANOM: AEF GGAEF 5D/269.

Africans might be drawn to Islam, Colombani characterized the vast majority of the one million Muslims in his territory as "illiterate *islamisés* of the bush, for whom a rudimentary, superficial Islam that incorporates properly African customs, constitutes above all a simple and convenient assortment of rules for collective life and a small spiritual comfort, free of complexities." He added that this syncretic, heterodox version of Islam "is perfectly suited to these latitudes and these populations."[107]

That stark racial paternalism governed Colombani's overarching approach to educating Muslims in Chad. He maintained that the smattering of Qur'an schools that dotted the countryside was wholly sufficient for the *"islamisés* of the bush,"* both in terms of their religious instruction and their general education. For the "handful" of Chadians who aspired to higher study, Colombani cited the founding of a new Franco-Muslim middle school in Ouddaï in the Arab north. He also conceded that a course could be offered in modern Arabic in the lone middle school in Chad's capital, Fort Lamy (contemporary N'Djamena), in the future, specifically to discourage Muslims in the territory from heading to al-Azhar. He had no doubt that these two middle schools (*collèges*) and the traditional Qur'an schools in rural areas would "surely suffice" for educating Chad's one million "illiterate, Islamicized" Africans.[108]

Global events had directly precipitated this exchange of views. On the eve of the Bandung Conference, Minister of Overseas France Pierre-Henri Teitgen asked Chauvet to increase surveillance of potential "Islamist" agents and political movements in AEF. At the same time, Teitgen also insisted that they must find a way to "retain our Muslim co-citizens within the French community by emotional ties, freely accepted." In that vein, he urged Chauvet to focus on education reform. Following the "theory of the specificity of *Islam noir*," Teitgen called on Chauvet to devise some kind of "adapted" religious instruction that would "attract children and adolescents to our culture, our techniques, and more generally, our civilization."[109] The Colombani-Chauvet exchange was a response to that directive. Like the ill-conceived "counter-reform" campaign in AOF, their correspondence illustrates how international pressure from Bandung to Cairo strengthened some French officials' investment in *Islam noir*, even as it encouraged others, especially those who considered Islam a potential ally in the global struggle against Communism, to consider alternative approaches

---

107. Chef du Territoire du Tchad Ignace Colombani à Gougal-AEF Paul Chauvet, May 23, 1955, ANOM: AEF GGAEF 5D/269.

108. Chef du Territoire du Tchad Ignace Colombani à Gougal-AEF Paul Chauvet, May 23, 1955, ANOM: AEF GGAEF 5D/269.

109. Ministre Teitgen à Gougal-AEF Chauvet a/s affaires musulmanes et Bandoeng, April 8, 1955, ANOM: AEF GGAEF 5D/269.

to educating African Muslims. But the window for French-directed experimentation with Franco-Muslim or Franco-Arabic schooling was closing quickly. The 1956 *Loi Cadre* gave the territorial assemblies more control over primary and secondary education. Two years later, the Algerian crisis in May 1958 led to the total dissolution of the Fourth Republic and French Union. The looser framework of the French Community that took its place devolved even more authority over school policy to the African-led governments of "member-states," which were not part of the new Fifth Republic.[110] That institutional arrangement was also short-lived. All African member-states acceded to independence during 1960, and the French Community was effectively defunct by the end of the following year.

Colonial anxieties about young Africans on the world stage, fueled by a potent combination of Cold War and Third Worldist geopolitics and racist stereotypes about Africa, Africans, and Islam, inhibited educational development in France's African territories in the crucial years in the run-up to independence. Given Colombani's dim view of his constituents' educational needs, it should not be surprising that when he stepped down as Chad's governor in 1956—the same year that the territories assumed more responsibility for local schooling—only 4.8 percent of school-age children in the territory attended primary school.[111] The situation did not improve in the liminal years that followed. Raising the rates of schooling as quickly as possible was therefore a vital national priority in postindependence Chad.

The swift disintegration of the French Community in 1959–1960 pushed Chad's leaders to look beyond France for educational support. In June 1961, Marc Dounia, who had represented Chad in the ephemeral Senate of the French Community and was then vice president of Chad's National Assembly, returned to his former metropole with an urgent appeal for investment in Chad's educational infrastructure. "Everything" remains to be done, he lamented, despite the efforts made by France, "our tutor until now."[112] This

---

110. Laurent Manière, "La politique française pour l'adaptation de l'enseignement en Afrique après les indépendances (1958–1964)," *Histoire de l'éducation*, no. 128 (2010): 163–190, https://doi.org/10.4000/histoire-education.2281.

111. Note a/s le développement de l'Enseignement primaire dans les TOM et le problème de la langue arabe, unsigned (1956), ANOM: 1AFFPOL/2256. This report tabulated combined rates of schooling in the territoires d'outre mer with Muslim majorities (Chad, Mauritania, Soudan, Guinée, Senegal, and Niger) and those with Muslim minorities (Ivory Coast, Upper Volta, Dahomey, Cameroon, Madagascar, Togo, Gabon, Moyen Congo, and Oubangui-Chari). The contrast—8.4 percent in Muslim-majority territories versus 31.8 percent in Muslim-minority ones—is stark.

112. Exposé sur la coopération technique et les échanges culturels, presenté par M. Dounia, Conférence de l'APE avec les parlements d'États Africains et de Madagascar, Strasbourg, June 19–24, 1961, CAC: 19771470/100.

appeal was pitched not to France but to Europe during a five-day "Eurafrican Parliamentary Conference" at the European Assembly in Strasbourg that included representatives of sixteen associated African states and Madagascar (EAMA) that had been attached to the European Communities in the 1957 Treaty of Rome.[113] Dounia endorsed the old idea of a "Europe-Africa Community," but he cautioned that Chad could not afford to wait until that grand dream was realized. He asked instead for immediate European aid for student scholarships, professional training, and local schools.[114]

Dounia found a sympathetic audience. Italian Christian Democrat Mario Pedini invoked the "humanism of the European tradition" in his call for the European Communities to prioritize the development of education in the associated states. Expanding African access to education was the fundamental prerequisite for any further "cultural exchange" and "technical cooperation" between Europe and Africa, Pedini argued; increasing the number of the schools in the EAMA should therefore be the focal point of European development policy. In his detailed proposals, Pedini emphasized reciprocity and the mutual benefits of cultural cooperation. He hoped that more Europeans would study and train in Africa and that European universities would create centers and professorships in African Studies. Like Senghor, he proclaimed that all cultures and civilizations possess "universal values" that should be shared and passed on. In that spirit, Pedini urged that schools in the EAMA "embrace their 'Africanness' and the universal cultural values within." However, his affirmation of cultural pluralism rested on the reassertion of European particularism. Pedini concluded, "At the end of the day, the school should produce Africans, not black Europeans."[115] According to the logic of postwar racial common sense, the very notion of "Black Europeans" had already become a

---

113. The EAMA included all of France's ex-African colonies, including trust territories Togo and Cameroon, as well as Madagascar, Congo-Léopoldville, Rwanda, and Italian Somalia.

114. Dounia, Exposé sur la coopération technique et les échanges culturels, CAC: 19771470/100.

115. "La coopération technique et les échanges culturels" document du travail élaboré par Mario Pedini, Conférence APE avec les Parlements EAMA, June 1961, European Commission Archives: CEAB 5, no 888. Alain Peyrefitte, whom we encountered at the beginning of this chapter promoting European unity in French-occupied Germany, was a colleague of Pedini's on the European Assembly's Committee on Cooperation with Developing Countries. In preparation for the 1961 Eurafrican Conference, Peyrefitte compiled a summary of the European Development Fund's activities since it came into force with the Treaty of Rome. According to his accounting, the fund had supported, at the cost of $122 million, 132 projects, 108 of which were in ex-French Africa and Madagascar. Social programs, primarily in education and professional development, accounted for more than half of the projects, but cost only $54 million. In his report, Peyrefitte characterized the goal of the fund in exclusively economic terms: to raise the national revenue and internal generation of capital in the associated states as quickly as possible. "Le Fonds de développement et sa gestion," document de travail élaboré par Alain Peyrefitte, Conférence APE avec les Parlements EAMA, June 1961, European Commission Archives: CEAB 5, no 888.

contradiction in terms. With African independence and the rise of a more mature institutional Europe, that could be admitted more freely.

For close to two decades, French and African leaders, policymakers, educators, and students fought bitterly over how to reconfigure youth and education policy to sustain new modes of belonging across African and European France. The ostensible object was to transcend historic racial and religious divides, but those divisions hardened as the imperatives of Franco-African and European integration collided and converged. While some African leaders held out hope that the establishment of the French Community might turn things around, younger generations of Africans were less optimistic, if not outright hostile, to continuing France-Africa relations in that form. For many, that stance may have been ideological, reflecting deeply held nationalist or pan-Africanist commitments; but it was also rooted in more than a decade of lived experience of enduring racial and religious domination across African and European France and beyond, specifically as *young* people trying to pursue their educations, obtain professional training, and participate in the wider world of organized youth and youth internationalism.[116] The failure of Franco-African integration precisely as a *generational project* preceded, and helps us better understand, the astonishingly rapid unraveling of France's African empire in just a few short years.

The breakdown of the Franco-African generational project breathed new life into the faltering European one. The cascading political and institutional denouement of African France in 1956–1960, from the *Loi Cadre* to formal independence, coincided with the acceleration and intensification of European institution building. Disappointed hopes for political European unification with the failure of the European Defense and Political Communities in 1954 were channeled into cultural integration projects that aggressively targeted young people. In 1956, pro-Europe educators formed the Association of European Teachers, whose transnational membership ran into the tens of thousands by the mid-1960s. The 1957 Treaty of Rome stipulated the creation of an explicitly transnational European university as part of EURATOM, the planning for which began the following year. Then, in 1960, the Council of Europe set up several permanent education committees, established the European Cultural Fund, and began preparations for a permanent European Youth Office to coordinate regular and expansive youth and student exchanges. The elaboration of European development policy, first laid out in the articles of association with the EAMA in the Treaty of Rome, initially ran parallel to this burst of transnational youth and education initiatives, but European youth and development

---

116. Marker, "African Youth on the Move."

policy converged in the 1960s. After more than a decade of failing to get young people excited about the European project, pro-Europe officials saw development, especially in Africa, as a new opportunity to engage European youth in transnational politics and encourage them to feel more "European." Inspired by the founding of the US Peace Corps (1961), from 1962 onward the Council of Europe enlisted European youth as the frontline workers of European development aid, hopeful that "by responding to the needs of developing countries, young Europeans can find the sense of purpose they are looking for."[117] As the opening of this book made clear, the proposition that young Europeans would best appreciate their distinctive Europeanness by traveling to French Africa had been fiercely contested at the gathering of European youth in Brest in the early 1950s. A decade later, the cleavage between Europe and Africa was institutionally instantiated and back to being common sense.

---

117. Jeunesse et Aide au Développement, Étude introductive, préparée par le Secrétaire du Conseil de l'Europe sur l'aide que de jeunes Européens commencent à porter aux PVD, unsigned, Colloque Conseil de l'Europe/OCDE, Paris, December 3–4, 1962, CAC: 19780596/65.

Epilogue

In July 2007, newly elected French president Nicolas Sarkozy made his first official state visit to sub-Saharan Africa as part of a highly publicized campaign pledge to take Franco-African relations in a new direction. The tour concluded in Senegal, where Sarkozy spoke before hundreds of students at the University of Dakar. After exhorting his young African audience to recognize that French colonialism in Africa had not been wholly bad, Sarkozy outlined the "new" paradigm in Franco-African relations that he envisioned. He declared:

> What France wants to embark on with Africa, is to prepare for the coming of Eurafrica, that great common destiny that awaits Europe and Africa. . . . What France wants to build with Africa is an alliance, an alliance between French youth and African youth so that the world of tomorrow will be a better world.

International reaction to these remarks was swift as critics denounced this speech as rank neocolonialism. Ivorian senate president Mamadou Koulibaly's stinging rejoinder, "To *Eurafrique*, no. To *Librafrique*, yes!," dominated the headlines of the francophone African press. Nevertheless, French media presented Sarkozy's Eurafrica as something new, heralding the transfer of responsibility for African development and Africa's relations with the wider world from a postcolonial French nation-state to a mature institutionalized Europe.[1]

In recent years, scholars have used Sarkozy's Dakar speech as a point of departure for thinking about the politics of Eurafrica in the 1950s.[2] We would do well to also take note of the venue—a university that the French hastily created on the eve of independence and that remained officially integrated into the French university system until 1968—as well as the audience, a group of francophone college students, an elite social milieu in contemporary Senegal whose particular relationships to France and Europe were not widely shared by the majority of Senegalese or young people in other parts of ex-French Africa.[3] As social historians of the region have argued, one of the greatest effects of French colonial education was the creation of new local forms of political domination and social inequality in African societies. As Louis Brenner has written of postcolonial Mali, "the bureaucratic bourgeoisie who inherited the mantle of state power and authority when Mali achieved its independence belonged to an educated social class that was invented during the colonial period primarily through the process of western schooling."[4] The concentration of political, military, and economic power in this small cadre of francophone elites, continually supported by French interventions since 1960, has posed a perennial challenge to African democracy.[5]

This book has shown that Sarkozy's particular appeal to youth in charting a "Eurafrican" future for France and Africa has a long and complicated history that dates to the postwar conjuncture. Postwar French officials approached imperial renewal in Africa and European unity as generational projects that enlisted youth as critical agents in the establishment of new kinds of pluralist, democratic, and postnational polities. To overcome colonial domination in the empire and national division in Europe, French politicians, administrators and educators—in dialogue with francophone African and west European

1. "Nicolas Sarkozy propose aux Africains de faire 'l'Eurafrique,'" *Reuters*, July 7, 2007.

2. Gary Wilder, "Eurafrique as the Future Past of 'Black France': Sarkozy's Temporal Confusion and Senghor's Postwar Vision," in *Black France/France Noire: The History and Politics of Blackness* (Durham, NC: Duke University Press, 2012), ed. Trica Danielle Keaton, T. Denean Sharpley-Whiting, and Tyler Stovall, 57–60; Muriam Haleh Davis, "Producing EurAfrica: Development, Agriculture and Race in Algeria, 1958–1965" (PhD diss., New York University, 2015), 103–104.

3. Tony Chafer has argued that the creation of the University of Dakar in 1958 was a desperate bid on the part of the French to keep postcolonial African elites oriented toward France. See his *The End of Empire in French West Africa*. The University of Dakar ultimately broke with the French university system in the wake of massive student uprisings in spring 1968. See Aboudlaye Bathily, *Mai 68 à Dakar, ou la révolte universitaire et la démocratie* (Paris: Editions Chaka, 1992) and Hendrickson, *Decolonizing 1968*.

4. Brenner, *Controlling Knowledge*, 13–14.

5. Achille Mbembe, *On the Postcolony* (Berkeley: University of California Press, 2001).

elites—proposed a vast array of education reforms and youth programs in the hopes of stimulating European integration and imperial renewal from the ground up. The proposals shared a good deal in common, despite the radically different political and material situations of postwar French Africa and Western Europe. Both looked to curricular and pedagogical reforms, textbook revisions, new institutions of higher education, and youth and student exchange programs to unite diverse populations. Indeed, French colonial reformers and European unity activists alike hailed the slogan "unity in diversity" as the mantra of their respective projects.

These entangled initiatives to turn African subjects into French citizens and national citizenries in Europe into "Europeans" in the 1940s and 1950s did not produce the desired effects. Implemented unevenly and on a small scale, these initiatives provided formative experiences for small cohorts of future French, francophone African, and West European leaders, but the majority of French people and other Europeans who came of age during this period did not develop a strong European political identity, just as most French and African youth did not forge a shared sense of common destiny. Those outcomes are interconnected. Concerns about holding on to France's African empire initially restrained French support for robust political union in Europe, and transnational campaigns for European unity helped consolidate an exclusivist vision of Europe that limited the scope and effectiveness of French education reforms and youth initiatives in Africa.

From today's vantage point, it might seem obvious that these two projects would be intrinsically at odds, but in the dramatic, albeit brief, opening of the postwar conjuncture, the boundaries between the French Republic, French Africa, and the nascent European Community were not yet firmly fixed. This was in fact a pivotal moment when French leaders seriously asked themselves whether Black Africans and African Muslims could be French *and* European, and what that might mean for republican France and transnational Europe more broadly. One of the central objectives of this book has been to analyze how and why the incompatibility of a Franco-African polity and united Europe became so naturalized—at the very moment when there was an apparent global renunciation of racism and religious discrimination—that this incompatibility now seems like common sense.

The definitions of Europe and European civilization that crystallized in youth and education initiatives in the 1940s construed Europe as raceless (read: white), secular, *and* culturally Christian. Those founding definitions helped locate France more firmly in Europe and provided a basis for future European integration, even as concrete efforts to create supranational European political institutions in the 1950s faltered. At the same time, those understandings of what it meant to be European contributed to the hardening of conceptions of African racial difference and older oppositions between French and European identity and Islam. The distance between France and Africa was not only widened but also reconstituted: what it meant to be African and what it meant to be European came to be defined against each other in the postwar period in powerful and enduring new ways.

That new conceptual repertoire influenced how French officials evaluated initiatives for young Africans in metropolitan France, the African Federations, and the wider international arena in the 1950s. French officials interpreted the disappointing results of their efforts as confirmation of unbridgeable "civilizational" boundaries and the incommensurability of African difference, rather than the consequence of the officials' own policies and lack of political will to make the kind of material investments needed for these efforts to truly succeed. And so, despite the fact that French imperial governance was indeed becoming more democratic in certain ways, officials' own negative assessments of their programs and policies for African youth contributed to a growing fatalism in the mid-1950s that France's postwar empire was destined to dissolve along racial and religious lines. The critical interplay between colonial and European youth initiatives is therefore key to explaining why, despite France's efforts to strengthen ties with its African colonies in the 1940s and 1950s, France became both more French and more European during precisely those years.

The divergent fates of the "unity in diversity" rhetoric that had been a hallmark of postwar youth and education policy in both the colonial African and transnational European spheres bring the legacies of that interplay into focus. Even now, as the fallout of the 2008 financial collapse and the 2015 European refugee crisis continues to throw the foundations of the European project into doubt, "united in diversity" remains the official motto of the European Union. The motto has perhaps lost some of its potency in these increasingly unsettled, post-Brexit times. Nevertheless, that rhetoric still exercises a powerful grip on the political imagination of most mainstream politicians and intellectual elites on the continent today, who continue to believe that the vision of "Europeans united in their diversity" is both possible and eminently desirable.[6] And while frustration with, indifference to, and in some cases outright contempt for the EU power structure in Brussels continues to rise, the enduring success of the ERASMUS student exchange program indicates that young

---

6. On the contemporary cultural politics of European integration, see Ekavi Athanassopoulou, ed., *United in Diversity? European Integration and Political Cultures* (New York: I.B. Tauris, 2008); Monica Sassatelli, *Becoming Europeans: Cultural Identity and Cultural Politics* (London: Palgrave Macmillan, 2009); Michael Bruter, *Citizens of Europe? The Emergence of a Mass European Identity* (London: Palgrave Macmillan, 2005).

people's disenchantment with political Europe has not turned them off from helping to build a transnational European civil society.[7] In 2013–2014, more than half of the thirty thousand United Kingdom students who studied abroad did so through ERASMUS.[8] Consistently high British annual enrollment in the program perhaps helps explain why fully three-quarters of Britons under twenty-four voted to remain in the EU in the 2016 Brexit referendum.[9] ERASMUS has been an even greater success in continental Europe; since its creation in the late 1980s, more than five million students have participated in the program.[10] In 2014, the EU committed 14.7 billion euros to the new ERASMUS Plus initiative, which has since enabled four million more European university students to study abroad within the EU.[11]

The postwar movements for united Europe envisioned just this kind of program and Europeanized universities as a crucial complement to institutions like the Common Market. As French academic and delegate Michel Mouskhély put it before the Council of Europe in 1956, Europe-wide student exchanges and transnational universities would endow Europe with its own "spiritual infrastructure," a necessary corollary to economic integration for rising and future generations to "feel European."[12] Though a proper European university did not come into being in the immediate postwar years, the early pro-Europe movements did establish the College of Europe in Bruges in 1950, which continues to train top EU personnel today. The movements also laid the groundwork for the eventual creation of the European University Institute (EUI) in Florence. Since the EUI opened its doors in 1971, it has played a central role in producing transnational European networks of academics, researchers, and students who have helped delineate a distinct European research sphere.[13] ERASMUS, the College of Europe, and the EUI—as well as an in-

---

7. In classic Eurocratese, ERASMUS stands for the European Region Action Scheme for the Mobility of University Students, as well as invoking the early modern Dutch philosopher.

8. Aisha Gani, "UK Students Increasingly Opting to Study Abroad," *Guardian*, May 27, 2015.

9. A majority of Britons ages 25–49 also voted to stay. For a complete breakdown of the Brexit vote by age, see Hortense Goulard, "Britain's Youth Voted to Remain," *Politico—Europe Edition*, June 25, 2016.

10. By contrast, only 325,000 foreign students have participated in Fulbright exchanges worldwide since 1946. "Fulbright Community," Fulbright US Student Program, accessed May 4, 2021, http://us.fulbrightonline.org/fulbright-community.

11. "Key Figures," Erasmus+, accessed May 4, 2021, https://ec.europa.eu/programmes/erasmus-plus/about/key-figures_en.

12. *Les universités et la communauté spirituelle de l'Europe, Rapport présenté par Michel Mouskhély*, Assemblée consultative du Conseil de l'Europe, Commission des questions culturelles et scientifiques, 2ème Réunion Spéciale a/s universités européennes, June 11–13, 1956, AN: 70AJ/27.

13. As Jean Palayret has shown, a European university had been one of the earliest demands for European intellectual and cultural cooperation from the European movements. See his *Une université pour l'Europe: Préhistoire de l'Institut Universitaire Européen de Florence, 1948–1976* (Présidence du Conseil des Ministres de l'Union européenne, 1996).

creasingly robust EU information policymaking apparatus that has developed since the 1960s—are all continuing the work of "uniting Europeans in their diversity" in the present.[14]

We would search in vain for a similarly optimistic framework for Franco-African relations today, as suggested by Sarkozy's maladroit resurrection of Eurafrica in Dakar in 2007 and current French president Emmanuel Macron's more recent reprise of Eurafrica in spring 2018.[15] The collapse of an overarching formal political-institutional relationship between postcolonial France and ex-French Africa in the 1960s has rendered the slogan "united in diversity" meaningless in that context. However, that rhetoric has also been abandoned with regard to diversity *within* France, even as the number of Africans and children of African descent born in France has risen into the millions. While the multicultural ethos of "unity in diversity" had always been rejected by the nationalist Far Right, since the 1980s a growing cadre of ultrarepublican intellectuals have assailed those values with equal vehemence, charging that identity politics, what they call "communitarianism," is eroding the foundations of the French Republic.[16] This is in stark contrast to postwar aspirations for a more pluralist republic.

For the past three decades, French debates about pluralism have centered largely on the supposed failure of the republican school to integrate the descendants of France's ex-colonial populations into contemporary French society. In the mid-2010s, a spate of sensational acts of terror forced France's leadership class to confront a starker reality. In the wake of the Charlie Hebdo and Hyper Cacher attacks in January 2015, French interior minister Manuel Valls defied a deep-seated French taboo against explicit references to race in his characterization of the spatial segregation between wealthy and poor, "native" French people and communities of "immigrants" and their descendants, as a state of "geographic, social and ethnic apartheid."[17]

While Valls's blunt allusion to apartheid stunned French pundits at the time, the analogy had been put forth a decade earlier by prominent leftist theorist and philosopher Étienne Balibar in an important essay, "*Droit de cité* or Apartheid?" In that piece, Balibar reflected not only on the ethnicization and

---

14. Oriane Calligaro, *Negotiating Europe: EU Promotion of Europeanness since the 1950s* (New York: Palgrave, 2013).

15. On Macron's more recent usage, see Édouard de Mareschal, "Immigration: les thèses à rebours de Stephen Smith, l'africaniste cité par Macron," *Le Figaro*, April 16, 2018.

16. Pierre-André Taguieff and Alain Finkielkraut are key examples. For an excellent analysis of the evolution of Taguieff's thought, see Chris Flood, "Nationalism or Nationism? Pierre-André Taguieff and the Defense of the French Republic," *South Central Review* 25, no. 3 (Fall 2008): 86–105, https://www.jstor.org/stable/40211281.

17. Cited in Sylvia Zappi, "Manuel Valls, l'apartheid et les banlieues," *Le Monde*, January 26, 2015.

"recolonialization" of immigrants in France but also on the way that stipulations in the 1992 Maastricht Treaty restricting "European citizenship" to citizens of EU member-states created a fundamentally new register of exclusion for noncitizen residents of Europe. The result was a specifically *European* form of racism and the production of an amorphous category of "less than white" for populations who were not white, Christian, *or* secular. The danger, Balibar warned, was that those populations would become a permanent underclass, effectively instantiating a system of "European apartheid."[18]

Balibar's reflections are part of an ongoing conversation among social scientists about how the evolving juridical framework of the European Union and revived efforts to define Europe in civilizational terms has shaped and will continue to shape the ability of former colonial subjects and their descendants to claim political and cultural membership in the national communities of their ex-metropoles.[19] This conversation has centered overwhelmingly on Islam. In an important essay originally published in 2004, anthropologist Matti Bunzl argued that Islamophobia has replaced anti-Semitism as the dominant logic of exclusion in contemporary Europe as the continent has transitioned from a national to a postnational order. If Jews once represented the archetypical Other of European nation-states, Bunzl claims they now constitute the veritable embodiment of European postnationality, whereas observant Muslims are construed as an existential threat to the secular, liberal "European civilization" that is presumed to anchor the supranational EU.[20] Bunzl bases this argument on the evolution of the explicit politics of exclusion peddled by extreme Right movements across the continent that have largely abandoned outright anti-Semitism in favor of attacks on Islam as fundamentally incompatible with Europe's "Judeo-Christian humanist culture."[21] However, if we shift our focus to the aspirational politics of *inclusion* in the European mainstream, as this book has done for the early postwar era, the deeply ambiguous position of the "Judeo" in that formulation rises to the forefront.

Jews occupy a liminal place in the story I have told here, a kind of present absence. If reason and common sense lead us to assume that the attempted

---

18. Etienne Balibar, *We the People of Europe? Reflections on Transnational Citizenship* (Princeton, NJ: Princeton University Press, 2004), 44.

19. See, for instance, Asad, *Formations of the Secular*; Douglas Holmes, *Integral Europe: Fast-Capitalism, Multiculturalism, Neofascism* (Princeton, NJ: Princeton University Press, 2000).

20. Matti Bunzl, *Anti-Semitism and Islamophobia: Hatreds Old and New in Europe* (Chicago: Prickly Pear Press, 2007). For a more recent spin on this argument, see Dorian Bell, "Europe's 'New Jews': France, Islamophobia, and Antisemitism in the Era of Mass Migration," *Jewish History* 32 (2018): 65–76, https://doi.org/10.1007/s10835-018-9306-4.

21. Bunzl cites Dutch nationalist Pim Fortuyn's use of this phrase as an example. *Anti-Semitism and Islamophobia*, 38.

destruction of European Jewry must have been a key subtext of postwar efforts to combat racism and religious persecution, we are nevertheless confronted with postwar policymakers' near-absolute silence on the matter.[22] How Jews might fit in a united Europe, or the place of Jews and Judaism in European history, was simply not discussed in transnational European forums on youth and education after the war. To the contrary, "European civilization" was explicitly defined as both Christian and secular, and secularism itself was construed as a Christian invention. As we saw in chapter 2, in one of the rare instances when actual Jews were mentioned in postwar French debates about state funding for private religious education, education officials insisted that French Jews had been "Christianized" precisely insofar as they had become French and secular.[23] If that was the true basis of the inclusion of Jewish survivors in the postwar republic, it follows that as Jewish religiosity has experienced a dramatic revival in France in recent years, Jews' place in the republic has been thrown into question once more.[24]

The legacy of the culturalization of Christianity in the postwar era is an unambiguous double standard in how Christianity and other faiths are treated in both contemporary France and Europe more broadly. In 2004, the French legislature passed a law banning students from wearing "ostentatious" religious symbols or religious dress in public schools. As many observers have noted, this law disproportionately affects, and indeed intentionally targeted, Muslim schoolgirls who wear the hijab, or Islamic headscarf.[25] The successful passage of this law was the culmination of fifteen years of heated public debate after a principal in the suburbs of Paris dismissed two Muslim students for wearing the hijab in his establishment in 1989. This incident proved to be the first of a series of so-called "Headscarf Affairs," in which a specifically Muslim religious practice was construed as incompatible with the bedrock republican principle of laïcité.

And yet, another controversy over questions of religion and education in France seemed to point to significant countervailing trends in public sentiment just a few years earlier. In 1983, Alain Savary, then minister of education in the Socialist government of François Mitterrand, proposed a law that would

---

22. Sam Moyn has famously explored this issue with regard to postwar human rights. See his *The Last Utopia: Human Rights in History* (Cambridge, MA: Belknap Press of Harvard University Press, 2010).

23. This dovetailed with many survivors' own sublimation of their Jewish identities in the immediate postwar era. See Alain Finkielkraut, *The Imaginary Jew* (Lincoln: University of Nebraska Press, 1994). We might then say that postwar French Jews were doubly disappeared, from within and from without.

24. For an excellent discussion of racial and religious identity among Jewish youth in private Jewish schools in contemporary France, see Kimberly Arkin, *Rhinestones, Religion, and the Republic: Fashioning Jewishness in Contemporary France* (Stanford University Press, 2013).

25. Keaton, *Muslim Girls and the Other France*; Joan Scott, *The Politics of the Veil* (Princeton, NJ: Princeton University Press, 2007).

have forced all religious schools to adopt the public school curriculum and require teachers in religious schools to have the same credentials as their public school counterparts. Catholic leaders, educators, and parents vociferously denounced this proposal. The bill sparked massive grassroots mobilizations across the country, with between one and two million people participating in demonstrations in Paris alone.[26]

The postwar culturalization of Christianity helps explain the radically different ways opponents of these two measures have been represented in the French public imagination. While those who defend the rights of Muslim girls to wear the headscarf in public schools were and continue to be subject to attacks that question their patriotism and their identity as truly French, the national loyalties and "Frenchness" of opponents to Savary's law were rarely challenged in mainstream public debate. Significantly, "French" was not the only relevant category in the controversy. Jean-Marie Le Pen, who was then a member of the European Parliament, went a step further, denouncing Savary's Law as *un-European*. In an appeal to parents and teachers to mobilize for the "freedom of education," Le Pen cast France as a bastion of Communist unfreedom in an otherwise pluralist, tolerant Europe: "The European Parliament gives us the opportunity to show all of Europe that, in the face of the progress of liberty and the examples of the Netherlands, Belgium, and Germany, Socialist France chose the Gulag and the sinister concatenation: *École Unique, Parti Unique, Dictature.*"[27] In the end, the government not only retracted the bill, but Mitterrand himself went on French national television—on Bastille Day no less (July 14, 1984)—to publicly request Savary's resignation. During this unusually public and symbolic dismissal of a cabinet member, Mitterrand declared his decision was motivated by overwhelming opposition to the bill; the protests had made clear to him that a significant segment of the French population did not approve of the measure, and he did not want to go against the wishes of "the people."[28]

---

26. "La 'manif pour tous' est le troisième plus gros cortège depuis 1984," *Le Monde*, last accessed January 27, 2020, http://charts-datawrapper.s3.amazonaws.com/QdQTZ/fs.html.

27. Open Letter from Jean-Marie Le Pen to parents and teachers, June 6, 1984. AHC: Fonds Savary, 3/SV/70.

28. The presidential address can be viewed on YouTube: "JA2 20H: Emission du 14 Juillet 1984," INA Actu, published July 2, 2012, https://www.youtube.com/watch?v=JECJemPrYRo. Alain Savary homed in on the hypocrisy of his opponents' posturing with regard to religious pluralism in personal reflections after his resignation. In a forty-five-page unpublished manuscript, he wrote: "It was discomfiting to listen to the highest authorities of Catholic education insist that they would happily see the creation of Muslim schools, like the Jewish schools founded after the return of North African Jews. . . . Isn't this at its core, with these ghetto schools, a good way to definitively manage the problem of schooling immigrants, especially Muslims, the least accepted by all those who are 'not racist, but . . . ?'" Savary, "Après la bataille," undated, AHC: Fonds Savary, 3/SV/70.

A similar pattern has emerged at the European level in recent decisions handed down by the European Court of Human Rights (ECHR). In July 2014, the ECHR upheld a 2010 French law that banned women from wearing the burqa and the niqab in public. The ECHR found that there had been no violation of individuals' rights to family and private life (article 8 of the European Convention) or respect for freedom of thought, conscience, and religion (article 9). The ECHR also ruled that the prohibition of discrimination (article 14) had not been violated with regard to either article 8 or 9. While acknowledging that the ban clearly "interfered" with individuals' rights to privacy and freedom of religion, the ECHR nevertheless declared that those infractions were justified in view of the higher purpose of the law "to ensure the conditions of living together." Specifically, the ECHR decision in *S.A.S. v. France* cited "public safety" and "the protection of the rights and freedoms of others" as legitimate concerns to that end.[29]

Three years earlier, the ECHR's decision in *Lautsi and Others v. Italy* upheld an Italian law that requires crucifixes to be displayed in public school classrooms.[30] The law had been challenged by secular Italian parents in Abano who protested that the crucifixes violated Italy's own secular laws, as well as their rights to freedom of conscience (again, article 9) and to educate their children according to their own convictions (article 2, provision 1). The ECHR ruled that there was no violation of either article because there was no evidence that the presence of crucifixes in classrooms had any actual influence on pupils. The ECHR accepted the Italian government's position that though the crucifix was a religious symbol, it was a symbol of Christianity, not Catholicism, and so it served as a point of reference for other creeds. The ECHR also accepted the Italian government's contention that the crucifix was also *more* than a religious symbol; it was a historical and cultural representation that had "identity-linked value" for "the Italian people," insofar as it "represented the historical and cultural development characteristic [of Italy] and in general the whole of Europe." The crucifix, the ECHR concluded, was "a good synthesis" of that development.[31]

The juxtaposition of *S.A.S v. France* and *Lautsi v. Italy* has become a focal point of interdisciplinary scholarly debate on European pluralism in recent years. Political scientists Christian Joppke and François Foret have pointed to

---

29. Press release issued by the Registrar of the Court, ECHR 191, July 1, 2014. http://hudoc.echr.coe.int/eng-press?i=003-4809135-5861652.

30. For a slightly different juxtaposition and interpretation of the politics of Muslim garb and crucifixes that focuses on France and Germany in the 1990s from a transnational European perspective, see Leora Auslander, "Bavarian Crucifixes and French Headscarves: Religious Signs and the Postmodern European State," *Cultural Dynamics* 12, no. 3 (2000), 283–309, https://doi.org/10.1177/092137400001200302.

31. ECHR, Judgment in the Case of Lautsi and Others v. Italy, Strasbourg, March 18, 2011, https://hudoc.echr.coe.int/app/conversion/pdf/?library=ECHR&id=001-104040&filename=001-104040.pdf.

these cases as an indication of a broader "culturalization of religion" in contemporary Europe.[32] By locating that process in the present, they suggest this is a fundamentally new, dangerous retreat from a well-established, institutionally instantiated, and equitable European religious pluralism. Conversely, anthropologist Saba Mahmood argues the cases illustrate a perennial, structural feature of modern secularism: the state's capacity to define the contours of "religion" according to the values of the majority religion at the expense of religious minorities.[33] For Mahmood, whose work focuses on Egypt, this is neither historically nor culturally specific to Europe. Historians, on the other hand, insist the cases are indeed the consequence of longer historical processes, which they most often associate with the Cold War. Samuel Moyn contends that the ECHR, which was born of conservative Christian Democratic politics in the 1950s, reflects not only the legacy of an exclusionary European secularism but also an exclusionary legacy of European *hostility* to secularism, rooted in the conflict between the "Christian West" and the Communist secular East.[34] Joan Scott also traces a seminal shift in European attitudes toward secularism to the Cold War, but for her that shift was not a rejection of secularism but rather the conflation of secularism and Christianity in a united front against Communist *atheism*.[35] Despite their differences, both Moyn and Scott argue that with the end of the Cold War, Islam simply took Communism's place as Christian/Christian-secular Europe's existential threat and Other.

All these insights are largely borne out in the interconnected history of decolonization and early European integration detailed in this book, even if my framing shifts certain emphases in important ways. Rather than a generalized culturalization of religion *tout court*, I have argued that a confluence of historical developments in the immediate postwar years contributed to the culturalization of European Christianity in particular. Secular European regimes may have always constituted themselves in relation to Christianity, but the postwar conjuncture created conditions to do so in new ways. Those conditions, I have argued, were bound up with contingent and entangled processes of postwar reconstruction, European integration, and decolonization. To be sure, those processes were all also profoundly linked to the Cold War, but none of them can be reduced to Cold War logics alone. In the middle decades of the

32. Joppke, *The Secular State Under Siege*; François Foret, *Religion and Politics in the European Union: the Secular Canopy* (Cambridge: Cambridge University Press, 2015).

33. Mahmood, *Religious Difference in a Secular Age*, 168–169. Mahmood's approach draws heavily on Talal Asad's foundational *Formations of the Secular*. For a critique of this intellectual tradition (which also cites the *Lautsi* case), see Udi Greenberg and Daniel Steinmetz-Jenkins, "Is Religious Freedom a Bad Idea?," *Nation*, March 16, 2016.

34. Moyn, "From Communist to Muslim."

35. Scott, *Sex and Secularism*.

twentieth century, as James Chappel, Darcie Fontaine, Elizabeth Foster, and Udi Greenberg have shown, Christians themselves fiercely debated the contours of European religious pluralism and the identity of Christianity and European culture as they confronted the rise of fascism and anticolonialism. Christians' positions may have often aligned with Cold War imperatives, but they had their own agendas.[36] As many of those same Christians became involved in the projects of imperial renewal and European unity, they brought those agendas with them into the world of postwar colonial and European youth and education policy and programs, where the ambitions and aspirations of Christian and non-Christian French, African, and other West European politicians, officials, educators, students, and youth leaders collided and converged. Understanding that world therefore gives us a fuller account of the emergence of a distinctly cultural, secularized Christianity in both late twentieth-century France and Europe more broadly.

The complex interplay between discourse and practice in that world produced a fundamentally new, specifically postwar racial common sense that widened the distance between France and Africa and cast Africanness and Europeanness as diametrically opposed. Postwar racial common sense fatally undermined the new French Union, which many French and African leaders alike hoped would turn the page on France's colonial past and transform the empire into a new kind of multiracial democracy. Forged at the crossroads of the tangled imperatives of colonial reform and European unity, postwar racial common sense located France more firmly in a Europe that desperately wanted to see itself as race*less*. The drive toward racial erasure in Europe encouraged representations of African protest over ongoing structural and everyday racism in both France and French Africa as rac*ist*. Contemporary discourse about "anti-white racism" emerged from these postwar dynamics. In France today, French students of color—who since the early 2010s have mobilized across the country on an unprecedented scale and have been shining a spotlight on systemic racism in French education in particular—are frequently disparaged in this way.[37] Reactions to activism by students of color, like broader debates about race and racism in contemporary France more generally, still tend to be framed in national terms, as scholars and pundits alike invoke a distinctly French tradition of

---

36. Chappel, *Catholic Modern*; Fontaine, *Decolonizing Christianity*; Foster, *African Catholic*; Greenberg, "Catholics, Protestants" and "Protestants, Decolonization, and European Integration."

37. This has been an effective strategy to discredit and demonize movements like the 2016–2018 "Camps d'été décolonial" in Paris and Reims and "Paroles non blanches" (PNB) events that began at the Université de Paris-8 in Saint-Denis. On the PNB, see "Paroles non blanches : rencontres autour des questions de race, travail et mobilisation," *Paris-Luttes.info*, April 12, 2016, https://paris-luttes.info/paroles -non-blanches-rencontres-5334?lang=fr. On the decolonial summer seminars, see "Camp d'été décolonial," Facebook community, accessed November 14, 2021, https://m.facebook.com/cedecolonial/.

colorblind universalism with ritualistic precision. However, much like contemporary iterations of republican *laïcité,* French colorblindness in its current form has a much more complex, conjunctural, and transnational origin story at the crossroads of late colonialism, European integration, and decolonization. The study of postwar youth and education initiatives across metropolitan French, colonial African, and transnational European contexts reveals that though French and European officials learned to rhetorically denounce religious and racial discrimination in powerful new ways in the wake of World War II, their practices and policy choices laid the groundwork for the processes of exclusion and the structural inequalities that continue to organize politics and social life in France, ex-French Africa, and the EU today.

BIBLIOGRAPHY

Archives

Archives Diplomatiques—La Courneuve, France (AMAE)

EU-Europe, 1949–1955: Conseil de l'Europe
Guerre 1939–1945 / Londres-CNF
Guerre 1939–1945 / Londres-Alger
Haut-Commissariat en Allemagne: DG-Affaires Culturelles
Haut-Commissariat en Allemagne: Service de l'Enseignement
K-Afrique, 1944–1952
Nations Unies et Organisations Internationales (NUOI): Secrétariat des Conférences
Relations Culturelles, Scientifiques et Techniques (DGRCST): Échanges culturels
Relations Culturelles, Scientifiques et Techniques (DGRCST): Enseignement, 1945–1961
Y-International, 1944–1949
Z-Europe, généralités, 1944–1949

Archives de l'Histoire Contemporaine—Paris, France (AHC)

1-2/DE	Fonds Michel Debré
1-3/SV	Fonds Alain Savary
EN	Fonds Étudiants Nationalistes
UEF	Fonds Fédéralistes Européens

Archives Historiques de l'Union Européenne—Florence, Italy (AHUE)

AEDE	Association européenne des enseignants
CENYC	Council of European National Youth Committees
CIFE	Centre international de formation européenne
EN	Fonds Emile Noël
JEF	Jeunesse européenne fédéraliste
ME	Mouvement européen
MFE	Mouvement fédéraliste européen
OFME	Organisation française du Mouvement européen
UEF	Union européenne fédéraliste

Archives Nationales de France—Paris, France (AN)

These materials were consulted at the Centre Historique des Archives Nationales in Paris. They have since been moved to the new archival center in Pierrefitte-sur-Seine.

382/AP	Fonds Cassin
560/AP	Fonds Pleven
625/AP	Fonds Philip
AJ/69	Office du sport scolaire et universitaire
AJ/70	Office national des universités et écoles français
AJ/71	Musée Pédagogique
C//	Assemblée Nationale, Assemblée de l'Union française; Assemblée consultative provisoire (Alger; Paris), 1er/2ème Assemblée nationale constituante
F1a	Cabinet du ministre de l'Intérieur / Commissariat de l'Intérieur (Londres; Alger)
F17	Éducation Nationale
F41	Information
F44	Jeunesse et Sports
F60	Secrétariat Général du Gouvernement et Service du Premier Ministre, Gouvernment provisoire de la République française

Archives Nationales d'Outre-Mer—Aix-en-Provence, France (ANOM)

1AFFPOL/	Affaires politiques et sociales
100/APOM/	Comité Central français pour l'Outre-Mer
AGEFOM/	Agence économique de la France d'Outre-Mer
AEF GGAEF	Afrique équatoriale française

Archives Nationales du Sénégal—Dakar, Senegal (ANS)

17-21G/	Politique et Administration Générale
O/	Enseignement—AOF

Centre d'Archives Contemporaines—Fontainebleau, France (CAC)

These archives have since moved to Pierrefitte. At Fontainebleau, the cataloging system was organized by the year the material was deposited rather than the competent institution (e.g., 197701981/1).

DOM-TOM
Éducation Nationale
Jeunesse et Sports
Premier Ministre

European Commission Archives—Brussels, Belgium

CEAB 1	Service juridique de la Haute Autorité de la CECA—Politique d'information et publicité
CEAB 2	CECA / Conseil de l'Europe
CEAB 5	CEE / Pays et territoires d'outre-mer et états associés

UNESCO Archives—Paris, France

CAME/Correspondence/I/
CAME, London 1942–1945 vol. 1: Records of plenary meetings
CAME, London 1942–1945, vol. II: General Series Documents I
CAME, London, 1942–1945, vol. III: General Series Documents II
CAME, London 1942–1945, vol. III: Books and Periodicals Commission: History
  Committees and Subcommittees

Periodicals

Annales de la propagation de la foi
Bulletin de la Direction de l'enseignement et de la jeunesse du MFOM
Cahiers de Jeune Europe
Climats
*Courrier de France et d'Outre-Mer: Bulletin mensuel de liaison et d'information de la Région
  d'Outre-Mer des Scouts de France*
Dakar-Étudiant: Journal de l'Association générale des étudiants de Dakar
L'éducation africaine: Bulletin officiel de l'enseignement en AOF
L'Étudiant de la FOM: Chronique des foyers
L'Europe en formation
Festival d'Afrique. Organe du 1er festival de la jeunesse d'Afrique
Le Figaro
Jeunes d'Europe. Bulletin d'information—Jeunesse européenne fédéraliste
Jeunesse d'Afrique. Organe mensuel de l'Association des étudiants catholiques de Dakar
Jeunesse. Organe du progrès de Dakar. Théâtre-Sports-Musique
Mer et outre-mer des jeunes: Revue des jeunes de la Ligue maritime outre-mer
Le Monde
Nous les jeunes: Mouvement jociste
La nouvelle revue française d'outre-mer
Pensée française
Peuple européen / Evoluzione Europa / Europaïsche Volk
Rythme et Clarté: Bulletin mensuel de la jeunesse féminine catholique d'AOF-Togo
Scout AOF
Tam-Tam
Tropiques
*UNEF Informations internationales: Bulletin international de l'Union nationale des étudiants
  de France*
Vers l'Islam: Bulletin mensuel de l'Association musulmane des étudiants d'Afrique noire
La Voix des jeunes: Bulletin officiel du Rassemblement de la jeunesse démocratique africaine

Published Primary Sources

Barker, Ernest, George Clark, and Paul Vaucher. *The European Inheritance: A History
  of European Civilization,* 3 vols. Oxford: Clarendon Press, 1954.
Bekemens, Léonce, Dieter Mahncke, and Robert Picht. *The College of Europe: Fifty
  Years of Service to Europe.* Bruges: Europacollege, 1999.

Capelle, Jean. *L'éducation en Afrique noire à la vieille des Indépendances (1946–1958).* Préface de Léopold Senghor. Paris: Editions Karthala, 1990.

Capitant, René. *Face au Nazisme: Écrits, 1933–1938; Textes réunis par Olivier Beaud.* Strasbourg: Presses Universitaires de Strasbourg, 2004.

——. *Pour une constitution fédérale.* Paris: Renaissances, 1946.

Cardaire, Marcel. *L'Islam et le terroir africain.* Dakar: Institut français d'Afrique Noire, 1954.

Cassin, René. *Les hommes, partis de rien. Le réveil de la France abattue.* Paris: Plon, 1974.

Césaire, Aimé. *Discours sur le colonialisme.* Paris: Présence Africaine, 1955.

Commission Langevin-Wallon. *Rapport Langevin-Wallon,* réédition commentée par Claude Allègre et al. Paris: Mille et une nuits, 2002.

Dadié, Bernard. *Un nègre à Paris.* Paris: Éditions Présence Africaine, 1959.

Danckwortt, Dieter. *Une jeune élite de l'Asie et de l'Afrique comme hôtes et élèves en Europe (problèmes de la communication d'une image de la culture européenne aux étudiants et stagiaires en Europe, venus de pays en voie de développement de l'Asie et de l'Afrique): Une étude sociologique sur l'ordre de la Fondation Européenne de la Culture.* Institut Psychologique de Hambourg, August 1959.

Debré, Michel. *Trois républiques pour une France: Mémoires.* 5 vols. Paris: Albin Michel, 1984–1995.

Éboué, Félix. *La nouvelle politique indigène pour l'AEF.* Paris: Office Français d'Édition, 1945.

Fanon, Frantz. *Peau noire, masques blancs.* Paris: Seuil, 1952.

Halévy, Daniel. *Essai sur l'accélération de l'histoire.* Paris: Editions Self, 1948.

Huxley, Julian. *We Europeans: A Survey of "Racial" Problems.* New York: Harper & Brothers, 1936.

Kane, Cheikh Hamidou. *L'Aventure ambiguë.* Paris: Julliard, 1961.

Kaziendé, Léopold. *Souvenirs d'un enfant de la colonisation,* vol 4. Porto Novo: Editions Assouli, 1998.

Konaté, Abdourahmane. *Le cri du mange-mil: Mémoires d'un préfet sénégalais.* Paris: L'Harmattan, 1990.

Sadji, Amadou Boooker. *Le rôle de la génération charnière ouest-africaine—indépendance et développement.* Paris: L'Harmattan, 2006.

Saurat, Denis. *Watch over Africa.* London: J.M. Dent & Sons, 1941.

Wright, Richard. *The Color Curtain: A Report on the Bandung Conference.* Jackson: University of Mississippi Press, 1956.

Secondary Sources

Acanfora, Paolo. "Christian Democratic Internationalism: The *Nouvelles Equipes Internationales* and the Geneva Circles between European Unification and Religious Identity, 1947–1954." *Contemporary European History* 24, no. 3 (August 2015): 375–391, https://doi.org/10.1017/S0960777315000211.

Adler, Karen. "Children as a Tool of Occupation in the French Zone of Occupation of Germany, from 1945 to 1949." *Nottingham French Studies* 59, no. 2 (2020): 191–205, https://doi.org/10.3366/nfs.2020.0284.

Ageron, Charles-Robert. *La décolonisation française.* Paris: Armand Collin, 1991.

———."L'idée d'eurafrique et le débat colonial franco-allemand de l'entre-deux-guerres." *Revue d'Histoire Moderne et contemporaine* 22 (1975): 446–475, https://doi.org/10.3406/rhmc.1975.2329.

Ageron, Charles-Robert, and Marc Michel, eds. *L'Afrique noire française: L'heure des Indépendances.* Paris: CNRS, 1992.

Agulhon, Maurice. *The Republican Experiment, 1848–1852.* Translated by Janet Lloyd. Cambridge: Cambridge University Press, 1983.

Ahearne, Jeremy. *Intellectuals, Culture and Public Policy in France: Approaches from the Left.* Liverpool: Liverpool University Press, 2010.

Aitken, Robbie, and Eve Rosenhaft. *Black Germany: The Making and Unmaking of a Diaspora Community, 1884–1960.* Cambridge: Cambridge University Press, 2013.

Al Dib, Fathi. *Abd El Nasser et la révolution algérienne.* Paris: L'Harmattan, 1985.

Aldrich, Richard J. "OSS, CIA, and European Unity: The American Committee on United Europe, 1948–1960." *Diplomacy and Statecraft* 8, no. 1 (March 1997): 184–227.

Aldrich, Robert. *Greater France: A History of French Overseas Expansion.* New York: St. Martin's Press, 1996.

Allorant, Pierre. "Lettre de Jean Cassou à Jean Zay." *Parlement(s): Revue d'histoire politique,* 11, no. 3 (2016): 177–182.

Amougou, Emmanuel. *Étudiants d'Afrique noire en France: une jeunesse sacrifiée.* Préface de Christian de Montlibert. Paris: Harmattan, 1997.

Amselle, Jean-Loup. *Affirmative Exclusion: Cultural Pluralism and the Rule of Custom in France.* Ithaca, NY: Cornell University Press, 2003.

Anderson, Benedict. *Imagined Communities.* New York: Verso, 1983.

Appadurai, Arjun. *Modernity at Large: Cultural Dimensions of Globalization.* Minneapolis: University of Minnesota Press, 1996.

Arkin, Kimberly. *Rhinestones, Religion, and the Republic: Fashioning Jewishness in Contemporary France.* Stanford, CA: Stanford University Press, 2013.

Artaud, Denise. "France between the Indochina War and the European Defense Community." In *Dien Bien Phu and the Crisis of Franco-American Relations, 1954–1955,* edited by Lawrence S. Kaplan, Denise Artaud, and Mark R. Rubin, 251–268. Wilmington, DE: Scholarly Resources, 1990.

Asad, Talal. *Formations of the Secular: Christianity, Islam, and Modernity.* Stanford, CA: Stanford University Press, 2003.

Assmann, Aleida. "Europe: A Community of Memory?" *Bulletin of the German Historical Institute* (Spring 2007): 11–26.

Atangana, Martin. *The End of French Rule in Cameroon.* Lanham, MD: University Press of America, 2010.

Athanassopoulou, Ekavi, ed. *United in Diversity? European Integration and Political Cultures.* New York: I.B. Tauris, 2008.

Atkin, Nicholas. "Church and Teachers in Vichy France, 1941–1944." *French History* 4, no. 1 (1990): 1–22, https://doi.org/10.1093/fh/4.1.1.

———. "France in Exile: The French Community in Britain, 1940–1944." In *Europe in Exile: European Exile Communities in Britain, 1940–1945,* edited by Martin Conway and José Gotovitch, 213–228. New York: Berghahn Books, 2001.

——. *The Forgotten French: Exiles in the British Isles, 1940–1944.* Manchester: Manchester University Press, 2003.

Auslander, Leora. "Bavarian Crucifixes and French Headscarves: Religious Signs and the Postmodern European State." *Cultural Dynamics* 12, no. 3 (2000): 283–309, https://doi.org/10.1177/092137400001200302.

Babiracki, Patryk, and Kenyon Zimmer, eds. *Cold War Crossings: International Travel and Exchange across the Soviet Bloc, 1940s–1960s.* College Station: Texas A&M University Press, 2014.

Babou, Cheikh Anta. *Fighting the Greater Jihad: Amadu Bamba and the Founding of the Muridiyya of Senegal, 1853–1913.* Athens: Ohio University Press, 2007.

Bailkin, Jordanna. *Afterlife of Empire.* Berkeley: University of California Press, 2012.

Balibar, Étienne. *Equaliberty.* Durham, NC: Duke University Press, 2012.

——. *We, the People of Europe? Reflections on Transnational Citizenship.* Princeton, NJ: Princeton University Press, 2004.

Balibar, Étienne, and Immanuel Wallerstein. *Race, Nation, Class: Ambiguous Identities.* New York: Verso, 1991.

Bancel, Nicolas. "Scoutisme catholique contre scoutisme laïc? Les activités physiques dans le développement comparé de deux mouvements de jeunesse en AOF (1947–1960)." In "Le Sport dans l'Empire Français: Un instrument de domination coloniale?," sous la direction de Driss Abbassi. *Outre-mers* 96, no. 364–365 (2009): 143–161, https://doi.org/10.3406/outre.2009.4418.

Bancel, Nicolas, Daniel Denis, and Youssef Fates, eds. *De l'Indochine à l'Algérie: La jeunesse en mouvements des deux côtés du miroir colonial.* Paris: La Decouverte, 2003.

Banting, Keith, and Will Kymlicka. *Multiculturalism and the Welfare State.* Oxford: Oxford University Press, 2006.

Baofu, Peter. *Beyond Civilization to Post-Civilization: Conceiving a Better Model of Life Settlement to Supersede Civilization.* New York: Peter Lang, 2006.

Barreau, Jean-Michel. *Vichy contre l'école de la République: Théoriciens et théories scolaires de la "Révolution nationale."* Paris: Flammarion 2000.

Barthélémy, Pascale. *Africaines et diplômées à l'époque coloniale (1918–1957).* Rennes: Presses Universitaires de Rennes, 2010.

——. "Macoucou à Pékin: L'arène internationale; Une ressource politique pour les Africaines dans les années 1940–1950." *Le Mouvement Social*, no. 255 (2016): 17–33, http://www.jstor.org/stable/26322022.

Bathily, Aboudlaye. *Mai 68 à Dakar, ou la révolte universitaire et la démocratie.* Paris: Editions Chaka, 1992.

Baubérot, Arnaud, and Nathalie Duval. *Le scoutisme entre guerre et paix au XXe siècle.* Paris: L'Harmattan, 2006.

Baubérot, Jean. *Laïcité 1905–2005, entre passion et raison.* Paris: Seuil, 2004.

Bauman, Zygmunt. *Globalization: The Human Consequences.* Cambridge: Polity Press, 1998.

Bell, Dorian. "Europe's 'New Jews': France, Islamophobia, and Antisemitism in the Era of Mass Migration." *Jewish History* 32 (2018): 65–76, https://doi.org/10.1007/s10835-018-9306-4.

Bellefroid, Diane. "The Commission pour l'Etude des Problèmes d'Après-Guerre (CEPAG), 1941–1944." In *Europe in Exile: European Exile Communities in Britain,*

1940–1945, edited by Martin Conway and José Gotovitch, 121–134. New York: Berghahn Books, 2001.

Berenson, Edward. "Making a Colonial Culture? Empire and the French Public, 1880–1940." *French Politics, Culture and Society* 22, no. 2 (Summer 2004): 127–149, https://www.jstor.org/stable/42843344.

Berezin, Mabel, and Martin Schain. *Europe without Borders: Remapping Territory, Citizenship and Identity in a Transnational Age.* Baltimore: Johns Hopkins University Press, 2003.

Betts, Raymond. *Assimilation and Association in French Colonial Theory.* New York: Columbia University Press, 1961.

Bhambra, Gurminder, Dalia Gebrial, and Kerem Nişancıolu, eds. *Decolonising the University.* London: Pluto Press, 2018.

Biess, Frank, and Robert G. Moeller, eds. *Histories of the Aftermath: The Legacies of the Second World War in Europe.* New York: Berghahn Books, 2010.

Birnbaum, Pierre. *Destins Juifs. De la Révolution française à Carpentras.* Paris: Calmann-Lévy, 1995.

——. *Les fous de la République: Histoire politique des Juifs d'État de Gambetta à Vichy.* Paris: Fayard, 1992.

Bitsch, Marie-Thérèse, and Gérard Bossuat, eds. *L'Europe Unie et l'Afrique: De l'idée d'Eurafrique à la convention de Lomé I.* Brussels: Bruylant, 2005.

Blanchard, Pascal, Nicolas Bancel, and Sandrine Lemaire, eds. *La fracture coloniale: La société française aux prises de l'héritage colonial.* Paris: Cahiers Libre, 2005.

Blanchard, Pascal, and Gilles Boëtsch. "La France de Pétain et l'Afrique: Images et propagandes coloniales." *Canadian Journal of African Studies/Revue Canadienne des Études Africaines* 28, no. 1 (1994): 1–31, https://doi.org/10.2307/485823.

Blanchard, Pascal, and Sandrine Lemaire, eds. *Culture impériale: Les colonies au coeur de la République, 1931–1961.* Paris: Editions Autrement, 2004.

Blum, Françoise. "L'indépendance sera révolutionnaire ou ne sera pas: Étudiants africains en France contre l'ordre colonial." *Cahiers d'histoire: Revue d'histoire critique* 126 (2015): 119–138, https://doi.org/10.4000/chrhc.4165.

——. "Transfers of Knowledge, Multiple Identities: The Example of Students from the FEANF (Fédération des Étudiants d'Afrique Noire en France)." *African Identities* 16, no. 2 (2018): 1–16, https://doi.org/10.1080/14725843.2018.1449719.

Boittin, Jennifer Anne. *Colonial Metropolis: The Urban Grounds of Anti-imperialism and Feminism in Interwar Paris.* Lincoln: University of Nebraska Press, 2010.

——. *Undesirable: Passionate Mobility and Women's Defiance of French Colonial Policing, 1919–1952.* Chicago: University of Chicago Press, 2022.

Boltanski, Luc. "America, America . . . le plan Marshall et l'importation du 'management.'" *Actes de la recherche en sciences sociales* 38 (1981): 19–41.

Borstelmann, Thomas. *Apartheid's Reluctant Uncle: The United States and Southern Africa in the Early Cold War.* Oxford: Oxford University Press, 1993.

——. *The Cold War and the Color Line: American Race Relations in the Global Arena.* Cambridge, MA: Harvard University Press, 2001.

Bossuat, Gérard. "Des lieux de mémoire pour l'Europe unie." *Vingtième siècle: Revue d'histoire* 61 (January–March, 1999): 56–69, https://www.jstor.org/stable/3771459.

——. *L'Europe des français, 1943 à 1959: La IVe République aux sources de l'Europe communautaire.* Paris: Publications de la Sorbonne, 1996.

——. *Faire l'Europe sans défaire la France. 60 ans de politique d'unité européenne des gouvernements et des présidents de la République française (1943–2003).* Brussels: Peter Lang, 2005.

——. *La France, l'aide américaine et la construction européenne, 1944–1954,* 2 vols. Paris: Institut de la gestion publique et du développement économique, Comité pour l'histoire économique et financière de la France, 1992.

——. "French Development Aid and Co-operation under de Gaulle." In "Europe and the First Development Decade: The Foreign Economic Assistance Policy of European Donor Countries, 1958–1972." Special issue, *Contemporary European History* 12, no. 4 (November 2003): 431–456, https://www.jstor.org/stable/20081177.

Bowden, Brett. *The Empire of Civilization: The Evolution of an Imperial Idea.* Chicago: University of Chicago Press, 2014.

Bradley, Mark. *Imagining Vietnam and America: The Making of Postcolonial Vietnam, 1919–1950.* Chapel Hill: University of North Carolina Press, 2000.

Brenner, Louis. *Controlling Knowledge: Religion, Power, and Schooling in a West African Muslim Society.* Bloomington: Indiana University Press, 2001.

Brown, Callum. *Religion and Society in Twentieth-Century Britain.* Harlow: Pearson, 2006.

Brown, Jacqueline Nassy. *Dropping Anchor, Setting Sail: Geographies of Race in Black Liverpool.* Princeton, NJ: Princeton University Press, 2005.

Brown, Megan. "Drawing Algeria into Europe: Shifting French Policy and the Treaty of Rome." *Modern and Contemporary France* 25, no. 2 (2017): 191–208, https://doi.org/10.1080/09639489.2017.1281899.

——. *The Seventh Member State: Algeria, France, and the European Community.* Cambridge, MA: Harvard University Press, 2022.

Bruter, Michael. *Citizens of Europe? The Emergence of a Mass European Identity.* London: Palgrave Macmillan, 2005.

Bryant, Kelly Duke. *Education as Politics: Colonial Schooling and Political Debate in Senegal, 1850s-1914.* Madison: University of Wisconsin Press, 2015.

Bunzl, Matti. *Anti-Semitism and Islamophobia: Hatreds Old and New in Europe.* Chicago: Prickly Pear Press, 2007.

——. *Symptoms of Modernity: Jews and Queers in Late Twentieth-Century Vienna.* Berkeley: University of California Press, 2004.

Buruma, Ian. *Murder in Amsterdam: Liberal Europe, Islam and the Limits of Tolerance.* New York: Penguin, 2006.

Byrne, Jeffrey James. *Mecca of the Revolution: Algeria, Decolonization, and the Third World Order.* Oxford: Oxford University Press, 2016.

Caldwell, Christopher. *Reflections on the Revolution in Europe: Immigration, Islam and the West.* New York: Doubleday, 2009.

Calhoun, Craig. *Social Theory and the Politics of Identity.* Cambridge, MA: Blackwell, 1994.

Callahan, Michael D. *Mandates and Empire: The League of Nations and Africa, 1914–1931.* Brighton: Sussex Academic Press, 1999.

Calligaro, Oriane. *Negotiating Europe: EU Promotion of Europeanness Since the 1950s.* Basingstoke: Palgrave, 2013.

Camiscioli, Elisa. *Reproducing the French Race: Immigration, Intimacy and Embodiment in the Early Twentieth Century*. Durham, NC: Duke University Press, 2009.

Campt, Tina. *Other Germans: Black Germans and the Politics of Race, Gender and Memory in the Third Reich*. Ann Arbor: University of Michigan Press, 2009.

Casanova, José. *Public Religions in the Modern World*. Chicago: University of Chicago Press, 1994.

Castells, Manuel. *The Rise of the Network Society*. Oxford: Blackwell, 1996.

Cauchy, Pascal, Yvan Combeau, and Jean-François Sirinelli. *La Quatrième République et l'Outre-mer français: Actes du colloque tenu au Centre d'histoire de Science Po les 29 et 30 novembre 2007*. Paris: Publications de la Société française d'histoire d'outre-mer, 2009, https://hal.univ-reunion.fr/hal-01243952.

Cesare, Nicole. "An African in Paris . . . and New York and Rome: Bernard Dadié and the Postcolonial Travel Narrative." Master's thesis, Villanova University, 2007.

Chabal, Émile, ed. *A Divided Republic: Nation, State, and Citizenship in Contemporary France*. Cambridge: Cambridge University Press, 2015.

——. *France since the 1970s: History, Politics, and Memory in the Age of Uncertainty*. New York: Bloomsbury, 2015.

Chafer, Tony. *The End of Empire in French West Africa: France's Successful Decolonization?* New York: Berg, 2002.

Chaplin, Tamara, and Jadwiga E. Pieper Mooney, eds. *The Global 1960s: Convention, Contest, Counterculture*. New York: Routledge, 2018.

Chapman, Herrick. *France's Long Reconstruction: In Search of the Modern Republic*. Cambridge, MA: Harvard University Press, 2018.

Chapman, Herrick, and Laura Frader, eds. *Race in France: Interdisciplinary Perspectives on the Politics of Difference*. New York: Berghahn Books, 2004.

Chappel, James. *Catholic Modern: The Challenge of Totalitarianism and the Remaking of the Church*. Cambridge, MA: Harvard University Press, 2018.

Childers, Kristen Stromberg. "The Second World War as a Watershed in the French Caribbean." *Atlantic Studies* 9, no. 4 (2012): 409–430, https://doi.org/10.1080/14788810.2012.719323.

——. *Seeking Imperialism's Embrace: National Identity, Decolonization, and Assimilation in the French Caribbean*. New York: Oxford University Press, 2016.

Chin, Rita, Heidi Fehrenbach, Geoff Eley, and Atina Grossmann, *After the Nazi Racial State: Difference and Democracy in Germany and Europe*. Ann Arbor: University of Michigan Press, 2009.

Clavel, Isabelle. "Réformer l'École après 1944: Du consensus au *dissensus* entre la SFIO et le MRP." *Histoire@Politique: Politique, culture, société* 3, no. 18 (September–December 2012): 129–143, https://doi.org/10.3917/hp.018.0129.

Cocquery-Vidrovitch, Catherine. "Jean Suret-Canale (1921–2007)." *Outre-mers: Revue d'histoire*, no 358–359 (2008): 395–397, https://www.persee.fr/doc/outre_16310438_2008_num_95_358_4806.

Collins, Michael. "Decolonization and the 'Federal Moment.'" *Diplomacy and Statecraft* 24, no. 1 (2013): 21–40, https://doi.org/10.1080/09592296.2013.762881.

Colonna, Fanny. "Educating Conformity in Colonial Algeria." Translated by Barbara Harshav. In *Tensions of Empire: Colonial Cultures in a Bourgeois World*, edited by

Frederick Cooper and Ann Laura Stoler, 346–370. Berkeley: University of California Press, 1997.

Conklin, Alice. *In the Museum of Man: Race, Anthropology and Empire in France, 1850–1950*. Ithaca, NY: Cornell University Press, 2013.

——. *A Mission to Civilize: The Republican Idea of Empire in France and West Africa, 1895–1930*. Stanford, CA: Stanford University Press, 1997.

Connelly, John. *From Enemy to Brother: The Revolution in Catholic Teaching on the Jews, 1933–1965*. Cambridge, MA: Harvard University Press, 2012.

Connelly, Matthew. *A Diplomatic Revolution: Algeria's Fight for Independence and the Origins of the Post–Cold War Era*. Oxford: Oxford University Press, 2002.

——. "Taking Off the Cold War Lens: Visions of North-South Conflict during the Algerian War for Independence." *American Historical Review* 105, no 3 (June 2000): 739–769, https://doi.org/10.2307/2651808.

Conway, Martin. "Legacies of Exile: The Exile Governments in London during the Second World War and the Politics of Postwar Europe." In *Europe in Exile: European Exile Communities in Britain, 1940–1945*, edited by Martin Conway and José Gotovitch, 255–274. New York: Berghahn Books, 2001.

——. *Western Europe's Democratic Age, 1945–1968*. Princeton, NJ: Princeton University Press, 2020.

Conway, Martin, Pieter Lagrou, and Henry Rousso. *Europe's Postwar Periods—1989, 1945, 1918: Writing History Backwards*. London: Bloomsbury, 2018.

Conze, Vanessa. "Facing the Future Backwards: 'Abendland' as an Anti-liberal Idea of Europe in Germany between the First World War and the 1960s." In *Anti-liberal Europe: A Neglected Story of Its Europeanization*, edited by Dieter Gosewinkel, 72–89. New York: Berghahn Books, 2015.

Cooper, Frederick. *Africa since 1940: The Past of the Present*. Cambridge: Cambridge University Press, 2002.

——. "Citizenship and the Politics of Difference in French Africa." In *Empires and Boundaries: Rethinking Race, Class and Gender in Colonial Settings*, edited by Harald Fischer-Tiné and Susanne Gehrmann. New York: Routledge, 2009.

——. *Citizenship between Empire and Nation: Remaking France and French Africa, 1945–1960*. Princeton, NJ: Princeton University Press, 2014.

——. *Colonialism in Question: Theory, Knowledge, History*. Berkeley: University of California Press, 2005.

——. *Decolonization and African Society: The Labor Question in French and British Africa*. Cambridge: Cambridge University Press, 1996.

Cooper, Frederick, and Randall Packard, eds. *International Development and the Social Sciences: Essays on the History and Politics of Knowledge*. Berkeley: University of California Press, 1997.

Daily, Andrew M. "Race, Citizenship and Antillean Student Activism in Postwar France, 1946–1968." *French Historical Studies* 37, no. 2 (2014): 331–357.

D'Almeida-Topor, Hélène, and Odile Georg, eds. *Le Mouvement associatif des jeunes en Afrique noire francophone au XXe siècle*. Paris: L'Harmattan, 1989.

Daughton, J. P. *An Empire Divided: Religion, Republicanism and the Making of French Colonialism, 1880–1914*. Oxford: Oxford University Press, 2006.

Davidson, Naomi. *Only Muslim: Islam in Twentieth-Century France.* Ithaca, NY: Cornell University Press, 2012.

Davis, Muriam Haleh. "'A Distinctly French Universalism': Translating *Laïcité* after Charlie Hebdo." *Jadaliyya* (January 26, 2015). https://www.jadaliyya.com /Details/31702.

——. *Markets of Civilization: Islam and Racial Capitalism in Algeria.* Durham, NC: Duke University Press, 2022.

——. "Producing EurAfrica: Development, Agriculture and Race in Algeria, 1958–1965." PhD diss., New York University, 2015.

Davis, Muriam Haleh, and Thomas Serres, eds. *North Africa and the Making of Europe.* London: Bloomsbury, 2018.

Deacon, Valerie, ed. "The French Resistance in Transnational Perspective." Special issue, *French Politics, Culture and Society* 37, no. 1 (Spring 2019).

De Grazia, Victoria. *Irresistible Empire: America's Advance through Twentieth-Century Europe.* Cambridge, MA: Belknap Press of Harvard University Press, 2005.

Delanty, Gerard. *Inventing Europe: Idea, Identity, Reality.* New York: St. Martin's Press, 1995.

Delbreil, Jean-Claude. *Centrisme et démocratie-chrétienne en France: Le Parti Démocrate Populaire des origines au MRP, 1919–1944.* Paris: Publications de la Sorbonne, 1990.

Dieng, Amady Aly. *Les grands combats de la Fédération des Étudiants de l'Afrique Noire: De Bandung aux indépendances, 1955–1960.* Paris: L'Harmattan, 2009.

——. *Les premiers pas de la Fédération des Étudiants d'Afrique Noire en France (1950–1955): De l'Union française à Bandoung.* Paris: L'Harmattan, 2003.

Dimier, Véronique. "Bringing the Neo-patrimonial State Back to Europe: French Decolonization and the Making of European Development Aid Policy." *Archiv für Sozialgeschichte* 48 (2008): 433–457, https://www.fes.de/index.php?eID =dumpFile&t=f&f=46875&token=b7cbf72149fd16efd967b632d62d31d4914fb944.

——. *The Invention of a European Development Aid Policy: Recycling Empire.* Basingstoke: Palgrave, 2014.

Dinan, Desmond. *Europe Recast: A History of the European Union.* London: Lynne Rienner, 2008.

Diouf, Mamadou, and Mara Leichtman, eds. *New Perspectives on Islam in Senegal: Conversion, Migration, Wealth, Power, and Feminity.* New York: Palgrave, 2009.

Dorn, Charles, and Kristen Ghodsee. "The Cold War Politicization of Literacy: Communism, UNESCO, and the World Bank." *Diplomatic History* 36, no. 2 (April 2012): 373–398.

Downs, Laura Lee. *Childhood in the Promised Land: Working-Class Movements and the Colonies de Vacances in France, 1880–1960.* Durham, NC: Duke University Press, 2002.

Dubois, Laurent. *Colony of Citizens: Revolution and Slave Emancipation in the French Caribbean, 1794–1804.* Chapel Hill: University of North Carolina Press, 2004.

——. *Soccer Empire. The World Cup and the Future of France.* Berkeley: University of California Press, 2010.

Dueck, Jennifer. *The Claims of Culture at Empire's End: Syria and Lebanon under French Rule.* New York: Oxford University Press, 2010.

Duranti, Marco. "A Blessed Act of Oblivion: Human Rights, European Unity and Postwar Reconciliation." In *Reconciliation, Civil Society and the Politics of Memory: Transnational Initiatives in the 20th and 21st Century*, edited by Birgit Schwelling, 115–140. Bielefield: Transcript Verlag, 2012.

——. *The Conservative Human Rights Revolution: European Identity, Transnational Politics, and the Origins of the European Convention*. Oxford: Oxford University Press, 2017.

Ekbladh, David. *The Great American Mission: Modernization and the Construction of an American World Order*. Princeton, NJ: Princeton University Press, 2011.

Elias, Norbert. *The Civilizing Process*. New York: Pantheon Books, 1982.

——. *Quest for Excitement: Sport and Leisure in the Civilizing Process*. Oxford: Blackwell, 1986.

——. *Time: An Essay*. Translated by Edmund Jephcott. Oxford: Blackwell, 1992.

El-Tayeb, Fatima. *European Others: Queering Ethnicity in Postnational Europe*. Minneapolis: University of Minnesota Press, 2011.

Escobar, Arturo. *Encountering Development: The Making and Unmaking of the Third World*. Princeton, NJ: Princeton University Press, 1995.

Faucher, Charlotte. "From Gaullism to Anti-Gaullism: Denis Saurat and the French Cultural Institute in Wartime London." *Journal of Contemporary History* 54, no. 1 (2019): 60–81, https://doi.org/10.1177/0022009417699866.

Faucher, Charlotte, and Laure Humbert, eds. "Beyond de Gaulle and beyond London: The French External Resistance and Its International Networks." Special issue, *European Review of History* 25, no. 2 (2018).

Featherstone, Kevin, and C. M. Radaelli, eds. *The Politics of Europeanization*. Oxford: Oxford University Press, 2003.

Fehrenbach, Heide. *Race after Hitler: Black Occupation Children in Postwar Germany and America*. Princeton, NJ: Princeton University Press, 2005.

Ferguson, James. *The Anti-Politics Machine: Development, Depoliticization and Bureaucratic Power in the Third World*. Cambridge: Cambridge University Press, 1990.

Fernando, Mayanthi. *The Republic Unsettled: Muslim French and the Contradictions of Secularism*. Durham, NC: Duke University Press, 2014.

Fields, Karen E., and Barbara Fields. *Racecraft: The Soul of Inequality in American Life*. New York: Verso, 2014.

Finkielkraut, Alain. *The Imaginary Jew*. Lincoln: University of Nebraska Press, 1994.

Fligstein, Neil. *Euroclash: The EU, European Identity and the Future of Europe*. Oxford: Oxford University Press, 2008.

Flood, Christopher. "Nationalism or Nationism? Pierre-André Taguieff and the Defense of the French Republic." *South Central Review* 25, no. 3 (Fall 2008): 86–105, https://www.jstor.org/stable/40211281.

Fontaine, Darcie. *Decolonizing Christianity: Religion and the End of Empire in France and Algeria*. Cambridge: University of Cambridge Press, 2016.

Foret, François. *Religion and Politics in the European Union: The Secular Canopy*. Cambridge: Cambridge University Press, 2015.

Forlenza, Rosario. "The Politics of *Abendland*: Christian Democracy and the Idea of Europe after the Second World War." *Contemporary European History* 26, no. 2 (2017): 261–286, https://doi.org/10.1017/S0960777317000091.

Foster, Elizabeth. *African Catholic. Decolonization and the Transformation of the Church.* Cambridge, MA: Harvard University Press, 2019.

———. "'Entirely Christian and Entirely African': Catholic African Students in France in the Era of Independence." *Journal of African History* 56, no. 2 (July 2015): 239–259, https://doi.org/10.1017/S0021853715000201.

———. *Faith in Empire: Religion, Politics and Colonial Rule in French Senegal, 1880–1940.* Stanford, CA: Stanford University Press, 2013.

Foster, Elizabeth, and Giuliana Chamedes, eds. "Decolonization and Religion in the French Empire." Special issue, *French Politics, Culture and Society* 33, no. 2 (Summer 2015).

Foucault, Michel. *The Birth of Biopolitics: Lectures at the Collège de France, 1978–1979.* New York: Palgrave, 2009.

———. *"Society Must Be Defended": Lectures at the Collège de France, 1975–1976.* New York: Picador, 2003.

Frank, Robert, ed. *Les identités européennes au XXe siècle: Diversités, convergences et solidarités.* Paris: Sorbonne, 2004.

Fransee, Emily Lord. "'I May Vote Like All Women': Protest, Gender, and Suffrage in French Senegal." *French Colonial History* 20 (2021): 119–144.

———. "Without Distinction: Gender and Suffrage in the French Empire, 1943–1962." PhD diss., University of Chicago, 2019.

Gadjigo, Samba. *École blanche, Afrique noire: L'école coloniale dans le roman d'Afrique noire francophone.* Paris: L'Harmattan, 1990.

Gamble, Harry. *Contesting French West Africa: Battles over Schools and the Colonial Order, 1900–1950.* Lincoln: University of Nebraska Press, 2017.

———. "La crise de l'enseignement en Afrique occidentale française (1944–1950)." *Histoire de l'éducation* 128 (2010): 129–162, https://doi.org/10.4000/histoire-education.2278.

Garavini, Giuliano. *After Empires: European Integration, Decolonization, and the Challenge from the Global South, 1957–1986.* Oxford: Oxford University Press, 2012.

Gendzier, Irene. "Play It Again, Sam: The Practice and Apology of Development." *New Political Science* 20, no. 2 (June 1998): 159–183.

Genova, James. "Constructing Identity in Postwar France: Citizenship, Nationality, and the Lamine Guèye Law, 1946–1953." *International History Review* 26, no. 1 (March 2004): 56–79, https://doi.org/10.1080/07075332.2004.9641024.

———. "The Empire Within: The Colonial Popular Front, 1934–1938." *Alternatives* 26, no. 2 (2001): 175–209, https://www.jstor.org/stable/40645015.

Gerbi, Alexandre, ed. *Décolonisations de l'Afrique ex-française. Enjeux pour l'Afrique et la France d'aujourd'hui.* Paris: L'Harmattan, 2010.

Getachew, Adom. *Worldmaking After Empire: The Rise and Fall of Self-Determination.* Princeton, NJ: Princeton University Press, 2018.

Giddens, Anthony. *The Consequences of Modernity.* Stanford, CA: Stanford University Press, 1990.

———. *Europe in the Global Age.* Cambridge: Polity Press, 2007

Gienow-Hecht, Jessica. "Shame on US? Academics, Cultural Transfer, and the Cold War—a Critical Review." *Diplomatic History* 24, no. 3 (Summer 2000): 465–494, https://www.jstor.org/stable/24913837.

Gienow-Hecht, Jessica, and Frank Schumacher, eds. *Culture and International History.* New York: Berghahn Books, 2003.

Gildea, Robert. *France since 1945.* Oxford: Oxford University Press, 2002.

Gillingham, John. *European Integration, 1950–2003. Superstate or New Market Economy?* Cambridge: Cambridge University Press, 2003.

Gilroy, Paul. *"There Ain't No Black in the Union Jack": The Cultural Politics of Race and Nation.* Chicago: University of Chicago Press, 1991.

Ginio, Ruth. *French Colonialism Unmasked: The Vichy Years in French West Africa.* Lincoln: University of Nebraska Press, 2006.

Giolitto, Pierre. *Histoire de la jeunesse sous Vichy.* Paris: Perrin, 1991.

Girardet, Raoul. "L'apothéose de la 'plus Grande France': L'idée coloniale devant l'opinion française (1930–1935)." *Revue française de science politique* 18, no. 6 (December 1968): 1085–1114, https://doi.org/10.3406/rfsp.1968.393128.

Girault, Jacques. *Pour une école laïque du peuple! Instituteurs militants de l'entre-deux-guerres en France.* Paris: Publisud, 2009.

Girault, René, ed. *Identité et conscience européennes au XXe siècle.* Paris: Hachette, 1994.

Girault, René, and Gérard Bossuat, eds. *Europe brisée, Europe retrouvée: nouvelles réflexions sur l'unité européenne.* Paris: Sorbonne, 1994.

Goldberg, David Theo. *Are We All Postracial Yet? Debating Race.* Cambridge: Polity, 2015.

——. *The Threat of Race: Reflections on Racial Neoliberalism.* Oxford: Wiley-Blackwell, 2009.

Goldstein, Jan. *The Post-revolutionary Self: Politics and Psyche in France, 1750–1850.* Cambridge, MA: Harvard University Press, 2008.

Goldstein Sepinwall, Alyssa. *The Abbé Grégoire and the Making of Modern Universalism.* Berkeley, CA: University of California Press, 2005.

Gosewinkel, Dieter, ed. *Anti-liberal Europe: A Neglected Story of Its Europeanization.* New York: Berghahn Books, 2015.

Gould, Andrew C., and Anthony Messina, eds. *Europe's Contending Identities: Supranationalism, Ethnoregionalism, Religion and the New Nationalism.* Cambridge: Cambridge University Press, 2014.

Grossmann, Johannes. "The Comité International de la Défense de la Civilisation Chrétienne and the Transnationalization of Anticommunist Propaganda in Western Europe after the Second World War." In *Transnational Anticommunism and the Cold War,* edited by Stéphanie Roulin, Giles Scott-Smith, and Luc van Dongen, 251–262. London: Palgrave, 2014.

Greenberg, Udi. "Catholics, Protestants, and the Violent Birth of European Religious Pluralism." *American Historical Review* 124, no. 2 (2019): 511–538, https://doi.org/10.1093/ahr/rhz252.

——. "Protestants, Decolonization, and European Integration, 1885–1961." *Journal of Modern History* 89, no. 2 (June 2017): 314–54, https://doi.org/10.1086/691531.

Greenberg, Udi, and Daniel Steinmetz-Jenkins. "Is Religious Freedom a Bad Idea?" *Nation,* March 16, 2016.

Gueldry, Michel. *France and European Integration: Towards a Transnational Polity?* Westport, CT: Praeger, 2001.

Guieu, Jean-Michel, Christophe le Dréau, Jenny Raflik, and Laurent Warlouzet. *Penser et construire Europe au XXe siècle: Historiographie, bibliographie, enjeux.* Paris: Belin, 2006

Guillen, Pierre. "L'avenir de l'Union française dans la négociation des traités de Rome." *Relations internationales* 57 (Spring 1989): 103–112, https://www.jstor.org/stable/45344281.

Guillou, Michel. *Francophonie-puissance.* Paris: Ellipses, 2005.

Guimont, Fabienne. *Les étudiants africains en France, 1950–1965.* Préface d'Odile Goerg. Paris: L'Harmattan, 1997.

Guisan, Catherine. *A Political Theory of Identity in European Integration: Memory and Policies.* New York: Routledge, 2012.

Guyomarch, Alain, Howard Machin, and Ella Ritchie. *France in the European Union.* New York: St. Martin's Press, 1998.

Halls, W. D. *Education, Culture and Politics in Modern France.* Oxford: Pergamon Press, 1976.

Hansen, Peo, and Stefan Jonsson. *Eurafrica: The Untold History of European Integration and Colonialism.* London: Bloomsbury, 2014.

Harismendy, Patrick, and Erwin Le Gall, eds. *Pour une histoire de la France Libre.* Rennes: Presses Universitaires de Rennes, 2010.

Harrison, Christopher. *France and Islam in West Africa, 1860–1960.* Cambridge: Cambridge University Press, 1988.

Hartog, François. *Regimes of Historicity: Presentism and the Experience of Time.* New York: Columbia University Press, 2015.

Harvey, David. *The Condition of Postmodernity.* Cambridge: Blackwell, 1989.

Hazareesingh, Sudir. *From Subject to Citizen: The Second Empire and the Emergence of French Democracy.* Princeton, NJ: Princeton University Press, 1998.

Hecht, Gabrielle, ed. *Entangled Geographies: Empire and Technopolitics in the Global Cold War.* Cambridge, MA: MIT Press, 2011.

——. *The Radiance of France: Nuclear Power and National Identity after World War II.* Cambridge, MA: MIT Press, 2009.

Hecht, Jennifer. *The End of Soul: Scientific Modernity, Atheism and Anthropology in France.* New York: Columbia University, 2003.

Hedetoft, Ulf, ed. *Political Symbols, Symbolic Politics: European Identities in Transformation.* Brookfield: Ashgate, 1998.

Hendrickson, Burleigh. *Decolonizing 1968: Transnational Student Activism in Tunis, Paris, and Dakar.* Ithaca, NY: Cornell University Press, 2022.

——. "The Politics of Colonial History: Bourguiba, Senghor, and the Student Movements of the Global 1960s." In *Global Sixties: Conventions, Contests, and Countercultures,* edited by Tamara Chaplin and Jadwiga Pieper, 13–32. New York: Routledge, 2018.

Hessler, Julie. "Death of an African Student in Moscow: Race, Politics and the Cold War." *Cahiers du Monde russe* 47, no. 1–2 (January–June 2007): 33–63.

Hine, Darlene Clark, Trica Danielle Keaton, and Stephen Small, eds. *Black Europe and the African Diaspora.* Urbana: University of Illinois Press, 2009.

Hodeir, Catherine. *Stratégies d'Empire: Le grand patronat colonial face à la décolonisation.* Paris: Belin, 2003.

Hoerber, Thomas, ed. *A Converging Postwar European Discourse: War Experience, Changing Security Concepts, and Research and Education.* London: Lexington Books, 2014.

Hogan, Michael J. "The Search for a 'Creative Peace': The United States, European Unity and the Origins of the Marshall Plan." *Diplomatic History* 6, no 3 (Summer 1982): 267–285, https://www.jstor.org/stable/24911272.

Holmes, Douglas R. *Integral Europe: Fast-Capitalism, Multiculturalism, Neofascism.* Princeton, NJ: Princeton University Press, 2000.

Holt, Thomas. *The Problem of Freedom: Race, Labor and Politics in Jamaica and Britain, 1832–1938.* Baltimore: John Hopkins University Press, 1992.

Hoogvelt, Ankie. *Globalization and the Postcolonial World: The New Political Economy of Development.* Baltimore: Johns Hopkins University Press, 1997.

Huntington, Samuel. *The Clash of Civilizations and the Remaking of World Order.* New York: Simon & Schuster, 1996.

Iriye, Akira. *Cultural Internationalism and World Order.* Baltimore: John Hopkins University Press, 1997.

Ismael, Tareq Y. "Religion and UAR African Policy." *Journal of Modern African Studies* 6, no. 1 (1968): 49–57, https://www.jstor.org/stable/158676.

Jackson, Robert H. *Quasi-States: Sovereignty, International Relations and the Third World.* Cambridge: Cambridge University Press, 1990.

Jarausch, Konrad. *Out of Ashes: A New History of Europe in the Twentieth Century.* Princeton, NJ: Princeton University Press, 2015

Jarausch, Konrad, and Thomas Lindenberger. *Conflicted Memories: Europeanizing Contemporary Histories.* New York: Berghahn Books, 2007.

Jardin, André, and A.-J. Tudesq. *La France des notables,* 2 vols. Paris: Éditions du Seuil, 1973.

Jean-Baptiste, Rachel. "Miss Eurafrica: Men, Women's Sexuality, and Métis Identity in Late Colonial French Africa," *Journal of the History of Sexuality* 20, no. 3 (September 2011): 568–593, https://www.jstor.org/stable/41305885.

Jean-Hesse, Philippe, and Jean-Pierre Le Crom. *La protection sociale sous le régime de Vichy.* Rennes: Presses Universitaires de Rennes, 2015.

Jennings, Eric. *Free French Africa in World War II: The African Resistance.* Cambridge: Cambridge University Press, 2015.

——. *Vichy in the Tropics: Pétain's National Revolution in Madagascar, Guadeloupe and Indochina, 1940–1944.* Stanford, CA: Stanford University Press, 2001.

Jézéquel, Jean-Hervé. "Histoire des bancs, parcours d'élèves: Pour une lecture 'configurationelle' de la scolarisation à l'époque coloniale." *Cahiers d'Études africaines* 169/170 (2003): 409–433, https://doi.org/10.4000/etudesafricaines.207.

Jobs, Richard Ivan. *Backpack Ambassadors: How Youth Travel Integrated Western Europe.* Chicago: University of Chicago Press, 2917.

——. *Riding the New Wave: Youth and the Rejuvenation of France after the Second World War.* Stanford, CA: Stanford University Press, 2007.

——. "Youth Movements: Travel, Protest, and Europe in 1968," *American Historical Review* 114, no. 2 (2009): 376–404, https://www.jstor.org/stable/30223784.

Jobs, Richard Ivan, and David Pomfret, eds. *Transnational Histories of Youth in the Twentieth Century.* New York: Palgrave, 2015.

Johnson, R. W. "Forever on the Wrong Side." *London Review of Books* 34, no. 28 (September 27, 2012), https://www.lrb.co.uk/the-paper/v34/n18/r.w.-johnson /forever-on-the-wrong-side.

Joppke, Christian. *The Secular State Under Siege: Religion and Politics in Europe and America*. Cambridge: Polity Press, 2015.

Joseph-Gabriel, Annette. *Reimagining Liberation: How Black Women Transformed Citizenship in the French Empire*. Urbana: University of Illinois Press, 2020.

Judt, Tony. *The Burden of Responsibility: Blum, Camus, Aron and the French Twentieth Century*. Chicago: University of Chicago, 1998.

——. *A Grand Illusion? An Essay on Europe*. New York: Hill and Wang, 1996.

——. *Past Imperfect: French Intellectuals, 1944–1956*. Berkeley: University of California Press, 1992.

——. *Postwar: A History of Europe since 1945*. New York: Penguin, 2004.

Kaba, Lansiné. *The Wahhabiyya: Islamic Reform and Politics in French West Africa*. Evanston, IL: Northwestern University Press, 1974.

Kahan, Alan. *Liberalism in Nineteenth-Century Europe: The Political Culture of Limited Suffrage*. New York: Palgrave, 2003.

Kaiser, Wolfram. *Christian Democracy and the Origins of the European Union*. Cambridge: Cambridge University Press, 2007.

Kane, Ousman, and Jean-Louis Triaud. *Islam et islamismes au sud du Sahara*. Paris: Karthala, 1998.

Kantrowitz, Rachel. "'So That Tomorrow Would Be Better for Us': Developing French-Funded Catholic Schools in Dahomey and Senegal, 1945–1975." PhD diss., New York University, 2015.

Katsakioris, Constantin. "The Soviet-South Encounter: Tensions in the Friendship with Afro-Asian Partners, 1945–1965." In *Cold War Crossings: International Travel and Exchange Across the Soviet Bloc, 1940s–1960s*, edited by Patryk Babiracki and Kenyon Zimmer, 134–165. College Station: Texas A&M University Press, 2014.

Keating, Michael, ed. *Regions and Regionalism in Europe*. Cheltenham: Elgar Publishing, 2004.

Keaton, Trica Danielle. *Muslim Girls and the Other France: Race, Identity Politics, and Social Exclusion*. Bloomington: Indiana University Press, 2006.

Keaton, Trica Danielle, T. Denean Sharpley-Whiting, and Tyler Stovall, eds. *Black France/France Noire: The History and Politics of Blackness*. Durham, NC: Duke University Press, 2012.

Kent, John. *The Internationalisation of Colonialism: France, Britain and Black Africa, 1939–1956*. Oxford: Clarendon Press, 1992.

Kepel, Gilles. *Allah in the West: Islamic Movements in America and Europe*. Stanford, CA: Stanford University Press, 1997.

Kergomard, Pierre. *Histoire des Éclaireurs de France de 1911 à 1951*. Paris: Éclaireuses et Éclaireurs de France, 1983.

Kiamba, Claude-Ernest. "Construction de l'état et politiques de l'enseignement au Congo du 1911 à 1997: Contribution à l'analyse de l'Action Publique en Afrique Noire." PhD diss., Université Montesquieu-Bordeaux IV, 2008.

Klimke, Martin. *The Other Alliance: Student Protest in West Germany and the United States in the Global Sixties*. Princeton, NJ: Princeton University Press, 2011.

Klose, Fabian. "Europe as a Colonial Project: A Critique of Its Anti-liberalism." In *Anti-liberal Europe: A Neglected Story of Its Europeanization*, edited by Dieter Gosewinkel, 47–71. New York: Berghan Books, 2015.

Kobo, Ousman. *Unveiling Modernity in Twentieth-Century West African Islamic Reforms.* Leiden: Brill Academic Publishing, 2012.

Kølvraa, Christoffer. *Imagining Europe as a Global Player: The Ideological Construction of New European Identity within the EU.* Brussels: Peter Lang, 2012.

Koopmans, Ruud, Paul Statham, Marco Giugni, and Florence Passy. *Contested Citizenship: Immigration and Cultural Diversity in Europe.* Minneapolis: University of Minnesota Press, 2005.

Koselleck, Reinhardt. *Futures Past: On the Semantics of Historical Time.* Cambridge, MA: MIT Press, 1997.

Kozakowski, Michael. "From the Mediterranean to Europe: Migrants, the World of Work, and the Transformation of the French Mediterranean, 1945–1974." PhD diss., University of Chicago, 2014.

Kuisel, Richard. "Americanization for Historians." *Diplomatic History* 24, no. 3 (Summer 2000): 509–515, https://www.jstor.org/stable/24913840.

——. *Seducing the French: The Dilemma of Americanization.* Berkeley: University of California Press, 1996.

Kymlicka, Will. *Multicultural Odysseys: Navigating the New International Politics of Diversity.* Oxford: Oxford University Press, 2007.

Lebovics, Herman. *Bringing the Empire Back Home: France in the Global Age.* Durham, NC: Duke University Press, 2004.

——. *Mona Lisa's Escort: André Malraux and the Reinvention of French Culture.* Ithaca, NY: Cornell University Press, 1999.

——. *True France: The Wars over Cultural Identity.* Ithaca, NY: Cornell University Press, 1992.

Lee, Christopher, ed. *Making a World After Empire: The Bandung Moment and its Afterlives.* Athens: Ohio University Press, 2010.

Lee, Daniel. *Pétain's Jewish Children: French Jewish Youth and the Vichy Regime.* Oxford: Oxford University Press, 2014.

Lentin, Alana. *Race and Antiracism in Postwar Europe.* London: Pluto Press, 2004.

Le Sueur, David. *Uncivil War: Intellectuals and Identity Politics during the Decolonization of Algeria.* Philadelphia: University of Pennsylvania Press, 2001.

Levsen, Sonja. "Authority and Democracy in Postwar France and West Germany, 1945–1968." *Journal of Modern History* 89, no. 4 (December 2017): 812–850, https://doi.org/10.1086/694614.

Loncle, Patricia. *L'action publique malgré les jeunes: Les politiques de jeunesse en France de 1870 à 2000.* Paris: L'Harmattan, 2003.

Lorcin, Patricia. *Imperial Identities: Prejudice and Race in Colonial Algeria.* New York: I.B. Tauris, 1999.

——. "Rome and France in Africa: Recovering Colonial Algeria's Latin Past." *French Historical Studies* 25, no. 2 (Spring 2002): 295–329, muse.jhu.edu/article/11923.

Louis, William Roger, and Roger Owen, eds. *Suez 1956: The Crisis and Its Consequences.* Oxford: Clarendon Press, 1989.

Lozac'h, Alain. *Visages de la résistance bretonne: Réseau et mouvements de libération en Côtes-d'Armor.* Nancy: Coop Breizh, 2003.

Ly, Boubacar. *Les instituteurs au Sénégal, 1903–1945,* 6 vols. Paris: L'Harmattan, 2009.

Mahmood, Saba. *Religious Difference in a Secular Age: A Minority Report.* Princeton, NJ: Princeton University Press, 2015.

Manela, Erez. *The Wilsonian Moment: Self-Determination and the International Origins of Anticolonial Nationalism.* Oxford: Oxford University Press, 2007.

Manière, Laurent. "La politique française pour l'adaptation de l'enseignement en Afrique après les indépendances (1958–1964)." *Histoire de l'éducation,* no. 128 (2010): 163–190, https://doi.org/10.4000/histoire-education.2281.

Mann, Gregory. *From Empires to NGOs in the West African Sahel: The Road to Nongovernmentality.* Cambridge: Cambridge University Press, 2015.

——. *Native Sons. West African Veterans and France in the Twentieth Century.* Durham, NC: Duke University Press, 2006.

Mann, Gregory, and Jean Sébastien Lecocq. "Between Empire, Umma, and the Muslim Third World: The French Union and African Pilgrims to Mecca, 1946–1958." *Comparative Studies of South Asia, Africa and the Middle East* 27, no. 2 (2007): 367–383, https://www.muse.jhu.edu/article/220772.

Marker, Emily. "African Youth on the Move in Postwar Greater France: Experiential Knowledge and Decolonial Politics at the End of Empire." *Know: A Journal on the Formation of Knowledge* 3, no. 2 (Fall 2019), 283–303, https://doi.org/10.1086/704620.

——. "Obscuring Race: Franco-African Conversations about Colonial Reform and Racism after World War II and the Making of Colorblind France." *French Politics, Culture and Society* 33, no. 3 (Winter 2015): 1–23, https://doi.org/10.3167/fpcs.2015.330301.

Marker, Emily, with Abosede George, Clive Glaser, Margaret D. Jacobs, Chitra Joshi, Alexandra Walsham, Wang Zheng, and Bernd Weisbrod. "*AHR* Conversation: Each Generation Writes Its Own History of Generations." *American Historical Review* 123, no. 5 (December 2018): 1505–1546, https://doi.org/10.1093/ahr/rhy389.

Marseille, Jacques. *Empire colonial et capitalisme français: Histoire d'un divorce.* Paris: Albin Michel, 1984.

Matasci, Damiano. "Une 'UNESCO africaine'? Le Ministère de la France d'Outre-Mer, la coopération éducative intercoloniale, et la défense de l'empire." *Monde(s)* 13, no. 1 (2018): 195–214, https://doi.org/10.3917/mond1.181.0195.

Matasci, Damiano, Miguel Bandeira Jéronimo, and Hugo Gonçalves Dores, eds. *Repenser la "mission civilisatrice." L'éducation dans le monde colonial et postcolonial au XXe siècle.* Rennes: Presses Universitaires de Rennes, 2021.

Matera, Marc. *Black London: The Imperial Metropolis and Decolonization in the Twentieth Century.* Oakland: University of California Press, 2015.

Matusevich, Maxim. "Soviet Antiracism and Its Discontents: The Cold War Years." In *Alternative Globalizations: Eastern Europe and the Postcolonial World,* edited by Mark, James, Artemy M. Kalinovsky, and Steffi Marung, 229–250. Bloomington: Indiana University Press, 2020.

Mazon, Patricia, and Reinhild Steingrover, eds. *Not So Plain as Black and White: Afro-German Culture and History, 1890–2000.* Rochester, NY: University of Rochester Press, 2009.

Mazower, Mark. *Dark Continent: Europe's Twentieth Century.* New York: Vintage, 1997.

——. "The End of Eurocentrism." In "Around 1948: Interdisciplinary Approaches to Global Transformation," edited by Leela Gandhi and Deborah L. Nelson. Special issue, *Critical Inquiry* 40, no. 4 (Summer 2014): 298–313, https://doi .org/10.1086/676409.

——. "An International Civilization? Empire, Internationalism and the Crisis of the Mid-Twentieth Century." *International Affairs* 82, no. 3 (May 2006): 553–566, https://www.jstor.org/stable/3874268.

——. *No Enchanted Palace: The End of Empire and the Ideological Origins of the United Nations.* Princeton, NJ: Princeton University Press, 2009.

Maza, Sarah. "The Kids Aren't All Right: Historians and the Problem of Childhood." *American Historical Review* 125, no. 4 (October 2020): 1261–1285, https://doi .org/10.1093/ahr/rhaa380.

Mazrui, Ali A. "Africa and the Egyptian's Four Circles." *African Affairs* 63, no. 251 (April 1964): 129–141.

Mbembe, Achille. *On the Postcolony.* Berkeley: University of California Press, 2001.

McKenzie, Brian A. "The European Youth Campaign in Ireland: Neutrality, Americanization, and the Cold War, 1950–1959." *Diplomatic History* 40, no. 3 (June 2016): 421–444, https://doi.org/10.1093/dh/dhv010.

Michon, Jacques. "Les éditeurs de littérature française aux États-Unis et en Amérique latine durant la Deuxième Guerre mondiale." *Papers of the Bibliographical Society of Canada/Cahiers de la Société bibliographique du Canada* 33, no. 2 (Fall 1995): 165–188, https://doi.org/10.33137/pbsc.v33i2.17964.

Migani, Guia. *La France et l'Afrique sub-saharienne, 1957–1963: Histoire d'une décolonisation entre idéaux eurafricains et politique de puissance.* Bern: Peter Lang, 2008.

Misa, Thomas, and Johan Schot. "Inventing Europe: Technology and the Hidden Integration of Europe." *History and Technology* 21, no. 1 (March 2005): 1–19, https://doi.org/10.1080/07341510500037487.

Mitchell, Timothy. *Rule of Experts: Egypt, Techno-Politics, Modernity.* Berkeley: University of California Press, 2002.

Montarsolo, Yves. *L'Eurafrique, contrepoint de l'idée de l'Europe: Le cas français de la fin de la deuxième guerre mondiale aux négociations des Traités de Rome.* Aix-en-Provence: Presses Universitaires de Provence, 2010.

Moore, Celeste Day. *Soundscapes of Liberation: African American Music in Postwar France.* Durham, NC: Duke University Press, 2021.

Moyn, Samuel. *Christian Human Rights.* Philadelphia: University of Pennsylvania Press, 2015.

——. "From Communist to Muslim: European Human Rights, the Cold War, and Religious Liberty." *South Atlantic Quarterly* 113, no. 1 (Winter 2014): 63–86, https://doi.org/10.1215/00382876-2390428.

——. *The Last Utopia: Human Rights in History.* Cambridge, MA: Belknap Press of Harvard University Press, 2010.

Muracciole, Jean-François. *Les enfants de la défaite: La Résistance, l'éducation et la culture*. Paris: Presses de Sciences Po, 1998.

——. "La Résistance, l'éducation et la culture." *Vingtième siècle: Revue d'histoire* 58 (April–June 1998): 100–110, https://doi.org/10.3406/xxs.1998.3747.

Musselin, Christine. *The Long March of French Universities*. New York: Routledge Falmer, 2001.

Mylonas, Denis. *La genèse de l'Unesco: La Conférence des Ministres Alliés de l'Education (1942–1945)*. Brussels: Bruylant, 1976.

Ndiaye, Pap. *La condition noire: Essai sur une minorité française*. Paris: Calmann-Lévy, 2008.

Neave, Guy. "War and Educational Reconstruction in Belgium, France and the Netherlands, 1940–1947." In *Education and the Second World War: Studies in Schooling and Social Change*, edited by Roy Lowe, 84–127. London: Routledge, 1992.

Nkwengue, Pierre. *L'union nationale des étudiants du Kamerun: Ou la contribution des étudiants africains à l'émancipation de l'Afrique*. Paris: L'Harmattan, 2005.

Nora, Pierre. "Between Memory and History: *Les Lieux de Mémoire*." In "Memory and Counter-Memory." Special issue, *Representations* 26 (Spring 1989): 7–24, https://doi.org/10.2307/2928520.

Nord, Philip. *France's New Deal: From the Thirties to the Postwar Era*. Princeton, NJ: Princeton University Press, 2010.

Norwig, Christina. "A First European Generation? The Myth of Youth and European Integration in the Fifties." *Diplomatic History* 38, no. 2 (April 2014): 251–260, https://doi.org/10.1093/dh/dhu006.

Olender, Maurice. *The Languages of Paradise: Race, Religion, and Philology in the Nineteenth Century*. Cambridge, MA: Harvard University Press, 1992.

Omi, Michael, and Howard Winant. *Racial Formation in the United States from the 1960s to the 1980s*. New York: Routledge, 1994.

Orkibi, Eithan. *Les étudiants de France et la guerre d'Algérie: Identité et expression collective de l'UNEF*. Paris: Editions Syllepse, 2012.

Otayek, René, ed. *Le radicalisme islamique au sud du Sahara: Da'wa, arabisation et critique de l'Occident*. Paris: Karthala, 1993.

Oulmont, Philippe. "Félix Éboué, un jaurésien inattendu." *Cahiers Jaurès* 200, no. 2 (2011): 147–161, https://doi.org/10.3917/cj.200.0147.

Ozouf, Mona. *L'école de la France: Essai sur la Révolution, l'utopie de l'enseignement*. Paris: Gallimard, 1984.

Palayret, Jean. *Une université pour l'Europe: Préhistoire de l'Institut Universitaire Européen de Florence (1948–1976)*. Rome: Présidence du Conseil des Ministres de l'Union européenne, 1996.

Palmer, R. R. *The Improvement of Humanity: Education and the French Revolution*. Princeton, NJ: Princeton University Press, 1985.

Parsons, Craig. "Showing Ideas as Causes: The Origins of the European Union." *International Organization* 56, no. 1 (2002): 47–84, https://doi.org/10.1162/002081802753485133.

Parsons, Timothy H. *Race, Resistance, and the Boy Scout Movement in British Colonial Africa*. Athens: Ohio University Press, 2004.

Passerini, Luisa. *Europe in Love, Love in Europe: Imagination and Politics in Britain between the Wars*. London: I.B. Tauris, 1999.

Patel, Kiran Klaus. *Project Europe: A History*. Cambridge: Cambridge University Press, 2020.

Peabody, Sue, and Tyler Stovall, eds. *The Color of Liberty: Histories of Race in France*. Durham, NC: Duke University Press, 2003.

Pearson, Jessica. *The Colonial Politics of Global Health: France and the United Nations in Postwar Africa*. Cambridge, MA: Harvard University Press, 2018.

Pedersen, Susan. *Guardians: The League of Nations and the Crisis of Empire*. Cambridge: Cambridge University Press, 2015.

——. *Family, Dependence and the Origins of the Welfare State: Britain and France, 1914–1945*. Cambridge: Cambridge University Press, 1993.

Perry, Kennetta Hammond. *London Is the Place for Me: Black Britons, Citizenship and the Politics of Race*. New York: Oxford University Press, 2015.

Pitts, Jennifer. *A Turn to Empire: The Rise of Imperial Liberalism in Britain and France*. Princeton, NJ: Princeton University Press, 2005.

Plaza, Arthur. "Paix ou guerre scolaire? Les divisions du Mouvement Républicain Populaire 1944–1960." In *Politiques de la laïcité au XXe siècle*, edited by Patrick Weil, 481–504. Paris: Presses Universitaires de France, 2007.

Poiger, Uta. *Jazz, Rock, and Rebels: Cold War Politics and American Culture in a Divided Germany*. Berkeley: University of California Press, 2000.

Pomfret, David M. *Youth and Empire: Trans-Colonial Childhoods in British and French Asia*. Stanford, CA: Stanford University Press, 2016.

Poucet, Bruno, ed. *L'état et l'enseignment privé: L'application de la loi Debré (1959)*. Rennes: Presses Universitaires de Rennes, 2019.

Prost, Antoine. *Du changement dans l'Ecole: Les réformes de l'éducation de 1936 à nos jours*. Paris: Seuil, 2013.

——. *Education, société, politiques: Une histoire d'enseignement en France de 1945 à nos jours*. Paris: Seuil, 1992.

Prost, Antoine, and Pascal Ory. *Jean Zay, le ministre assassiné*. Paris: Taillandier/Canopé, 2015.

Rabinow, Paul. *French Modern: Norms and Forms of the Social Environment*. Chicago: University of Chicago Press, 1989.

Raffin, Anne. *Youth Mobilization in Vichy Indochina and Its Legacies, 1940–1970*. Lanham, MD: Lexington Books, 2005.

Rémond, René. *Religion and Society in Modern Europe*. Oxford: Blackwell, 1997.

Rempe, Martin. "Decolonization by Europeanization? The Early EEC and the Transformation of French-African Relations." *KFG Working Paper Series* 27 (May 2011): 1–21, http://dx.doi.org/10.17169/refubium-22834.

Rice, Louisa. "Between Empire and Nation: Francophone West African Students and Decolonization." *Atlantic Studies* 10, no. 1 (2013): 131–147, https://doi.org/10.1080/14788810.2013.764106.

——. "Cowboys and Communists: Cultural Diplomacy, Decolonization and the Cold War in French West Africa," *Journal of Colonialism and Colonial History* 11, no. 3 (Winter 2010), https://doi.org/10.1353/cch.2010.0023.

Richard, Anne-Isabelle. "The Limits of Solidarity: Europeanism, Anticolonialism and Socialism at the Congress of the Peoples of Europe, Asia and Africa in Puteaux, 1948." *European History Review* 21, no. 4 (2014): 519–537, https://doi.org/10.1080/13507486.2014.933187.

Rist, Gilbert. *The History of Development: From Western Origins to Global Faith.* Translated by Patrick Camiller. New York: Zed Books, 2002.

Robert, André D. "La commission Cathala et le modèle anglais, Londres, 1942–1943." *Carrefours de l'Éducation* 41, no. 1 (2016): 65–80, https://doi.org/10.3917/cdle.041.0065.

Roberts, Richard. *Two Worlds of Cotton. Colonialism and the Regional Economy in the French Soudan, 1800–1946.* Stanford, CA: Stanford University Press, 1996.

Robinson, David. *Paths of Accommodation: Muslim Societies and French Colonial Authorities in Senegal and Mauritania, 1880–1920.* Athens: Ohio University Press, 2000.

Robinson, David, and Jean-Louis Triaud, eds. *Les temps des marabouts: Itinéraires et stratégies islamiques en Afrique occidentale française, 1880–1960.* Paris: Karthala, 1997.

Rosa, Harmut, and William E. Sheuerman, eds. *High-Speed Society: Social Acceleration, Power, and Modernity.* University Park: Pennsylvania State University Press, 2009.

Rosenberg, Clifford. *Policing Paris: The Origins of Modern Immigration Control between the Wars.* Ithaca, NY: Cornell University Press, 2006.

Rosenhaft, Eve, and Robbie Aitken, eds. *Africa in Europe: Studies in Transnational Practice in the Long Twentieth Century.* Liverpool: Liverpool University Press, 2013.

Ross, Kristin. *Fast Cars, Clean Bodies: Decolonization and the Reordering of French Culture.* Cambridge, MA: MIT Press, 1995.

——. *May '68 and Its Afterlives.* Chicago: University of Chicago Press, 2002.

Rothberg, Michael. *Multidirectional Memory: Remembering the Holocaust in the Age of Decolonization.* Stanford, CA: Stanford University Press, 2009.

Rousso, Henry. *The Vichy Syndrome: History and Memory in France since 1944.* Cambridge, MA: Harvard University Press, 1991.

Rutter, Nick. "Unity and Conflict in the Socialist Scramble for Africa." In *Global Sixties: Conventions, Contests, and Countercultures*, edited by Tamara Chaplin and Jadwiga Pieper, 33–51. New York: Routledge, 2018.

——. "The Western Wall: The Iron Curtain Recast in the Summer of 1951." In *Cold War Crossings: International Travel and Exchange across the Soviet Bloc, 1940s–1960s*, edited by Patryk Babiracki and Kenyon Zimmer, 78–106. College Station: Texas A&M University Press, 2014.

Rye, Lise. "The Origins of Community Education Policy: Educating Europeans." In *The History of the European Union: Origins of a Trans and Supranational Polity, 1950–72*, edited by Wolfram Kaiser, Brigitte Leucht, and Morten Rasmussen, 148–166. New York: Routledge, 2009.

Saada, Emmanuelle. *Les enfants de la colonie: Les métis de l'empire français entre sujétion et citoyenneté.* Paris: Découverte, 2007.

Sabot, Jean-Yves. *Le syndicalisme étudiant et la guerre d'Algérie: L'Entrée d'une génération en politique et la formation d'une élite*. Paris: Éditions L'Harmattan, 1995.

Said, Edward. *Culture and Imperialism*. New York: Knopf, 1993.

——. *Orientalism*. New York: Vintage Books, 1979.

Saint Martin, Monique, Grazia Scarfò Ghellab, and Kamal Mellakh. *Étudier à l'Est: Expériences de diplômés africains*. Paris: Éditions Karthala, 2015.

Sartori, Andrew. "The Resonance of 'Culture': Framing a Problem in Global Concept History." *Comparative Studies in Society and History* 47, no. 4 (2005): 676–699, https://doi.org/10.1017/S0010417505000319.

Sassatelli, Monica. *Becoming Europeans. Cultural Identity and Cultural Politics*. London: Palgrave Macmillan, 2009.

Scaglia, Ilaria. *The Emotions of Internationalism: Feeling International Cooperation in the Alps in the Interwar Period*. Oxford: Oxford University Press, 2020.

Schierup, Carl-Ulrich, Peo Hansen, and Stephen Castles. *Migration, Citizenship, and the European Welfare State: A European Dilemma*. Oxford: Oxford University Press, 2006.

Schmidt, Elizabeth. *Cold War and Decolonization in Guinea, 1946–1958*. Athens: Ohio University Press, 2007.

Schnappeur, Dominique. *Juifs et israélites*. Paris: Gallimard, 1980.

Schreurs, Rik. "L'Eurafrique dans les négociations du Traité de Rome, 1956–1957." *Politique africaine* 49 (March 1993): 82–92, http://www.politique-africaine.com/numeros/pdf/049082.pdf.

Scott, Joan Wallach. *The Politics of the Veil*. Princeton, NJ: Princeton University Press, 2007.

——. *Sex and Secularism*. Princeton, NJ: Princeton University Press, 2017.

Scott-Smith, Giles, and Hans Krabbendam, *The Cultural Cold War in Western Europe, 1945–1960*. Portland, OR: Frank Cass, 2003.

Seck, Papa Ibrahima. *La stratégie culturelle de la France en Afrique: L'enseignement colonial (1817–1960)*. Paris: L'Harmattan, 1993.

Segal, Daniel. "'Western Civ' and the Staging of History in American Higher Education." *American Historical Review* 105, no. 3 (June 2000): 770–805, https://doi.org/10.1086/ahr/105.3.770.

Segalla, Spencer D. *The Moroccan Soul: French Education, Colonial Ethnology, and Muslim Resistance, 1912–1956*. Lincoln: University of Nebraska Press, 2009.

Séréni, Frank. "La Cité internationale universitaire de Paris, 1925–1950: De la Société des Nations à la construction de l'Europe." *Relations internationales* 72 (Winter 1992): 399–407.

Serra, Enrico, ed. *The Relaunching of Europe and the Treaties of Rome: Actes du Colloque de Rome 25–28 Mars 1987*. Brussels: Bruylant, 1989.

Sewell, William H. *The Logics of History: Social Theory and Social Transformation*. Chicago: University of Chicago Press, 2005.

Shaev, Brian. "The Algerian War, European Integration, and the Decolonization of French Socialism." *French Historical Studies* 41, no. 1 (February 2018): 63–94, https://doi.org/10.1215/00161071-4254619.

Shennan, Andrew. *France: Plans for Renewal, 1940–1946*. New York: Oxford University Press, 1989.

Shepard, Todd. "À l'heure des 'grands ensembles' et de la guerre d'Algérie. L''État-nation' en question," *Monde(s): Revue d'histoire transnationale* 1, no. 1 (2012): 113–134.

——. "Algeria, France, Mexico, UNESCO: A Transnational History of Anti-Racism and Decolonization, 1932–1962." *Journal of Global History* 6, no. 2 (July 2011): 273–297, https://doi.org/10.1017/S174002281100026X.

——. *The Invention of Decolonization: The Algerian War and the Remaking of France.* Ithaca, NY: Cornell University Press, 2006.

Shipway, Marin. "Thinking Like an Empire: Governor Henri Laurentie and Postwar Plans for the Late Colonial Empire-State." In *The French Colonial Mind*, vol. 1, *Mental Maps of Empire and Colonial Encounters*, edited by Martin Thomas, 219–250. Lincoln: University of Nebraska Press, 2011.

Shore, Cris. *Building Europe: The Cultural Politics of European Integration.* London: Routledge, 2000.

——. "Inventing the 'People's Europe': Critical Approaches to European Community 'Cultural Policy.'" *Man* 28, no. 4 (1993): 779–800, https://www.jstor.org/stable/2803997.

Siegal, Mona, and Kristen Harjes. "Disarming Hatred: History Education, National Memories, and Franco-German Reconciliation from World War I to the Cold War." *History of Education Quarterly* 57, no. 3 (August 2012): 370–402, https://doi.org/10.1111/j.1748-5959.2012.00404.x.

Sierp, Aline. *History, Memory and Trans-European Identity: Unifying Divisions.* New York: Routledge, 2014.

Silverman, Maxim. *Deconstructing the Nation: Immigration, Racism and Citizenship in Modern France.* London: Routledge, 1992.

Silverstein, Paul. *Algeria in France: Transpolitics, Race and Nation.* Bloomington: Indiana University Press, 2004.

Simpson, A. W. Brian. *Human Rights and the End of Empire: Britain and the Genesis of the European Convention.* Oxford: Oxford University Press, 2001.

Slobodian, Quinn. *Foreign Front: Third World Politics in Sixties West Germany.* Durham, NC: Duke University Press, 2012.

Smith, Andrew, and Chris Jeppesen, eds. *Britain, France and the Decolonization of Africa: Future Imperfect?* London: University College London Press, 2017.

Snow, Nancy, et al. *Routledge Handbook of Public Diplomacy.* New York: Routledge, 2009.

Solomos, John, and John Wrench, eds. *Racism and Migration in Western Europe.* Oxford: Berg, 1993.

Sot, Michel, ed. *Étudiants africains en France, 1951–2001: Cinquante ans de relations France-Afrique, quel avenir?* Paris: Karthala, 2002.

Stern, Fritz. *The Whitewashing of the Yellow Badge: Philosemitism and Antisemitism in West Germany, 1945–1952.* Oxford: Pergamon, 1992.

Stolcke, Verena. "Talking Culture: New Boundaries, New Rhetorics of Exclusion in Europe." *Cultural Anthropology* 36, no. 1 (1995): 1–24, https://www.jstor.org/stable/2744220.

Stoler, Ann Laura. *Along the Archival Grain: Epistemic Anxieties and Colonial Common Sense.* Princeton, NJ: Princeton University Press, 2009.

———. *Race and the Education of Desire: Foucault's History of Sexuality and the Colonial Order of Things.* Durham, NC: Duke University Press, 1995.

Stovall, Tyler. *Paris Noir: African Americans in the City of Light.* Boston: Houghton Mifflin, 1996.

Stratton, Clif. *Education for Empire: American Schools, Race, and the Paths of Good Citizenship.* Berkeley: University of California Press, 2016.

Sue, Derald Wing. *Microaggressions in Everyday Life: Race, Gender and Sexual Orientation.* Hoboken, NJ: Wiley, 2010.

Sutton, Christopher. "Britain, Empire and the Origins of the Cold War Youth Race." *Contemporary British History* 30, no. 2 (2016): 224–241, https://doi.org/10.1080/13619462.2015.1079489.

Taguieff, Pierre-André. *La force du préjugé: Essai sur le racisme et ses doubles.* Paris: Gallimard, 1987.

Tapia, Claude. *Les jeunes face à l'Europe: représentation, valeurs, idéologies.* Paris: PUF, 1997.

Tedga, Paul John Marc. *L'enseignement supérieur en Afrique noire francophone: La catastrophe?* Abidjan: PUSAF; Paris: L'Harmattan, 1988.

Tévoedjrè, Albert. *L'Afrique révoltée.* Paris: Présence Africaine, 1958.

Therborn, Göran. *European Modernity and Beyond: The Trajectory of European Societies, 1945–2000.* London: Sage, 1995.

Thomas, Martin, ed. *The French Colonial Mind,* vol. 1, *Mental Maps and Colonial Encounters.* Lincoln: University of Nebraska Press, 2011.

Thomas, Martin, B. Moore, and L. J. Butler, *Crises of Empire: Decolonization and Europe's Imperial States, 1918–1975.* London: Hodder Education, 2008.

Thompson, Elizabeth. *Colonial Citizens: Republican Rights, Paternal Privilege, and Gender in French Syria and Lebanon.* New York: Columbia University, 2000.

Thompson, Virginia, and Richard Adloff, *The Emerging States of French Equatorial Africa.* Stanford, CA: Stanford University Press, 1960.

Todorov, Tzvetan. *On Human Diversity: Nationalism, Racism, and Exoticism in French Thought.* Cambridge, MA: Harvard University Press, 1998.

Trachtenberg, Marc. *A Constructed Peace: The Making of the European Settlement, 1945–1963.* Princeton, NJ: Princeton University Press, 1999.

Triandafyllidou, Anna, Tariq Modood, and Nasar Meer. *European Multiculturalisms: Cultural, Religious and Ethnic Challenges.* Edinburgh: Edinburgh University Press, 2012.

Tribalat, Michèle. *Faire France: Une grande enquête sur les immigrés et leurs enfants.* Paris: Editions La Découverte, 1995.

Tumblety, Joan. *Remaking the Male Body: Masculinity and the Uses of Physical Culture in Interwar and Vichy France.* Oxford: Oxford University Press, 2012.

Valliant, Jerôme, ed. *La Dénazification par les vainqueurs: La politique culturelle des occupants en Allemagne 1945–1949.* Lille: Université de Lille, 1981.

Von Eschen, Penny. *Race against Empire: Black Americans and Anticolonialism, 1937–1957.* Ithaca, NY: Cornell University Press, 1997.

———. *Satchmo Blows up the World: Jazz Ambassadors Play the Cold War.* Cambridge, MA: Harvard University Press, 2004.

Wacquant, Loïc. "For an Analytic of Racial Domination." *Political Power and Social Theory* 11 (1997): 221–234.

Wagnleitner, Reinhold. *Coca-colonization and the Cold War: The Cultural Mission of the United States in Austria after the Second World War.* Chapel Hill: University of North Carolina Press, 1994.

——. "The Empire of the Fun, or Talkin' Soviet Union Blues: The Sound of Freedom and U.S. Cultural Hegemony in Europe." *Diplomatic History* 23, no. 3 (Summer 1999): 499–524, https://www.jstor.org/stable/24913677.

Wall, Irwin. *France, the United States and the Algerian War.* Berkeley: University of California Press, 2001.

Ware, Rudolph T., III. *The Walking Qur'an: Islamic Education, Embodied Knowledge and History in West Africa.* Raleigh: University of North Carolina Press, 2014.

Webber, Frances. "From Eurocentrism to Euro-Racism," *Race and Class* 32, no. 3 (1991): 11–17, https://doi.org/10.1177/030639689103200303.

Weber, Eugen. *Peasants into Frenchmen: The Modernization of Rural France.* Stanford, CA: Stanford University Press, 1974.

Weinstein, Brian. *Éboué.* Oxford: Oxford University Press, 1972.

Werner, Michael, and Bénédicte Zimmerman. "Beyond Comparison: *Histoire Croisée* and the Challenges of Reflexivity." *History and Theory* 45, no. 1 (February 2006): 30–50.

Westad, Odd Arne. *The Global Cold War: Third World Interventions and the Making of Our Times.* Cambridge: Cambridge University Press, 2006.

White, Bob W. "Talk about School: Education and the Colonial Project in French and British Africa (1860–1960)." *Comparative Education* 32, no. 1 (1996): 9–26, https://doi.org/10.1080/03050069628902.

White, Owen. *Children of the French Empire: Miscegenation and Colonial Society in French West Africa.* Oxford: Oxford University Press, 1999.

White, Owen, and J. P. Daughton, eds. *In God's Empire: French Missionaries and the Modern World.* Oxford: Oxford University Press, 2012.

Whitehead, Clive. "The Impact of the Second World War on Education in Britain's Colonial Empire." In *Education and the Second World War: Studies in Schooling and Social Change*, edited by Roy Lowe, 151–158. London: Routledge, 1992.

Wilder, Gary. *Freedom Time: Negritude, Decolonization and the Future of the World.* Durham, NC: Duke University Press, 2015.

——. *The French Imperial Nation-State: Négritude and Colonial Humanism between the Two World Wars.* Chicago: University of Chicago Press, 2005.

——. "From Optic to Topic: The Foreclosure Effect of Historiographic Turns." *American Historical Review* 117, no. 3 (June 2012): 723–745, https://doi.org/10.1086/ahr.117.3.723.

Winant, Howard. *The World Is a Ghetto: Race and Democracy since World War II.* New York: Basic Books, 2001.

Winter, Jay and Antoine Prost. *René Cassin and Human Rights: From the Great War to the Universal Declaration.* Cambridge: Cambridge University Press, 2013.

Wolf, Eric. *Europe and the People without History.* Berkeley: University of California Press, 1982.

Woloch, Isser. *The New Regime: Transformations in the Civic Order in France, 1789–1820s.* New York: Norton, 1994.

Zahra, Tara. *The Lost Children: Reconstructing Europe's Families after World War II.* Cambridge, MA: Harvard University Press, 2011.

Zancarini-Fournel, Michelle, and Christian Delacroix. *La France du temps présent, 1945–2005.* Paris: Belin, 2010.

Zauner, Stefan. *Erziehung und Kulturmission: Fransreichs Bildungs-Politik in Deutschland, 1945–1949.* Munich: R. Oldenbourg Verlag, 1994.

Zeghal, Malika. "Religion and Politics in Egypt: The Ulema of Al-Azhar, Radical Islam, and the State (1952–1994)." *International Journal of Middle East Studies* 31, no. 3 (1999): 371–399, https://doi.org/10.1017/S0020743800055483.

Zielonka, Jan. *Europe as Empire: The Nature of the Enlarged European Union.* Oxford: Oxford University Press, 2006

Zimmerman, Andrew. *Alabama in Africa: Booker T. Washington, the German Empire and the Globalization of the New South.* Princeton, NJ: Princeton University Press, 2012.

——. *Anthropology and Antihumanism in Imperial Germany.* Chicago: University of Chicago Press, 2001.

Zubryzcki, Geneviève. *The Crosses of Auschwitz: Nationalism and Religion in Post-Communist Poland.* Chicago: University of Chicago Press, 2006.

INDEX

AEF: colonial education in, 50–61, 70–71, 88–95, 108–109, 124–127, 131; Muslims, 89, 209–212

African political participation, 80–81, 94–95, 183–185, 196–197. *See also* African students; democracy

African student associations, 135–137, 202; Association Musulmane des Étudiants d'Afrique Noire (AMEAN), 208–209; Fédération des étudiants d'Afrique noire en France (FEANF), 140–142, 171, 182, 197–198

African students: activism, 134–137, 140–147, 154–160, 171–175, 200–20; experiences, 101–102, 123–124, 139–145, 149–150, 156–158; housing, 123–124, 147–150, 157; newspapers, 135–136, 142, 156–158, 172–174, 197–198; surveillance of, 123–124, 141, 144, 148–149, 196–197

al-Azhar University, 202–207

Algeria, 78, 96–97, 185, 211–212

alienation, 33, 110, 207–209

anticlericalism, 26–30, 41–44, 57–58, 66–69. *See also* laïcité

anticolonialism: anticolonial uprisings, 9, 96–97, 129, 185; Cold War anticolonial politics, 58, 93–94, 183–185, 194–203; critiques of colonialism, 84, 106–108, 141, 156–158. *See also* African students: activism.

antiracism, 102–107, 111, 141, 153–157, 160–161, 197–199

anti-white racism, 102, 129–130, 227

AOF: colonial education in, 33–34, 52, 57–64, 71, 83, 108–109; Muslims, 95–100, 203–209

assimilation, 33–34, 119–121, 163–165, 174

Atlantic Charter, 38, 58–59

Aubineau, Yves, 62–63

Aujoulat, Louis-Paul, 162–164

Bandung, Afro-Asian Conference in, 201–203, 209, 211

Bayet, Jean, 75, 78–79, 84–86

belonging, 2–6, 20–23, 65, 84–85, 193, 212–214, 218–219

Berveiller, Michel, 38–40, 45

Bony, Nazi, 130–131, 148

Brazzaville Conference, 33–35, 59–65, 83–84, 118–125, 131–132

Brugmans, Hendrick, 87–88, 183n9, 188

Cabrière, Edmond, 61–62, 102–103, 122, 195

Capelle, Jean, 108–110, 129, 134

Capitant, René, 71–73, 96

Cassin, René, 25–27, 34–42, 46–48, 50–51, 54–55, 57n112

Cassou, Jean, 48–49

Catholicism: and ecumenism, 18–19, 48–49, 64–65, 67–68; and republicanism, 28–33, 41–44, 66–71, 75–79, 94–96; social Catholicism, 67, 166n72; students, 139, 158–159

Chauvet, Paul, 209–212

Cheick Hamidou Kane, 207

Chéruel, Abbé, 77–78, 95n98

Christian Democracy, 3, 10–11, 18, 41, 85, 155

Christian tradition, 19, 44–46, 77–78, 86–88

Christian: Europe, 18–19, 67–68, 84–87, 190–191; France, 26, 57–58, 64–65, 76–80, 99–100

Cité Universitaire Internationale in Paris, 34, 147–148

citizenship, 2–3, 12–13, 105–106, 165, 221–222

civil status, 89–91

civilization: European, 45–47, 61–62, 66–68, 81–85, 114–120, 166–167; French. *See* civilizing mission

civilizing mission, 4, 32–34, 83–84, 164–165

Cold War, 76, 93–94, 196, 226–227;
    anti-Communist front, 18–20, 67–68, 140;
    Cold War youth race, 182–186, 189–193,
    196, 200. *See also entries for individual
    nations*
College of Europe, 82, 85n59, 86–88
Colombani, Ignace, 209–212
colonial discourse. *See* civilizing mission
colonialism, 4, 7–9, 39–40, 193, 216–217;
    indigenous policy, 57, 70–71, 89–90;
    legacies of, 143, 177–179, 212–213. *See also*
    anticolonialism
colorblindness. *See* racelessness
Commission for Technical Cooperation in
    Africa (CCTA), 195
Communism, 74–78, 170–172, 224–226.
    See also Cold War; Soviet Union
Conference of Allied Ministers of Education
    (CAME), 34–35, 46–48, 81, 112–115.
    See also United Nations: UNESCO
confessional schooling: Qur'anic schools, 5;
    121n64; 204–209; 211; mission schools,
    32, 52–53, 56–57, 60, 89–90; state
    funding for, 75–76, 79, 88, 91–95, 139,
    191, 223
cooperation: transnational, 34, 37–39, 44–46,
    81, 195, 213; International Institute for
    Intellectual Cooperation (IIIC), 34–35, 47
Coste-Floret, Paul, 119, 124
Coudenhove-Kalergi, Richard, 39
Council of Europe, 9, 81, 141, 176–179,
    215–216
Cournarie, Pierre, 59, 103, 122–124, 132,
    148–149
culturalization of Christianity, 19–20, 66,
    84–91, 209–210, 222–227
curriculum, 29–30, 33, 64, 86–87, 163–164,
    199; civic and moral instruction, 42–45,
    58, 78; history instruction, 44–47, 85,
    101–102, 110, 115, 189

Dadet, Jean, 108, 124, 126, 138
de Gaulle, Charles, 34, 36, 37n37, 53–54.
    See also Free France
Debré, Michel, 2–4, 68, 76n35, 85
decolonization, 21–23, 106–107, 111,
    182–184, 212–216; consequences of, 168,
    177–179; in historiography, 7–8, 12–14
Delavignette, Robert, 15, 176–177
democracy, 9–11, 36, 43–45, 49, 77–78;
    democratization of education, 30–32,
    60–61, 73–74; as multiracial, 5–6, 141,
    160–161, 194–197, 227–228
denazification, 47, 112–113, 116, 187–189

development, 5, 14–15, 172–178, 182, 195,
    212–217; FIDES, 109, 162, 166–167
Diop, Alioune, 173–174
Diop, Thomas, 158–160
diversity: brassage, 142–148, 152–153,
    169–170, 177, 186–187; "Unity in
    Diversity," 45–46, 72–73, 84–87, 219–221.
    See also pluralism
Dounia, Marc, 212–213

Éboué, Félix, 55–58, 70–71, 91–92
education reform: Capitant-Durry
    Commission (Algiers), 72–75, 78,
    185–186; Cathala Commission (London),
    41–46, 49, 55, 58; Langevin Commission
    (Paris), 75, 131–132; Langevin-Wallon
    Plan, 76, 93n87; Philip Commission
    (Paris), 75–79, 93, 95n98. *See also*
    Brazzaville Conference; CAME
van Effenterre, Henri, 86–88
Eugene, Jacques, 168–169. *See also* European
    Youth Campaign
Eurafrica: challenges to, 142, 171–172,
    181–184; conceptions of, 13–17, 39,
    48–49, 161–170, 212–213; postcolonial
    resurrection of, 216–217, 221
European Coal and Steel Community, 1–3,
    141, 161–162, 192
European Defense Community, 1–3, 162,
    167–168, 214
European Economic Community (EEC), 15,
    141, 144n10, 169–170, 181
European federalism, 37–40, 45, 183–184,
    188–189; Juventus, Young European
    Federalists, 191–193; Union of European
    Federalists, 116, 166, 175, 184; United
    States of Europe, 34, 38, 183–184, 189
European integration: as generational
    project, 7, 21–24, 26, 80, 190, 214–218; in
    historiography, 7–8, 16–17; as political,
    45–46, 141–142, 161–162, 165–168; as
    social and cultural, 16–17, 45, 192–193,
    214–215, 219–220
European Movement, 1–3, 21, 84–85, 116,
    165
European unity, 38–39, 115–118, 178,
    186–190; religion in, 18, 85–87. *See also*
    pluralism
European Youth Campaign, 1–2, 18, 161,
    165, 167–170, 191–193
Europeanization, 16–17, 20
Europeanness, 2–4, 163–164, 172–175, 188,
    213–215
évolués. *See also* Francophone Africans

foreign policy, 47–48, 179–180, 186–187, 198–203
Fournier, Vincent, 125–127, 128n87
francophone Africans, 104–107, 110–112, 137–138, 197–203; elite, 33, 54, 60–61, 64; and Eurafrica, 161–165, 184; generational divide, 140, 147, 169, 181; representations of, 124–131, 145–149, 156
Free France, 25–27, 34–41, 47–50, 57, 69–70; governments in exile, 37–38, 40; Resistance, 58, 74. *See also* World War II; cooperation
Frenay, Henri, 184–185
French Union: Assembly, 10–11, 15n34, 81n47; collapse of, 212–214; founding, 2–4, 10–11, 80–81; reforms, 107–112, 164–165; Youth Council, 198–200

gender, 21–22, 101, 107, 149, 192
generations, 7, 21–22, 60, 126, 132, 173; generational conflict, 169, 176–177, 196
Germany: French occupation zone in, 186–192
Giacobbi, Paul, 94, 118, 122–123, 131
globalization, 172–175, 179–180, 183
Great Britain, 25, 40–41, 50–51, 186–187, 194–195, 219–220

Halévy, Daniel, 172–173
Hauck, Henry, 36–38, 57n112
higher education, 60, 175–176, 189, 195, 218–221; European University Institute, Florence, 220–221; Institut des hautes études de Dakar (IHED), 134–136; University of Dakar, 131–134, 216–217
history, acceleration of, 172–176
Houphouët-Boigny, Félix, 5, 105–106, 143n9
human rights, 27, 133, 223n22; European Court of Human Rights (ECHR), 141, 225–226; right to education, 54, 63, 107, 201, 208–209
Huxley, Julian, 45. *See also* scientific racism

identity. *See* belonging
illiteracy, 94–95, 108, 138
integration (national), 64, 83–84, 88–92, 153–155, 221–222
international aid. *See* development
international opinion, 4–5, 118–119, 131, 194–199
international order, 13–14, 20, 41–49, 68, 137, 183–186
international oversight. *See* League of Nations; United Nations

international socialism, 183–184
internationalism, 37–38, 44–45; youth role in, 185–191, 214; Cold War, 192–193
interracial sex, 123, 149
Islam, 19–20, 89, 95–99, 160, 185, 202–206; racialization of, 20, 98–99, 167, 204–206, 208–212

Jews, 77–79, 222–223, 224n28; antisemitism, 19n50, 36–37, 49, 69, 113; Jewish youth programs, 69, 72, 96, 187n19. *See also* religious education

Kaziendé, Léopold, 104–106, 117–118
Ki-Zerbo, Joseph, 174–175
Konaté, Abdourahmane, 104–105, 110–11, 117, 119
Kutuklui, Noé, 171–172

labor, 55, 57n112, 105–106
laïcité, 30–32, 66–69, 73–77, 88–93, 95–100, 209–210; querelle scolaire, 28–30, 41–45, 75
language of instruction, 33, 63, 83–85, 187, 208–211
Laurentie, Henri, 55–61, 91, 124, 155
Lawrence, Antoine, 128–129, 168
League of Nations, 34, 37–39
Loi Cadre, 148–149, 168–171, 212–214
Lorelei Rally, 192–193
Lycée Van Vollenhoven, 101–103, 195

Ministry of National Education (MEN), 30, 75–76, 107
missionaries, 50–55, 57, 80–90, 94–95
Mouskhély, Michel, 175–176, 220

Nasser, Gamal, 201–203
nationalism, 20–21, 32, 61, 77, 189
Ndiaye, Samba, 142, 171–172
neocolonialism, 170–172, 216

pan-Africanism, 4, 102, 140, 166, 214
pedagogy, 42–43, 53, 85, 125–127, 163–164, 205–207
Peyrefitte, Alain, 81–82, 189–191, 213n115
Philip, André, 1, 75–76, 88, 183, 188
Planchais, Louis, 170–171
Pleven, René, 83–84, 122
pluralism: cultural, 115–116, 165; debates surrounding, 20, 77–78, 174–178, 221, 225–227; religious, 18–20, 67–69, 72, 86–87, 158. *See also* diversity
Pré, Roland, 165–167

primary education: expansion of, 29–30, 59–60, 63, 139–140

public/private education, 57, 91–92, 95

Puteaux "Congress of European, African, and Asian Peoples," 183–184

Qur'anic schools. *See* confessional schooling

race: and African difference, 52–54, 118–122, 125–127, 144–153, 210–211; as category, 3, 17, 51–52, 114–118, 136–137; and citizenship, 54–55, 105–107, 125–126, 143, 221–222. *See also* whiteness

racelessness, 17, 103, 114–119, 188–189, 227–228

racial common sense, 17, 103, 134–135, 138, 213–214, 227

racial discrimination, 107–112, 157, 199, 225–228

racial minorities, 153, 199

racism: in education, 103, 108, 110; experience of, 104–105, 155–160. *See also* antiracism; anti-white racism, scientific racism; structural racism

religious education: Catholic, 28–30; Islamic, 78, 95–99, 205–211; Jewish, 36–37, 78–79; in official state curriculum, 29–30, 42–44, 98, 206–209, 223–224; right to, 191, 208–209

republican ideology, 20, 27, 32, 41, 44; limits of, 124, 221

revolutionary tradition, 27–28, 44–46, 125

Sadji, Amadou Booker, 145, 181–182, 196n45, 197, 201

Sarkozy, Nicolas, 216–217

Sarraut, Albert, 10n18, 15

Saurat, Denis, 36, 45–46, 49–53, 55, 57–58

Savary, Alain, 183n9, 223–224

Schmittlein, Raymond, 186–189

scholarships, 131, 139–140, 182, 202; representations of boursiers, 144–149

Schuman, Robert, 67, 192

scientific racism, 51–52, 112–115, 115n49; and Nazism, 112–117. *See also* Huxley, Julian

scouting, 31, 43, 60, 82, 69–75, 96–98

secondary education: access to, 53–54, 60–63, 83, 101–103, 122–124, 130–131; expansion of, 73, 107, 127–129, 139. *See also* Lycée Van Vollenhoven

secularism. *See* laïcité

self-determination. *See* decolonization

Senghor, Léopold Sédar, 12–14, 33, 106–107, 132–134

single school system, 28–30, 42–43, 77–79, 224

Socé Diop, Ousmane, 9, 161–162

social mobility, 4, 62, 128

Socialist Movement for the United States of Europe (MSEUE), 183

solidarity, 7, 160, 183–184, 191–193, 201–202

Sommerfelt, Alf, 113–114, 116–117

sovereignty, 12–14, 39–40, 48–49

Soviet Union, 19, 129, 182, 185–186, 197–198, 202n73

Spaak, Paul-Henri, 37–39, 172

structural racism, 112, 138, 141–144, 153–159

supranationalism, 1–3, 18, 45, 175–176, 218

Suret-Canale, Jean, 101–102

teaching. *See* curriculum; pedagogy

Teitgen, Pierre-Henri, 3, 203, 211

Tévoedjrè, Albert, 157–159

Tévoedjrè, Isabelle, 156–157

textbooks, 45–47, 85, 113–115, 189n23, 199, 217–218

Third Republic, 28–34, 66–67; Popular Front, 30–31, 33, 108n28

Third World, 182–185, 192–193, 201–203

totalitarianism, 27, 51, 167

Treaty of Rome, 141–142, 181, 212–215

United Nations, 93–94, 106, 133; UNESCO, 34–35, 48, 113–116, 133, 195–196

United States, 47–48, 58–59, 93–94, 124–126, 199–200

universalism. *See* pluralism; racelessness

university. *See* higher education

Vangrévelinghe, Raphael, 43–44, 49

Vaucher, Paul, 47, 115

Vialle, Jeanne, 21, 107, 147

Vichy, 29–31, 33–34, 53, 58, 69, 74–76, 104–105. *See also* Free France; World War II

Wallerstein, Immanuel, 200

Western Europe, 17–20, 45–46, 67–68, 84, 166–167

whiteness, 3, 16–17, 61–62, 120–121, 218–222. *See also* race; racelessness

World Festival of Youth and Students, 182, 192, 197

World War II, 4, 7–9, 23; June 1940 defeat, 29, 57; postwar moment, 8–11, 22–24, 31–32; wartime Brazzaville, 56–57; wartime London, 35–40. *See also* Free France; Vichy

Yaméogo, Antoine, 143–146
Youla, Nabi Ibrahima, 169–170
youth and education policy, 26, 31–33; in French Africa, 51–55, 58–64, 109–110, 163–164, 217–218; transnational European, 45–46, 84–85, 113–117, 175–179
youth exchanges, 5–6, 185–187, 199; internship and training, 154–155, 162–163, 168, 182; student exchanges Africa-metropole, 139–144, 153–154; student exchanges Africa-Europe, 144, 168–169, 178–180, 182, 186; student

exchanges within Europe, 188–189, 193, 219–220; South-South exchanges, 182–183, 200–204
youth leaders, 82, 168n76, 186–188, 200. *See also* Lawrence, Antoine
youth organizations, 5, 30–31, 43, 78, 157n49; World Association of Youth, 168, 186, 198–200; World Federation of Democratic Youth, 182, 186, 197. *See also* scouting
youth political participation, 97–98, 167–170, 182–186, 192–194, 197–200
youth programs, 30–31, 42–43, 59–60, 167–169, 187–193
youth: appeals to, 182–186, 197, 215–218; as a category of analysis, 12–13, 16; myth of, 30, 150–152, 173–174, 177–178, 190

Zay, Jean, 30–31, 73

www.ingramcontent.com/pod-product-compliance
Lightning Source LLC
Chambersburg PA
CBHW032346280326
41935CB00008B/466